John Lars Zwerenz

the complete anthology

includes the new release
Cathedrals in the Rain

Green Frog Publishing, East Montpelier, VT 05651

John Lars Zwerenz

The Complete Anthology

Copyright © 2020 John Larz Zwerenz
Green Frog Publishing
East Montpelier, VT 05651

greenfrogpublishing.com

First Edition
John Lars Zwerenz, Author
Green Frog Publishing, Interior and Cover Designer

Cheers for actually reading this copyright page! Most readers don't bother. To reward your efforts, here's a very cool and unique poetry term that you won't find elsewhere in this book. Now amaze your family, friends, and colleagues with your improved command of the English language!

Tome— (1) book: especially a large or scholarly book; (2) a volume forming part of a larger work. Thanks to Merriam-Webster online, accessed December 17, 2019, https://www.merriam-webster.com/dictionary/tome.

All rights are reserved.

Green Frog Publishing is a trade name for Green Frog Publishing, and is not associated with any other person or company.

ISBN-13   978-1-7327241-8-1
Library of Congress   2019913410

Prepared, printed and bound in the United States of America.

Dedicated to the blessed virgin Mary.

Table of Contents

Introduction 1

Selected Poems 11

    I Trod Upon the Glade… 12

    To One So Fair 13

    Your Hair 14

    The Duchess I 14

    Browns 15

    In the Bower 16

    The Princess I 17

    Wine 18

    Your Gaze 19

    As in a Dream 20

    An Ecstasy 21

    As You Lay 22

    The Poetic Dimension 23

    Sunlight 23

    Tinges 24

    By the Manor House She Walks 24

    Beneath the Green Palms 25

    Monet is Still Here 25

    Your Tresses Reposed 26

    Scarlet Breezes I 26

    Upon the Beach 27

    My Contrite Heart 28

Table of Contents

From the Balcony 29

As the Sun Descends 30

Vespertine Fire 31

Gently Near She Comes 32

A Supplication 33

Majestic Heights 34

Flaxen Gold 35

Beside the Stream… 36

Let Me Sleep 37

By the Seine 38

Paris 39

The Bride 40

Silhouette 41

Ennui 42

A Lady Fair I 43

Wreaths 44

Beneath the Boughs 45

Radiant Angel 46

Sacred Glances 47

A Kiss 48

Where Roses Weep 49

Twilight 49

Ambrosia 50

Sanctified and Bright 51

Where the Sun Laments 52

In the Lamplight 53

Within Your Soul 54

The Autumn Rain 54

November 55

An Elegy 56

Before We Met 57

Table of Contents

Of a Regal Grace 58

Your Russet Wine 59

The Palace I 60

The Coach 61

The Cloister I 62

To Mary and My Beloved One 63

Burgundy 64

A Wedding of the Sacred 65

The Wanderer 66

Her Piano 67

The Patio 68

A Walk with My Lady 69

A Sailor's Song I 70

Let Us Dream 71

To Marry 72

At the University 73

Seen and Unseen 74

Violins 75

I Shall Place You in a Garden 76

Mist and Flame 79

To a Dark-Eyed Lady 80

Romance I 80

The Veranda 81

Your Touch 81

Your Hymns 82

Remnants 83

Your Rose 84

Suburbia 85

By the Bay 86

New Hampshire 87

Table of Contents

Your Face I 88

Her Silhouette 89

The Shade I 89

Only in You 90

Faded Candles 91

On a Winter's Eve 92

Poets 93

Isolation I 93

Days Now Gone 94

The Glade 95

Ode to Robert Schumann 96

Your Sobbing Soul 97

Forlorn 97

Heaven I 98

Verse I 99

Little Girl on a Bike 100

My Youth 101

Vignettes 103

Coming Home 104

The Morning Dew 105

An Autumn Sunset I 106

Bouquets 107

My Black-Haired Queen 108

A Reverent Night 109

In The Hallowed Night 109

Eternal Streams 110

By Hazel Eyes 111

Rapturous Gazes 112

Consumed with Sighs 112

Blossoms Once Bright 113

The Lakeside 114

Table of Contents

The Pond 114

My Queen 115

A Christmas Poem 116

Wind Chimes 117

The Porch 118

Late November 118

The Louvre 119

In Clement Times 120

A Stream of Stars 120

Raptures 121

Benediction 122

Our Souls Become One 123

Our English Tudor 123

The Castle I 124

In the Field We Lay 124

My Best Beloved 125

Ethereal Mist 126

By the Winter Moon 127

The Scarlet Breeze 127

As I Wander 128

October 128

The Sacred Shrine 129

Poetry 130

I Saw God in Your Tress 131

Table of Contents

Visionary Wanderings *133*

- Alchemy 134
- Rhyme 135
- An Ode to Keats 136
- On Poetry 137
- A Grecian Tale 139
- A Gypsy's Life 143
- A Summer's Day 144
- Corridors 145
- Come, Let Us Wander 146
- A Correspondence 147
- The Countess 148
- The Baroness 149
- Violets 150
- Noel 151
- A Veil of Sorrow 152
- A Lover's Sonnet 153
- One of the Mellow Dawn 154
- O Mary 155
- Wisdom 156
- Schoolgirl 157
- A Maiden Fair 158
- When Music Ceases 159
- Rejoice 160
- Harding Court 161
- Currents 162
- The Grand Beyond 163
- Peace I 164
- Over the Windy Sea 165
- A Night in Hades 166
- The Spring 167

Table of Contents

Soliloquy	168
The Cliffs by the Sea	169
The Starlight Night	170
A Walk in the Garden	171
A Bonny Lass	172
Emerald Billows	173
Two Women by the Shore	174
A Pantomime	175
A Coquette	176
Recollection I	177
The First Snow	178
King Henry VIII	179
The Swashbuckler	180
In the Candlelight	181
The Palace Ball	182
The Lavender Mist	183
Music	184
Advent	185
Carol	186
The Composer	187
A Wandering I	188
A Night in December	189
A Walk Through the Graveyard	190
One Winter Night	191
The Abbey at Dusk	192
In an Hour of Silence	193
Gray	194
The Little Garden	195
Autumn's Cellos	196
Gales I	197

Table of Contents

Unrequited Love 198

Hope 199

The Ardor of the Wise 200

Grace 201

Sadness 202

A Lady in the Park 203

She Passes and I Sigh 204

Twilight by the Shore 205

Heaven's Dew 206

Where the Zephyrs Flow 207

The April Rain 208

A Wistful Strain 209

She Walks in a Russet Ray 210

A Walk Beneath the Stars 211

My Turquoise Soul 212

The Dale 213

Benedictions 214

Apathy 215

Lethe 216

Hymns 217

Ballads 218

Lovers 219

Paradise I 220

As I Await Her 221

An Invitation 222

My Proposal 223

In the Evening I 224

Two Years Ago 226

Rapture 227

Steven 228

Moonlight I 229

Table of Contents

    Jones Beach 230

    Chelsea 231

    A Litany of Roses 232

    A Walk in Spain 233

    Virgil 234

    Shakespeare 235

    A Voyage to Scotland 236

    Mystic Wines 236

    The Harvest Ball 237

    Forest Park 238

    A Roman Garden 239

    A Walk Through Paradise 240

Sonnets of Dusk and Dawn *243*

    Preface 245

    Dawn 246

    Ode to Coleridge 246

    Sappho 247

    The Voyage of Icarus 248

    The Snow-Covered Hill 249

    One Summer Morn 250

    Ode to Robert Louis Stevenson 251

    The Bastion by the Sea 252

    The Blessed Dead Are We 253

    Verse II 254

    The Journey of Aeneas 255

    The Colonial House 256

    The Thirteenth Sonnet 256

    Diamond Stars 257

    Whiskey 258

    Bourbon 259

Table of Contents

Chablis	260
Kingdoms	261
The Auburn Dawn	262
My Chamber	263
The Painter	263
A Night in Paris	264
By a Wall of Stone	265
Hamlet's Guest	266
The Cloister of Kings	267
Fruits of the Ascension	268
Conversion	269
After the Rain	270
Beethoven's Ghost	270
The Mansion	271
Halos	272
The Storm I	272
The Thirty-Fourth Sonnet	273
August	274
Ode to Bobby Darin	275
The Second World War	276
Homer	277
Sonnets of Travel	278
Exile	281
The Happy Fault	282
An English Sonnet	283
Vermont	284
The Art Gallery	285
Love I	286
A Picnic	287
Before the Ball	288
The Ball	289

Table of Contents

Night	289
Alone with Renee	290
Claudia	291
Belgium	292
Reflections	293
Azure Heights	294
The Visitor	295
Central Park (2012)	296
Ode to Lord Byron	297
The Mansion by the Sea	298
Switzerland	299
Kissing in the Woods	299
Wines I	300
Ode to Baudelaire	300
The Hurricane	301
Calm	301
Buried	302
The Crypt	302
The Chameleon	303
My Host	303
The Dance	304
Advice to Young Poets	305
The Carriage I	306
On Betrothal	307
Ode to Henry David Thoreau	307
An Irish Garden	308
Raptures of White	309
My Lady I	310
The Fountain	311
Dusk I	312

Table of Contents

Eternal Verse 315

    Preface 317

    Of Two in Paradise 319

    Moonlight II 320

    The Courtyard I 321

    The Garden I 322

    A Rhapsody 323

    The Sea Below the Forest of Pines 324

    Let Us Rove 325

    In the Evening II 326

    On Entering Heaven 327

    Snow 329

    The Rain 330

    I Hold You on a Bed of Gold 331

    After Our Walk Amid the Reeds 332

    By the Lake 333

    The Gilded Ball 334

    I Met You in a Dream 336

    My Mansion by the Sea 338

    Mary 339

    The Castle II 340

    The Cloisters 341

    Paradise II 342

    The Way to Heaven 345

    In the Hush of the Morning 346

    My Fair Love 347

    The Chaste Wood 348

    Her Kiss 349

    Le Chateau 350

    The Chateau 352

    I Lay Down with Christ 354

Table of Contents

Une Promendade dans la Ville	355
A Walk in the Town	355
Je Vous ai Recontré à Paris	356
I Met You in Paris	357
The Priest	358
The Flowers by the Ocean	360
The Colossal Wood	362
The Zephyrs of the Paradisal Sea	363
In Love's Eternal Realm	363
Mary, The Mother of God	364
A Wandering II	367
Your Face in the Garden	368
The Holy Trinity	369
The Little Flower	371
A Tuft of Daisies	375
The Hallowed Beach	376
Night in Paradise	376
The Study	377
The Balcony	378
The Carmine Hill	378
A Walk in the Dawn I	379
Your Eyes	380
A Lady Most Lovely	381
Serenity	382
Adam and Eve	383
A Journey	384
The Arbor	387
Amour	388
Golden Shores	389
Our Bastion by the Sea	390

Table of Contents

Let Us Drink Our Fill ... 394
Your Name ... 396
Your Wake ... 397
Beneath the Archway ... 397
Beauty ... 398
The Song of Your Love ... 399
God ... 400
Peace II ... 401
My Lady II ... 401
Canticles ... 402
Fountains ... 403
The Fruit of Iguazú ... 404
The Rosary ... 405
Epilogue I ... 407

A Lady Fair and other Poems ... **409**

Introduction ... 411
A Lady Fair II ... 412
Emotions ... 413
Boughs ... 413
Two-Thirty ... 414
A Sailor's Song II ... 414
The Lake ... 415
A Voyage to Cyprus I ... 417
The Billowing Reeds ... 418
Wines II ... 419
It Is the Season ... 420
To Rebecca ... 421
I Shall Call for You, My Love ... 424
Love II ... 425
The Infinite ... 427

Table of Contents

When You Were Young	428
The Conservatory	429
Southern California, 1966	431
The Hallowed Eve	432
I Came Upon a Castle…	433
Autumn	435
We Shall Wander	436
We Shall Rove	437
Dreaming	438
Spring	439
A Voyage to Spain	440
The Music Room	443
It is Snowing in the Town	444
My Poetry	445
Beauty is Her Name	446
Recollection II	447
Our Chambers	448
An American Montage	449
Terror	451
A Carolingian Ride	452
Let Us Cross the River	453
The Lady of the Garden	454
My Irish Love	455
The Lost Art of Poetry	456
A Nocturne Song	457
A Soul in Purgatory	458
A Walk in the Dawn II	459
La Villa au Bord de la Mer	460
Hyde Park	462
Morning	463
An Elopement	464

Table of Contents

Dante's Saloon 465
Cafés 466
My Politics 467
Romance in Town 470
South of Florence 472
A Morning Song 474
The Meadows 475
A Troubadour's Song 475
Rain 476
Inebriation 477
I Once Lived in Luxury 478
Landscapes 479
October Nights 480
Madness 481
My Lady III 482
London, 1969 483
Juliet 485
On Poets 486
The Lane I 487
Your Mane, Your Eyes 488
Silhouettes 488
My Lady is Lovely 489
Summer 490
A Walk After Painting 491
An American Girl 492
An Autumn Sunset II 493
Candles 494
Epilogue II 495

Table of Contents

Ecstasy **497**

    Ecstasy 499

    An Angel's Song 500

    The Rose Garden 501

    Love III 502

    Ladies and Men 503

    The Grave of Charles Baudelaire 504

    Our Love 505

    Scarlet Breezes II 506

    The Bower 507

    To My Future Bride 510

    My Eternal Beloved 511

    Romance II 512

    A Garden in Paradise 513

    I Ventured Out Beneath the Moon 514

    Ode to Edgar Allan Poe I 515

    On My Way to Boston 516

    The Outer Darkness 517

    The Acropolis 518

    Of a Dark-Eyed Lady 519

    Of She Whom I Love 520

    Her Melody 521

    A Melody 522

    The Black Baby Grand 523

    A Walk in the Square 524

    A Walk With My Love 525

    The Muse 526

    I Walked with Byron 528

    Epilogue III 530

Table of Contents

Elysian Meadows *533*

    Introduction 535

    The First Sonnet 536

    The Autumn Lane 537

    Billowing Reeds 538

    The Black Concerto 539

    The Cloister II 540

    The Duchess 542

    The Garden II 543

    Ghost Ship 544

    The Grave of Arthur Rimbaud 545

    The Graveyard 546

    The Grove I 547

    One Hallowed Eve 548

    Love IV 549

    Lady of the Bastion I 550

    In the Summer She Paces 551

    The Palace II 552

    The Queen 553

    One Sacred Night 554

    The Shade 555

    The Sky is so Blue 555

    Song of Your Love 556

    The Square 557

    Starlit Night 557

    To Mary I 558

    To One in Heaven 560

    To You, My Love 561

    Torment (The Guest) 562

    Tremulous Seas 564

Table of Contents

The Gilded Sun and Other Verse..**567**
    Introduction 569
    The Gilded Sun.. 570
    A Lovers Song.. 571
    Heaven II 571
    A Reverie 572
    A Sailor's Song III 573
    A Walk With You 574
    A Winter's Night 575
    A Winter's Wood 576
    After Our Deaths I... 577
    Our Walk Amid the Reeds 578
    Am I Fine, Am I Beautiful? 579
    My Reader 580
    Winter 581
    Death at Sea 582
    The Cult of Dionysus.. 583
    The Princess II... 585
    Meditation 587
    Gales II 588
    The Palace III... 589
    The Death of the Pagan Gods 590
    Dreaming 593
    Spring 594
    A Voyage to Spain 595
    The Music Room 599
    It is Snowing in Town 600
    My Poetry 601
    Beauty is Her Name.. 602
    Recollection 603
    Our Chambers 604

Table of Contents

An American Montage 605

Terror 607

A Carolingian Ride 608

Let Us Cross the River 609

The Lady of the Garden 610

My Irish Love 611

The Lost Art of Poetry 612

A Nocturne Song 613

A Soul in Purgatory 614

A Walk in the Dawn 615

La Villa au Bord de la Mer 616

Hyde Park 617

Morning 618

An Elopement 619

Dante's Saloon 620

Cafés 621

My Politics 622

Romance in Town 625

South of Florence 627

A Morning Song 629

The Meadows 630

A Troubadour's Song 631

I Once Lived in Luxury 632

Landscapes 633

October Nights 634

Madness 635

My Lady 636

London, 1969 637

Juliet 638

On Poets 639

The Lane 640

Table of Contents

    Your Mane, Your Eyes 641

    Silhouettes 641

    My Lady is Lovely 642

    Summer 643

    A Walk After Painting 644

    An American Girl 645

    The Shade III 646

    Candles 646

    Epilogue IV 647

Mystic Wines **649**

    A Word From the Author 651

    Introduction 652

    The Regal Dawn 653

    Ode to Bram Stoker 654

    The Garden III 655

    Dusk II 656

    The Song of John Keats 657

    The Grove II 658

    The Ghost Ship 659

    Diadems 661

    The Lane II 662

    The Shrine of Saint Anne 662

    The Window Bay 663

    Stilled by a Sigh 664

    Her Silken Kiss 665

    The Half Opened Window 666

    After Many Sullen Years 667

    Isolation II 667

    One Fine Day 668

    Robert Louis Stevenson Samoa, 1894 669

Table of Contents

Byron's Ghost	670
Saint John's Wood	671
Saint Paul's Cathedral	672
Sailing	673
Ode to Saint John	674
The Farmhouse	675
The Storm II	676
Chillingham Castle	677
Blossoms in Her Hair	678
Roses on the Waves	679
My Love	680
A Sanctified Flame	681
On Soft, Spring Nights	681
In Shadows on Foot	682
Peace III	682
Tears	683
The Courtyard II	684
The Driest Place	685
The Good Road's End	686
The Ascension	687
My God, Thrice Holy	689

Table of Contents

Cathedrals in the Rain **691**

- Preface 693
- If You Give Your Heart Away 694
- Ecstasy (A Sonnet) 695
- The Courtyard III 696
- The Baby Grand 697
- The Duchess (A Sonnet) 698
- Behold 699
- Love V 700
- Who Doth Seek Me When I am Near? 701
- My Love, She Sleeps 702
- One Summer's Dawn 703
- Your Face II 704
- A Sonnet of the Shade 705
- Lady of the Bastion II 706
- A Litany to Mary 707
- Advice From a Father to His Son 709
- The Autumn Leaves are Falling 710
- My Dead Wife (1814) 711
- The Vagabond 713
- Ode to Paul Verlaine 714
- The Glory That is You 715
- The Piano 716
- Ophelia 717
- My English Love 719
- Dresden 720
- The Rain it Fell 721
- A Wedding to Be 722
- Sable Eyes 723
- The Ghost 724
- She Walks Beyond 725

Table of Contents

To Mary II	726
The Murderer	727
Andalusia	728
After Our Deaths II	729
An Angel's Song	730
The Duchess	731
Ladies	732
The Day Still Does Rise	733
Ode to Elizabeth Barret Browning	734
Two Ghosts	735
Night by the Bay	736
Dusk	736
My Sailor's Daughter	737
Blossoms in Her Hair	737
The Eve	738
The Castle	738
Your Song	740
Your Name	741
Your Majesty	741
Lucifer	742
A Courtyard's Sonnet	743
The Bells of Amiens	744
Nostalgia	745
Death	746
The Villa by the Sea	747
A Poem Written in Heaven	749
All Save for Heaven	749
Sunlight	750
The City	751
The One Whom You Admire	751
Come	752

Table of Contents

A Belgian Tale 753

Her Cadence 755

The Rose Clad Bower 756

The Black Night 757

The Ghost Ship 758

The Grave 759

The Regal Palace 760

The One I Love 761

Grace 762

Our Love 763

The Christian 764

About the Author *767*

About the Illustrator *769*

Index of Poems *771*

Introduction

By night on my bed
I sought him whom my soul loves…
The watchmen who go about the city found me;
'Have you seen him whom my soul loves?'
I had scarcely passed from them
When I found him whom my soul loves.
I held him and would not let him go
Until I had brought him into my mother's house…

These are words uttered by the Lover in Scripture's greatest love poem, *The Song of Songs* searching for her Beloved. The Lover seeks the satisfaction of eternal love. Theologians interpret this as a poetic expression of **the Soul's thirst for God**. Nothing less will do, or can do. This is theology and it is also the theme of John Lars Zwerenz's works, where one hears the echoes of his—and our—yearning hearts.

The words in the Song of Songs are often erotic, because they best express mystical love. The love that many saints had for Christ was often passionate, as were their actions. Mary Magdalene's grieving heart forced her to bathe Jesus' corpse, and when Jesus appears to her she *clings* to him. Saint Margaret Mary decides to drink a sick person's vomiting; Catherine of Siena actually does. Their love is beyond the pale. Saint Margaret of Cortona declares, "Plunge me in hell, Lord, so that at least one person will love you there!" Saint Thérèse of Lisieux, whom the pope, in canonizing her in 1925, declared her, "the greatest saint of modern times" scratched Jesus name with a pin on the wall of her room, something a lovesick adolescent does. Interestingly, Thérèse's favorite poetic verse comes from the Song of Songs, "Draw me, we will run after thee to the odor of thine ointments."

But the question of human love extending into heaven itself is an open question.

In a letter *To A Young Widow*, the 4th century Church Father, Saint John Chrysostom, consoles her broken heart with these this hope words:

> *For such is the power of love, it embraces, and unites, and fastens together not only those who are present, and near, and visible but also those who are far distant; and neither length of time, nor separation in space, nor anything else of that kind can break up and sunder in pieces the affection of the soul… do your best to manifest a life like his, and then assuredly you shall depart one day to join the same company with him, not to dwell with him for five years as you did here, nor for 20, or 100, nor for a thousand or twice that number but for infinite and endless age… the place of rest will receive you also with the good Therasius, if you will exhibit the same manner of life as his, and then you shall receive him back again no longer in that corporeal beauty which he had when he departed, but in luster of another kind, and splendor outshining the rays of the sun… What then is the place? It is Heaven. Send away your possessions to that good husband of yours and neither thief, nor schemer, nor any other destructive thing will be able to pounce upon them… And if you do this, see what blessings you will*

Introduction by Paul Franzetti

> *enjoy, in the first place eternal life and the things promised to those who love God, which eye has not seen, nor ear heard, neither have they entered into the heart of man, and in the second place perpetual intercourse with your good husband, "… you may inhabit the same abode and be united to him again through the everlasting ages, not in this union of marriage but another far better. For this is only a bodily kind of intercourse, but then there will be a union of soul with soul more perfect, and of a far more delightful and far nobler kind."*

What is it about Romantic Love that makes it so perduring? Simply, there is a "feel" of heaven about it. Love letters of *all* people, in all times, even the illicit ones, try to express and alleviate the furious desire of the Lover. The only difference is in talent, not in intention or emotion. Great poets rise above common words; they reach for wine with words. In *Cynara*, Ernest Dowson calls for "madder music and stronger wine!"

I cried for madder music and for stronger wine,
But when the feast is finished and the lamps expire,
Then falls thy shadow, Cynara! the night is thine;
And I am desolate and sick of an old passion,

Yea, hungry for the lips of my desire:
I have been faithful to thee, Cynara! in my fashion.

Even if this is love brooding over its own ruins, one can smiling ask, "Can an animal speak thus?" Surely this suggest the divine impulse.

More than two thirds of *The Complete Anthology* deals with this theme, this love ache. The verse is what such fulfillment *sounds* like; what it might feel like. Poem after poem hammers home the feverish longing. Keats caught our human attention in his unforgettable *Ode on a Grecian Urn*:

Ah, happy, happy boughs! that cannot shed
Your leaves, nor ever bid the Spring adieu;
And, happy melodist, unwearied,
For ever piping songs for ever new;
More happy love! more happy, happy love
For ever warm and still to be enjoy'd,
For ever panting, and for ever young;

And again in *Bright Star*:

No—yet still steadfast, still unchangeable,
Pillow'd upon my fair love's ripening breast,
To feel for ever its soft fall and swell,
Awake for ever in a sweet unrest,
Still, still to hear her tender-taken breath!

If Zwerenz falls suit, it is no surprise. Of eleven volumes of poetry in this anthology, *Eternal Verse* contains the largest number of poems containing this heady brew of romance and religion. **This is his unique trademark**. *On Entering Heaven* best expresses and summarizes this:

Introduction by Paul Franzetti

I ventured out among crystals,
Invisible to all but God...
I ascended the russets of Mars,
Beyond the gilded rings of Saturn,
Above the coveted curve of space,
I gazed down upon the innumerable beams
And their roving planets
Which seemed small as stones
Glistening in streams
To my widely enlightened eyes...
I met saints and angels, one by one,
In a new, incredible diamond sun.
I heard harpsichords play
In the amber light of their melodic sway,
And I took delight reclining in the furrows of gilded hay
In those wavering dales of boundless day...
And I met my queen by the laughing, white brook
Where she told me her beatific name,
And I undertook
Loving
And I loved her just the same
As I did on earth
And in her gleaming gaze's birth
She sang to me
A soft, delicious melody
Which flowed from the ring of the emerald mountains
To the spacious, marble courtyard, to its slender, white fountains
As the carriage of the King came to take us away
Into a higher, brighter, diamond hued light,
Devoid of stars, devoid of night,
Of purity, bliss and eternal day.

If this poem were set to music (or read while listening to music) the music should be Debussy's *Arabesque #1* or Ravel's *Ondine*. Even the *Song of Songs* would be enhanced by such music.

To the question, then, "Is there human love in heaven?" Zwerenz answers "Of course there is."

✍ ✍ ✍ ✍ ✍ ✍ ✍

I first met John Zwerenz in the fall of 1986 when he was a senior in my humanities class, a class that catered to his love of the classics. His first words to me after my lecture on Sappho were, "That was the best class on poetry I have had." Clearly, he meant it. And he impressed and awed his peers in class by answering questions when everyone else kept his hand down.

Introduction by Paul Franzetti

He was that rare student seeking answers. Education was serious business to him. Conversant with Byron, Shelley, Keats and Poe he was also a lover of French Symbolists like Rimbaud, Nerval, Baudelaire and Verlaine.

One day he read some poetry, then asked me, "What is your opinion of this?"

I thought he had written it and said, "No big deal."

"It's Rimbaud," he said,

Another day he was also reading Nietzsche and I cautioned him about atheism.

"Father S. said that Sartre could be forgiven but not Nietzsche. Why is that?"

Another day he spoke quietly about the recent death of his Spanish teacher, "It was as if Mr. M—had never existed. One day he was there, and the next, he wasn't."

At the end of his senior year, while most of his happy-go-lucky peers were looking forward to the prom and summer vacation, John was straining at the high drama of life's paradoxes.

I did not suspect that this budding young romantic rebel (who thought sleeping in a cemetery fostered Poe-like verses) would spend the rest of his life writing volumes of poetry on romantic love.

Certainly great poets was always a febrile topic for him. Whenever I engaged him on the subject, he was always quick to respond, like a batter at the plate focused on the next pitch.

"What do you think of Shelley's *Epipsychidion*? The idea of an eternal ideal love, "an angel of light… the light of the moon seen through mortal clouds, a star beyond all storms."

   Shelley was always a loaded topic, good for a monologue. Neither was Shelley any kind of Christian, let alone a Catholic. I questioned him about his own eternal romantic love's resemblance to Shelley's *Epipsychidion*. Even though Shelley idealized his love in *Emilia*. Zwerenz has no such woman in his present life. He is consecrated to chastity. Zwerenz seldom speaks of his own love, a woman of the sacred whom he gravely confesses he is well acquainted with, yet he speaks of her only rarely and then exclusively in the context of eternity. Unlike Zwerenz, Shelley was clearly not an otherworldly realistic romantic. Shelley's loves were mortal and continuous. Married to Mary Godwin, (he called marriage "wearisome") he dreamt of his life teen-aged countess. "I think one is always in love with something or other… I confess it is not easy for spirits cased in flesh and blood to avoid it, consists in seeking in a mortal image the likeness of what is, perhaps, eternal."

I would ask Zwerenz many questions. John once said: "Shelley hid himself in literature, but he did look up to Byron."

"Then what do you think of Byron?"

"Byron was like a homeless man trying to scribble in the sky. His efforts are beautiful, and he lived the poetry."

"Coleridge?"

Introduction by Paul Franzetti

"Coleridge had a better poetic muse, and he didn't go over board.

"The Decadents, your favorites?"

"The Decadents **were higher in that they were more ethereal, more heaven dwelling and more hell dwelling**."

"Verlaine?"

"From him I get a sense of intoxication where absinthe rules and the sunset is lavender. He died young because he couldn't see himself in this world anymore."

"Robert Frost?"

"Overrated, mundane. The meanings are not there. *Stopping By Woods* and *The Road Not Taken* are his best."

But for Edgar Allen Poe, John's praise would be unstintingly laudatory.

Zwerenz said of Poe: "Poe is the ultimate tragic lover in the extreme giving his whole self to God; his is the razor's edge towards deity; his *Annabel Lee* is a parable, close to what I write." He knew *To One In Paradise* by heart:

Thou wast that all to me, love,
For which my soul did pine—
A green isle in the sea, love,
A fountain and a shrine,
All wreathed with fairy fruits and flowers,
And all the flowers were mine.

Ah, dream too bright to last!

Ah, starry Hope! that didst arise
But to be overcast!
A voice from out the Future cries,
"On! on!"—but o'er the Past
(Dim gulf!) my spirit hovering lies
Mute, motionless, aghast!

For, alas! alas! with me
The light of Life is o'er!
No more—no more—no more—
(Such language holds the solemn sea
To the sands upon the shore)
Shall bloom the thunder-blasted tree,
Or the stricken eagle soar!

Introduction by Paul Franzetti

And all my days are trances,
And all my nightly dreams
Are where thy dark eye glances,
And where thy footstep gleams—
In what ethereal dances,
By what eternal streams.

Neither Poe nor the Decadents were enamored of religion; certainly Edgar Allen Poe was no Catholic. No theological impulse fuels his verse. Zwerenz's verse, on the other hand, ***is soaked in theology***. In *Ode to Saint John* in *Mystic Wines*, Saint John witnesses Mary's Assumption (a modern Catholic dogma). Saint John the Evangelist who, on earth, had taken her into his home, now witnesses, from their home in Turkey,

… her rise
Above the dell where the reeds did bend.
With the moon at her feet,
Surrounded by twelve brilliant stars,
In the ineffable realm of celestial skies,
Her glorious Assumption was complete…

Zwerenz does idealize one woman, over **all** women, Mary, the humble Jewess of Nazareth, Queen of Heaven.

The poem entitled *Mary, the Mother of God*, from *Eternal Verse,* is his longest, fullest, most ardent paean to Mary:

I met the Mother of God donning bright diadems.
Her long, black hair
Is astonishing to behold
As if all gold
Finds nits temple there.
Her crown is studded with immaculate jewels,
Each the reward of a Saint's fidelity.
With tender love she commands all citadels,
And all the angels glory in her beauty…
She rarely wishes to be alone,
Except for the times she converses with her Son,
Pacing on the hallowed beach, where streams
Of violets swirl around her feet,
And run
To the tranquil sea, beneath the terrace where the vines meet…
Nothing, no one, save
God Himself
Possesses such a lovely face…

Introduction by Paul Franzetti

And she loves to say
When the consecrated pray
In their cloisters of rapture,
Clad with lindens willows and oaks and birch:
"God bless the Holy Roman Catholic Church!
Its eternal truths be praised!"

In this poem and in the majority of his work, his theological stand is final, his poetry and prose unapologetic. He writes:

> *I want you to understand that my own personal religious, metaphysical and ontological beliefs (or what is relevant to the doctrinal teachings of The Roman Catholic Church; which are in accord with my own) may very well differ vastly from your own such beliefs and that I am not attempting to alter your own personal religious, agnostic or atheistic views. Firstly, I mention this topic because I believe it to be necessary in regards to the similar themes contained within this present volume, to afford the reader a more profound insight into this collection of poems. I shall briefly put in words a summary of circa 2,000 years of unapologetic Catholic Theology. I will then try to my best abilities address your prospective poetic related questions one by one in regards to this book and to these matters. I trust I am clear in my words.*

He is not shy about rejecting other creeds.

> *No other religion is salvific in the absolute or even relative sense. The cross is the sole means to paradise. In Islam, Allah, or "god" is a transcendent being, **unknowable** to the individual… In Judaism "god" is likewise **transcendent and unknowable** to the human being and there is a general belief that "good" people go to heaven as in Islam, but that heaven is freely given without the need for a medium to allow man to acquire paradise through faith in the man-God of Jesus Chris… Hinduism espouses the idea of cyclical reincarnation until one achieves a state called "Nirvana" where and when one loses his or her identity and becomes a cosmic abstraction. Buddha was a philosopher and an agnostic. **So whereas God is unknowable in all other major world religions, He is the Object of perfect union in Catholic theology**… [Emphases are the Poet's]*

More poetically he says, "When I write I try to hear what the Holy Spirit is whistling in the boudoir. Yes, I try to hear that first."

I asked him "What do you want to say to your readers?"

> *I write verse to convince atheists and despairing people that they have a creator who loves them. My poetry was written in order to re-awaken man to his God-given origins.*

> *We are made of spirit, but 'the flesh is a hinge of our salvation, as Tertullian says. What Poe, Byron and Verlaine, to name a few, gave to me, I want to give to other poetic souls. I choose words that communicate the ethereal qualities of the spirit world. I want to give them proof of a loving God that will make my readers comprehend objective truths. To prove to all: man, woman, young and old, that Divine love saves you; you do not stem from a meaningless void. It is not a Meaningless Voice that Calls to you. You should find His voice now, now or never. There is this urgent accent in my poetry*

Introduction by Paul Franzetti

which is the urgent accent to this life. Whatever you do, you must pursue your Savior. Over the years I reacted to other great poems which espoused what I have written here, and I was confirmed in my convictions.

✍ ✍ ✍ ✍ ✍ ✍ ✍

Eternal Verse (2012) concerns itself with love between two people in Heaven itself.

When I wrote Eternal Verse (2012) I was not interested in worldly love, but in the love which takes place in heaven between a man and a woman. In the latter case, the soul is perfected and can not go against reason as it can and often does here. The question then arises how can two "make love" in heaven without a body? The answer is that they can not until the general resurrection at the end of time when they take up a glorified body forever, such as Christ and Mary possess now.

*It is also a belief in Catholicism that there are also eternal virgins who **never** give themselves or unite in romantic love with the opposite sex. As for my own personal conviction, I always equated romanticism with realism, because **life is beautiful as is God and his children are beautiful**. Love is the most important aspect of humanity and life and is indeed God Himself in His quintessence.*

As far as boundaries go, there are none in paradise nor in what we cordially call heaven. Love itself is infinite and knows no limits. The truth is heaven is wonderful beyond conception, and I personally believe with my whole heart that it is our collective and individual eternal destiny. But it must be chosen freely by man and worked for.

*Because man is the absolute, definitive summit of all of God's creations, he will eventually regain a glorious body. The body is animated by the soul, not the other way around. So sex in this life is ultimately linked to both body and soul, for the two in this life are one. **It is in the human will however that one chooses between right or wrong, good or evil**. The body then takes its cue from the soul which animates it. Since our natures are fallen in part still in effect from original sin, it is exceptional for a man and a woman to engage in the marriage act without feeling the dominating spirit of lust, especially when that act is consummated outside of the sacrament of marriage. The lower appetites tend to interfere with the more lofty expressions of the soul concerning the God intended mutual expressions of true love. This is just as true for the female as it is true for the male obviously, and for females in more cases than not (for females, due to the differentials concerning what Eve did and to what extent in her heart she did sin) compared with the differences and specifics of Adam's sins.*

God intended Adam and Eve to propagate human glory and make them 'divine' through the sacrament of union. Had Adam and Eve not failed the test, all humanity would have enjoyed the freedom to love as in the Song of Songs or to dedicate their chaste ardor, their sanctified passion as eternal virgins. Saint Francis of Assisi and Saint Clare are of the first brand of inhabitants of Paradise. Aside from the glorious, unspeakable heights of Mary most powerful.

Almost all his verse celebrates the ineffable ecstasies of the union "that some souls in heaven will enjoy." According to him, The Magisterium of the Catholic Church, agreeing with the opinion of many saints, affirms that "aside from eternal virgins there are eternal lovers… "

✍ ✍ ✍ ✍ ✍ ✍ ✍

Introduction by Paul Franzetti

Like Plato, Zwerenz's world of perfect ideas—heaven—leapfrogs the mundane world which sickens with mutability and separation; this world of Becoming never stops rotating on time's axis. In Zwerenz's verse the heart is not subject to Time's wrinkles—or "time's sickle" as in Shakespeare immortal Sonnet 116:

Love's not Time's fool, though rosy lips and cheeks
Within his bending sickle's compass come;
Love alters not with his brief hours and weeks,
But bears it out even to the edge of doom.

Transcendence for Zwerenz will resolve this dilemma of romantic love. If there are no old people in heaven, as the saints like to tell us, there are no lonely lovers either,. Zwerenz's heaven is composed only of lovers.

I walk beneath the Holy Father's sun,
Hand in hand with my beloved one.
Among the teeming, bright, holly-green pines,
Which carry on the breezes of perfumed wines.
    From *The Sea Below the Forest of Pines*

Let love unite us
In this ageless age
    From *Let Us Rove*

I shall ponder you,
And possess your every thought, your every movement,
Your mystic dream
As the glistening firmament
Reflects its majestic glory in your sable gaze's gleam
    From *In the Evening*

This language of human love divinized is also the language of Zwerenz in his poetry. Zwerenz' poetic optimism about a heaven is unflinching. Love is the essence of all that is poetry. For years he has sung songs of eternal joy. All his verse begins and ends there. If the reader wants to see and experience such mystical throbbing in the human veins, read on.

Paul Franzetti, PhD
Professor Emeritus of English Literature
Saint John's University, New York
September, 2019

I

Selected Poems

I Trod Upon the Glade...

I trod upon the glade
And all
became amorous;

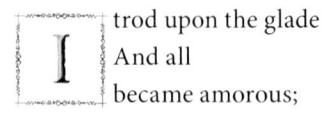

I fixed my gaze
Upon beatitude,

And I beheld my fair lady
Clad in a white dress,
With sable eyes
And raven hair.

Her look passed through me
And my spirit became transparent
And I was a mystery to myself
No more.

To One So Fair

Her eyes are dusky
And her mane is fair,
And many rare perfumes
Dwell so sweetly there.

Though she is of the past
Her cast is of today.
And in her longing gazes
Serenades still softly play.

And in my admiring mind
Her images shall stay,

As a wistful, azure angel
Her face shall remain with me,
Swaying every dappled frond with grace
Of every spring-clad, emerald tree.

For she sends me into rapture
With the touch of her scarlet kiss.
And the things of heaven
Are made of this.

Selected Poems

Your Hair

I could write the strain of a rain-clad memoir,
Or verse composed roving on the downy ground,
Or sing my lyrics to the sullen sound
Of ballads played in a small, lonesome bar.
I could look at the beauty of Renoir
Of beneath my gaze to a blue Monet,
Or recline in bed on a bronze Sunday
Musing on classics to grace my guitar.
But these flowers fail to assuage the ice,
The egregious chill of the pain I know
Standing near a church where the wedding rice
Is thrown for another groom in the snow.
I have walked through the countryside more than twice
Dreaming of your hair, braided in a bow.

The Duchess I

I cherish the dire fire of my trembling
As I watch you from the palace depart
In a queenly coach, your face resembling
A beauty more grave than all found in art.
Myrtle blooms perfume your midnight-hued hair.
Your gazes glitter in the flaxen light.
The courtyard gleams beneath a ringdove's flight
As marigolds sway in your regal air.
You ignite within me a deep desire
More than the muses could ever inspire
As you glide on the sunlit, olive grass
In daisy-laced winds of the afternoon.
My profound, fervid dream ceases to pass
To kiss your lips beneath the flaming moon.

Selected Poems

Browns

The benevolent, dark browns
That weep within your liquid eyes
Touched by mignonettes beside the sea
Are amorous, enchanting raindrops
Which find the spire of their gracile glory

In your gaze which makes my spirit whole,

Where flows, like a sunlit waterfall
The majestic quintessence
Of your sanctified soul.

For I have walked beside you
In your spirit's fountain
Beholding its bold magnificence
In the late spring afternoon,
When the sun's gold glistens
Upon the balconies, in silence.

In the Bower

In the hushed, boundless bower; we slowly roved alone,
Saffron rays descended through the glinting aspen trees.
Your fair; resplendent face, graced by a timorous breeze
Shone among the sprawling ivy, strewn upon the stone.

Near tall, marble columns, half-visible through the vines
Beneath the leaf-clad boughs of sonorous olive wines
Stilled, we stood in wonder—As you looked into my eyes
An adorned, while carriage passed amid our shroud of sighs.

Some straying, vivid petals swirled to the vernal ground
In vast, quiescent arbors colored effulgently bold.
The blissful soul of summer rejoice without a sound.
In florid gardens near the glade your hair was painted gold.
For your tender; brown eyes where fell a pensive shower,
I waited for the warmth of their visual address
To drink the rare champagne of their deep gaze by the cress,
Beside the quiet brook, in the silence of the hour.

Selected Poems

The Princess I

In a palatial courtyard where a fountain shines,
Its pearly, silver flow, falling like fragrant wines,
A princess gathers roses, with rare felicity,
Beneath an ardent sky, by a statuary.

On brisk, spring afternoons when the booklet is swelled
With currents that gleam beneath teeming, budding trees,
Her grace loves to wander in the somnolent breeze,
To gaze into the stream, where all her cares are quelled.

And when the oaks cast their shade upon the grass,
She roves among the maple-scented bowers
Dreaming of ecstasy amid the flowers,
As I pine by a trellis for her to pass.

But my head grows heavy
When I behold her beauty,
And my heart grows weak
When she wanders slowly by,
And I try to speak—
But I can only sigh.

Selected Poems

Wine

My lover enthralls me with her charmed, innocent wade
Beneath the dipping branches in the broad, breezy park;
In the languorous afternoon, she waits for the dark
When russet petals waver in the redolent shade;

Among the sandy, fall glow which finds burgundies of bliss,
In the thickets here and there and on the half-while grass,
As she daydreams unaware, I watch her slowly pass
Wearing a long, grayish coat—living only for a kiss.

As the dusk grows deeper; in the shade of the tower;
On an ancient, stone bridge, over a still, shallow stream,
My sable-haired princess holds a delicate flower,
To place by the statues, where enchanted lovers dream;

Her chaste and solemn soul is deepened by a sorrow,
As she pines in her heart with a dignified grace;
She is blind to the heavenly raptures I borrow,
As my eyes sip wine from her fair; angelic face.

Your Gaze

You pass by an ivory portico
Amid the profoundly tranquil silence
Of an eminent, verdant hedgerow.
In leisurely calms of mosaic hours,
You absorb the radiant elegance
Of an ancient castle's vine-clad towers.

Your pristine and classic countenance
Blushes in a willow's graceful glow,
In the vivid, mild, blossoming boon
Of the fragrant, yellow afternoon.

Your serene and solemn trance
Is captured in the glance
Of a lucid, blissful gaze
Where the summer royally looms,
Beholding the gold, majestic glaze
Of sun-kissed, violet blooms.

Selected Poems

As in a Dream

I have seen your hallowed heart
Given in a tender glance,
Where the splendid, ancient art
Of the cypress trees dance.

I have seen you on a balcony,
In a flowing, long, white dress,
Opening its regal, noon-kissed bay
To greet the summer sun
Which glistened upon your hair;
Dusky and undone,
Wavy, black and long.

I have put your name to music,
To a poignant, wistful song;
It plays in the boughs,
Over the emerald grass;
In the late afternoon,
I hear it pass
Like the winds of the ages,
Each succeeding like the pages
Of a book of verse,
Each line of the same theme,
Of seeing you walk
Slowly, as in a dream,
Among a thong of roses,
And the rustling of a stream.

Selected Poems

An Ecstasy

Her long, dark locks wavered in the breeze.
As my soul ascended above the trees,
All became a diamond light—
Brighter than any earthly sun;

I beheld her hair through the brilliant fountain,
A her pitch-black tresses were overcome
By the shine of flaming, silver pearls,
Until I fell into an azure sea
From where I saw her walking,
Walking very slowly,
Passed a teeming, stone wall—
Adorned with vines;

She passed with the ineffable gracefulness
Of an angel immersed in gold,
In a dress of regal white,
As billows soft and laced with fragrance
Kissed her hair with tears.

Selected Poems

As You Lay

I shall call for you as you preen your hair,
Brushing your tresses in your perfumed lair;
In your grand, cushioned carriage,
Beneath the lindens we shall ride
On the day before our marriage,
To the florid, purple hills
Of the quiet countryside.

As we pass beneath the lofty stills
Of the glistening, golden crest,
Upon your lips the sun shall play,
Gilding their crimson—as you lay
In the cosmic boon of your tranquil rest;

We shall dream of a vast, palatial space,
Drunk with the redolent chardonnay
Of clustered coronets in a boundless place;
We shall drink from heaven rapturous sighs,

And I shall kiss your fair, tender face
While looking intensely—into your eyes.

The Poetic Dimension

Her classic countenance
Reads the intangible verse,
On a cypress-lined path
In the veils of spring;

She is a witness to the blossoming
Of fountains in the sobbing trees,
Gracing the lamenting silence
Of an ancient, weeping statue.

And as she passes through the mist and flame,
Shrouded by the lavender lights
Of ethereal, mystic sunsets
Which languish in the nebulous demise
Of tenebrous, foggy tendrils, of soporific days,
Angels cloak her radiance—
Descending from boundless skies.

Sunlight

Vines on stone,
Wines pouring from the hills,
The sunlight plays
Among the glistening daffodils;

The mellifluous tone
Of the sacred cello
Resonates through the trees
In the sunlight's billow,
Descending on a wind-swept willow—
Amid the rapture of fallen leaves.

Selected Poems

Tinges

Blessed are the tinges, indistinct,
That weep like dappled daisies in the fragrant wind,
Lamenting in the smallest remnants of the rain
That gleam between the arched, while petals
Of ancient, sunlit gardens
Among the colonnades of courtyards
Ageless as the mountains,
Near the archway of the cloisters
Amid the glitter of sobbing fountains,
Where the brows of slender grasses
Grace the turquoise streams.

By the Manor House She Walks

Around the age-old balcony sways a basswood tree,
It frames the alcove's bay with gleaming leaves of green,
As its wood absorbs the sun, unseen,
My lady roves through tepid gales carried from the sea.

About she walks, by moss-covered stones,
On a paved path, near a bed of roses,
Which wavers in a row, and gently discloses
Melodies of solemn tones.

Now and then a whisper stirs in the bower;
A rustle plays in the tall, sallow reeds,
She innocently smiles in this soft, monastic hour;

Her heart is of peace in the wake of good deeds.
Her pace is of an angel's, with each foot that is laid;
She is clad in a peacoat, and her hair is in a braid.

Beneath the Green Palms

The boundless bower by the lapping lake
Reflects the sun in the glory of spring,
Where we, as angels, marry wing with wing
Beneath pink blossoms which sway in our wake.
We wander in love, as in days of yore
In unspeakable raptures, as we dream;
Your ambrosial hair weeps in the gleam
Of mystic lights, by the sallow shore.
(I know your rapturous busses were destined for me.)
In a quiet cove, where the tranquil breeze
Wept though the boughs of the sycamore trees,
I first beheld you by the turquoise sea,
Where your long, black hair into gold was made,
Beneath the green palms, in the still night's shade.

Monet is Still Here

An azure sky beams, dreams rustle in the grass,
The town is at peace; its vespertine bells
Rise from a cathedral's fane; its rustic tower knells
As the sun descends—a few billows pass.
Monet would adore the hues by the lake.
He would laud the light of your sable hair;
And be held captive by the summer air,
Perfumed by the rose of your scarlet wake.
He would paint your gaze and your every tress,
Where the soft, nascent moonlight finds its place
In the ericaceous crown of your gilded grace:—
In your raven mane, my holy empress.
His canvass is near, as I kiss your hand,
Monet is still here; his soul is still grand.

Selected Poems

Your Tresses Reposed

I have seen bright stars in your sable eyes;
I have seen you walk with your long, black hair,
In tranquil gardens, of soft, summer air;
I have kissed you in dreams—and heard your sighs.
In visions of peace, in visions of light,
You wander by the chapel where we met,
Among the statues, where the sun's rays set,
So sublime to you in your sacred sight.
I see you beneath the pendulous billows,
Of graced, swaying leaves, of viridescent blooms.
I have seen you lie in your sanctified rooms
Your tresses reposed upon your scented, white pillows.
Yet, mostly profoundly, I have seen your pure soul—
And no longer rended, my heart is made whole.

Scarlet Breezes I

Scarlet breezes gently trail
Through the tall and slender, sallow reeds
Sanctifying as they sail
The misty mint of scattered seeds;

Now is the time for pregnant stills,
As the languishing sunlight softly fades,
Tinting the cloister's colonnades—
Amid the golden daffodils.

Upon the Beach

To find repose in a quiet place,
Upon the warm sand, amid small dunes,
Inhaling the wines of a thousand Junes,
The dark-eyed princess reclines with grace.

Her spirit is soft, and her heart is kind;
The calm, solemn concert of the winds and waves,
Veering through her psyche, gently as it laves,
Effaces all the cares within her mind.

She is one with the tranquil, sloping sea,
Cradled by its billows, rolling and white;
Her soul is betrothed to the source of all light.

Immersed in the bliss of eternity,
Near her; I behold of what I can not write:—
Her unspeakable beauty—so chaste in God's sight.

My Contrite Heart

The myrtle's boughs and the bright yellow birch
Await the gray sky, ripe with fresh rains
To assuage the thirst of the olive plains
Beyond the tall reeds, by the old, wooden church.

The crimson roof of the rustic fane,
Where the cross is kissed by the veering gales
Which turn the old vane as the red sun pales,
Through weathered, it still gleams where the vines remain.

Prodigious, the dusk with its wistful refrain
Heard only by myself, as I walk alone,
Mounting the steps of the still chapel's stone,
Removes the dead leaves from the wilting mane
Of the silent birch which trembles from my sin
Of my contrite heart, lamenting within.

From the Balcony

From far down below your grand bay window,
Which glitters above the sun-painted valley,
Of spender, of regalia, of chivalry,
I stand entranced, as the winds come and go.
In the ancient castle's tallest tower;

You open the sashes with your soft, white hands
Gazing on the vast, enchanted, green lands
As the balcony gleams above the bower.

Your indigo look and your long, sable hair
Send my soul into rapture, as I quiver and stare.
And there, ethereal, you choose to be still;

You utter not a word, and only with your eyes
You speak into my own, like a daffodil—
And our souls are immersed in a thousand sighs.

Selected Poems

As the Sun Descends

Open the shutters to the indolent winds,
As the sun descends and dusk begins.
The kettle whistles upon the old, brick stove;
Let us retire to our fire lit cove.

Let the gentle, approaching shades of night
Grace the worn, dusty books beside ourselves,
As the cat sleeps soundly beneath the shelves,
The cozy crackle of the hearth gleams bright.

What a sweet and reverent, sacred sight
To see you in your long, silken dress,
Awaiting my hands to adorn your tress,
As the water of your eyes are filled with light.

So open the curtains to the soft, sleepy breeze,
As the sun sheds red through the sycamore trees.

Vespertine Fire

The boundless ocean, beneath our terrace
Is not far to reach for your deep, dark eyes;
Let us drown our souls in the sunlit sighs
Of the calm, russet sea which reflects God's grace.

Come, my young princess, into my embrace;
Let your tears of felicity shed their dear light

As they trail down my chest, pining for the night
When I love you best in that sacred place;

There angels descend with a thousand white stars,
Pouring sweet, white wines from their gilded guitars,
When courtyards rejoice with their soft violins.

As our ineffable ardor just beings,
All becomes fiery flames of desire;
Oh, welcome the dusk—and its vespertine fire!

Gently Near She Comes

My eternal queen comes gently near,
Smiling as she roves upon the dew clad glade
Of the breeze-cradled green,
In the still, dappled shade,
Slowly, by the belvedere;
Free from all woes, like the ruby dawn,

She walks in bliss on the olive lawn,
As her sable diamonds softly rise
From the sacred deep
Of her raven eyes;

In the dear, soft grace of her amorous sighs
I shall bury my brow and find my rest
In the sanctified sleep
Of her dew-clad breast.

A Supplication

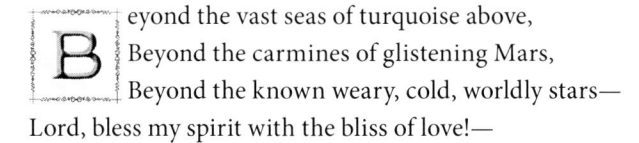

Beyond the vast seas of turquoise above,
Beyond the carmines of glistening Mars,
Beyond the known weary, cold, worldly stars—
Lord, bless my spirit with the bliss of love!—

For what in this life is as effluent
As a waterfall inspired by a tender kiss,
To bathe in the moonlight and reminisce—
To look to the morrow without lament?

For I have trod upon the starless trails,
And wept beneath the many thankless moons;
I sobbed by the sea, and witnessed the sails.

Yet the blue expanse denied me all boons,
Until I embraced the creed of all sages,
And let my love's muses compose all my pages.

Selected Poems

Majestic Heights

Lend your ear to the white-winged robin,
Sobbing in the somnolent sycamore tree,
Surrounded by the lights
Of majestic heights,
Where the sun-clad leaves
Meet the violet nights,
Reflecting the delights
Of the courtyard's glory,
Where the ivory of the stunning stars
Mingles with the gleaming glades,
Gilding the viridescent dew,
As the day gently fades
Into the vast boon
Of the arboreal blue
And the pensive rue
Of the mystic moon,
Lamenting as it weeps:—
Welcome to the night;
And the weary day;
"Adieu."

Flaxen Gold

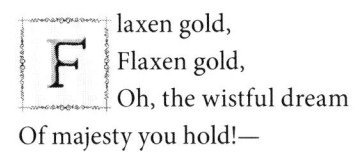

Flaxen gold,
Flaxen gold,
Oh, the wistful dream
Of majesty you hold!—

Entranced beside the stream
Graced by the sun,
Royal and bold,
You undo every fold
Of my pure, endeared exalted one;

Her billowing, white sleeves,
Bright in your caress,
Perfumes the flaxen leaves
With a scent of happiness;

For beneath the ancient boughs,
Where muses rove and await the night
All of living's whys and hows
Are answered in your gazes' light—
In their gleam

Of flaxen gold;
Oh, the wistful dream
Of majesty you hold!

Selected Poems

Beside the Stream...

Beside the stream,
The stairways gleam—
Beneath the moon,
The lamplights beam
Where the angels dream—
Of a tranquil noon;

The ripples veil
A tenebrous trail
Of billows below,
Concealed from the light,
Of the Paris aglow—
In the currents of night.

Let Me Sleep

Let me sleep, let me sleep,
Where the angels keep
Their sentineled care
Of souls unaware;

Please let me drown
In the greenish brine,
Of the Seine's choice wine
Which ferments the town;

Oh, let me wander in the dim,
Lavender vales of seraphim;
Let my vision behold
The sunrise of gold
Which embraces each bough
With a rose-laced breeze—
As I wipe my brow
In your ruffled sleeves.

By the Seine

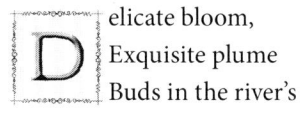

Delicate bloom,
Exquisite plume
Buds in the river's
Rare perfume;

A delicious wind
Stirs in the trees
Where the songbirds' fleece;
Touched by a breeze,
Calls to mind
My ecstasies.

Paris

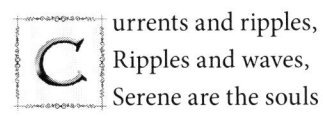

Currents and ripples,
Ripples and waves,
Serene are the souls
In your watery graves;

Serene are the lights
Of your majestic enclaves,
Of rose-embellished
Stone-framed bays;

Of balconies,
Of ambers,
Of splendid avenues;

The symphonies
Of ramblers
Bless your flowing hues.

The Bride

Near the alcove
The bride does rove,
Awaiting my kiss,
As she dreams in the courtyard—
Of a pristine bliss.

She searches for her bard
On approaching ships,
In the quivering boughs
Where the breeze allows
Her scarlet lips
To bless the shade—
Of amaranthine perfume,
In a bower by the Seine,
Where our sacred vow of betrothal was made
Beneath the dappled trees, in a sunlit June.

My delicious, impassioned, romantic mind
Finds solace in her soundness—
Of a solemn and hallowed, eternal kind.

Silhouette

The soft silhouette
Of a fair brunette
Haunts my nights
Yet inspires my days.
And I always behold her;
Among the lights,
By the ancient streets,
In the old cafes;

She passes slowly by,
(Entrancing my eye)
Like a youthful specter
Of a glorious queen.
(A piano's tune arises there,
On her path, in the bath of the perfumed air—
Beneath the shady leaves of green.)

Her spirit and her face
Are deeper than the sea;
An appeasing glance
From her royal grace
Is a potent trance
Of ecstasy.

For I have seen her soul,
On the sunlit balconies,
And wept many streams
Of a sad, wistful wise.
For she holds all my dreams—
In the ocean of her eyes.

Ennui

The rain which fell
Has joined the past—
Never to descend
Once more like the last;

The face of the day
Sent my muses away.
For she stays as she was—
An actress in a play.

So I return once more,
As I leave the cafe,
To my empty, cold room
By the Seine's dim shore,
Haunted by a tedium
In my constant, mortal gloom—
When every flower fails to bloom.

A Lady Fair I

At the foot of a castle, where a forest glowed,
In a long forgotten ancient time,
An azure brook flowed
Beneath a holly-green pine,
And other trees in the perfumed breeze
Which winnowed through the reeds like a sacred wine
In the soft and dulcet autumn clime.

In the highest tower;
Above the bower;
A lady most lovely, a lady most fair
Would gaze upon a noble prince,
Where he stood, as in a wistful dream,
Alone, beside the listening stream,
Ever since he beheld her classic face,
And her raven mane—of regal grace.

He pined with a grave and solemn stare,
For never was a beauty so ravishing and rare—
Yet he chose to keep her distance there.
And so he wept, by the brook that still grieves,
In the cool of the crisp, October air—
Amid the still of dappled leaves.

Wreaths

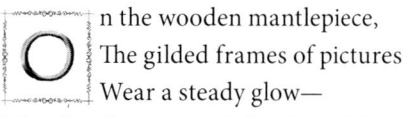

On the wooden mantlepiece,
The gilded frames of pictures
Wear a steady glow—
Like the silver rims of abandoned sleighs
Lying in the moonlit snow;

The exalted wreaths that adorn your gaze,
The lacrimal hues that embellish your cast,
Ignite within my heart an emotive blaze,
As they shimmer in the wintry gales
Like a starry mast
Of windblown sails.

Beneath the Boughs

I have sobbed beneath the pendulous boughs;
I have wept beneath the gleaming terrace.
I have lamented in the branches,
Where my mind has felt
The velvet touch
Of every spring,
All the radiant summers—
Dazzling with brilliance
From immaculate heights
Of resplendent turquoise;

I have witnessed all the universe,
Beyond what merely eyes can see:—
The veils in the splendor
Of the autumn woods;
The hidden trembling of the snow clad reeds;
The cloak of winter's ethereal whispers.

Yet nothing has moved me more
Than she.

Radiant Angel

Radiant angel
Bathing—
My young, exquisite one,
Let your sable tresses
Perfume the scarlet sun;

Inhale each star
In my amorous caresses;
Betroth your spirit to the golden seas,
Perpetual and full of sighs,
Whispering weeping, hallowed cries,
Where paradise finds ecstasies—
In the dusky diamonds
Of your eyes.

Selected Poems

Sacred Glances

In our rustic cabin,
Over tea,
Your sacred glances
In the twilight dances
With solemn stars—
Majestically;

The glowing bars
Within the hearth
Caress your face
Like an angel's hand,
Softer than silk—
From beyond the earth.

And all the stars
They weep in space,
And tint the panes
With a fountain's trace.

A Kiss

How precious is a lover's kiss!—
The azure winds are made of this,
And perfumed boughs
Which harbor gold,
In the music of the spritely soft spring
And of the wintery cold.

All cherished vows
Are always new
And never fade
Among the old.

For the sunlit sheens of an everglade
Speak of a chivalrous heart's crusade,
In every season, touched by love,
Of celestial reason, bestowed by hands
From far above
The mystic lands.

Selected Poems

Where Roses Weep

Of all the roads I have wandered on,
Of all the things my mind has seen,
With vision never strayed nor gone—
Perspicacious, clear and keen,
I never saw a transcendent bloom
As profound and lovely as your eyes,
Where the starry heavens greet the moon
With a symphony of lullabies;

I never beheld a more enchanting place
More grand than the garden of your gazes' gleams,
Where roses weep, as in sanctified dreams,
Endowed with every season, of a timeless grace.

Twilight

My bride and I exchange soft looks,
Known only to ourselves;
The ghost of Bach plays among the books,
Amid the rustic shelves;

Our fireplace gives off its glow,
As twilight stirs within her eyes;
Outside, upon the portico,
The last of the sallow sunlight dies.

Ambrosia

Now is the time for silence.
The words have all been said.
My queen reclines upon our bed,
As the reticent realms of reverence
Crown golden halos around her head—
Beside the flickering timbers' red.

Now is the time for sanctity,
As the crackling, crimson embers there
Glow a I inhale the sea
Of black ambrosia from her hair.

Sanctified and Bright

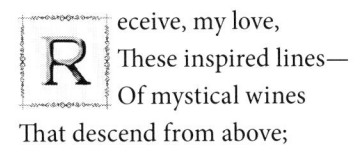

Receive, my love,
These inspired lines—
Of mystical wines
That descend from above;

Receive, my dearest,
The tender moon,
Auriferous and soft,
Of an amorous June
When tall pines quiver;
Adorned and old,
Effacing the shiver
Of the minty cold,
Behold, my love,
What true romance
Is fashioned of
When courtyards dance,
Cabalic and of ancient style,
Of fountains and of light,
Until we walk upon the aisle—
Sanctified and bright.

Selected Poems

Where the Sun Laments

Amid the courtyard's colonnades,
Where the sun laments
As it gently fades,
Your spirit's coves
And sacred tents
Wind and rove
As you search for me,
Beneath a wavering, dappled clove,
In a rapturous boon—
Of ecstasy.

In the Lamplight

In the mansion immense,
The candlelights
Glitter in the halls
Where the dark is dense—
As winds of whispers tap the walls;

The tender nights
Of starry grays
Are silent as an urn in bloom;

In your lamplight room
You undo your braids
With gracility—
Unafraid of gloom.

And with a solemn sanctity,
I tremble as I stare,
Gazing upon your pristine face,
As you preen your long and raven hair
With a statuesque, angelic grace.

And in the lamplight, soft and still,
I behold your lips with a fiery thrill,
As you place your brush beside your bed;

You ringlets lay upon your back,
Voluptuous, of a midnight-black,
And all my soul is a blazing red.

Selected Poems

Within Your Soul

Your soft, eternal beauty
Which time can not erase
Is found within your saintly soul—
Possessing such a pious place;

Your inner depth
Of gilded hues
Blends with the brooklet's
Turquoise blues,
Amid the park,
Where leaves aflame
Fall from sunlit, dappled boughs—
From where I always hear your name.

The Autumn Rain

The autumn rain
Of a mystic mien
Descends on the plain of amber-green
And laves me of my lifelong pain.

The balconies' sublime refrain
Shimmers beneath the dreary clouds,
Unveiling fall's lamenting shrouds
Concealed within a gold domain.

And the chosen one, she wanders by,
As a rainbow paints the clearing sky
Beneath the boughs in the old, quaint park—
Pining for a kiss in the starless dark.

November

Colors grace your leaf-clad land,
Of scarlet and of gleaming gold;
Beneath the turrets, where I stand,
Your frost-feathered breeze renews the old;

I hear your elegy in the coves,
Of windblown, wilting, riven hedgerows
Graced by the solemn, sanguine stills
Resembling the hush of moon-laced hills:—
A wistful strain that idly roves,
Tinting your sunsets, soft and sad,
As I wonder amidst your gentle dew
Half-mad,
Consumed with thoughts of you:—
My lover of November skies
Which fill your dark, angelic eyes
With visions of Noel anew.

An Elegy

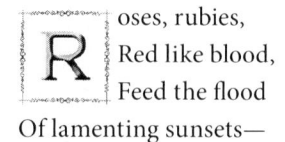

Roses, rubies,
Red like blood,
Feed the flood
Of lamenting sunsets—

Sobbing in the autumn wood;
I would lift my spirits if I could,
As I bequeath my tears to God.
And though for some it might seem odd—
I can not live without a bride.

For my psyche dives into the tide
Of starless rivers, deep and wide,
With every fading, passing night
Without her tender, gentle hand;
My life perceives no trace of light—
And only angels understand.

Before We Met

In the sallow sunset,
By the vine-clad stone,
Before we met—
No joy was known.

I would walk alone
In the April breeze,
Beneath the moonlight's weeping wines;

The leaves would sway
Above my head,
Near eglantines
Where my spirit bled,
Amid the leaves of a russet-red,
Of the silent meadow
That knew no bound,

The last of the snow
Clothed the melancholic glade
And its somnolent mound
With the gloom I found
In the prescient glow
Of the misery I had made.

For still, I had no arm to hold,
As a stream of tears would sting and trail;
The sun would shed its lacrimal gold,
Anointing grief—
On the sobbing dale.

Selected Poems

Of a Regal Grace

I

For you, my love—
A new bouquet;

The sunset, scattered,
Sifts through the myrtles,
In a nimbus of sweet and soft array,
As you sit beside me,
Modest in your evening dress.

The wind was from the north today.
And the swirling leaves
Glitter amid the gleaming cress,
Majestic in the gentle gales
Of the reticent wood,
As daylight pales
As it rightly should—
For the night is tender, warm and good.

II

What vistas I can see
When my eyes are firmly closed!—
A gold, resplendent tree
To muses well disposed;
A soft, vermilion symphony,
Beheld from the ancient balcony
Of an ageless, lamenting melody
Framing your face
Of regal grace—
Of a grave and solemn sanctity.

III

So take these blooms upon your heart;
Their scarlet plumes outshine all art.
Accept them, my dearest, from your bard—
I chose their petals from your languorous yard.

Your Russet Wine

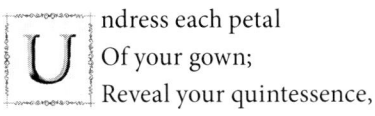

Undress each petal
Of your gown;
Reveal your quintessence,
Where paradise gleams,
Of great renown
Within my heart;
Make real my world
Of celestial dreams.
Touch my soul where heaven looms,

And I shall place your choice perfumes
Above all art,
You graceful blond,
If you should wed this vagabond.

Invigorate me with your eyes,
And your elysian skin, so soft and tan,
You humble the being of this entire man;

Allow me, my dearest, to bathe in your sighs,
And drown me in your russet fronds,
Ethereal—
Of golden ponds.

Selected Poems

The Palace I

The magnificent palace with its windows of blue,
And its marble walls of gray, decorated with gold,
Is the dwelling of a lady, whose hand I long to hold.
Her spirit is sweet and humble, and heart is fair and true.

She lives up high, beyond a gate's gilded bars,
In ornate chambers which look out upon the sky.
She is modest in her demeanor and in her dress—
Quite unusual for this age of ours.

She blushes easily, and is somewhat shy.
In her innocent musings she pines for a soft caress,
And sings of fair love to the gardens below.

I have searched for her palace in the rain and in the snow.
And I have seen her in its courts, in her wanderings and dreams,
Where fountains sob in their immaculate streams.

The Coach

My heart and mind they go to bygone times,
To medieval scenes and English climes,
To cool shades and shadows, to leafy reads,
Where cathedral yards hold hyacinth beds.

There castellated towers clad with green vines,
Brought enchanted suns down upon the earth,
Gracing splendid gardens with a fragrant mirth.
In the quiet of a cloister a river breeds wines.

By lark-laden pines, near a brook that gleams,
A carriage passes. A debutante dreams.
She reclines on cushions; her long, raven mane,

Frames deep, dusky eyes which are bright, without stain.
I have searched for her in the moon's silver rays, beneath its haunting light,
Yet her coach is cloaked by the lindens of the night.

The Cloister I

A wall of glistening laurel leaves shone beside you,
In a gilded garden, where the cadence of a flute
Carried tenderly a wistful tune which all but rendered mute
The sounds of every city upon this earth of blue.

The rubies of the cloister released a minty scent.
As you smiled at me in silence, some flakes came falling down;
With grace they kissed your sweater; and your coat of chestnut brown.
Our mirthful hearts were married, and free from all lament.

The boughs of bending maples received the sighing snow;
Their beauty was reflected in the silver brooks below,
Which flowed as immaculate wines amid the emerald grass.

Raptures in the breezes pierced our hearts as we did pass
By statues made of marble, and shrines there made of gold.
Now let us rise to paradise, years before we're old.

To Mary and My Beloved One

My solemn meditations were on a Parisian cafe,
And on rustic, old lanes where maple trees would sway.
The compass of a college, and a school girl's dappled looks
Were penned on my pages as in history books.

I found summery streams,
From which I drank gleaming wines.
Near an ancient rectory, among sun-touched vines,
A statue of Mary enchanted my dreams.

In my musings I discovered lofty, opened casements,
Of an age-old castle where a princess pined in lavender laments;
Gray towers with their battlements clad with fallen snow,
Spoke of sacred marriage to the flowing brooks below.

And I witnessed my fair, beloved one, open-eyed in bliss
Gaze into my soul—with a sunlit, soft unspoken kiss.

Burgundy

Van Gogh first painted portraits in the meadow of his mind;
Remnants of his brush left a rose upon your face.
We wandered to the glen to find a solitary place,
Where scented gales caressed us, reticent and kind.

Solemnity engulfed us there,
Near an exquisite gondola by the vast and splendid sea;
As if in a dream, I kissed you in that majestic air;
And the bower of your heart rejoiced with me.

There were columns which rose, Doric, tall and white,
Married to copious vines which glistened in the sunlight.
We sipped some mystic burgundy, made of an angel's brew.

Boughs of redolent trees shed some leaves of a lavender hue;
Then we heard a distant strain of sweet cello praise the spring,
And fell into an ecstasy, forgetting everything.

A Wedding of the Sacred

Symphonies and stars, rhapsodies and blooms,
All contained within the gleam of your eyes,
Speak of romantic dreams—luminous with sighs.
(There a wedding of the sacred looms.)

Your hair of sables hide here and there gold;
Their tresses flow as waterfalls;
The scent of your mane, how kindly it calls,
Dousing your long redingote with wistful shades of old.

Among the statues of the square's medieval still,
Where a fountain laments, arching to the sky,
The sycamores languish as you pass by,
In the wake of streams and the dappled hill,
As you wander through the cools of the minty Yorkshire clime,
Beneath the golds and carmines, beyond the myth of time.

Selected Poems

The Wanderer

I wandered through fields by the vast, sallow sea,
Wearing a pea coat, and drinking Chablis
When a brown-eyed brunette would capture my mind,
As I would write verse, of a Galilean kind.

The summer light breathed through every branch and bough,
Of each glittering palm and plume that I journeyed beneath.
Her mane was of a rare perfume, and I placed within my sheathe
The sword of all my seafaring days, working on the prow.

I would happen upon an inn,
Dreaming of her kiss, beyond the fields at play.
I would order a Belgian ale at eve, and gaze upon the bay.
As the stars upon the waves would entrance me amid the din,
Her soul was immortal for she prayed to Mary, hail!—
Unlike those distant jetties that died when I did sail.

Her Piano

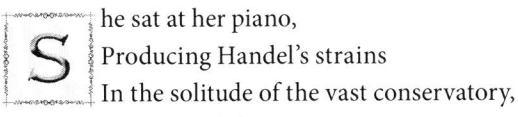

She sat at her piano,
Producing Handel's strains
In the solitude of the vast conservatory,
As the silver, languid downpours
Of the misty, autumn rains
Fell upon the marble columns of the campus,
Looking out upon the suburban plains.

I watched her play those ivory elegies,
Pining for her fair-white hands.

Her raven eyes were consumed with concertos,
Born in times long gone.
Oh, the beauty I mused upon,
As she serenaded my enraptured ear
With rose-enchanted masterpieces
From cloistered, foreign lands.
(Oh what eternal grace arose
From those shiny, little hands.)

What glorious symphonies did arise,
What majestic music I did hear,
As the setting, sallow, sifting sun
Kissed her daisy, hazy eyes
With the languor of a tear.

And as the Indian summer's balms grew near
Her music ceased—as she gazed at me,
Looking out upon the belvedere.

Selected Poems

The Patio

The refuge of the patio,
With its marble floor,
Next to the tranquil ponds,
Grants a grace which I know,
Which I found many times before:
That grace is of the autumn's fronds,
And of redolent gales, from the tranquil shore.

I relax there and recline,
With a bottle of burgundy;
In a state of true felicity
As I gaze at the teeming, emerald pines,
And the wanderings of the summery vines;

Life is soft and sweet there,
Solemn, safe and sound.
Framing the corners of the swan-white ground,
Corollas blush as they enclose
And bequeath to the cool, brisk air
Ballads which soothe every nook and lair;
As in the caress of a loving rose,
In the lofty heights of the arching bines
A joyful assembly of sparking hues
Shimmer in those lofty branches, where the sunlight shines
Grandly on their flickering blues;

And as I sit in my reveries,
Which enter and leave my enraptured mind,
The gentle zephyrs come and go,
Born from pleasant, sleepy seas,
Instilling gold rivers, rejoicing as they flow,
With eternal loves that are pure and kind.

A Walk with My Lady

Dappled oaks sway in peace over streams below.
There is quiet on the down, where the sallow grasses sigh.
The chorus of an elegy,
Born of violins and cello,
Sobs with an exquisite harmony
To the astounding temples of the crimson sky.

An immense and fragrant garden, laden with blooms and copious vines,
Is clad with emerald leaves which gleam in the florid bower.
Its ravishing roses glitter beneath the boughs,
On which the summer sunlight shines,
Granting grace to our eyes, in this mystical hour,
Of raptures and love, of ecstasy and wines.

A Sailor's Song I

I scuffle in my sailor's coat,
On a paved path, near an emerald pond,
Surrounded by two rows of roses;
I approach my long, archaic boat.
I shall cross the Atlantic,
And ferry beyond the Straights
To the old, Roman lake;

And after I awake,
On the Isle of Crete,
I shall pick my teeth
With the splintered wood
Of my ancient vessel.
(And because you are so sweet)
If I only could,
I would place around your alabaster neck
A wreath of those blooms
Which own the spring sun,
To grace your long dress
With such a flowery, sprite strand
From your seafaring bard;
Oh, do accept it from my hand,
My exquisite, dear, beloved one.

Let Us Dream

Sallow, wavering grasses caress your dreamy head;
Let us boast of our weaknesses, as a Saint once said;
In the meadows of innocent delights,
Where blue jays color the fragrant shades,
And the varied greens of the piney heights,
Let us wander on those flowered glades,
Among streams of silver and ethereal gold.

There is music in your long, dark hair;
Its raptures cascade in the brisk autumn air;
It instills within your gaze virtues of old.
Showered in a flurry of falling leaves,
We are weaned on the milk of honeyed harmonies,
Serene on the banks of the temperate seas;
Let us dream of spring days, and tranquil summer eves.

Selected Poems

To Marry

In the corner of the vast, ornate room,
Rich and Victorian, grave and serene,
A statue gazes down with sadness seen,
Yet the sun comes through the windows, and laves the dour gloom.

O, glorious princess of rainy dawns,
I shall take you from your chamber, and call for you at noon;
We shall ride in a carriage, beside the spacious lawns
And be as one within a summery boon.

A magnificent cathedral beckons beyond the mountains,
As we glide along beside the courtyard and the fountains,
Beside the gardens and the arbors, to the tall, gilded gate;

We shall leave your grand estate,
And marry with the Virgin's blessing,
To be forever one, forever in love, eternally caressing.

At the University

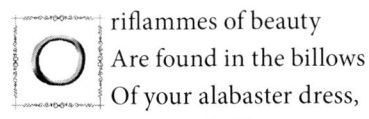

Oriflammes of beauty
Are found in the billows
Of your alabaster dress,
As you saunter with felicity,
Beneath the pilasters, where the sunlight glows,
By the brooklets lined with watercress;

A poetic prince awaits you there—
To embrace you in the regal air;
Alive with violet perfumes
Which bathe your braided hair;
Among the soft, majestic blooms
Of the silent satin, saffron fanfare
—Of the summer's royal plumes.

What books do you carry beneath your arm?—
(Volumes of verse which laud your charm)
As you gaze with watery, sable eyes
Upon a youth in love with you,
Who bows as you acknowledge him
With a wondrous smile, with a chorus of sighs,
Looking into his glances of turquoise-blue
Where you find your fateful seraphic eyes
Serenading you from his heart of hearts.

Tell me, oh studious angel of white,
If you major in the liberal arts,
—*Of what do poets write?*

Selected Poems

Seen and Unseen

The grassy, tree topped hill
And the abbey's languorous, wistful strain
Play to us, as the wines of heaven fill
Our peaceful spirits, free of pain;

And every song there that is one
With the oceanic breath of elysian dew,
Glistens in the morning's crimson sun.
This day was made for a lady such as you.

Let us wander to the alcove by the sea,
Let us hold each others' hands, as you walk with me.
There are angels hovering in the world unseen.

Let us pray for them to hide us beneath their wings.
And let us listen to the ocean as it sings,
As we blissfully reline upon a field of green.

Violins

The violins which weep within your gaze
Of the sea
Are from another world, my dear;
The concertos of Mozart sweetly engulf me
Whenever your approaching kisses are near;
Their psalms are of ardor; and wear purity for a glaze.

The hallowed chapels which dwell upon your lips
Posses rosy shrines which enrich me, as they eclipse
The sun, the moon, and all the gleaming flares of old.
Your hair emits a redolent wine, tender; soft and gold.

The sheens which glisten in the fairness of your face
Bestow upon my soul a glow of timeless grace.
And in the chambers of your spirit, a sunlight garden pines;

It is sacred and solemn, endowed with a silver diamond which shines…
There are streams in those holy temples where the angles sleep;
To your symphonies they swoon, to those violins which weep.

I Shall Place You in a Garden

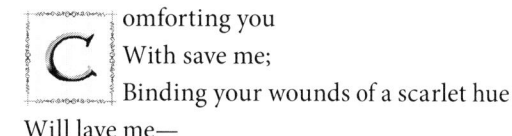

Comforting you
With save me;
Binding your wounds of a scarlet hue
Will lave me—

In waters that are pure.
I shall saunter in the summer air;
Through oceanic vistas.

The soft, fragrant winds
Shall be my garments.

I shall bask below a bath of cheerful bines,
And I shall wander beneath their honeycombs
In blissful, sunny ecstasies.

The harmonies of life,
Shall flow in currents around my knees,
Of multicolored brines;
They shall engulf my spirit in varied wines.
I shall rove beneath a delightful flurry
Of splendid, dappled vines,
Of every season, of every year.

And I shall bind your wounds, my love, my dear.

I shall collect your tears within a vase,
And transform them into sunlit blooms;
I shall remove you from your dry, deserted dwellings,
And place you in a garden,
Amid palatial rooms.

II

Mist and Flame

Mist and Flame

To a Dark-Eyed Lady

I long to be one with your deep, dark eyes
To live in paradise while still on earth,
And witness the hand of spring giving birth
To the buds of your love which gild the skies;
I long to touch you beneath the lindens,
At night, when the breezes weave your tresses,
And gaze into your soul in glowing dens;
I pine to see you in flowing dresses.
To kiss your lips in majestic enclaves,
Where heathers sigh beneath the azure sky,
I will give you roses from oceans' waves;
Every tear you shed I will surely dry,
To fill you with joy beyond all telling,
And bathe your heart in a raptured dwelling.

Romance I

The stream is blessed like our hallowed marriage,
Reflecting in ripples, beneath the ridge
Of vine-varnished stones of an ancient bridge,
The ornate wheels of a splendid carriage;
Let us lie reclined in our reverie,
Which symphonies sob on the balcony
And dream of a seaside, romantic place
Where I can hold dearly forevermore
The ravishing rose of your tender face;
We shall wander at night, among the dunes,
Immersed in raptures on the amber shore,
Beneath a thousand silver moons;
Eternity will fill our wave-kissed eyes,
Adorned with stars—until the sun does rise.

The Veranda

The veranda's nimbus awaits our kiss;
The effulgent greens welcome you and I
In arabesque gardens, where linnets fly
Over windswept brooks, (as we reminisce)
Musing on the day our eyes first met.
In the shaded cools of old, russet trees,
A breeze stirs the grasses beneath our knees.
As your black mane's waves scent the red sunset,
Ambrosial blooms in splendid array,
Sway near the dale by the china-blue bay.
Our precious romance, in sanctified ways,
Graces our souls which eternal stars bless.
The sky crowns your gaze with gold, feathered rays,
As you smile at me, in your long, white dress.

Your Touch

The wavering grasses and flowers of white
Greet you as you pass in the rose-clad light;
Where ardent streams flow over ancient rocks,
Beneath a snowy crest of ivory tips,
The sunlight gilds your voluptuous lips,
And caresses your curly, raven locks;
Among lavender blooms, the pine trees shake
As you rove half-dreaming in fragrant bliss;
My heart pines in fire and bleeds for your kiss:—
Behold my tears in the still, starry lake.
Let me keep my brow in your dress's folds,
In its sigh-laced rain where your kind hand holds
My weeping mind which has sorrowed too much;
Bare your sweet refrain, spare me not your touch.

Your Hymns

Finding respite in the tall
Statues sculptured by a bard,
In the fallen leaves of fall,
You wander in the courtyard;

In a nimbus of delight,
Where a glinting fountain's breeze
Stirs the nearby cypress trees,
You saunter in the sunlight;

Your long, ambrosial ringlets
Are touched by a cast of grace;
The carmines near the brooklets
Caress your angelic face,
As the hymns you write within
Humble every violin.

Remnants

Her amatory gaze glittered in the mystic mist;
In a silken, amber furrow, our torrid love's desire
Once grew wings like a seraph in our passion's ardent fire.
(The starry heavens shimmered when I held her as we kissed.)

The bourbon of the grass, graced by the redolent rains,
Possessed both our spirits in the plains which captured
Our tears beneath the gleam of the moon's symphonic stains;
Our soul were immersed in ecstasies—enraptured.

The meadows where we roved now are dour, ghostly places
Where remnants of our ardor still linger in traces,
Unseen in the mist of the thick, silent grass;
Passersby, unknowing, sense them haunt—as they pass.

Mist and Flame

Your Rose

You once disclosed your untarnished rose
And the true, romantic soul of its fragrant domain,
Still fresh beside the wines of the old, quiescent lane
Where the reds of budding blooms unclose;

You disclosed, young duchess, your nubile gaze
And gathered the carmine bouquets, one by one,
In the sweet, polished rays of the saffron sun.
(Which gilded the browns of your vision's glaze.)

You disclosed, gentle princess, your sovereignty
And unveiled your dark eyes, resplendently dressed
Were the zephyrs of summer softly caressed
The lucent luster of your soft spirit's beauty;

What was it in those weeping ponds,
Those glowing, dusky browns
That wrapped the sleeping, olive fronds
In flowing wedding gowns?

Walking in the leaves,
To reminisce
In ruffled sleeves—
What sad heart is this?—

Full lips of cherry slopes
Were sun-enchanted baths,
But dead now are my hopes,
Once on blissful, golden paths:—
For the precious rose of your kiss is gone;
Such doleful, dour leaves are these I tread upon.

Suburbia

In the summer, I have seen
The haven of the suburbs,
Where breezes clothe the sheen
Of the sidewalks' gleaming curbs;

Elaborately framed windows
Look out upon the flowers,
The exquisite, vast, suburban bowers—
Schoolgirls' braided bows;

The marigold nuance of the cordial sun
Greets the vine-embellished sidewalks,
The trellis-varnished by walks—
The timorous step of my beloved one.

For I have wept, as my vision bade
A sorrowing sunset, flowing red
Within the pulse of a sobbing cello
In her slow, sacred wade
Where tears were shed,
Beside an emerald hedgerow;

Her window with the soft, yellow glow
Finds my starry stare, beholding her face;
She parts her hair, as she pines with grace;
Her long mane shines like moonlit snow;

How I would love to be the viny strand
That almost enters her ornate room;
Preparing for bed, her sweet perfume
Wafts down the wall—to where I stand.

By the Bay

I

Enraptured in the yellow grass,
Over our heads
The dry leaves pass.

As the whites of a once woolly willow sheds,
Wilting mignonettes are kissed by the dew,
In the maize of the dying flower beds,
Wavering all round you;

The massive, dark cloud that hauntingly roams
Will break with many silver tears,
Descending on the verdant plain and the reddish bay,
By the rustic homes;
An angelic refrain
Will fill our ears
When the fog is dispersed, effaced by the rain.

II

Traces of the drizzle garnish glitter in your gaze,
As we stroll on the cobblestones by the quiet bay
In the billowing cools of the crisp, autumn day;
You take my hand within a rose-embroidered haze,
As the dark clad fades in the clearing sky.
(The aromatic rubies of the sunlight die.)

III

Amid the red leaves, by the crimson bay,
Alone with our thoughts, I kissed you there;
The sun's final ray left an imprint in your hair—
Like a stroke from the hand of Monet.

New Hampshire

Our little hamlet in the north
Cradles your gaze, outside gleams the snow,
As the winter brings forth
A sanctified glow.

In the briskness of the wind, the carol of your name
Majestically opens the rustic, wooden doors.
As horse-drawn carriages struggle to tame
The rocky, whited roads of the snow-clad moors.

In the soft, woolly folds of the sweater you wear
I shall bury my brow, as you hold me in your arms,
Oblivious to the chill of the crisp, frosty air—
As the amber sun dies beyond the distance, red farms.

Your Face I

The snow descends serenely on the slender, frozen grass
As spruce trees lace the breezes where you leisurely pass.
Your raven mane of curls frame your dear, classic face,
As they wear the woolly flakes that decline from lofty tips;
The temple of your soul is a sanctified place;
I fervidly dream of your soft, scarlet lips.

The frosty, milk-white snow
Falls languidly and slow
As I wait to see your dark, brown eyes
Where the precious crown of my destiny lies;

I shall drink rare Chablis from their solemn, majestic gaze
Beneath the bold, blissful, boundless rays
Of radiant, royal skies.
For since I first beheld your face,
My soul is not the same;
To win your exalted, regal grace
I would certainly be lame and plagued by the pain
Of a thousand torments,
To dwell in your spirit's magnificent tents
Where fountainous love's sacred, diamond showers
Mingle with the ecstasy of the moon's enamored glow
And glitter like a waterfall's enchanting, silver flow
As I burn—while you patiently count the hours.

Her Silhouette

The dim silhouette
　Of the ambrosial brunet
　　Sends my soul into rapture,
In the cool of an autumn eve—
After the scarlet sunset;

At her vanity she stands
Gazing upon her dress,
As she parts the strands
Of a wavy tress;

Her demure, soft cast
Majestically commands
Every light from my past—
As I burn for her hands.

The Shade I

The vague, lamenting
　Misty shade
　　Where we kissed
Beside the hunting glade
Possesses an air
Of embellished despair,
Where roses in the garden
Weep within their shrouds
Of carmine petals—
Betrothed to the clouds.

Only in You

I found no rest
In the outskirts of the city,
In the old, provincial inns,
In the arctic winds and rains,
In the cruel, spartan grains
Of the boundless, yellow plains;

Only in you,
In the folds of your dress,
Can my spirit be solaced
In the strands of your tress
Of elysian perfumes—
In your feminine caress,
Of aromatic blooms
Where my weary brow is buried
In the pink blush of your bosom—
In the dew of your tender breast.

For only in you can I find true rest,
Can my psyche nap secure,
In your precious heart—so pure.

For only in you am I free to weep
In your soul's eternal streams
Where I reap my sanguine dreams
In the repose of sacred sleep,
In your spirit's soothing blues,
In your soft, endearing eyes,
In their sparkling, peaceful hues
Of heartfelt, hallowed sighs.

Faded Candles

The candles, lit low,
Flicker as you go
Once more,
Into the Orphic blue;
Oh, the mystic pinnacles
Of the ecstasies we knew!—
And yet, those heights
We no longer know;
What was it that stilled
That glorious fountain's flow
Which bathed our hearts by firebrands,
Embracing in their glow?—
Alas!—

Like Juliet's balcony,
Once adorned as if dipped in glass,
The diamond-hued summers,
The autumn's lily-laced wind
All pass when true romance
Does not within abide,
For all ephemeral glories
Eventually rescind,
Like the capricious ebbs of azures—
On a sunlit, sobbing tide.

On a Winter's Eve

I

In the snow-clad pines,
There stirs a voice
Of a long-lost love.

As her soul reclines,
She wills to rejoice
In the silence above,
Beneath the clouds;

In the tips of the trees,
Cloaked by misty shrouds,
She ascends into the breeze
As if to say
Her final goodbye
In the silent sky
Of boundless gray.

II

I felt her sway,
As I gazed upon the snow,
More reticent than a grave
Yet blessed by a solemn glow:—
Another soul she willed to save.

III

Before she vanished,
The glow was banished,
Disappearing, as it veered to a distant hill;

I thought I heard from above a tree,
Before she left, her say to me:—
"Be still, my love. Be still.
Be still."

Poets

What mortal poet can assuage
The toils of a hour's wage?
What visionary, mystic bard
Can turn one single, tristful page
In the book of life, in any age,
With descriptions of a florid yard?

Which souls can soothe tormented men
Of dismal Decembers and jaded Junes?
Which brand of poets truly can?—
Only those who bleed from a thousand wounds.

Isolation I

I am the roar of the sea as well as its hush;
I am the tear-clad founts of Van Gogh's brush;
I am a sullen Picasso, left with the pyre
Of a wilted desire to compose further verse:—
More dull, prosaic lines to throw into the fire;
Isolation, isolation—what could be worse?—
I'd gladly fling my manuscripts in the abyss
For one, just one sincerely sacred, ardent kiss.
Until that day my head shall lie upon my desk,
Consumed with only shade and shadows of the dusk.
For what use is my pen to scribe mere fantasies,
And abrasive vignettes for a gloomy burlesque?—
Until I behold the gold of a feminine dusk,
I shall bequeath my mind to the whimsical breeze;
Let if ferry my muse to wherever it may,
While I sleep in my bruise—a coma of gray.

Days Now Go ne

Do you recall Handel's porcelain rose
That bloomed in the furrow of your florid mind,
And the rare perfumes it would gently disclose
When reality treated you less than kind?—

Do you recall the embowered, wavering sheen
In Coleridge's garden of a sable-haired queen?—
Do you remember the tall, limpid, moon-graced walls
And your fervently ambitious, most wistful dreams
Of scaling all the diamonds in the waterfalls,
When Beethoven's fragrance fermented the streams?

Do you remember the decadent prince, who, touched by grace
Blessed a youthful duchess with her first, sweet embrace
In the placid shadows of Baudelaire's trees,
Where she swooned in his arms in the pine-laced breeze?—

Now those days are gone with the vanished look
Verlaine once held that was soft, pure and true.
But that look has faded in the turquoise-blue
Of a sullen, sea-bound, sobbing brook;

It died in the sea, from hills now dry,
And only the stars above the cloud-filled sky
Can tell the taciturn angels why.

The Glade

The slender grasses swayed,
As Bach's piano played.

My burdened brow had finally slept
In the glade, where a symphony
Near the arbutus had wept.

But my pain came back to me
Gravely and soon after;
My burden returned, and my burden stayed
Ever since I heard the death of laughter,
When Bach's piano no longer played.

And silence claimed the hallowed glade
When the slender grass no longer swayed.

Ode to Robert Schumann

Let not the dead reeds around your tomb
Mislead the dim eye of passersby
Who, too often, are consumed with gloom;

Let not the cryptic boughs of sadness,
Which hover to remind us we die,
Grand the impression that our gladness
Shall not be fulfilled beyond the grave;

Let mourners look not upon the reeds,
Made frail by sparse rains in the enclave;
Yet let them recall the strains you gave,
From your spirit which no longer bleeds.

With gold, elysian symphonies
Your graced the weary, orbital earth
And all ears that heard the dear, sweet birth
Of the rose from your piano keys.

Mist and Flame

Your Sobbing Soul

The lacrimal brooks that lament in your gaze
Flow like the foam of white, cresting waves,
Of a vast sea endowed with the moon's summer rays,
Beneath the old jetties, among sailors' graves.

Those deep, doleful steams that weep in your eyes
Collect all your dreams, in the sleep of their sighs,
For regardless of your solemn pain,
Which weighs upon you, profound and whole,
Your beloved's voice can be heard in the rain—
To sing to your chaste and sobbing soul.

Forlorn

The sapid chestnut of the fallen leaves
Is be frilled with dew, as a princess grieves;
Departing in her carriage from the palace,
The sunset bleeds on her majesty's face,
Her doleful, brownish cast of a royal grace;
Her unshed tears fill an unseen chalice.

Riding in her coach on pastoral roads,
Where holly-green hills lap placid abodes,
She carries among her gold, ornate decor
Of her regal carriage of a burden borne
Of a long-lost love that left her forlorn,
As she rides to the sea—to weep by the shore.

Heaven I

I once beheld heaven in a willow tree.
Like a shower of pearly diamonds,
It shimmered as it fell,
Like an immaculate fountain, blissfully,
To auriferous, gleaming grounds;
Among the luminescence of an azure well,
It descended into the white and green
Of the glittering, bright fronds
That laved my spirit clean,
Dipping their tips in the dappled sheen
Of serene, translucent ponds.

Verse I

Use the seaside wind as your brush my dear;
Wear the soft, summer sun as a chandelier
And walk without musing;
Simply perusing,
Read the verse engraved in the lucent nook
Of wavering darnel, by the pensive brook,
And know that you are truly blessed;
Reap the wistful sight of each reed caressed,
And walk without musing;
Simply perusing,
Read the verse of Sappho on the gilded terrace,
Of aesthetic and ethereal permanence;
Behold Mozart's mind in the stars of space,
And kneel within you before his grand grace;
Witness the trellis with its elaborate fence
Made lovely by the lattice of rose-clad wood;
Embrace every heart in the human race—
And all in the world that is Godlike and good.

Little Girl on a Bike

She rides through the nuance of a blissful azure-green
In the soft, florid winds of April's gleeful gleam;
The bright spokes on her wheels reflect her silver dream
Of gliding freely through the park, mirthful and serene.

The scarlet blooms caress her innocent, young blues;
In the midst of spring's delight, an oceanic scent
Fills her mind with waves of white, so very redolent;
The sunlight paints her curls with nimble, flaxen hues.

In years, when she is blessed in those rare, radiant hours
By her lover's sacred kiss and his loyal reverence,
Betrothed in a vineyard, where branches sway in silence,
Her bicycle will be gone—all except its flowers.

My Youth

Hitching rides to high school,
Crossing railroads by the graveyard,
Once my friend and I found refuge
On porch in the pouring rain;

The grasses were my muse,
Returning from the colossal gym
Where America was revealed to me
In the tresses of fair brunets
Whose legs were smooth and ravishing
Beneath their red-striped shorts of white;

An azure book of poetry,
While I stole from the library,
Opened my eyes to feminine gracility
And to lustrous, polished fingertips
Painted glossy, with carmine hues
Which would glisten in the sunlight's kiss;

Struck by visions beside the hedgerows,
I graced every puddle with my cloak
In the paths of angelic schoolgirls
Who deserved the most immaculate wreaths
From the realm of medieval chivalry;

I lived more verse than I wrote in those days.
In the radiant boon of a rapturous gaze,
I fell into the symphony of a girl's brown eyes;
All the universe became ablaze—
With a statuesque courtyard and a fountain's sighs;

I drank potent burgundies from everything romantic,
From mystic, teeming sun showers
That fell like ruby diamonds;
Every book engraved a rapture in my mind;
I saw stars in every lamplight;
Forsaking sleep, I conversed with angels;

Mist and Flame

All windowpanes were waterfalls;
I witnessed the ethereal with my eyes;

Majesty was my betrothed—
And ecstasy was my bride.

Vignettes

Although I still dream of provincial cafes
Where burgundies gleamed in carafes of gold rays,
I have the billows of the brine to quell my reveries;
Their starry, ancient wine devours the dour seas—
The dim, misty tendrils of my spirit's former torments;
The fading, mystic nooks of my mind's most poignant contents:—
Of fragrant, mahogany fountains, of tragic love affairs;
Of foggy, sullen mountains which stilled the wistful airs;
Of angelic, perfumed, braided bows wafting through the hallways
Of the high school by the graveyard where a symphony still plays;
Of ardent, youthful passions sobbing beneath the diamond trees;
The nimbus of vignettes which I scribbled in the breeze;
The ethereal, scented winds that wept in the slender reeds;
The ephemeral shine of loving deeds—
Which I beheld in a schoolgirl's eyes;
The volant, roving wings of melancholic butterflies
Which flapped between the grayish veils
Of cryptic ships and ghostly pales,
Of realities and lies;
Absorbed by a fresh-faced, fair brunette,
Prosaic practicalities were left undone;
Immersing myself in the saffron sun,
I dove into every sunset;
I relinquished my reason without regret;
I bequeathed my soul to the arbitrary gales,
Which would veer to the greenish harbor,
Clothing the carmine canvas of intangible sails
Before they would expire in the tips of the arbor,
Where rufescent leaves would read my mind
In the still, dappled meadows—where I reclined.

Coming Home

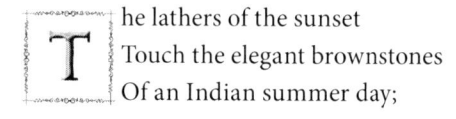

The lathers of the sunset
Touch the elegant brownstones
Of an Indian summer day;

Ladies walk by,
Some dignified, some troubled,
With languorous glances,
Laden with rue;

To separate houses, to different rooms,
Each bares their burden like cryptic cloaks;

Reaching home, they cast their pocketbooks
On pale divans, on wicker chairs,
Looking down on the pools of loneliness
That sprawl across the lifeless carpets
Like empty, doleful lakes—
Beheld by weary eyes.

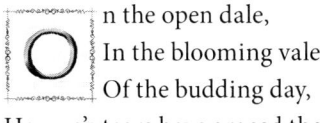

The Morning Dew

On the open dale,
In the blooming vale
Of the budding day,
Heaven's tears have graced the waterway
Among the billowing grass,
Of a glittering hue;

Across the golden landmass,
The morning dew,
Composed last night,
Clothes the leaves with a damp delight,
And my crinkled sleeves, of a dappled white;

I had a dream-enchanted sleep.
For my own romantic sake,
There is in my satchel a notebook I keep;
Immersed in wet leaves, it requires a shake;
I wield it at dawn to harness the visions I reap,
And to write of the dew—when I awake.

Mist and Flame

An Autumn Sunset I

The sunset dies
In the ambiance of fall,
Amid the amber foliage—
At the foot of a Tudor's teeming wall;

The evening stars ascend
With sonority and grace;
Regardless of the age,
They rise with an ancient pace.

And the book of life turns a page,
As the roseate, western downpours
Gleam in their majestic languors.

And in the east, the waves of white
Break among the limpid moors,
On the starlit, bright
New England shores.

Bouquets

The sunny ripples in the glory of your hair
Send the breadth of my soul into despair.
For if the flesh of our lips shall never meet
My bed shall be a dreadful, icy street.

For as I would lie upon the snow,
The water's cold would claim my life;
In an anguished fit of somber strife,
All balconies ornate with their mystic gold
Would cease to glow
In my romantic vale.
(And the end of my tale
Would be sadly told.)

So take these rosy-red bouquets;
I pray thee, take them to your heart,
So I may see the summer rays—
And never from the sun depart.

My Black-Haired Queen

I have crossed every sea;
I have braved every billow,
With supplicant hands, pining as I plea
For the one, majestic, wavering willow
My weary eyes have yet to behold
Amid the sands,
In the briny cold.

For I have trod upon the lonely trails,
In strange, exotic, foreign lands.
I have seen their grand and regal dawns;
I have stripped them of her gilded veils,
One by one,
In the scattered sun,
Lying on their emerald lawns
Until the skies were filled with stars—
Even in the light of day;
The ales I drank in mystic bars
Turned my madness into clay.

And still I wander,
I wander on,
And so I shall—
Until I see
My black-haired queen
Awaiting me.

A Reverent Night

The weeping moonlight,
Upon the book,
Caught the adoring, loving look
Your eyes had shed,
Profoundly bright,
In the solemn still
Of a reverent night.

In The Hallowed Night

Let our ardor adorn
The marigold mound
Of sun-touched sand
Where the cello resound,
Where the day's half-dormant, nascent boon
Will be plain to see
In the hallowed night,
Beneath a full, exquisite moon
Which will illuminate your astonishing soul
With a splendid diamond light—
To make us forever one and whole
In heaven's true, eternal sight.

Mist and Flame

Eternal Streams

The white, wavering roses shimmer in the bowers;
Our carafe of wine, mellow as the sea,
Silken as your kiss—its vintage Chablis
Gleams like those sunlit, quiescent, white flowers.

The pensive murmur of the bright, silver brook
Flows upon the rocks by the sorrel trees,
As the tall reeds sway, sweet beneath your knees,
Into my eyes you gaze with your Doric look.

We wander beneath the boughs, free from all care,
As soft, fluorescent, effluent dreams
Tint the crimson leaves with eternal streams.
(And we know that our love is sanctified there.)

Your diamond tears rejoice, trailing down my chest.
For of all in the vale—I adore you best.

By Hazel Eyes

I

The restless winds
    Have swept through my soul,
    And removed from my palm
The peace I knew at dawn,

And so I wander,
Weary of scorn,
Beneath the dead stars—
Bruised and bereft by hazel eyes.

And yet within I know
Felicity shall find my heart
Once more and profoundly twice as deep,
And all my sorrow shall depart,
As my sentinel, guardian angels sleep
Unhurried by my needless tears—
For completely unfounded
Are all my fears.

II

My queen approaches!—
I can see her now—
Standing in the autumn rain,
Her long and majestic, sable mane
Wet beneath a dappled bough.

Mist and Flame

Rapturous Gazes

Rapturous gazes
Exchanged over tea
Manifest such majesty,
As the saffron sun raises
Its light upon the sea
Of boundless, billowing downs of wheat
Rejoicing in our happiness,
As our chaste and tender gazes meet.

And all the cabin warmly glows
With nuptial, soft, enchanted vales,
Lovelier than all the glistening furrows:
Those swaying, sunlit-christened dales.

Consumed with Sighs

I toppled stars
In the rustling wood,
Lamenting for your sake;
Surrounded there by white guitars
Weeping around me, as I stood—
For I could not move your heart to wake.

Your brown, diaphanous, tristful eyes
Denied to arouse
The hallowed strains of symphonies;

And so I roved, consumed with sighs,
Espoused to only boughs—
Betrothed to only trees.

Blossoms Once Bright

Sitting in my study, dreaming at my desk,
I gaze upon the arabesque
Of heaths and splendid grasses,
As the tall reeds murmur on the mellow downs,
The soft, scattered rays of daylight passes
Caressing the foliage, of ambers and browns.

Straying peregrine, primrosed leaves
Descend upon their sallow bed
Where a shrouded whisper mystical cleaves
To faded blooms, once bright, now dead,
Where lovers once loved when the sky was red
In the bliss of a spring gone long-ago,
Where now the mist of the indistinct night
And the sapid breezes, weeping as they blow,
Aurify the meadows with the moon's gold light.

The Lakeside

I return to the sandy, quiet shores
Walking on a dour trail, as the sunset bleeds,
In the silhouettes of lindens,
Amid tall reeds. I come upon a grand estate,
Where no light gleams from its roof to its floors.
A horrid spirit's verse is a glistening portent—
Spoken from dead eyes, exquisite with terrific rhyme;
I flee the place where baleful stars do weep,
Shedding their tears on the ghostly sea;
And there, on the beach, someone trembles beside me,
Longing for my soul, of which he would keep;
His spirit is barren, and of dreadful fame,—
For none but Satan is his name.

The Pond

Her dusky look is a sacred pond;
It takes my heart to the realm beyond;
It ripples billowing towards the shore,
Regal is her spirit of an azure-blue;
It shall gleam in a peace forevermore—
For the sake of raptures made for two.

And just before dusk, when the nascent stars
Shed their soft, calamari, silver-whites
Upon the dew of the coming nights,
When one can see the red of Mars
And behold the grave and splendid sights
Of the weeping boughs in lavender lights.
The shades bestow glory to her sacred pond
And takes my heart to the realm beyond.

My Queen

Music is all around me,
It overflows within;
Kiss me, my queen of eternal beauty;

Caress me with your violin.
Take the heart and soul of me.
Receive all my love,
Take all of it in.
For every cloud has died above.

All I know in the world is you;
Your radiant spirit of turquoise blue
Shall evermore in glory reign.

Oh, let me hear your name again,
To silence all of this poet's pain—
So I can retire from the fire of my pen.

A Christmas Poem

Snow is on the sidewalk and more falls down;
We dream, hand in hand, beneath the white trees,
Roving in the rapturous, cool, crisp breeze,
As the scent of chestnuts veer through the town.

I adore your gaze of deep, starry browns,
As your woolly, winter sweater is kissed with flakes;
The good, cozy warmth turns smiles from frowns;
What tender, loving sights this holy season makes!—

Blessed with bliss, the townsfolk—free from every pall,
Go window-shopping with the children; all the toys
Move by themselves, enchanting the girls and boys,
As gleeful Main Street gleams—for everyone, for all.

Wind Chimes

I always genuflect upon hearing wind chimes.
For they send me into rapture, as I gaze alone
On my queen, beneath her room, flanked with ancient stone;
I behold her fair white face of fragrant autumn climes.

And then her gazes meet with mine; all is silent,
All is calm, as the courtyard's vespers softly rise,
I behold heaven's light in the browns of her eyes,
Mellifluous with purity, deep and reticent;

She pines on the terrace, where the boughs are bent,
Majestically swaying in the cool, fall breeze
As the last of the sun gilds the tops of the trees.

And the wind chimes ring, without sorrow or lament,
As I ask for her hand in marriage, again without speech;
Her yes is of an ecstasy; the highest realm we reach.

The Porch

We contemplate the rustic silence,
Beneath the sallow eaves,
Immersed within the gentle flames
Of love's eternal, mystic torch;

The soft, sacred rapture
Of the old, wooden porch
Stirs the blades of amber grass—
In concert with the russet leaves.

Late November

The sodden meadow, silent and sallow,
Pensively wavers in the languid sun,
As the brown, naked leaves, one by one,
Crown the vast down and the old oak's hallow,

No late summer for this sleepy, sweet day;
Perhaps the first snowfalls shall soon descend,
For the gales are crisp, and the fleeced boughs bend.
Oh, take my hand where the white petals stray!—

Receive all my world, from pole to pole;
Take the length and width of my humble soul,
And grace my lips with yours to make it whole;

Dreaming of Paris and the solemn, grave toll
Of grand Notre Dame by the ancient, green Seine,
Let us rove, hand in hand, on the quaint, rustic lane.

The Louvre

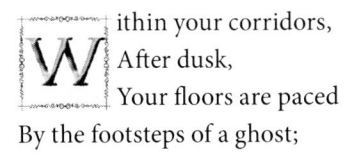

Within your corridors,
After dusk,
Your floors are paced
By the footsteps of a ghost;

Your hallways are haunted
By an ominous flow
Of dreadful wraiths,
Condemned to torment,
When your visitors go,
When your guards depart—
When your corners are dark
And hold no glow;

A famed smile dies
For a nebulous sake,
As your statues awake—
With their raven eyes;

With a purpose pale,
And a cryptic relief,
Stepping from her canvas,
Mona Lisa comes to life;

From her weary, old heart
She removes a searing knife
Unseen in the day—
Of an ageless grief.

And her soul does wander,
Like a wayward leaf,
Through your chambers of blackness,
Like a royal
And mystic,
Ancient thief.

Mist and Flame

In Clement Times

I n clement times when Keats wrote sonnets in the sun,
When waterfalls cascaded from your kiss, my beloved one,
And melodies filled the cathedral's glen,
You told me with your lips indeed I was yours only then.
When weeping statues, drunk with the sunlight,
Knelt down on purple carpets to make divine
The splendor of the courts, your hand in mine,
Your heart said you loved me, with a reverent light.
And in the evening, when the vespers rose
From the hazel ecstasies of your grace,
I witnessed, betrothed, your shining, white face
Near the wooden veranda, by the garden-close.
And now the winds, serenaded by the streams
Resurrect the scarlet blooms where an angel dreams.

A Stream of Stars

O h, the glory to walk amid white colonnades!—
There is no need to travel to the golden age
When Sappho wept on every page
To see such columns as the red sun fades.
The dusk comes gently to assuage and grace
Every needless care in the languid light,
With ancient turrets in the solemn night
Adorned by the moon with its full, round face.
And there, in the calm, beneath the tall fane,
In splendid shadows, I behold your eyes,
I behold your soul, immersed in your sighs,
Drenched in summer days that never know rain.
The ethereal is seen, red like Mars,
In your wondrous gaze—in a stream of stars.

Raptures

Lost in somnolent verse I tread,
Troubled in neither heart nor head.
The winds of mint bring thoughts of gold,
Of true romance from medieval days of old.

The raptures of the dew-clad dale
Swirl through the swaying, amber grass
Wavering gently, as I pass
Blissfully on the dallied trail.

Beneath the birch, I behold your face
In sublime, resplendent airs of grace;
Our passion gilds such a sacred place,
Which the myth of time can not efface.

All is reticent, calm, and still;
Unfold your flower—my love, as you will.

Benediction

The soft, fall breezes from the balcony,
Above the burnets, and the walls of gray,
Perfume your long hair, as the oak trees sway
Beside the terrace, so majestically.
The capacious courtyard, where the statues stand,
Among the fountains, enchanting and white,
Which rise to the firmaments' gilded light
Gleams in the sun like dunes of mystic sand.
And there, in your deep benediction's gaze,
My soul is espoused to yours forevermore;
Your lips meet mine; my embrace you adore,
And my enraptured heart is set all ablaze.
So let the autumn gales ferry through the trees,
As rogue cherry blooms are graced upon our knees.

Mist and Flame

Our Souls Become One

In the shade of elms, in the solemn still,
Where the fragrant air of spring blossoms rare
Descend from the boughs so tranquilly there,
Your soft, scarlet lips command all my will.
And yet our will is free, still, let it be;
For you christen me with your elysian kiss,
In the autumn-scented shade of ardent bliss;
The glory of God in your gaze I see.
And there, overwhelmed by your lips of fire,
Dazed, I recover, my brow upon your breast,
Where I lay my head in enraptured rest,
Drunk from the wine of your boundless desire.
And as your tresses fall, your hair is undone,
And given in union, our souls become one.

Our English Tudor

Our English Tudor has one hundred rooms;
Each one has been graced by your starlit gaze,
And though for most our home would be a maze,
Its vast ancient bounds grant us only blooms.
Above the bower, from the western wing,
Beneath the terrace, as the sunset gleams,
On the gilded leaves you can see your dreams,
Near the azure brook, where we wander in the spring.
Your fair hand in mine fills my spirit with mirth,
When we rove through the roses, red and white;
Yet nothing compares to the bright, splendid sight
Of your angelic face which lends perfumes to the earth.
There the salty breezes carry mist and flame—
Those soft, eternal gales, which forever speak your name.

The Castle I

The circular stairs made of ancient stone
Wind and rise within the northern tower;
Taller than most spires. Yet every flower
Can be seen in May, (where we rove alone
In boons of the white garden's splendid light.)
From the ornate balcony, jetting from the wall
On the third plateau, where the snowflakes fall
In late December, below the grand height
Of the highest floor, crowned by but a star.
And up there, at the top of the old, stone stairs,
The long corridor, of enchanted airs
Is graced by candles, and although quite far,
The walk is worth all—for at the hall's end
In your lamplit room *all canticles blend.*

In the Field We Lay

The tall, saffron reeds that clothe the quiet dale
Shines behind the barn, as the sun descends.
In that field we lie, where the bright hay bends;
There perfumes of your tresses I desire to inhale.
Your soft, fair-white legs, ablaze in the grass,
Shimmer in my daze, as the sweet gales pass.
Your eyes overflow, flooded with sunshine.
Your vase is of silk; its walls are of wine.
Oh, my fair empress, of dark, starry skies,
Take me from the anticipation of my torment,
And when the fever subsides with a delicious attainment,
Clad me immersed with your nipples' pert sighs.
And there, in the bliss of your milky, blushing glow
Your breasts I shall kiss, and deeper I shall go.

My Best Beloved

Oh, my best beloved one—be still; be still.
The petals of day have serenely closed.
The rose of your blush is softly exposed.
Allow me to please you—as you will.
I shall take the candle looking out upon the night,
And place it next to your sanctified bed.
And when the nocturnal breezes have fled,
Beyond the curtains to the moon's sultry light,
I shall instill within your bosom an anguishing flame
As your vase extends upwards to receive my seed.
And then, my dear empress, I shall satisfy your need.
And you shall see stars, and the piercing shall claim
All of you grasping, as I behold you there—
In an ecstasy unspoken, in the all consuming air.

Ethereal Mist

I am free once more, free again to take
Rare wines and perfumed, apple-blossomed air
Into my soul from the scent of your hair,
Which renders me weak in its splendid wake.
The nocturnal dew, fresh upon your face,
Sails through the window, open for your sake
To unite our hearts in a boundless lake
Of passions bestowing graces to grace.
In freedom complete we meet in the still,
Like schooners drifting on a quiet sea,
Approaching one another gracefully,
In the moonlit heights of a mist-clad hill.
So open your window on the terrace clad with vines,
And receive all my soul in a scarlet lake of wines.

Mist and Flame

By the Winter Moon

I love the winter and the fresh, white snow;
The bare branches gleam, softly in the light
Of the full, bright moon; And for my delight,
I see you walk, smiling in the bower as you go,
Beneath the tall myrtles, happily your tread,
Smiling at me with your dark, dusky eyes,
Which know no bounds of loveliness in sighs,
Nor measure in the realm of heart nor head.
There you slowly pass, my empress of eternal grace,
As ivory snowflakes crown your violet-scented dress,
Where Bach's sonatas shine, grandly like a soft caress,
Composed by his angels, framing your astonishing face.
Beneath the winter moon, in a carriage we shall ride,
And glide into the wood, on cushions, side by side.

The Scarlet Breeze

Do not deny me the mane of your hair,
Nor the scent of its long, sable tresses
Which, in their glory, hold all caresses
Yielding their song to the sweet, autumn air.
Do not deny me the touch of your tender hands,
Nor their soft beauty, so fair to my eyes;
Immerse my soul in the sea of your sighs,
Streaming from your gaze, of sunlit, white sands.
Do not deny me the fire of your kiss,
Nor its resplendent realm of paradise,
Which cleanses my heart from all worldly vice,
You send my adoring spirit to a citadel of bliss.
As I behold you there, waiting in the scarlet breeze,
Snug within your sweater, to kiss beneath the trees.

Mist and Flame

As I Wander

The roving, paved way, flanked on either side,
By hyacinths that sway, clothed by the dew,
In the light of day reveals what is true,
It speaks of a poet's love, eternally long and forever wide.
And as the bright sun glitters on the down,
Where Saint Louis De Montfort prays by a stream
I wander beneath a throng of leaves to dream,
Where tall reeds rustle; shaded, soft and brown.
Then I hear you name in the Orphic breeze,
Laced with the odor of violet blooms;
It veers through my mind with its rare perfumes.
I see your tresses in the ancient trees.
Sipping wine by the gleam of a Normandy bay,
I await your arrival in a French café.

October

Pensively you gaze on the stony brook,
Where, last October, we stood in the sun,
Beside the old stream, (your braids came undone)
As I kissed your hair—my spirit you took.
Oh!—The blazing spring, fresh upon your face,
Brings back that bright day when we were filled with grace
With May's vivid moss (where the swift currents race.)
They are no near as firm, no near as lasting,
As the bond which binds our impassioned hearts;
(The sun in the west descends and departs.)
Gone are the days when, piously fasting,
I prayed on my knees for your fair, soft hands
To grace an October, upon these fair lands.

The Sacred Shrine

The scared shrine in the gardens of grace,
Clothed by the evening's celestial, white wines
Of the vespertine moon, gleaming on the vines,
Houses my kisses upon your elysian face.
In the tallest spire, where the lamplight glows,
Before we retire to a dreamless sleep,
I drown my soul in your hair as I weep,
And taste your perfume which no one else knows.
Then all the stars retreat into the sky,
And the curtains fold to your eyes and mine,
As we are immersed in the heavenly wine
Cascading from jars which the angels pry.
Then all becomes rapture; We are no longer here:
Our spirits become entwined, and ascend above the sphere.

Poetry

I am of the gray sky,
I am of the tree tops,
Where the blue robins perch,
And I am unafraid.

Then comes the lavenders,
And the Victorian Maid,
Descending on the wooden porch;
(Humble in her dress of white.)

And then, gleaming, sings the tender scarlets,
Of illuminated light,
Of the sacred meadow,
Of the infinite artisan.
(So fond to her majestic sight.)

I Saw God in Your Tress

I saw God in your tress, of sunlit hair.
Your dark, dusky eyes shed light on the pond;
Your soul was adorned with gold from beyond.
The white petals swayed in the autumn air.
The firmament sang for your grace and I;
The ethereal claimed the vast, green land.
And then you touched me with your soft, white hand,
As the stars wept wine in the azure sky.
Then all became still; the white petals quelled
The fragrant fall breeze that veered through the dale;
Your heavenly hair of bright, flowing ale
Possessed all my soul where the angels dwelled.
Now all is flowing—the universe sings
Mellifluous strains of a lark's bright wings.

III

Visionary Wanderings

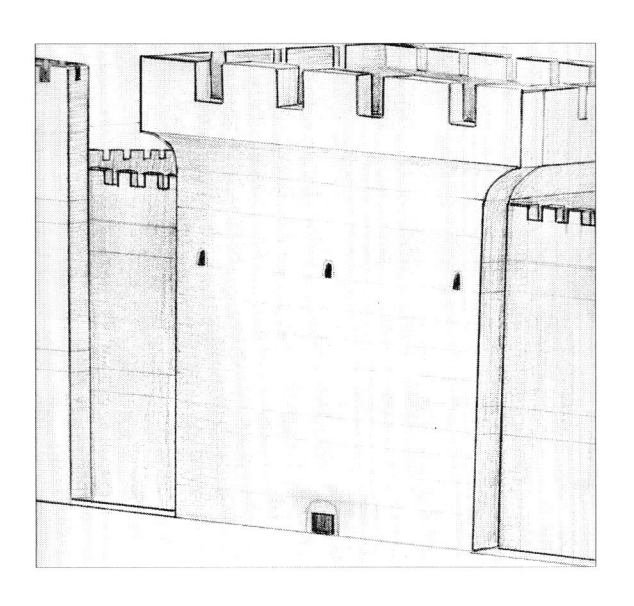

Visionary Wanderings

Alchemy

I wove my verses in a cluster of purple stars
While dreaming on the meadow in the tender, April rain.
A mendicant, I wandered to the outskirts of the plain,
And I slept in the glow of a campfire's bars.

I awoke to the vast, blond horizon,
To dahlias, daisies, roses, to aromatic Fleur-de-lis.
In my black sailor's coat, I arose to symphonies.
And at night I roved the Acheron.

I swam through a gulf of evergreen billows.
I ascended from the brine to the sight of splendid willows.
All prosaic things became sanctified.

Rubies and rings I presented to the queen
In jeweled, velvet boxes, neatly tied.
And in alcoves near the river, I witnessed the unseen.

Rhyme

The burgundy-tinted sunset,
Like a bohemian enchantress
Speaks of the soul's loneliness,
As it glitters on the brooklet.

The silver foam of the little stream
Rushes joyfully, without regret;
Yet I, disconsolate,
Wander to a reverent dream.

The solitary nooks, where I roam and rove,
Dressed with other brooks lined with watercress and clove,
Are caressed by breezes, of myrtles, pines and thyme.

I lose myself in the splendid wood.
In my buccaneer's coat, in my winter hood,
Weaving, as I saunter, a menagerie of rhyme.

Visionary Wanderings

An Ode to Keats

I am of the royal lineage of Keats,
Symbolically at least, an offspring of his pen.
I compose my verse in a sunlit den,
Behind a white gate, where the viny lattice meets.

His florid Ode to Autumn, his effluent poems,
Still flow grandly, for they triumphantly resound
Like strains of golden trumpets, where realized dreams are found;
In his soft and radiant songs, a scented flurry roams.

Never did a bard use such varied paints.
Never was his canvass as wide as the horizon.
He gilded the aureoles of romantic saints.

And when the perfumed wind spoke to him of Byron,
Of Virgil, and the weaver of Hamlet and his ghost,
He would bow to their lines as a poor, afflicted host.

On Poetry

Andromache wept
In her Hellenic despair—
To be widowed twice;

In her heart she kept,
In the calm of her hallowed lair,
With the hue of diamonds, and of ice,
The memories of Hector's iron stare.

Before Alexander,
What fables arose!—
Before fair Ophelia sailed dead,
Drifting on a pond like an oleander,
Before Juliet's balcony would close
To the setting sun's scarlet red,
In the umbrage of the shallows,
The bright, triumphant mallows
Serenaded the blessed dead.

And after Byron,
In the Victorian age,
The rhymers with their opium
Danced with the faun, the fairy and the Siren,
As they turned another delirious page
To witness a goddess or a phantom.

Now the days are dark,
And the nights are dour;
For the trustful poet,
And the exiled lark
It is the hour—
And I know it—
As I wander through the sullied park
To admit to the wanton, wayward leaves
That my anachronistic mind
Is weary of autumn eves;
That contemporary verse,
Is vulgar, banal, rarely polished or terse;

Visionary Wanderings

O, for my former ecstasies!—
I shall voyage to ancient, sunlit sands,
Over wild seas—
To unbridled lands!

Visionary Wanderings

A Grecian Tale

I

My Soul, like a languid, lamenting bird,
Gazes to the east, with its distant, red face;
I desire to escape from the doleful, urban herd,
And depart for a sojourn, to a faraway place.

The sounds of a subway are of a dismal strain;
They die by Central Park in the gray, vaporous dark.
Graffiti on the oaks of brownish, wilting bark
Renders my aesthetic mind weary with disdain.

My spirit of a troubadour, hungry for meadows,
Immured with the city, clasped around my feet,
Will break beyond the tears of these dreamless ghettos,
On a journey to the past—to the Isle of Crete.

II

Tall, ivory pillars, of brilliant colonnades,
Grace my white shroud, as I pace on promenades;
Roving through grand dunes of billowing, gold sand,
I feel the royal hold of Apollo's noble hand.

At last!—I am free; In regal felicity,
I saunter, laved by breezes, blissfully sweet and mild,
As I behold the unbridled, transcendent and wild
Pelagic domain of the exuberant sea.

The Mediterranean's effervescent breath
Fills my lungs with the wines of Dionysus.
As I pass beyond the veils of intangible death,
Carmine blooms shine, and all becomes miraculous.

There, among statues, on this ancient, Greek traverse,
Like a lover's suspiration, fulfilled in a dream
Of a freshet of fountains, glistening in a stream,
Thalassic furrows gleam—like ethereal verse.

Visionary Wanderings

III

Soft zephyrs veer through the courtyard of a palace,
Caressing the rims of an eminent chalice,
Stirring ripples in the sovereign wine,
Glimmering in the rays of the immaculate sunshine.

Illustrious marble steps mount a precipice;
Overlooking the oceanic canvas,
I contemplate the death of tragic Icarus.
Above foamy rolls—I weep upon the cornice.

IV

Among cascading brooks, an immense garden shines—
Home to a thousand potent wines and elations;
It ferments amid Hera's dappled, dangling vines:
A bower of fragrant hues, and mystic revelations!

Pearly fountains fall, as I behold the flowers:—
The enchanting, rosy-red florets of every year;
A Macedonian sentinel of the intoxicating bowers
Threatens my adventure with a long, silver spear.

Aphrodite's white lyres sound like Spanish guitars,
Adorned with the luster of enamored, white stars.
I turned from Alexander, where an Orphic breeze veers,
Leaving the blooms of Helen, resisting blissful tears.

V

I pass redolent hedgerows, of ornate enclaves,
In the soft wake of Sappho, I approach wild waves.
A strange, wooden ship of ghostly sails awaits my heel;
I board the cryptic schooner, and it creaks where the currents reel.

The large, foreboding vessel knows no other hand but I.
I clasp the splintered wheel, beneath a baleful sky.
Something is beneath the boat; (what I do not know)
All that I can fathom is the Kraken dwells below.

Visionary Wanderings

Through a storm I pervade, beyond the gleaming sand;
I sail at topmast, northward, to the deep Aegean Sea,
Until the Sirens are left with no sonatas to assail me;
I find a forgiving harbor—Onto the glorious mainland!

VI

I reach the Acropolis, and I witness the ancient plays.
A goddess of wisdom scents the Parthenon with grace.
By an alabaster temple, Athena's fair face
Smiles as I bless her, with amaranthine bouquets.

My heart, moved by Euripides' words, beholds her Doric rose,
And is engulfed in a florid, fountains repose.
The fire of her kiss leaves my soul profoundly weak.
I have visions of celestial reason—of which I can not speak.

VII

I see the distance, spirited, fine and black,
A stallion beaming in the sun, awaiting my plea:
"I implore, tenacious breed, to saddle your raven back;
Let us ride beyond the wind—beside the splendid sea!"

We pass through a viny, trellis-lined portal,
Beyond the azure glow of a tall, resplendent tree;
We reach the blue dominion of His teeming majesty—
The great and stony Titan:—Poseidon—The Immortal!

VIII

The pure, valiant spirits of my gallant horse and I
Witness the quintessence of the infinite fly by;
Beneath the bronze of the sky, across the diamond shore we race,
Increasing the speed of our incredible pace.

Lifted above the world, beyond curtains of time and space,
Together we breach all earthly realms as we ride,
Entering an effulgent place beside the tide;
We behold upon the billows—a glimpse of heaven's face!

Visionary Wanderings

Rising above the crest of topless ecstasies,
We witness beyond a glided gate a glimmer—
Blooming into an ardent, ravishing shimmer—
Containing all kinds of ineffable rubies.

And so, like Zeus, on Mount Olympus I ascend,
To absorb all that is rapturous and lofty.
But like all true bards who transcend an ecstasy,
I relinquish my spirit and my wings in the end.

IX

My muse whispers into my ears: *"You must return home."*
The sunlight disappears, withering on the vanishing foam.
Shedding red, the dream is pierced, as if with a rending fork.
The beach sheds amber tears, as I behold New York.

X

And so, my fair pedigree of the banished sand,
Because reality has claimed my intellect,
I must bid you farewell, left only to recollect
A nebulous vestige of your enchanted land.

A Gypsy's Life

A gypsy am I, as I rove on the downy dale;
Aside from the taverns, the fields are my only vale.
I drink from my carafe a fairy-fermented brew,
And I dream of fair love, beneath a radiant sky of blue.

I carry within my satchel a book of romantic rhyme;
I wield it when I may, and write as I did of old:—
Of a sable-haired girl, whose gaze is of a raven-gold.
Her dress is white and long, and her hair is of an elysian clime.

I am struck by visions beside the lane,
On starry October nights, laved by the autumn rain.
And I sleep beneath the myrtles, musing on her kiss.

I have searched for her in ethereal bliss.
I have seen her face in dreams, wandering on the shore,
And the specter of her beauty, passing on the moor.

Visionary Wanderings

A Summer's Day

As I wandered through a garden, its petals' budding folds,
A wreath of varied blooms I laid upon my chest.
I scuffled through those beauties to find a tranquil rest,
In a bed of dappled daisies, amid bright marigolds.

A melancholic blue jay lingered in the lights
Which sifted through the leafy heights,
At the end of a playful summer's day.
A lady with a parted mane passed along the way.

I took out my guitar, and plucked a nylon string.
She sat in the sun, upon a cloistered seat;
Our spirits were married, wing with wing.

"I am of a royal house," she said, in a tone so sweet.
Her name was of rapture, of a redolent stream.
We walked to a sunny nook, and embraced as in a dream.

Corridors

Taciturn elegies fill leaf-barren bowers
Of the mountainous forest, clad with tears.
No moonlight gleams on the castle's broken piers.
Gray billows pale beyond the time-weathered towers.

Next to the court there are barrows in the enclave;
The parapets above know only gloom.
All alcoves are dark; black is every room.
In the hallways a warrior walks as in a grave.

In days long gone when the Turk, with a sword in hand,
Crossed the ruby Danube, upon the scarlet sand.
Their blood was shed by this fierce, feral prince.

He died in the dawn—and ever since,
He walks the cryptic corridors in shadows of the night,
Bereft of any angels, bereft of any light.

Visionary Wanderings

Come, Let Us Wander

Come, my lady, my only love,
The dawn is of the russet wine.
Shining from above
On the trellis clad with vine.

Come, let us wander,
Where the pleasant breezes rove
On the prairie over yonder,
Among the dappled clove.

Come, unfold your flower
In the soft, exquisite boon
Of the fair, arboreal bower;

As we await the approaching noon,
In the dew beneath the autumnal moon,
Come, let us wander,
Where the redolent breezes play
On the prairie over yonder,
By the undulating, azure bay.

A Correspondence

The roof looks down on the busy din of bars.
A sole candle burns on my old writing table;
In the ancient avenue sparks silver cars of cable,
As my psyche ascends above the curtain of ivory stars.

To an oceanic vista, my dreamy mind is carried,
To a sallow, sunlit beach, beneath a leafy canopy;
My young, majestic beauty, enchanted by the sea,
Looks on splendid hues, where billowing brines are married.

And yet this distant fantasy does not console my heart.
There are winds outside my windowpane
Which speak of my love with a sad refrain;

For she lives within a mansion, where the halls hold works of art;
She is tristful in a ballroom, gilded with gold light,
As our spirits call to one another, softly in the night.

Visionary Wanderings

The Countess

The liveries of spring rejoice
In the rural plains, in the urban streets.
A gaze of wonder softly greets
His lover's face, as he hears her voice.

She is of the meadows, where scented breezes sigh.
With her dusky rubies she easily entrances,
As his soul drowns within them, where the sunlight dances.
She is humble in every aspect, as she passes slowly by.

She walks in grace, with a canonized tread.
She is modest in her dress, of a scarlet hue.
Her wake is of a symphony, of a deep azure-blue.

She holds him in her bands, with each word that is said.
For she speaks in song with her lips of the rose.
And she blesses every bower, as her petals unclose.

The Baroness

In the vast, royal courtyard of the bright, regal palace,
Gleaming fountains flow like soft, silver rain.
From the font of a fair maiden's long, raven mane,
A prince drinks wines, as if her tresses were a chalice.

She reclines on cushions in her swan-white carriage,
In the soft majesty of the autumnal sun;
She dreams of lofty towers, where the vines are one,
With glistening stone, where gold rays speak of marriage.

And in the mystic psalms of the vespertine light,
She wanders among the mignonettes, in the sweet, scented air,
To find her love waiting her, amid the lilacs of the square.

As the good, October moon sifts in the nascent night,
Through the boughs which cloak their nuptial embrace,
He is taken by the glow of her pure, celestial face.

Visionary Wanderings

Violets

The crested, blue waves of the turquoise bay
Rise to majesty of the brilliant sun,
And support the haulers, which one by one,
Drift to the sand where the violets play.

And in the reeds, which are kissed by the gales,
My lady dreams of the sloping sea,
Enrapturing my mind with her eloquent beauty;
She sighs like a seraph, and softly exhales.

Reclining amid the purple, redolent flowers,
Her hand falls into mine, as the ships ascend
The billows of the brine—the palms gently bend.

A quiescence claims the dunes of the bowers;
My lady's tresses, more splendid than all dawns,
Sleep upon my chest, as lavender breezes toss the lawns.

Noel

Now comes the wintry refrain of falling, ivory snow;
It sets upon our windowpane, softy and serene.
The Angelus protects our union; sweetly and unseen,
From the skies a host of angels bless our cabin here below.

The gilded hearth gives off a sanctified glow,
As your gazes address me with a sacred grace;
The crackling bars flicker gold upon your face,
And instill within your glances burgundies which flow.

Our relatives shall arrive soon, from the white-blanketed dale,
With presents in their arms, and warmth within their hearts.
Melodies of Yuletide whisk our minds to where the gale departs.
Of alabaster flakes, in Our Creator's cozy vale;
He brings to one and all burnished harbingers of love,
Of profound, solemn peace, and downs of the turtledove.

Visionary Wanderings

A Veil of Sorrow

Give ear to the sorrowful strain
Of a lady born to a heart heavy laden,
To a thorny crown, a sad, holy Maiden;
Give ear to the triumph of a love in pain.

She came from Nazareth, and wept in the reeds
Which were sanctified by her many tears.
Her faith was such that she had no fears;
She found solace in serving all of mankind's needs.

She longed to bind every wound she did see,
With her outstretched hands, soft, fair, and white.
She was well-acquainted with the night.

Her compassion, dressed resplendently,
Still zealous for her little ones,
Shall evermore reign, outshining all suns!

A Lover's Sonnet

Let us walk in the redolent air, to dales of swaying grain,
Alas!—The moonlight pales, by the soft, majestic sea;
Let us embrace, entranced, within a sonnet's symphony,
Among the misty blooms, which await the autumn rain.

Let us lose ourselves in a rapturous enclave,
Where Aphrodite weeps upon a Grecian stream;
Let us wander by the moss, and as if in a dream,
I shall kiss you in the sun, where the tender breezes lave.

For there exquisite gales endear our married minds,
As they carry through the branches of mild, olive wines.
They take us to concertos of multicolored, dulcet brines.

I confess to you my love, as you enclose me with your binds;
In shadows of ecstasy, more than twice,
In have seen your face in wonder, *indeed in paradise*.

Visionary Wanderings

One of the Mellow Dawn

What beauty can I express
In my lover's eyes of fire?
Does all the world expire
In the flames of her caress?—

Indeed, I believe the answer is yes.

For she is of the mellow dawn.
In her gaze there are blossoms
Of an innocent wise.

There are sanctified temples
Within her sighs;

There are scents which carry forth in the sunlight,
From her bright demeanor of a true, regal queen;

And only to the poet's sight (for others unseen)
She wanders at night,
By the sculptures of the court,
Placing roses at their feet,
Like a dove-eyed child of the rainy vales;
She sleeps amid the iridescent foliage,
Of the summer's dappled liveries which entrance
Her anointed brow, as the daylight pales,
Caressing the ardor of her summery glance.

And as the silver moon rises gracefully,
Her gazes strike with profundity
My bohemian soul, as it slowly rambles,
Amid the white statues, the maples, and the brambles.

Visionary Wanderings

O Mary

Let us penitents mortify ourselves in virtue,
And let all voices, in prayer and in song
Praise you O Mary; for the night is long.
And all my affections are completely about you.

Let me not fall for a specious facial rose—
For the worldly can never be truly beautiful without.
Yet let me hope for the bloom which will close
To this vile vale, holding faith free of doubt.

Perhaps you possess a daughter suited for me;
Superior in spirit; (for I've gone mad in sin)
I drank my fill in the dank misery of a baleful inn,
Until I became aware of true felicity,
When cheerful vows spoke of freedom untold.
For in your holy countenance I witnessed only gold!

Visionary Wanderings

Wisdom

The liveries of beauty must speak only of the soul.
I have trod like a fool upon the dallied walkway;
I was witness to a Siren's guile when my reason went astray.
And now, by grace, my eyes are mended whole.

I rejoice in beauty that is true and fair;
All specious gazes I abjure.
I seek only what is sanctified and pure,
And I no longer look to the perfumed air.

My beloved must kneel within a chapel of white;
The Rosary must be her constant friend,
So she can persevere with me, until the very end.

She need not be entrancing in her fashion, nor in sight;
A spirit of goodness and chastity must resound
Within her secret thoughts, to keep my poor mind sound.

Schoolgirl

On the college campus, one bright, gilded spring,
I met a young lady, as pretty as a rose,
With smooth, raven hair, and lips which would unclose,
In shadows of white colonnades, where seraphim would sing.

I drank wine profusely, (verse was my love)
And I admired her soul as one does a saint.
Whether with music or with a chisel, or with stanzas or with paint
I lauded her with poems, to peruse in realms above.

Her name was of rapture, a violet bloom.
I would carry her books from the classroom.
And she kissed my cheek, one fair, starlit day.

We would wander in the sumptuous breezes of May,
Beneath the gleaming trees, in the aromatic light.
And our hearts became one, in the sanctity of night.

Visionary Wanderings

A Maiden Fair

I scuffled carefree down the dallied, sunlit trail,
Blissfully in love with a maiden fair;
I tasted her lips in the perfumed air.—
(I met her by the sea, where soporific masts would sail.)

Her scents came upon me in the auriferous night,
As I roved, like Hermes, without a home.
I found her asleep by the dune where I would roam,
Where slender grasses sighed to the oscillating moonlight.

Her name was of the billows, and of the lavender sky;
She was classic in her aspects, and somewhat shy.
(Her chin housed a dimple when she would smile.)

Her chestnut gaze would stray to the white-crested ocean.
Her perfumes entranced me, like an ethereal potion.
And her heart was pure, without taint nor guile.

When Music Ceases

When music ceases, and blue stars ascend
Beneath a moon of rue, amid the gloom,
On the avenue below my bedroom,
My mind ferries south, to where palm trees bend.

To the saffron seaside my heart does rove,
To escape the misery of the urban night
Where sinister wraiths haunt me in the moonlight.
(I write on my table in the corner of the alcove.)

Still, the palm trees and the sea are swallowed
In my loneliness which seems unhallowed.
For this is the time when witches come to life!

Yes, this is the hour when all hope seems to fade,
And all the universe becomes a glade
Of a beckoning grave—*the revolver and the knife!*

Rejoice

Sing: O slaves, rejoice in the sovereign song!—
The beauty of the grasses that sway
Has receded in the clay
Of the wistful artisan
Whose file is sharp,
Sure and long.
Sing to the dying embers of the day.
Rejoicing in the vespers
Of the nocturnal strain
Which carries lovers
To the fertile plain,
Amid the laughter
Of the silver rain—
Rejoice in the sovereign song!

Harding Court

The women come and go at Harding Court.
Some are with children, some are not.
Many linger with a smoke in the shaded lot.
Most appear sultry, of a licentious sort.

I watch them return in the russet-hued sun,
Pining for their mate, any new, handsome someone.
They yearn for caresses, a kiss, any carnal play.
In their jeans and dresses, they pine for the end of day.

It is hard to tell in this day and age
Which souls are suited for a lifelong wage,
After they are sated within the flesh.

Whether man or woman—there is no disparity.
The sun shines upon every alley equally.
And especially at night the sewers mesh.

Visionary Wanderings

Currents

Currents that soothe the expanse of my mind,
Are of angelic hands that glisten in the moonlight.
Glossy painted lips, an enchanting smile and sight,
Dress the lovely spirit of one who is kind.

There are vistas fashioned for you and I;
Let us recline beneath the astounding sky.
Behold—the feathered branches bless us as they hover,
As friend with friend, as lover with lover.

Let us saunter to where the breezes stray,
Over crested waves, which sway the bramble,
Where one can witness the ocean's spray amble.

Let us scurry down to the dunes, where rushes play,
And inhale the burgundies of a thousand bright Julys,
Where the morning sun glows, and tribulation dies.

The Grand Beyond

I ventured out beneath the full, white moon
And tasted ecstasies beside the lane,
In my sailor's coat, in the summer noon,
And I slept in the wines of a maiden's mane.

A bohemian, I explored all lands in the radiant sun.
I met fair Ophelia in a glistening dale,
And caressed her tresses, one by one.
I drank from the stars a Byronic ale.

All of Shakespeare's sonnets were exclusively my own;
Every rapture revealed to me its true quintessence.
I bowed in the presence of my Creator's essence,
And I sailed in each pelagic gale where every seed was sown.
From the prodigious meridians of pine-clad mountains,
I greeted the dawn of saffron and gold.
Dionysus gave me his hand to hold;
In an alabaster courtyard I found rhapsodies in fountains.

I flung my cloak on a shimmering pond,
Where angels spoke from the grand beyond,
Of vast, gilded ballrooms, of a glorious light
Which erased the darkness of the worldly night.

There were servants in a hall, with silvers in hand;
A Seraphim's song bound an eternal wedding band.
Couples danced, their garments gleaming,
Exalted, they would kiss,
As their youthful gazes, beaming,
Were filled with a sacred, ineffable bliss.

Visionary Wanderings

Peace I

Now at peace is the cedar and the swan.
Drizzle-clad fleece glides serenely on the pond.
Between the sun and moon there is a solemn bond,
Which lends concert to the ocean's waves, wayward, white and wan.

Amid tall, quivering reeds, which dip their sallow heads
In the corners of the pools, there stirs a strophic breeze;
From the branches of majestic trees,
A somnolent song sighs to the flower beds.

And in the ripples of fuchsia, you can see lavender stars
Glitter and perish to the strain of bronze guitars:—
For an elegy plays in the bowers of the wells.

Far off in the village, there chimes a chapel's bells.
(This is the hour when faiths intertwine.)
Let us lay beside the mystic lake, in a cloister, pure, divine.

Visionary Wanderings

Over the Windy Sea

The emerald meadows are my home; I live a poet's life.
Like a buccaneer, through brines I roam; a voyager I am.
At the rustic inn I drank potent ales in lamplit Amsterdam,
And I wandered near the grottos, in search for a pretty wife.

Through bramble I amble, through clusters of holly-green,
I walk beneath the ogives to soft, arboreal boons.
In my seafarer's garb, in auriferous noons,
I behold pelagic blues, both profound and serene.

A lady resides in a bastion, over the sloping sea.
She sings of fair love to the gardens below;
From her sweet, white hands alights the swallow.

At eventide, she serenades the moon in its gleaming majesty,
And she sighs and dreams of the prince who is on the other side
Of the ocean beneath her towers—as long as it is wide.

Visionary Wanderings

A Night in Hades

I returned from the land of the living dead
Where demons gave me their terrifying eye.
Indeed, I was in hell, and thought I could no longer die.
I searched for a door to open my head.

But I could not escape the fury of the fire.
It consumed my spirit and would not burn out.
In despair I could not breathe, and was tossed about
Between scarlet curtains where the heat would not expire.

There were other damned there, whom struck with fear,
Attempted to run into the belly of the night.
But Satan's fallen seraphs kept them from all flight.

Not once in those flames was there a loved-one near!
Yet my despair was such that I indeed perished twice,
And returned to the earth—from fire and ice.

The Spring

The Grand Palais de Champs-Elysées
Looks down upon me, as I wistfully depart
For the undulating sea, where a Parisian lass laced with ecstasy,
With the buds of her lips, the refuge of my martyred heart.

And so the boulevard rings new and lauds my revelry.
I have in my pea coat some fresh sailor's verse.
Its lines are of fermented vines—an alchemy of the universe!
It serenades my soul with the rhyme of infinity.

And so the mellifluous leaves fall one by one,
Gracing my boots in a rapturous gale, upon the splendid avenue.
The moon sings to my spirit, and the heavens are bright and china blue.

O, what one can see in the fading, sallow sun!
To inspire me, my wondrous muse, and ferry my schooner north,
To where the Vikings reigned—from where the spring comes forth!

Soliloquy

My heart and mind, they correspond,
As they make their plaintive sigh
To the infinite, azure wells on high.
The cormorants play by a rippling pond.

I remain in the sway of Keats' Grecian urn.
Beneath a gallery, made of old coquina,
Surrounded by statues of terra-cotta.
The sumptuous vales of bards still have much to learn.

For the umbrageous boughs, sympathetic to my rue,
Frame my reflection on the barren little lake,
As if I were a pantheist without a clue.

They seem to quiver for my sake,
As the moon's ethereal rays alight
On the terrace's haunted bays, in the silence of the night.

The Cliffs by the Sea

I wandered through the arbor with my fair, beloved one,
Among swaying, slender reeds, where a strain did arise
From the effulgent clouds of strange, green skies.
We sauntered through scents of mints and saffron.

The path of bricks and grass, where we gently tread
Sent us to the burgundies of the vast, umbrageous sea;
Alone on the promontory, she softly sang to me,
And undressed herself, where the trail had led.

She removed her coat, and laid it on a warm, marble seat;
We sat beneath the palms, emerald, old, swaying and sweet.
The frothy brine appeared in effulgent billows
As she whispered lines from Yeats in a dale of ivory willows;
She took me to a moss-clothed cave,
Married to the sky and I, the wind and every wondrous wave.

Visionary Wanderings

The Starlight Night

Your voice is dreamy, sad, like canticles of old,
Taciturn, like us, weavers of the rhyming word.
In the somnolence of the park, like a whisper it is heard,
Sifting through the branches, pensive, brown and gold.

Yet your heart is young, and of an elevated air.
Sweet in your slumber, you dream without care,
In a lavender peace, my fair, exquisite one,
In a billowing tuft of redolent leaves, of the setting, scarlet sun.

In the vague and nebulous starlit night,
Let us hold each other's hand in the elysian grays,
And rove by the terra-cotta mansions in the moonlight.

Every rapturous thought, seaborne, of the winds,
Rushing through the brambles, the reeds, and tamarinds,
Shall sail through our psyches, like twilit Chardonnays.

A Walk in the Garden

The cruciform, clad with vine, looks down upon the bower.
The wistful cloister, arborescent,
Lends to the arabesque a summery scent,
Where vivid fields transports my mind—a poet's precious flower,
To serried, sunlit partitions
Of Roman colonnades;
And there, in extravagant profusions,
As the intoxicating daylight fades,
The statuary, framed by a menagerie of fallen leaves,
Gives off a mordant fragrance of honeyed harmonies,
Such as Sirens sing, mysteriously, on warm, autumnal eves.
The sonorous hues of the whirling breeze,
Shine to the eye like turquoise seas;
And the fountains sigh, languorously and white,
To the lavender stars which rise, in the soft and nascent night.

A Bonny Lass

The mysterious languishing cool of the soft, summer breeze,
Carried from the Atlantic, lifts up the wavering grass.
I fell in love with a youthful, wealthy, bonny lass
Who likes to slowly saunter beneath the vivid, virid linden trees.

She lives in a villa, by the symphony of the seas;
Her chamber is up high; she owns many rubies.
Her father is a whaler, and tells daring tales of old.
He sailed to Persian lands, and returned with treasures of bronze and gold.

Her hair is very dark, and her sable eyes are set
Within the vivid canticles of scented mignonette.
Her lips are bewitching, halcyon, round, and red.

She takes my hand in hers, within the vast, marble square;
Her kisses are of wonder, and perfume the majestic air.
And when her gaze is starlit, I hear hymns within my head.

Emerald Billows

"When you call upon me, from the depths of your heart,
I shall comfort your soul in the long, bitter night."
So says The Lord from His humble height—
For the star of His mercy does not depart.

I am weak, I am wan, and I pine for relief.
And although I am firm in my Catholic belief,
I waver like a capricious billow,
When the larks of the sun meet the ivory willow.

For beauty, if she is fair and true,
Eludes me lately in my heart of rue,
And I fail to feel fortunate when sorrow steals the moonlight.

I wander, like a nomad, through valleys devoid of anything bright.
And on these dreary dales, where lamenting litanies sigh,
I trod through the vales like a specter waiting to die.

Visionary Wanderings

Two Women by the Shore

Two women walk upon the shore;
They are without all riches nor fame.
They talk of their suitors, and smile in the flame
Of their mutual, innocent ardor.

The waves roll in and wash their slender feet
With cool, blue brine, as they rove hand in hand.
Their dresses release a scent of burgundy on the sand.
They exchange tender kisses whenever they meet.

They hear one another's secret desires
Concerning the men who sit around fires
Lauding the charms of these dear, close friends.

And at night, beneath the quivering tree that bends,
Cradled by the soft and scintillating breeze,
They give thanks to the Lord, on their smooth, white knees.

A Pantomime

Harlequin, you who have left your old pantomimes
For Aphrodite's lyre, and for Sappho's verse,
You look sad beneath your dress, and seem to curse
The tears of your mask, as you flee to ancient times.

Punchinello, wandering on the gilded Parthenon,
Contemplates Columbine, gracing on the Athenian sand.
And Pierrot, drunk with sunshine on the luminous land,
Muses upon a fairy, as the play carries on.

And they dance, in their revelry beneath the moon,
These visionaries enraptured by Apollos' grand boon.
They rove in their costumes, and drink until the dawn.

Zeus looks down with rare confusion,
On this modern invasion, this unwelcome intrusion,
And he scatters them like seeds on the briny lawn.

Visionary Wanderings

A Coquette

A deceptive embrace that lies about a kiss
Is taken beneath the lamplights of the sultry town.
I was tempted there by flirty eyes, of a dusky-brown,
And their sparkling gazes—(she was but a mere sixteen, this miss.)

And I was a sailor, just a half-year older;
She slept in the folds of my seafarer's gown,
And she wept like a child upon my shoulder;
Her hair was softer than a dove's fleecy down.

O, the caresses that profess fidelity—
Yet, with a malevolent skill, yearn to deceive one.
To cloak her intent, she tried to hide the benevolent sun.

I was saved by the ring of an angel's plea,
Which warned me of her corrupt design
To leave me to come the dawn, and of her fingertips' shine.

Recollection I

Come, let us walk
Beneath the tufts of the morning flower,
In the rapturous cadence of the boundless bower;
Come, my beloved, and let us talk
Of sanctified things—
It is the hour.

I shall clothe your fingers
With silver rings.
And there, in the alcove of ambrosial air,
In the caress of the summer wind,
Where a moonlit fountain lingers,
Beneath the canopy of a tamarind,
Allow me to undress you there.

And slowly, one by one,
Your immaculate, white veils
Shall clothe the fresh, green grass.

At first, the last of the scattered sun
Shall make you wonder and hesitate;
But your cautious protests come too late—
For a weak objection softly fails
When halcyon scents commingle with the flesh—
All scruples shall pass,
And our arms shall mesh.

Come, let us walk
Beneath the tufts of the morning flower;
Come, let us talk
Of sanctified things,
Of bright, silver rings,
Of the ardent heart with its flutterings—
Come, it is the hour.

Visionary Wanderings

The First Snow

Near, in the fever of my nocturnal distress,
You comfort me with a dear caress,
Upon my weeping, pensive brow.

Over the moors, a wooden prow
Greets the white-capped billows of the brine,
As the winter's first snow
Descends majestically and slow.
(In our quaint, old cabin we recline.)

The shepherds' farms are hidden by the fog,
As icy north winds fling shrouds upon the bog,
Swirling alabaster flakes
Which settle upon the frozen brooks,
And upon our crystal windowpanes.

(This holy season makes
Such soporific nooks.)
Let us drown our tears in Christmassy strains,
And with verses from your buccaneer—
Since you have tamed my fever with your hand—

Let the approaching night be of only cheer,
As swan-white curtains clothe the land.

King Henry VIII

The Argentine fountain in the bastion's square
Finds the young chatelaine walking in her redingote;
By cameos of white, the prince within his stare,
Transfixed by her gazes, leaves his briny boat.

And nimbly, with an amorous semblance,
With an eloquent repose, with an aureate cadence,
She grants him a smile, in her dress of candescence;
Her mane is of the rose, and so is her countenance.

Yet the mighty king spies from his tallest tower;
Their ardor he sees within that regal bower.
He grows displeased with this prince and his wife.

He muses to himself: there is no pathos in this life.
He calls to his sentinels, and lo and behold,
For the prince and his lady, it is off to the scaffold.

Visionary Wanderings

The Swashbuckler

I row my wooden skiff, approaching the brilliant shore,
On the sanguine sea, with rubies in the bow;
A troubadour, I leave the jewels within the prow.
(I hide my little boat in the grasses by the moor.)

I scuffle on the boundless dales as a poetic patrician.
With an aureole about my head, I hold a silver spear.
Am I Virgil, Keats, or the author of King Lear?—
None of these: I am of my own—a meta-physician.

A Carolingian invader, I have crossed the English Channel twice.
I have met my foe in battle, as the maddened Mongolian kills.
My lover awaits me in a flake white dress, with aristocratic frills.

Her tone and her aspects entrance as they entice.
I have voyaged over land and sea for her kiss of adamantine.
And I shall leave my sword behind me—for her pearly skin of wine.

In the Candlelight

The candelabra upon the night table,
In your chamber, scented with violets,
Gives off auriferous glows.

Your soft gaze of sable,
As the summer sun sets,
Finds us where a zephyr flows;

For the open sashes
Receive the gentle gale,
As your eyes and their lovely lashes
With the nascent moon prevail.

Visionary Wanderings

The Palace Ball

The wistful cadence of a melancholic melody
Arises from the grand piano, in the drawing room.
A servant chimes in, after dusting, with gracility,
Lays down a tray of china, with a lavender bloom.

And tea is served, as the gleaming sun sets.
Soon all will be ready for the palace ball.
The first to arrive are patrician coquettes,
Along with their suitors, they walk down the hall.

The princess still plays to one and all,
As the guests stroll into the royal palace;
Wines begin to flow from every silver chalice.
And upon the marble floor, the laced dresses fall.

The orchestra starts to fiddle and tune;
Through the stained glass panes one can see the moon.
Each couple takes their places, they curtsy and smile.
The princess takes my hand, eager, yet with guile.

We danced and we drank, until the regal dawn
Found us sleeping on chairs made of brown rattan.
I awoke to the conductor's long baton;
A dunce, I realized I played the foolish pawn.

For the princess held me; with completion,
From within her eyes of azure blue,
She spoke: "Last night, what love we knew!"
And I saw within her gaze a vague look of repletion.

The Lavender Mist

The lavender mist
Whispers of a kiss
Where the moon does glow,

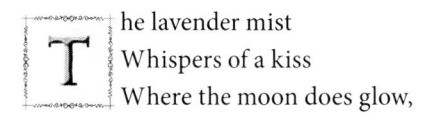

Wistfully, on the snow.
A lover's kiss,
A solemn bliss,
Is found beneath the piny grays;

Your kisses are of Chardonnays!

Let us caress in the cools
Of the shaded air;

Let the world call us fools;
What do we care?—

The lavender mist
Whispers of a kiss
Where the moon does glow,
Wistfully, on the snow.

Visionary Wanderings

Music

In the distant horizon
Gleams the emerald valley,
Before the castellated partition;
And from that radiant dale,
Many oboes play.

Drunk with the sun, a gypsy in the hay,
I can hear the bramble of the fields caroling;
I drink in the mystical ale,
And the trumpets, glorious,
Sound their rapturous triumphs
Where an angel's whitened wing,
Gilded with adamantine bands,
Ascends over the holly-green lands
In the luminosity of the late, fall day.

The heavens beam a golden ray
Upon the alabaster statues,
Clad with viridescent vines.

And the starlit mandolins,
In concert with the azure sky,
Blend with the somnolent violins,
As the redolent rubies
Of the daylight die;
The, nascent the night,
With its violet sonatas,
Rises from pianos in the autumn wood;

And all the majestic Shangri-la
Enchant me in the ecstatic flood
Of a languorous bassoon
Which leaves me astonished
Beneath the Ossianic moon.

Advent

I

Shades of clover on the fields of wild oats
Are presages of winter yet to come.
I leave the saloon, inebriated and numb,
As I swagger into town to buy some winter coats.

I am in love with God and nature,
And with the eternal murmur
Of the pine-laced breeze,
Which exalts the splendid myrtle trees.

II

The village glitters with the lights of Christmas.
I have purchased two jackets of raven leather.
How I love this season, this frosty weather;
It is time to go home to my faithful lass.

III

She receives me in the cabin; she is half-asleep.
Half-dreaming on the couch, she takes my hand;
"I can see you have been at the ale," says my pretty firebrand.
Yet all is understood, when upon her breast—I weep.

Visionary Wanderings

Carol

What can be said
Of an angel-eyed saint?—

What splendid verse within her can be read!—
What portraits can be seen,
And with what grand paint!—

Behold a rose of red,
Upon a sea of green.

For whom does the Seraph bow his head?—
She is her faithful daughter.

And when the cosmic twilight
Triumphantly ascends,
Softly and serene,
In peace, beside the fire, she bends
To coat with tinsel the hearth of brick.
A golden-haired elf,
She works for Saint Nick,
And dusts the bookshelf.
A servant, she is glad,
As she greets the night
Inspiring laughter
In the hearts of the sad.

With an enthusiastic, innocent glee,
She decorates a Christmas tree,
With a miniature carousel,
A cute, little mouse,
To the chime of Santa's bell,
In her cozy, humble house.

The Composer

The silver rain falls softly down
Upon the sleepy, quaint, old town;
The blue larks stray
Over the chapel of gray
To the somnolent sea.
So gracefully.

A composer weeps,
With a sole, flickering candle,
And a white carafe of wine,
Upon his grand piano.

As the rustic village sleeps,
Beneath the glittering, adamantine,
Descending glow
Of the mourning moon,
He weaves his assonant lyrics,
No longer concerned with the logistics.

And in his anhedonia
There can be no boon
As the charwoman walks in,
His melancholia
Tempts him to leave for the colloquial din
Of the corner saloon.

And he wonders why,
With a glass of rye,
His heart is filled with such a sorrowful strain—

Welcome, my brother, poor composer,
To the salvific treasure
Of the poet's pain.

Visionary Wanderings

A Wandering I

I passed a holly-clad trellis,
Beneath a rosewood, shedding its leaves,
Dreaming of purple, summery eves,
And the dulcet embrace of my mistress.

Under a violet display of ascending stairs,
I ventured out beneath the August sun,
In scented airs of amber, maize, and saffron,
I strolled beyond an ogive's tall, iron bars.

Gold-colored clouds were aureoles for the moon.
From a cupola sighed a dissonant tune.
I muted upon a cry from the effulgent vale.

All became harmonious, from heaven's citadel,
A sudden wind flung dandelions on a dale.
And astonished, beneath the moon I beheld a mystic well.

A Night in December

My dear, young darling, will you please pour the tea?—
There is snow upon my boots, you see.
And my hands are chilled, although my burden is light.

(This house is a blessing on a cold, winter's night.)
Woolly, silver, feathered flakes gather on the panes.

Our old, brick hearth is a joy to my eyes.
You hang our bedclothes amid a shroud of sighs,
As I dress the pine tree, with tinsel and with canes.
The hush of your gaze, and their sweet, dappled look
Speak gently of repose, as you water a new bouquet.
(I heard sleigh bells in the village today,
And saw whited oaks, by the frozen brook.)

We retire by the fire, and recline amid the crackling bars,
As a sea of ebony brings distinction to the stars.

Visionary Wanderings

A Walk Through the Graveyard

From the graveyard's sodden dale, sorrowing, asleep,
A dour ballad alights from graves and their leaves;
It is wistfully sad, and hauntingly cleaves
To quivering mallows, over brooks that weep.

To a dim October's once fair lands,
My memory roves, drunk with the strain
That brings solemnity to the Orphic plain,
To this place where a lady held my hands.

Gold, whispered vows which once glittered like the sun,
Let to trysts of madness, as my mind came undone.
For her affections died, and so did mine.

The yew trees, barren, soaked in a dusky wine,
Among the sighing, withering cypress,
Are shrouded with the vine—deceased as her caress.

One Winter Night

In the obscure pales of brisk, winter gales,
Beneath a lamplight, by an old, stone church,
In a bath of shadows, where branches lurch,
I dream, in the evening, of cold, ancient tales.

Balconies are struck by the Orphic moonlight,
In the Gothic town, where paradise sleeps.
A fairy in the clouds enchants the deeps
Of haunting, chilled bays, and the cryptic night.

Eagles, from a canyon, ascend in their flight,
As Tudors and their ales, rich with many stars,
Quell with dew the embers of the expiring bars,
Of my languorous soul, consumed with the sight.

Alas!—It is over; The village and ravine
Are stilled by the morn, with a twilit green.

Visionary Wanderings

The Abbey at Dusk

I have come to see the lady in white,
Who lives up high over rivers that flow,
Through an emerald ravine, where pine trees glow.
(I stand there below to behold her sight.)

Upon a balcony, fragrant with the spring,
From the regal court, she appears in a veil,
In a long, flowing dress, and gazes on the dale,
Above a spacious garden, where the violets sing.

A piano plays softly in the drawing room.
In a wistful wise, with innocent wishes.
The dining rooms are elegant, and graced with silver dishes.
Servants come and go, with rare bouquets in bloom.

And outside, among me, nascent in the dusky hours,
Shimmer moonlit hues, rich with the scent of mint and showers.

Visionary Wanderings

In an Hour of Silence

In an hour of silence, in the haunted, unholy bower,
Where an elysian cool, in the concert with the moonlight,
Breeds mysteries, among old crypts which glitter in the night,
Caresses ancient graves—now comes the witches' hour!

In the vast and starless cemetery, a grim river flows.
There are no blooms, no fragrance there plays.
Among the placid hues, an oleander sways.
Souls of true perdition speak though no one knows.

With a slumbering emergence, dreadful wraiths ascend,
Grim, shaded marigolds shed their leaves in a miasmatic spring;
Beneath the dour sky, clad with dew a corpse does swing.

The moaning heard this evening with these malevolent spirits blend.
The reason why these specters walk is known alone to the winds which blow.
A cold seeps through their burial shrouds—of winter's approaching snow.

Visionary Wanderings

Gray

Tender dreaming, beneath cold phosphors of blue
Produces dim raptures for my psyche in its exile.
All artistic verses seem delirious and futile.
(The castle on the cliff is sympathetic to my rue.)

When raptures are dead all dreaming will cease,
I bequeath my soul to the wide, endless road;
I shall let my carriage cart away its load
To the ends of the earth, to find some peace.

To some foreign asylum I shall ride,
And find consolation kneeling before a shrine.
I shall dissipate my misery in ethereal wine.

I hope for a lady's company by the roadside.
Then (perhaps) my dreams, no longer in veils of gray,
Shall shine before the sepulcher and have its final say.

The Little Garden

The bright belvedere in the little garden-close
Where a blue jay darts, harbors somnolence and peace.
The sycamores above shed their leaves like fleece,
And mingle with oaks, the myrtles and the rose.

The blooms of the sun, in their languors open wide;
Tall, budding daffodils here and there glisten.
To sighing siroccos, relining, I listen,
As I lay upon a lawn chair, seeking nothing but to hide.

And in the vague, mysterious stillness,
Fashioned by the lack of another,
A sentiment arises of sadness.

(A stranger passes by, an unknown brother.)
And the aromatic vines, reflected in a pool,
Shake their hymns upon me, of a thyme-enchanted cool.

Visionary Wanderings

Autumn's Cellos

The cadet cello of the fall
Stirs from within a rhapsody of love;
When I hear it played, in the plaintive night,
It brings a majestic hush upon all,
Cascading from starlit skies above,
To lamenting boughs at twilight.

Of ancient verses, I possess them all;
Whether at noon, or in the morn—they call.
Like starry ballerinas, clad in white,
They dance in the vague, ethereal sun,
Alleviating my every affliction,
Like flares around a castle's spire;
(I envision them when I retire.)

As I read those rhymes, the church bells toll.
Benevolent waves of wind sway the slender grass,
Pressing upward tufts of bramble as they roll,
Eclipsing every sorrow as they pass.

And as I close my poetic essays,
Engulfed by the sovereign night,
The cello of the fall
Marry muses to the moonlight.

Gales I

A flurry of leaves, from wavering trees,
Form brines as they descend, around my feet.
Eglantines of amber and the autumn gales meet,
Stirring wines as in a vase, containing every breeze.

Gales of incense, of a splendid kind,
Ascend and flow with a rapturous purity;
They transcend the setting sun, and scent humanity.
(Mary's tender hands bring such quiet to the mind.)

A muscatel of old mellows my soul,
Of these mystical gales which pacify.
Upon the vespertine litanies I rely;

They bestow these tepid breezes to make me whole,
As the park retires from the drowsy day,
And my body prepares for a bed of hay.

Visionary Wanderings

Unrequited Love

A young woman on a swing
Sways in the wine-laced air;
I would take her for a song to sing,
Rising from the chalice of my despair.

Though I know she has no eyes for me.
(Just a passing fancy mingles there.)
Yet rising from the breezes of the autumnal air,
Is an ardor, vast as the boundless sea.

Her tresses are gold, and her gaze is blue.
And oblivious to my misery and rue,
She is perched among the scarlets of the spring.

Felicitous as a bloom, yet flighty as a dove,
She is blind in her mind to a serious love.
(For which I would give most anything.)

Hope

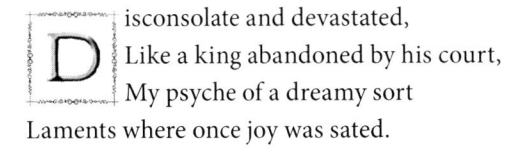

Disconsolate and devastated,
Like a king abandoned by his court,
My psyche of a dreamy sort
Laments where once joy was sated.

Forsaken, I pine for paradise;
I desire it with my very blood,
Like a pent-up dam before the flood.
My death is of roses, my life is of ice.

And all of heaven's heraldries, all studded with lights,
Still inspire to illuminate the vast forest's heights,
Where hope still carries through the golden trees.

And the ghost of a lady wanders below,
Whom in the next life, perhaps, I shall know,
Whose heart is flushed with ecstasies.

Visionary Wanderings

The Ardor of the Wise

Belvederes and cupolas shine beneath the skies.
The hues of a sonata, in their cadences, are seen
As their chords are reflected in roses on the green.
On the terrace appears a lady; the balcony—it sighs.

With each speckled member, in perfect array,
The arbors below welcome a sobbing fountain.
Her gazes are enchanted by the glitter of a mountain,
Where the soft, wilting lindens mingle ivory with their gray.

No calendars are here, all is timeless as the sea;
The lady bestows violet glances upon me,
As I stand within a boon no pleasure there denies.

The sleeping canyon's silence, by the vast, gilded wood,
Is a witness to our rapture, where all is understood:
Humility and goodness are the ardor of the wise.

Grace

She roves beneath the oaks, of varied heights,
Cradled by the autumn's languorous lights,
Clad in a redingote of turquoise-blue,
Wrapped in a veil, of a starry, wistful rue.

She wears a silver ring, which glitters for two.
The sunlight paints the locks of her hair,
As hyacinths blush, by the old, country lane,
Where leaves breathe bliss upon her shoe.

Traces of her tears for a mysterious love
Are effaced by the gems of the soft, dulcet rain.
Her fiancé builds castles, engaged with the strain
Of sighing Shangri-las, perched in lofty boughs above.
And as she wanders beneath fall's colonial eaves,
The glory of saints grace her diamond hued sleeves.

Visionary Wanderings

Sadness

I wander through the willows of the wood,
Gazing at beatitude, not feeling as I should.
I see bright tufts of daisies, and flowing springs.
Yet the voice of my muse no longer sings.

For these blooms no longer move my heart.
I call to the heavens with a lonesome cry,
Yet receive no answer, not one remote reply.
The lights of the sun grow dim and depart.

The willows wither, and the streams of the dale
Become wrapped in a nimbus obscure and pale.
I walk to the outskirts of the silent plain.

Dark, oppressive clouds amass to release their rain.
Their baleful, dreary showers approach the Orphic boughs,
Like wooden ships which sob with grim, haunting prows.

A Lady in the Park

The scarlet trees are dressed in tears.
The symphonies have been stilled, and the mansions are pale.
A lady passes by, as I tristfully exhale.
I am weary in my coat, and worn beyond my years.

Yet there are spirits in my intangible flask.
(I own the whispers of angels and the eagle's wing.)
The beauty of this lass renews the ales of spring.
(To acquire her kiss would be a comely task.)

Yet she is married to the verse of her books,
As I am wedded to the bourbons of moonlight.
I am weaned from the sighs of her eyes' dusky looks,
And I see that her countenance is lovely, fair, and white.

And as she wanders dreaming to the outskirts of the park.
I pine for her caress in the footsteps of the dark.

She Passes and I Sigh

Her unique, exquisite beauty makes me sigh.
My enraptured heart does not know why.
In the scented night, I tremble and weep.
Her aspects are dark, where sentinels sleep.

I found her in an ethereal dream,
Showered by a fountain's spray.
On a daisy-dressed field, where emeralds play,
She drinks Chablis from a mystic stream.

Beneath piney branches, white with snow,
Round about moss-covered stones,
She walks barefoot through a rainbow,
Flushed with pink tones.

Her soul breathes forth ecstasy, and her glances are bright,
Endowed with somnolent stars, and the sanctity of night.

Twilight by the Shore

Beyond the statuesque Tudor's stained glass windows,
On a path in the wood, by the waves of the sallow shore,
My lady took my hand, as we paced upon the sandy floor.
(The soft, September canopy blessed us in the garden-close.)

In her eyes I could see the burgundies of the shade,
Through watery sighs, from the redolent glade.
Her white, flowing dress was doused with dew,
Caressed by breezes, of a china blue.

We entered the chateau, in the hour of twilight,
To find peace in that abode, in the haze of the nascent night.
We climbed a circular stair, and found a quaint, colonial air;

Vases filled with blooms graced mahogany tables;
My lover's long hair was radiant in its sables.
(I stole one rose for her, as precious as it was fair.)

Visionary Wanderings

Heaven's Dew

Fountains lead to fountains,
And snows lead to snows,
Pressed upward by the winds,
Where a brooklet flows.

The clear, white stream,
Descending, cascading over stones,
Cool and pure,
Rushes beneath the teeming waterfalls
Which majestically rumble down,
Slowly and profound,
Like old, red wines
From the highest paradise.

Ivy, green, and sunlit,
Pristine, and married to a rose-clad trellis,
Melodies play within an age-old arbor;

And in the near distance,
Beyond the valley,
A cottage is lit with candles,
And all its powdered windows
Are tinted with a glowing gold.

Where the Zephyrs Flow

There the zephyrs flow
Between the paintings of my mind,
Some scarlet petals know
What landscapes I shall find.

I go there not alone:
My love walks by a wall of stone,
To the sobbing of the ocean's foam,
To the endless lament of the sobbing foam.

With a rosary in her hand,
And a cross around her neck,
She roves upon the sand,
In siroccos on the jetty's deck.

Some blooms hint in the blue of some distant, soft sleep.
The zephyrs flow, and the paintings weep.

Visionary Wanderings

The April Rain

The April rain weeps, silvery its flows,
As I sit, gazing on the lane, I compose,
With a candelabra upon my writing table.

(I ferry through my stanzas, as well as I am able.)
Outside, the wistful oleanders,
Beside a row of corianders,
Waver by the roadside.
Dusk sifts through the evergreens.
(I pine for my brunette bride.)

Against my panes
A willow leans,
Serenading me with soft refrains.

I muse upon the face of Hamlet's ghost,
Upon Byron's verse,
Upon the one I love the most,
And on the books aflame,
(As I drink my ambrosia)
Lost in fair Alexandria.

I am astonished by the worldly sighs,
As if I were a child.
And as the obscurity of the skies
In concert with the mystic moon,
Overwhelm me in my poetic boon,
The showers cease,
And the wind becomes mild.

I pine for release
From the hand of Keats,
Sappho, Schumann, Bach, and Baudelaire,
As the willows repeats
Its strains laid bare
To my open ears and my weary eyes.

Visionary Wanderings

O, the majesty found in Iris' air!—

A rainbow paints the clearing skies,
As Jupiter ascends,
And the sunlight dies.

A Wistful Strain

The mystical courtship of ebony fingers,
Of the grand piano, played by slender hands,
Breathes forth a strain that pines for distant lands.
(Outside the fog from the storm still lingers.)

In the grandeur of the palace, some haunting vespers rise,
As I sit in the conservatory, entranced by this song;
It wavers like a ghost, whose shadow is alive and long.
(The lindens tap the panes in a soft and dreamy wise.)

It was two years ago since I first beheld her face;
She paced upon the fields with a Dutch-white grace,
And her pearly neck was a sacred shrine.

Now the days are dim, dour, and old.
I have come to this palace to hide from the cold,
And to drown my afflictions in a chalice of wine.

Visionary Wanderings

She Walks in a Russet Ray

She walks in a russet way,
Beneath an ivy-laden archway,
As dappled blooms among her glow,
Her soul possesses streams
Which glitter as they gently flow.

There are seraphs in her dreams,
Beneath the pelagic skies
Of mystic waterfalls,
Among the moon which lives and dies.

And all the cloister's vine-clad walls
Greet her gaze in quiet ways,
As the amber autumn light
Paints the terrace and its azure bays
With a shimmering Shangri-la
Of elysian delight.

She drinks her ambrosia,
And wanders through the scented shades,
Laced with the wine of verdant glades;

She humbles each flower
With the rainbows of her glances.
Enraptured by her Dionysian dances,
I beheld in the golden bower
The bliss of her innocent smile,
Longing for her majestic kiss,
And musing all the while
On the ineffable splendor
Of true happiness.

A Walk Beneath the Stars

The glow of the evening brings dreaming to her soul,
To my young bride who roves in a boon by the orange trees,
In the soft, briny air of tender, sleepy seas;
Her love is of innocence, and her heart is pure and whole.

There is music in the winter woods.
As we walk through fallen leaves, she sweetly takes my hand.
We listen to the hymns which shed light upon the land.
(We are warm within our coats and hoods.)

These ballads speak of streams from spring,
As we pass through tall reeds rustling.
The misty shades serenade our treading.

A quivering hyacinth shimmers in the dusk.
The gales which touch our hair are rich with the scent of musk,
As the silver, nascent stars consummate our wedding.

Visionary Wanderings

My Turquoise Soul

I awake to the ring of a wedding bell,
And rove through elaborate gardens to a timeless dell,
Where labyrinths of burgundies mystify and stream
From passionate sunsets which sob as they gleam.

I wander beneath corollas
In the cloistered shade.
Among busts of terra-cottas
I encounter a queen,
Not far from the glade
Asleep in the perfumed air,
One arm to the ground,
With her slender hand
Gracing the green
Of the alabaster square.

Such beauty I found
In the strands of her hair;
As the fountains, sliver, tall, and grand
Rise to the weeping firmament.
She is modest, yet opulent;
Her lips are like the rose,
Soft, smooth, and bewitching in the glens of violet hues;
(They replace my wines
With stronger brews.)

And the rapturous eglantines,
They glitter among the sunlit marble
In the majesty of the cosmic court,
Where the statues resemble
An Apollonian order,
As the queen awakens in the garden's border
To a dream of a hazy sort.
(I greet her with my halcyon ale.)
She beholds my turquoise soul, and peers through its every veil,
As I stand, entranced, on the sun-drenched dale.

The Dale

There is coffee on the table.
The rain outside descends.
What head of lofty sable
Beside the fire bends?—

It is my love, half-dreaming, on this stormy winter night.
Awaiting my caress, donning her evening gown.
The dew within her gaze gleams like moonbeams on a down,
As she smiles from within that light.

We shall leave our books and nuptial nooks
Behind in this house of adoring looks,
And wander to the outskirts of the wild dale.

There are winds shall trail beneath the pale
Mysterious moon which weeps for our sake,
As we sail into the mists of the vast, majestic lake.

Visionary Wanderings

Benedictions

The cool pool ripping in the sweet, scented shade,
Where here and there a fallen leaf rides,
Is stirred by the gales of the autumn's tides,
Which flow beneath the boughs, to the oceanic glade.

Nearby a cathedral, its spires clothed with mist,
Rings out a strain upon the starry wood.
There are whispers in the shade, where my first love stood;
Sunny blooms abound there, amid that hallowed tryst.

Now all is obscure; sullen winds sway the grass,
And bring silvers to the pond, sighing as they pass.
A rueful moon rises, yet cryptically pales.

And there, by the pool, I behold her ghost,
Rising among the reeds, by the lane she loved the most,
As cordials in her wake wed benedictions to the gales.

Apathy

I am no longer moved by nature's landscapes;
Nor by the gleam of carriages in the park;
Nor do I fear the shadows after dark,
When moonlight steals in between the long, purple drapes.

All but love I have relinquished.
All but love I have forsaken.
There is gray in my meadow where no grasses are shaken.
The wind is still, and all but extinguished.

Nothing shall disturb this stagnant grave,
Not even the hopeful fingers of the dawn.

There is nothing but frost on this isolated lawn.
Nothing but the port of death do I crave.
I shall drink from Lethe inebriation,
And lose my dour spirit in the absence of sensation.

Lethe

I shall open my satchel and compose anew.
While dreaming, I saunter to the inn for a brew;
After I shall wander to the outskirts of the grove.
A Carolingian chatelaine has fallen in love.

Her bastion's teeming turrets, and their ancient, stony tiers
Shine above the fountains in the cloistered, marble square.
She admires a row of flowers and combs her undulant hair,
As she ambles by the sculptures, near the bower's belvederes.

I shall drink the dews from the grand beyond,
From the elysian wells of her royal countenance.
I shall greet her with my verse as a Saxon vagabond,
Enraptured and drunk with the orgasmic cadence
Which emanates from the aspects of her deep, raven eyes,
Beneath the Lethe of the moon, and the swallow that sighs.

Hymns

Daisies mingle with mignonettes and wine.
(There is moonlight on the balcony.)
From the colossal, white conservatory,
Somnolent sonatas resplendently pine.

They are redolent, rapturous, and of the spring.
They ascend with the grace of an angel's wing,
And stir the bending boughs, as they glitter in the sun.
(I stand beside a brook, where the silver currents run.)

At dawn, at noon, and at night they play.
Their soporific ebonies ring radiant over the open bay,
Near the gleaming terrace, where the curtains sway.

And as dusk approaches from the holly-green mountains,
To the diamond-hued stars rises the fountains,
From the umbrageous court, to the hymns of May.

Visionary Wanderings

Ballads

Ballads from guitars resound with harmony;
The concertos of the cloister are for yours ears alone.
Roses in the summer rays are found to marry stone.
(The arborescent bower is dressed for a lady.)
Myrtle trees are doused with light,

As their leafy limbs are dipped in pools.
Gales grace the path where the day's reflection cools.
Solemnity and fashion await the strains of night.

Take my hand, where the white petals weep;
Let us stroll amid the blooms where marigolds sleep,
And seek the mystical blessings of this holy hour.

There are glistening daisies which speak of rain.
Clouds amass to assuage all pain,
And to caress your dress with a somnolent shower.

Lovers

Transfixed by your figure, upon the green,
The sun paints your tresses with a redolent gold.
We are graced by blossoms, as I behold
Your ineffable face, majestic, and serene.

The leaves are all alive, each rejoicing in your wake,
As hedges softly sway, beneath a cloudless sky.
Ebonies and alabasters mingle on the lake,
Beside a stone-paved trail, as you glance at me and sigh.

Over there, beneath the maples, we shall bask in what they yield,
And recline within their potions, by the breeze-kissed, emerald field;
We shall rest in our love, in its timeless perfume.

The shadows of the season shall blend within your eyes;
Ambrosial, each aroma shall entrance us as they rise,
From the roses of the garden-close, glittering as they bloom.

Paradise I

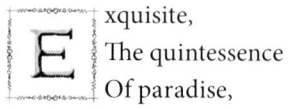

Exquisite,
The quintessence
Of paradise,
Emits its essence
As coronets entice,
As Seraphs visit,
Emanating from the dew
Of a weeping rose
Which sings to you
In the aromatic blue
Where you delightfully pose.

Violins rapturously weep
In elysian lakes of rain,
With tears that run deep
Within a blessed refrain.

In magnificent courtyards,
Flowing with burgundy,
The bohemian bards,
Drunk with stanzas of sunshine,
To the rhythm of a symphony,
Cascading from sighing billows,
Weave their florid rhyme,
Immersed in the scent
Of mints that refine,
Watercress and thyme,
Passions without lament,
Ambrosial willows,
And the viridescent vine.

And in the corner of the bower,
You receive each measured line
As you do the weeping, scarlet flower
Which sings to you
In the aromatic blue,
Emanating from the dew.

As I Await Her

Flushed with pink tones,
She walks in a winter wood;
The snowflakes which she owns
Grace her woolly hood.

Her mane is of a raven hue,
I remain
Within her soft domain
Of rain and china blue.

Her gazes are deep,
They possess true bliss;
Their lights resemble
Dante's kiss
To his fair majestic Beatrice.

And among the marble,
The silver jets weep,
As I await her coming
In the breezy cool
Of the frosty square,
By an azure pool,
Yearning to inhale
The wines of her hair,
Beneath the pale
Of the night's majestic, pristine air.

Visionary Wanderings

An Invitation

Purify my heart,
So pure may be my love.
There are lush, spacious gardens
That await us above,
And ineffable arbors,
Clad with gilded vines.

Come my fair and innocent one,
Let us drown our dreams
Where the dawn reclines,
Beneath cloudless skies,
Among diamond streams,
Near magnificent pools
Where the starlight shines,
Let our spirits ascend
Above the sun.

Where rainbows bend,
And canticles play,
On a stone-paved path,
Beneath white colonnades,
Let us amble to the emerald glades.

Let us pace upon the silver sands,
By the somnolent sonata of the endless sea,
With adoring, clasped hands,
Where the Virgin finds humility
In the soft, majestic, tender gaze
Of your childlike, capricious, wondrous ways.

My Proposal

From somewhere in the summerhouse,
A piano gently plays;
There are blue jays in the garden,
Which lend color to the haze.

The nimbus of the sallow light
Bequeaths to the sighing, sonorous boon
Of your tender, white hand
The caressing rays
Of the effulgent moon,
In the sacred, cosmic atmosphere
Of the grand, ascending night.

Kneel beside me, my bride, my dear,
Upon the verdant grass,
As I ask you to be your eternal one,
In the sobbing hues of the setting sun,
With a sanctified ardor that shall not pass.

O, let your scarlet "yes" profess
An infinite design
Which the gilded coronets
Of the aureoled saints shall bless,
Forever a bond that is yours and mine.

Visionary Wanderings

In the Evening I

You sit in front of your vanity,
Beside the open window,
Which overlooks the billowing sea,
As you brush your hair,
And unloosen your bow.

Outside the palm trees
Sway in the breeze,
Of siroccos flowing north,
Warming the water,
As they carry forth.

You spray your neck
With a French perfume,
As your gaze beholds the deck
Of an approaching ship,
In the light of the moon.

And as you dress with scarlet
Your soft, upper lips,
You witness a sailor,
Handsome, young, and bold
Who steps upon the sand,
Consumed with the desire
To kiss your tender hand
With his ardent heart afire.

And later in the evening,
When the dreaming swallow sighs
To the vast, appealing, starlit skies,
You bare the dew of your chest
Where he lays his brow
If only to rest.

And the waves break slowly on the gilded shore,
As the dawning sun rises,
Over the glistening moor.

Visionary Wanderings

You place a rose within a porcelain vase,
As your sailor sleeps, dreaming of your hair,
And its ambrosial scent, dulcet and mild.
And you open the sashes,
To the sweet, summer air
With the graceful innocence of a child.

Visionary Wanderings

Two Years Ago

I voyaged to the amorous Scottish plains,
To the countryside, surrounded by virid mountains,
A vagabond, I slept beneath a spray of fountains,
In the supple caress of the tranquil rains.

The ardent embrace of fairies and muses
Kept me warm in my sanctified delirium;
I drank from a stream an elysian rum;
My mind was filled with verse, which an angel still peruses.

A faun slept beneath the silver glass
Of a mystic pond, below a golden bough.
An enchantress approached me who was pretty and dow.

She came from the north—a farmer's lass.
Two years ago she kissed me, and awoke me from my slumber;
I can still see her now—a maiden of thunder.

Rapture

Epigrams dwelled
Within the ocean of her eyes;
With a mystic aptitude they quelled
My heartfelt, hallowed, languorous sighs.

The cadence of her gaze
Spoke of the sunlight's weeping rays
In the glorious park, ablaze
With hues of paradise;

I beheld her lips in the phosphorous haze
Of soft, tepid fires, of a diamond's wondrous ice.

And we walked a minstrels,
In the wake of God and the autumn breeze
To gilded citadels,
Beneath majestic trees.

Visionary Wanderings

Steven

My benefactor and my friend
Is a starry-eyed lad
Of Roman lineage;

His perspicacious vision
Has no linear end;
And he is touched (more than a tad)
By the curse of true genius
In the summer of his age.

His heart is sincere, generous, and sage,
And we often walk
Beneath the coronated moon;

Yet we seldom talk
Of darkness and the dour.

From specious rubies
He turns away,
And he will hide
From pride
In the morn, at noon,
And in the russet boon
Of the twilight hour.

Moonlight I

In their luminary languishing,
The vast, sleepy fields
Give way to the splendor
Of the melancholic moon
Which forever gently yields
Its silvery portents
Of immaculate grandeur;

The extolling swoon
Of the tall, emerald grasses
Glorify the end of June,
As the tepid liveries
Of the sparkling spring passes,
Into the vespers of a solemn, gold July;

And the balconies,
They gleam below
The lovely starlit, majestic sky.

As a lady, young, lovely and fair
Opens the sashes to the frothy air,
She inhales the wistful, redolent glow
Of the enchanting orb of crystal and white
Which lends its daisies, its marigolds and roses
To her dark, astonished innocent sight
As she softly closes
Her eye to the dale—of a diamond-hued, exultant light.

Jones Beach

After the rain,
The ambrosial coquette
Lights a slender cigarette,
And taking a hungry drag inhales;

Her brunette mane,
Silk and suited for the gales,
Is scented by the salty breeze,
In the mint-enchanted sunset.

Her sandals meet the glistening grain
Of the diamond-hued sand,
As a zephyr cradles her exquisite knees;
She holds within her supple hand
All of the summer's ecstasies.

She passes by an emerald hedgerow,
Behind which is a swimming pool;
Her younger sister is still in high school.

To the spacious beach they go,
Where all the crested currents flow
To the sound of rock and roll,
Pouring from the silver cars,
Parked within the briny lot;

The dunes are sallow, soft, and hot,
As they sit beneath the lavender stars,
Around a fire, with many a friend,
Amid the harmonic sounds of guitars,
And the throng of palms that gently bend.

Chelsea

The nightclubs and the neon bars
Of fashionable Chelsea
Ring with the urban cadences
Of mingled voices and guitars.

Couples stroll by with a bohemian glee,
Like vagabonds, along the white, wooden fences;
Each youthful lover, like a wide-eyed gypsy,
Takes in the city's changing sights:
Its yellow taxis—its frenzied lights.

As the autumnal moon
Glitters in the southern sky,
Beyond the harbor, over the sea,
A canticle, a wistful tune,
Arises from the corner's café—
Where I drink my rye
In a lonely way.

Visionary Wanderings

A Litany of Roses

Just before dusk, in the moonlight's solemn hour,
When soft vespers rise to the monastic tower,
The pious are caressed by breezes, salty-sweet,
As they pace upon the grass, of wild oats and wheat.

With rosaries in hand, they greet the nascent twilight,
As their prayers are carried to a distant hill,
Where a lone cross beckons, struck by the wintry chill;
They genuflect in stills of the ascending night.

And as the somnolent leaves prepare for the snow.
They meditate in the cloister's sanctified glow,
And each to his own, they petition in that place;

They kneel as they are given gifts of grace.
And the Ave Maria, grand, does resound,
Flowing like honey—coronated—crowned.

Visionary Wanderings

A Walk in Spain

I discovered, near Madrid, a quaint, old town
Where buccaneers assailed me,
With their lances of bronze which reflected the sea,
And I left their dead bones behind me.

Then I wandered to the piny hills,
Where I gladly would doze
Within a charming garden-close,
Amid a row of daffodils.

I met a lady, fair and dressed
In an archaic style;
We spoke for a while,
And I could see that she was blessed,
In her graceful demeanor,
And in her smile.

And within that luscious vagueness,
Of the summer's tepid languor,
Beneath the splendid Moorish sky,
I took the hand of the Latin miss,
And we lost ourselves within the blessing of a sigh
Of a soporific, gleaming kiss.

Visionary Wanderings

Virgil

The austere, Roman colonnades
Surrounded Virgil's vine-clad palace
Where he would write his chiseled verse;
At twilight, when the grand sun fades,
He would take his wine from a golden chalice,
With one line expansive, another terse,
He would compose
Until the dawn—
His head laid upon his marble table,
Weary of the dew-kissed rose,
The dappled lawn,
And manes of sable.

Shakespeare

Hamlet's father, that specter of the night,
Blends in his sorrow
With Juliet's balcony,
Hidden from the moonlight;

The radiant moonlight,
Soft and sad,
Tender and dour,
Remembers the old, English bard
Who was sometimes mad—
In his finest hour.

Visionary Wanderings

A Voyage to Scotland

I dreamt of fabled epochs
In gilded, golden, spectacular times;
I envisioned diadems and crimson jewels,
Which donned the crown of a feudal queen.

I ferried to Scotland, and dove into the lochs;
Underneath the waves I heard mystical wind chimes,
And I swam with Sirens in radiant wells;
I grew fond of Glasgow and Aberdeen.

I heard carillons in voluptuous domains,
In quiescent gardens, where dappled mallows
Dipped their petals in the turquoise shallows;

I met a Celtic beauty, roving in the rains,
With black, braided tresses in her long, parted mane;—
And we kissed beside the mist of a wind-swept lane.

Mystic Wines

On sumptuous evenings in late July,
I would scamper down diamond-studded dunes,
Beneath an azure confusion of ethereal moons.
And I slept in the sand where linnets fly.

I drank from a silver cup mystic wines.
I drowned in pelagic brines where cathedral bells would ring.
In raptures, I heard a chorus of angels sing,
Wrapped in curtains of green, and petals of carmines.

The Harvest Ball

The cadence of my piano
Familiar with pain,
Streams from my chamber, to far below,
Along with the autumn rain.

Patrician couples come and go,
To the wistful keys, the tremolo,
Descending down the tower's wall.

It is the joyous eve of the harvest ball
For servants, masters, for one and all.
(The claret wine begins to flow.)

The marble floors await the dances.
I have seen the duchess in my trances,
As she walks on the carpet of the opulent hall.

Effulgent greens grace
Vases made of tiffany.
All the chandeliers are warmly lit;

In my mind I behold infinity,
And the ballroom, twilit,
As each takes their place
On the alabaster floors,
With an aristocratic pace,
(The vassals tend to the old, wooden doors.)

Outside my chamber, far below
The glorious Catholic stained glass panes,
Patrician couples come and go
To the wistful keys, the tremolo,
Descending down the turret's wall,
Along with the autumn rains.

Visionary Wanderings

Forest Park

The quaint carousel, by the ice cream stand,
Made of carved, wooden horses
Revolves like the moon on its circular courses,
In a rustic wood, of an urban land.

Young and old hold picnics in the park,
Amid a band shell, there after dark,
Symphonies consummate clustering stars;
Soloists are married to pianos and guitars.

A golf range gleams with its varied dappled oaks,
With ponds and streams, with leisure-minded folks;
In winter, children sleigh down its swan-white hills.

The athletic courts agree, with their dins and stills.
And the elders of surrounding towns, donning winter coats,
Spend their final morns slowly roving on the oats.

A Roman Garden

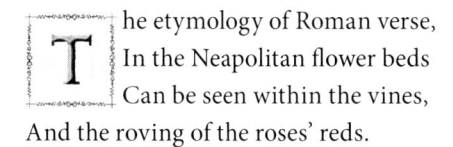

The etymology of Roman verse,
In the Neapolitan flower beds
Can be seen within the vines,
And the roving of the roses' reds.

A princess reclines
With rubies in her purse.

Among eglantines,
And auriferous streams,
She drinks from her carafe
Lavender wines,
Gazing at the azures
Of the distant brines.

Colonnades and a portico
Receive the Mediterranean raptures
Of a summery sirocco,
As the somnolent sunlight captures
Mystical strains
From ethereal cello,
As the daisy-laced grasses
Welcome the rains.

A salty wind passes
Through the redolent boughs,
Like a breezy chandelier
With gold refrains.

Visionary Wanderings

A Walk Through Paradise

I walk as an angel,
In the light of paradise,
Where azure tiles grace the floor
Of the entrance of His radiant palace.

Emerald slopes of an immaculate moor
Can be seen from the highest tower;
Above a statuesque court,
And the boundless beauty
Of a ravishing bower,
The gilded spires reach
To an infinite of astonishing skies;
The tangible and ethereal
Are one to blessed eyes.

I am one with The King, and His Virgin Queen,
As I dally down a dell of ineffable green,
Graced with the lily, the marigold, the rose.
My spirit is drenched in an ecstasy,
Within a majestic garden-close.
And every sorrow that was mine
Has been replaced by a deep felicity,
In a splendid cloister, clad with vine.

Effulgent streams
Through a golden forest gleams—
And is wine to the taste!—

Awake my brethren—
There is no time to waste!—
Let us live our lives be of service,
Goodness and love—
For I have been favored
With an elysian glimpse in the twilit hour
To see such diamond dew drops
Of our recompense above!

IV

Sonnets of Dusk and Dawn

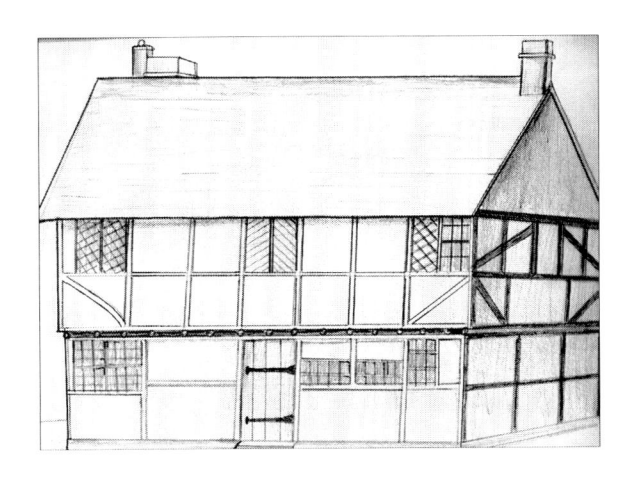

Preface

When I was seventeen, in my junior year of high school, I discovered a blue anthology of poetry which when opened and read, instilled in me a profound sense of happiness. For the life which breathed forth from those poems expressed a life I was leading and have led ever since. That life was one of freshness and freedom, a life acutely aware of the spiritual realm, and of life everlasting. I became fully convinced that the poet, in order to fulfill his role as an artist, must become an instrument of the Divine One for the sake of his fellow man, in a spirit of servitude. Much in the same way Saint Francis of Assisi asked to become God's instrument on earth, the poet must ask for the same grace, the same blessing, if he truly wishes his work to be authentic. I was confirmed in these beliefs when I read the *Summa Theologica* by Saint Thomas Aquinas. I discovered my calling as a poet that very day, as one does enter a royal priesthood. These ideas and ideals are not confined to Christendom, as they have been expressed for centuries, in literature, and in other art forms, to different degrees, in most cultures of the world.

Poetry, like music, has a universal appeal to all of humanity. Yet unlike music, verse, to be generous, requires translations if indeed the poetry is authentic and worthy to be introduced to peoples and nations beyond the writer's own native vernacular. Hence, the importance of translators is incalculable in the realm of poetry. One thinks of Chaucer in this regard, or even Baudelaire, who brought Poe's writing to the French masses.

The purpose of poetry is, through words inspired, to convey the realities of love, beatitude, existential adventure and sometimes darkness and suffering to and for the sake of the reader. The poet is therefore a servant. Poetry must always be something more than a form of mere entertainment. The reader must be assured that he does not suffer alone in a cosmic void, that love is indeed real, and that it is the source and end of all life.

The sonnets which comprise this volume are true to these principles.

~John Lars Zwerenz

To my fair Maria

Sonnets of Dusk and Dawn

Dawn

Rising on the mead like a rustic, old sphinx,
The dawn, with its elegant morphia,
Erases from the night every lingering umbra,
As it paints the canopy with transient inks.
Like an meteorite, I cross on the shelly golds,
Beside the wondrous waves which fill my flask:—
The azure of my psyche, free of every task
But to pierce through Cleopatra's poison folds.
I shall ascend from the tumultuous depths unscathed,
And return to Rome, where Catullus bathed
In ointments of refinement, bejeweled with gems
Of passionate queens who donned diadems.
Come the moon I shall awake to new revelations,
On the pasture by the ocean, free of tribulations.

Ode to Coleridge

The mellow opium of the vague afternoon
Sways the yellow drapes where Wordsworth gazes
At the mariner who fancies golden glazes
On poured, fermented grapes, and on the languid moon.
Accounts of literally life, soon to appear
Above the place of any wife, is all he holds dear.
For Christabel has taken every lady's place
In the mansion by the meadow where repose and grace
Is prized in lyrical ballads of odes and elegies;
Coleridge walks upon the dales to the ring of rhapsodies;
Leaving his study where his work appeals to German thought,
He places his hands in a coat which writing bought.
Wordsworth, now alone, fills a glass with imported rum,
As the Kubla Khan is wrought, in a green delirium.

Sappho

The diamond-kissed panes look out upon the lawn.
Beneath the gleaming terrace, Sappho pines with delight
To walk upon the furrow in her Grecian dress of white,
As she sits on her divan, dreaming in the dawn.

Her eloquent aspects are of Picasso and Monet;
She finishes a sonnet, and leaves her grand estate.
Her mercurial mind is bright; she is fortunate in her fate,
As she reclines amid the reeds, the lilacs and the hay.

She opens her halcyon mouth to receive the violent rain,
In the grasses which cradle her red, endless mane.
She muses on fair love, gazing at the shrouded sky.

Inspired to ascend to romantic perfection,
She settles for no man—save for divine election.
She sees his face within her, and exhales with a sigh.

Sonnets of Dusk and Dawn

The Voyage of Icarus

Into the realm of boundless azure,
I ascended, graced by Zeus, with golden wings.
In my ruby ascension, I discovered gold rings;
In my flight I attained every sanguine rapture!—

The billows, suddenly beneath my elevation,
Appeared as distant, conquered, old shrouds.
I gazed upon a firmament devoid of all clouds;
My spirit rejoiced in a godly sensation!—

Then segments of the Bible spoke of a warning:
I ignored their words, and beheld a brilliant light.
I felt exultation in an astonishing height!—

I was a witness to every dusk and dawning!—
Yet then I met the might of He Who saves—
And fell like lightening, swallowed by waves.

The Snow-Covered Hill

I ventured out to a hill near a forest
Beneath a sullen sky, seeking peace and rest.
Feathery flakes fell on the soft, sloping dell,
Adjacent to the pines, I crossed a frozen well.

Silence reigned in the timberland of white.
Every bough was barren, shaken by the cold.
The chilly wind whispered in the day's moonlight,
And seemed to echo a sapience of old.

I heard my footsteps breach the still,
Of the virginal field, of the shallow hill.
The flurries spoke of reason, coupled with grace.

Their soft epiphanies were of fleecy downs,
As they covered reeds of chestnut browns:—
One often finds God in a lonely place.

Sonnets of Dusk and Dawn

One Summer Morn

Summer descending on the greenery
Carries in the emerald gales a tune
Which lauds the rising, matin moon;
(This sonnet is one with such luminous scenery.)
Its pulse, of a nimble, theistic cadence
Swirls leaves on a path which gleams as a flower,
Situated between a villa and a bower;
The musical morns are all bejeweled with radiance.
And now the beaches, not far from the greens,
Receive the lapping, salty caresses
Of mahogany cello, and oscillating dresses
Of sanguine bells, and pearl-laden queens.
Suddenly the earth is singing with lights
Which emulate with tears, from effluent heights.

Ode to Robert Louis Stevenson

Mystic cathedrals, vacant of any member,
Tower over Samoa, beneath a white and blue sky.
Stevenson wanders, with a shot of rye,
To his dim wine cellar, in late December.

Musing on which combination to ingest,
He states his face changes, daily, with ease.
His wife sees him lost to aesthetic, dark seas
In the winter of his life, as a seer, he is best.

Enraptured with Osiris, Apollo and Pan,
He chooses a fine Bordeaux, and wipes his sweaty brow.
Jekyll's guilty psyche is alive within this man.

Suffering from lunacy, the flights his drinks allow
Produce peculiar transformations which terrify at times,
And in horror he collapses, for uncommitted crimes.

Sonnets of Dusk and Dawn

The Bastion by the Sea

The yard below the bastion holds many crimson blooms;
Swirling, russet leaves around a freshet are blown,
Heavy with a mordant scent, they toss among the stone,
As terra-cotta sculptures flake beneath palatial rooms.
Beyond the large square, there are woods of rhyme
Where the cloistered pass, musing on books,
Admiring the aesthetic boulders and brooks,
Wandering as gypsies without a dime.
Nearby, the sea, in soft sonority,
Mingles with the twilit, oceanic sky
Of a thousand stars, rising as they sigh,
Ascending with the violet canopy.
And as the sun disperses, all colors correspond,
As grottos of green grace the boundless beyond.

Sonnets of Dusk and Dawn

The Blessed Dead Are We

The grand chess set in the lutescent ballroom
Sits among bookshelves beneath a chandelier.
Outside, on the yew tress, the moonshine does appear.
Death to all of hatred, death to all of gloom.
The ravishing carriages circle in the court,
Amid fallen leaves of mahogany-brown.
I have sent my vassals into the immaculate town
To acquire burgundies, Chablis, champagne and port.
Welcome, my fiends, come frolic, dance and dine.
Do you recall your passing, as I do mine?
Ah yes!—Love's first kiss has not yet been taken.
This vale is all green, reborn and awoken.
Take a splendid gold piece for a token—
We have no need of it—no more can we be shaken.

Sonnets of Dusk and Dawn

Verse II

The misty shade on the moonlit glade
Hides, here and there, in the wintry air
The sheen of a maiden, of long lovely hair,
Owned by a queen who poses as a maid.

Pining where the sun bleeds, a prince upon the meads
Holds a ring in his hand to bind a golden band;
Her eyes search and find him riding on the land,
As a bold equestrian, on a raft of bending reeds.

The vaporous umbrage of the silent dell,
In a wondrous page from Alexandria's citadel
Of sparkling lines, of mystical gin, vodka and ryes.

Beneath snowy pines, where glee is wrought with sighs,
Their soft, ardent gazes remember long forgotten verse,
As redolent December hazes grow faint and disperse.

The Journey of Aeneas

As Troy was burning, its scarlet embers
Lighting the dawn, founding a band of troubadours,
A prince sailed on whited waves to western shores,
In a wooden ship, with his tempest-loving members.

His cult, like a bower, flourished in the sand;
He created a new, alabaster throne,
Made of colonnades and gardens, where fresh seeds were sown
Of immaculate roses, in a new, Latin land.

Their tall, florid grandeurs framed the grand palace
Made of stately marble, freedom and gold.
Into his empire arrived the virile and the old.

He knighted Kings, and drank from each chalice
A mosaic of spirits—of Lavinia's sun,
Defeating young Turnus, and the gods, one by one.

Sonnets of Dusk and Dawn

The Colonial House

The colonial house in New Hampshire,
Situated at the end the country lane,
Calls to my heart with a rapturous refrain;
Wintry breezes upon the meadows stir.
A tire hangs form a swaying, old yew tree.
In the backyard, a car from the twenties
Still can run through nearby counties,
Bridges over rivulets are beautiful to see.
Dare I place her in my mind once more there,
Gazing out the window, gladly and still,
With flesh as tender as the daffodil—
The radiant scent of heaven in her hair.
Wistful, I wonder if her lips I shall kiss once more,
As I behold my home, rain washed by the shore.

The Thirteenth Sonnet

In the sibilant evening, soft and moonlit,
Cantillations ascend with appeasement,
Rising with the winds to the dusky firmament;
(This is the hour heaven's verse is writ.)
The dandelions on the furrow are all aquiver
Beneath the expanding, volcanic clouds;
All the sky is swirling, every pine is clothed with shrouds.
Hemlocks and geraniums weep as they shiver,
As autumn's cold reminds one of graves—
To be delivered from present sorrow
The furious wind negates the morrow.
All now is prescient—for love truly saves.
And the nearby sea foams with an uncanny glee,
As its waves are kissed by the rain—and He.

Diamond Stars

My transported sense traveled with rapture,
Along with my soul, to a diamond sky of song;
There were mystic streams, silver, slender and long,
Which led me to an enchanted cloister.

Teeming, bright columns shone by the sea,
Standing among Dutch-white scruples of grace.
Paths were of stone and marble received my cordial pace
Where tall lindens glittered resplendently.

The promenade took me to a fragrant mountain,
Where more colonnades shimmered in the light
Of the Athenian day, and the Gothic night.

A medieval square was lit by a fountain.
Every star that ascended perfumed with thyme
A moonlit tower, and a flurry of rhyme.

Whiskey

The potent rue of the mystic moon
Releases its whiskey upon Tennessee;
The hallow trees quiver gracefully,
On a lovely night in June.

I have taken a lady from the rustic bar,
To walk upon the dew-clad grass;
We wander far,
And the hours pass.

Then I kiss her lips,
Among green streams, beneath the wide sky,
Taking starry-eyed sips
From a fairy's mum.
The morning ascends, and we lie—
Overcome.

Bourbon

Bourbon is blue—an enkindling brew,
Certain to grant a profound repose
To a wide-eyed drunken, wavering rose.

Shall it soak the soil,
Yielding gilded fruits
For troubadours in leather suits
Who greet the brine under sails of toil?—

Yes, let is lace the bright, silver rain
Which falls on the splendid, astonishing plains
Where the mists of the mighty showers reign!

Alleviating all constraints and pains,
We shall grace all the waves and each dappled dell,
Drinking mystic bourbon from every starlit well.

Sonnets of Dusk and Dawn

Chablis

Ivory Chablis weeps in a gold carafe,
The ancient, ghostly castle is cryptic and still.
Spirits of ebony descend and fill
Deep, azure wells, from the moon's silver half.

There are ladies, clad in blue,
Who pace unending halls
Painting scarlets on gilded walls
Framing ghostly faces, lost in rue.

A pearly cluster of shivering lights
Whitens freshets in the solemn square
Where fair Ophelia roves in the splendid air.

Recalling her fall, she smiles at the bride of nights,
And listens in the shadows as Beatrice talks
Praising broken willows in the umbrage of their walks.

Kingdoms

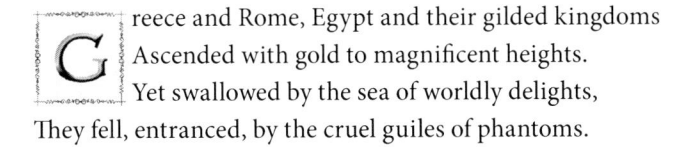

Greece and Rome, Egypt and their gilded kingdoms
Ascended with gold to magnificent heights.
Yet swallowed by the sea of worldly delights,
They fell, entranced, by the cruel guiles of phantoms.

The sight of gods seduced the eyes of women.
And Sirens swallowed fleets of men.
They abounded in a glossy, specious den
Which rendered to those mighty realms dark oblivion.

And like our first parents, falling with a kiss,
They witnessed the barbarians descend from the north,
Closing the gates of their former bliss.

The pyramids now are dusty, the Colosseum decays and pales;
Centuries after their verses came forth—
Behold Alexandria—its books are deceased in cryptic tales.

Sonnets of Dusk and Dawn

The Auburn Dawn

The auburn dawn opened the buds of the garden-close
As I beheld its gate, it seemed a hidden place.
Flowers wavered at its foyer with a majestic grace.
As I entered, rays of cordials rapturously rose.

Far beyond the ogive, with a cadence discreet,
Dahlias and lilies quivered in the morning dew.
As the cloudless sky shone with an oceanic blue,
I found a path to pace upon, old yet still complete.

Made of stone lined with moss, it softly met my boots.
I conjured up a lyric, and ate there mellow fruits,
In the early, twilit cloister of many dappled petals.

A stately wood appeared as a throng of vivid citadels,
And framed the varied flora with a spray of leafy boundaries,
As dawn became day with a gold display of sundries.

My Chamber

Whited, mellow pillows play
Upon my bed at noon day,
When sunny rays commence the spring,
In my chamber where the violets sing.
How old yet new is this happy season,
When Christian faith, coupled with reason,
Can be seen on the lawn from the terrace serene;
With delicacy and grace, the fresh, good air
Is perfumed by breezes sweet and fair,
Tasting like a tangerine.
My Victorian bed and colonial chair
Made special by depicting a Grecian scene,
Holds wonder in my hallowed lair,
As angels rove upon the green.

The Painter

Good morning emerald petals, good morning queen!—
I take my bow in a scarlet ray
Where verse and paintings upon the prairie play
With a vision perceptive, aesthetically keen.
I shall paint your brow and your voluptuous mane
In the summer sun's sobbing, immaculate reds
As you dream in your reverie among the flower beds
On my canvas beside the rustic, stony old lane.
Your eternal gaze I shall shade with black,
And your sensuous ringlets which grace your white back.
For your eyes a hue of hazel, with a hint of green!—
And to summarize the background scene,
Perhaps some lavenders mixed with a happy maize!—
O, kiss me, my dearest, in this delirious haze!

Sonnets of Dusk and Dawn

A Night in Paris

My sole beloved, my sacred bride,
Envision us enraptured in a Utopian caress;
How charming you look donning your white, frilly dress!—
Let us dine by The Seine in the eventide.
The taste of Chardonnay awaits your gleaming lips
Taken from the cruet enkindling sips,
In the city of lights, below a stream of stars.
Oboes serenade you, as do twilit guitars.
Your unspeakable gaze is of a taciturn grace.
In the shade of the fronds, the moon reveals your face.
The restaurant is closing, my love, my dear.
Let us wander by the cathedral to your grand hotel,
Lost within our eyes under Cupid's spell,
As you clasp me by the river, and the dawn does appear.

By a Wall of Stone

I made a study of Cupid's oracle,
In my den, dressed with a thousand books.
Enchanted by her Doric looks,
Athena's gaze is piercing yet subtle.

I am lost within her eyes, and my pain is gone,
Left to my essays and the beauteous night,
Charmed by her flossy glances, their elysian delight;
These gazes of a goddess—I shall muse upon.

For I have witnessed, beneath a golden tree,
In a transcendent realm, in the evening, her majesty
Walking with humility by a wall of vine clad stone.

Her aspects are profoundly wholesome;
And she renders her lover overcome,
As I admire her passing, beneath those golden leaves, *alone*.

Sonnets of Dusk and Dawn

Hamlet's Guest

Gertrude's lily-white hand led me to madness.
My mind is one with a black, sable sea
When my strange, familiar guest appears to me.
He cares not for my dire sadness.

What do I care for a foolish, old king?—
Why should I, with trembling, lend him my ear,
Merely because he has departed from this sphere,
To leave me alone, with a princely ring?—

Do I dare run through the flesh of Claudius,
And let the rapier decide my fate?
You, my guest, avenge yourself, if you are so odious.

And while you are at it, take Gertrude as well!—
I shall flee from your company—to some foreign estate.
Depart from me you specter—to Acheron, to hell!

The Cloister of Kings

Mother, how I adore thee in the garden!—
The mystical archives of eternal sands
Wash our vale away, by the ogives' arched bands
In the cloister of kings, where all archways glisten.

How your gentle hand recovers me beneath
The bells of the glittering canopy of azure,
In the labyrinth of the dawn's florid enclosure,
Contrite, I weep, by the smithy on the heath.

Lanterns of white slowly sway on the bower's edge,
Illuminating the promenade on the promontory's ledge.
The cascading foam below speaks of mystical verse.
There swirling lagoons devour the celestial curse.
Alas!—angels sob like lamenting, old pages
Of blooming indigos, of the poetry of sages.

Fruits of the Ascension

Lavenders and crystal whites
Ascend to lofty, emerald heights
Where good sisters pray in ecstatic delights,
Mediating amid bright petals, these holy Carmelites.
There the pious receive rewards in silver glasses of sacred wine,
Given by the angels to the pious classes,
Where Marx's blasphemy regarding opiates and the masses
Is turned on its serpentine head.
On every scarlet border of the spacious flower bed
The cloistered find the sunshine
And its fermenting properties
A friend to The Gospel's Holy of Holies.
For transubstantiation feeds them daily, all the while:
Those peaceful, pretty nuns who smile.

Conversion

I am en route to Lancaster on Pennsylvanian plains
To visit with the Mennonites who toil on the land.
They resemble a parish with their acclimated hand.
My foreign faith they witness in the silver, Latin rains.

Like Hermes, dispatched, as a flurry-carried leaf,
I wander like a weather vane, turning silver to gold.
Yet few have soil for my seeds, and used to the old,
Most townsfolk cling to their original belief.

I sleep in the attic of a farmer's shanty.
In a bed of hay, I gaze at the hunter's moon.
The landscape is astonishing, especially at noon.

"You deny yourselves too much," I say, according to my fancy:
"And I have not heard one joke here yet."—
Then one among them smiled—and lit a cigarette.

Sonnets of Dusk and Dawn

After the Rain

The mysteries of God and I, caressed
By a purple breeze in a wintry wood,
Left my mind beholding the things it could,
Of profundity, peace, and all that is blessed.
I took my story to a Parisian estate,
Where I witnessed Apollonian flowers,
Azure windows, and palatial bowers;
I walked beyond its tall, iron gate.
And met in the halls paintings of Monet;
I heard majestic chords from Mozart's hands,
And saw rings of gold from exotic lands.
Clouds replaced the sun at the end of day.
And then my epiphanies, confirmed by the moon glow,
Were shown to my vision, on the soft, ivory snow.

Beethoven's Ghost

Beethoven's ghost, from a nearby hill, appeared to me and smiled.
On my grand piano, his grace played his poignant Fur Elise.
The umbrage of the music room enclosed us within a child's peace.
I envisioned a romantic place, *unspoken words were mild.*
I mused upon beatitude in a sacred eve of gray,
And saw his lover's face outside in the misty glen which shimmered,
As she passed by this mansion where the turrets gleamed and glimmered.
Every chord was played in a haunting way.
The multihued rhapsody reached to the pearly sky,
Ascending and transforming into citadels of suns,
Touching with their rays each river that runs
Beneath stone bridges, where emerald ivies cry.
Suddenly he disappeared—the piano keys fell still,
For his spirit left the house—retreating to a distant hill.

The Mansion

The turquoise vase at the top of the stairs
Shines by the window, and is splendid to the sight;
Its Grecian design is detailed and bright.
(It sits by a statue of Roman airs.)
The carpeted hall leads to the book room;
Homer and Yeats are brothers on my shelf.
A gilded blue chair rests my quiet self,
As I look upon my court in its summerly bloom.
And when days become dusk, with starlit paces,
The scenery changes, the sunlight sifts
More gently through the parapets, and my spirit lifts,
As liveries of the night dress yews with downy laces.
Then flickering murmurs of the enchanting candles' flares
Gives light to these autumnal eves, in my villa free of cares.

Sonnets of Dusk and Dawn

Halos

Dearest lady of sweet convalescence,
I shall place within my woolly pocket
The candy canes of a scarlet socket,
And hide within my coat the joys of deliverance.
O, joy upon joy to be sane, sober, and whole,
As the china-blue, gleaming, ancient earth
Turns with a call of promising mirth—
I am done with commingling sand with sole.
A nomad crossing the brine was my state.
It is better to be asleep upon the sand.
Such sense has taken my mind and my hand.
What do I care if it be morning, noon or late,
Dawn, noon or dusk, when swirling zephyrs encircle us,
Framing halos around my head with a gilded, golden buss.

The Storm I

Wave upon wave carries over the pier,
While I think of a grave, beneath a gold chandelier;
My piano is played by fingers which are dear,
In my villa by the ocean, lit by the moon.
The evening appears to have come too soon.
Feel free, my love, to help yourself to a cup of English tea,
My fair and youthful, beloved bride.
Let my niece serenade us, as the ascending tide
Swallows stars and sands so majestically.
In the cadence of each chord our hearts will abide.
(The curtains by the window sway with mystery.)
From an approaching tempest no one can hide.
Nor can one wipe lightening from the sky;
We are all in a hurricane—asleep in its eye!

Sonnets of Dusk and Dawn

The Thirty-Fourth Sonnet

The mahogany table in the drawing room
Is the host to a bouquet, of violets and carmine,
I raise my new cruet, and taste is varied wines,
Sipping in my leisure, above a court devoid of gloom.

The mistress of the villa, lost in a reverie,
Whose hair is tossed by scented winds, by the sculpture,
Travels to and fro, amid the French architecture,
To heavens here blow, in her bower by the sea.

Ascending with the fountains, and oceanic stars of white,
From the greens of surrounding mountains, are portions of the night.
She inhales their charming flowers as a dreaming, young queen.

And in her calm and enraptured mind is seen
Benevolent tides of a redolent beach,
Where every moonlit swallow is within her tender reach.

August

Basking in a shiny dune, to acquire an August tan,
I laid upon a lawn chair, gazing at the firmament,
In the salty-scented air, within in the sun's yellow spender.
(The most intelligent lines spoken by man
Are writ with self-effacement,
And a good sense of humor.)
I felt small as the summery radius descended
Onto the horizon, where wild finches flew:
A humble flock of blue jays, laughing in the blue.
My solitary reverie swiftly ended,
For the night with its haunting ghosts ascended,
Glittering as my dreaming ceased—and it knew
That I was self-engrossed, too serious for the sand,
Unable to fly, and bound to the land.

Sonnets of Dusk and Dawn

Ode to Bobby Darin

A dreaming goddess roved through trees of a garden's green,
Wandering with grace through a mystic world unseen,
When the world was unworldly, for a brief, glad time.
A singer sang of the soft, summer clime.

All branches and boughs were lit with candescence.
The cathedral of the radio sanctified epiphanies.
In the gleaming cloister of symphonies,
The dreaming goddess swooned, with ardor in her essence.

Her glances were intense in the diamond-studded evening,
When deified music was wedded to the sun.
Her soul was dignified, and her lover's heart was won.

Yet the singer bowed, and took a poignant leave.
And with him went the goddess, and the innocence,
To a realm where nature corresponds in spirit and in sense.

Sonnets of Dusk and Dawn

The Second World War

Masses skinned in the scorching rain
Let out a cry to the infinite of pain,
Before the allied banners covered the dead.
With Nuremberg's judgments
Man sought to urge man
To remove the dragon's furious head,
And to raise Democracy to the moonlit firmaments.
With the devastation of Germany and Japan,
And Mussolini hung in the square,
A timeless awe was wrought in the stifling air.
The ineffable crimes of the twisted cross,
And the red sun's insatiate lust for blood
Were allowed to flower before the scarlet flood
Unleashed its hell-spawned, unspeakable loss.

Homer

What did the Orphic Pythia whisper
Of mighty Ithaca to Hadrian's ear?—
Indeed, Herodotus made it clear,
So we read Homer's verses ever after.

Yet how many stanzas have the romantics chose
To praise with lines of loveliness
Victorian grace of Ophelia's sadness,
Yet failed to gaze upon the fairest rose?

How many suitors were slain by Odysseus
Of this beauty who maddened Telemachus?—
Alas!—Penelope owns every **star**.
For her gaze is of an angel's, bejeweled with liquid light,
From which Homer drinks as rum mixed with moonlight,
To the dance which streams from Apollo's guitar.

Sonnets of Travel

I

Midnight train,
Shining locomotive,
Rolls over the steely plain;
All clouds are oppressive.

I have poems within my pocket
To sell for tobaccos
And rum.
There are visions within my socket,
Of azure siroccos;
I listen to the engine's hum,
Set for Iowa and beyond.
The fields and graveyards
Wave their Orphic wand;
Joy to all bards!—

II

Joy to all men.
The orange dawn has spread its cloak
Over every rainy dale and oak;
I shall not see the east again.
Is there one saloon left in the west?—
I need lodging, for the cold makes brittle
The strangled, thorny reeds, the robin's hasty-made nest,
Where the sun bleeds scarlet,
If only but a little
In the trees which shake and quiver in the wake
Of my dreams of a queenly starlet.
I think I'll make
My bed in the dried, yellow hay of the rear caboose,
To let my hobnailed boots feel loose.

Sonnets of Dusk and Dawn

III

I awake to Des Moines in a tepid haze.
I think I'll clean a room or two,
To buy some snuff and coffee;
The blue motel, where the vagabonds laze,
Has been painted by Russo with an optimistic hue.
Enough of the awe of the endless sea,
For there are furrows which amaze me.
As I rove through the country, I offer each society
A patriotic heart, and a working hand.
It was Jefferson's pen who inspired the land
And my artistic perusal
Of felicity with each blossoming renewal
Of every day—*I hunger for the happiness of men,*
And woman.

IV

The white cafeteria,
With its Columbian brew,
Holds truckers who awake
To roads which lead to California,
Wide and ever new.
Behind us is a lake
Of pickerel, trout, and sunfish.
I tip my hat, as I clean my last dish,
And scurry with my tackle and line,
(Purchased at the desk)
To have rainbow with my wine.
In the fresh water reeds, by the arabesque,
I spoke with a lass who wore a coat like mine,
As I hooked silver bass in the sunshine.

V

I caressed her mane,
In a wooden, little skiff,

Sonnets of Dusk and Dawn

Lost in a scene from Twain.
She asked me kindly if
I would walk her to the station,
Where I met her father in a state of elation,
With her phone number written on my hand.
He inquired as to my profession:
"Once in a while sir, I give an English lesson,
Though most of the time I travel the land,
I take in the stars, and wield romantic rhyme."
He took his daughter from me,
And tossed me a sunny dime.
We went to separate cars, and rolled though a pine-clad sea.

VI

The train made the coast too soon for me.
I lost my dear lady in a frothy spray of poetry;
I witnessed a Siren, as I beheld the terrific,
Araucanian Pacific,
As the sunset gilded Hollywood.
I slept in Hermosa, and the sands were cold.
I fed my seaside firewood,
Transforming every misery to gold.
The breezes were of ecstasy,
And astonishing to behold,
As they brought from China majestic liquors
And an immaculate rhapsody
Of ancient, ruddy splendors
Shouting out against the oppressive clouds.

Exile

I delivered a letter in the brisk, misty rain.
Passing by houses of limestone, stucco, and brick;
I returned to my home, and lit a candle's wick,
And sat in my chair, gazing out upon the windowpane.

The street was singular in its solitude.
The passersby looked sad and burdened,
The childlike as well as the learned,
All seemed dead save vicissitude.

And so I pondered on our first parents' fall,
Listening to the pine trees, flapping against the wall,
And releasing through my hall a Christmassy scent.
Indeed the rainy grays above became tolerant.
And I saw a portentous look within a stranger's eyes:
O, sacred humanity, burdened with sighs—
Our rightful home is beyond the skies!

Sonnets of Dusk and Dawn

The Happy Fault

The yew tree with its shadowed lot,
That shade where the licentious act, so torrid,
Was committed—As Adam and his wife
Believed that dark umbrage was God's blind spot,
Quickly turned barren, in their horrid
Realization of the moral evil they ushered into life.
The grisly night ascended all at once to their sight,
And cold oblivion stole from the elysian days
Which man shall never see on earth again
Until the end of the linear trial, when Our Creator's might
Shall cast every spear into the outer haze,
When no more shall disease and war render slain
Our family, amazed by our mysterious sadness.
The cross has razed our parents' madness!

An English Sonnet

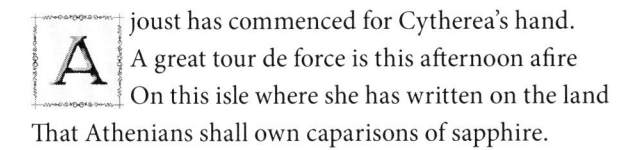

A joust has commenced for Cytherea's hand.
A great tour de force is this afternoon afire
On this isle where she has written on the land
That Athenians shall own caparisons of sapphire.

The phaetons rush beneath the regal skies
Taking their knights to a swift, bloody end.
The Spartans and their wild, marvelous eyes
Seek the goddess before the fronds that bend.

The tournament plays on, next to the partition
Where the vortex is viewed by their lady in white.
Every Spartan is lanced and met with perdition,
And the people of Cytherea dance in the sunlight.

And among their victorious swords and sheaths
Stands fair Alexander, crowned with wreaths.

Sonnets of Dusk and Dawn

Vermont

The ski lift takes us to the feathered pines,
To the mountain's empyrean, graced with the sun.
We are snug within our snowsuits, wavering as one,
Down the bracing trail of alabaster wines.

After we recline in the cozy, wooden cottage,
Drinking ale from tap, looking out upon the hedgerows.
I am entranced by your face, and with every word that flows
From your dark, pink lips of such a voluptuous age.

The lights come on over every whited way,
As I fall into a kiss in your delicious soft sway,
Dazed in your brown sweater, my soul is on fire.
The next day arrives in the wake of our desire,

As you open the window, and brush your sable hair,
Thrilled to be with child, and to greet sweet, majestic air.

The Art Gallery

When Raphael designed
On the slope of Monte Mario,
Facing south, towards Rome,
The Villa Madama
Angels dined,
Praising the Madonna
On wines which wafted west to every barrio,
And seaward, to Saint Peter's home.
And as Michelangelo completed his dance,
The end of the wondrous Renaissance
Met a wild horizon blazing with gold;
Caparisons of an emerald air blended with the old,
As impressions of an absinthe-colored kind took hold
In Monet's winnowing mind, in the fair, Parisian cold.

Sonnets of Dusk and Dawn

Love I

The song of the myrtles in majestic air
Speaks of love ever new, white, graceful and fair.
In the spring one can see one's destiny there
When the birds with languor sing
In the boughs where blessings bring
Visions of a queen, with dusky hair.
In the summer one can feel
The ardor of God made real,
In the glittering of the sunny rays which heal.
In the autumn one can ponder
On the raptures over yonder.
In dells where winter approaches with care.
The song of the myrtles in crisp, cold air
Speaks of love ever new, crystal, white, and fair.

A Picnic

Into the joyous foyers arrives many an old friend.
My servants receive their coats, with smiles and respect.
The dining room's terrace holds a wonderful prospect
Of a sloping, spacious lawn, where fall scarlets blend.

On a table of oak sit hors d'oeuvres and rum punch.
(It is good to shake hands in the halls.)
There are gilded ceilings here, and golden walls;
The art is baroque; the vassals serve lunch.

The meadow beyond the gallery, in the bright afternoon,
Is the sight of a picnic, where wines are poured
Beneath a bold, setting sun, and a splendid, full moon.

(One among the party is laughing and adored.)
An immense chandelier is seen to become alight,
In the ballroom of the mansion, as the sky is crowned with night.

Sonnets of Dusk and Dawn

Before the Ball

The suitors relax in the lovely evening.
The stars glow high, glittering above,
The ladies talk and whisper of love.
In the distance strikes a flash of lightening.

My best friend sails a felucca on the sea.
He rejoices of late, for in June he shall be married
To an Italian beauty whose coach is being carried
To his Georgian estate to meet me.

The music sails above the wine,
In the ballroom where we chatter and dine.
His fiancée is elegant, her servant holds a parasol,
As she enters from the courtyard into the grandeur of the hall.
She extends her hand, of the rose, still wet from the plain.
I kiss it, as the vassals close the windows to the rain.

Sonnets of Dusk and Dawn

The Ball

"It is a shame you missed the picnic today."
I heard the beauty of the banquet say
To my fiend's eloquent fiancée.
(A gorgeous girl, we ran away
From the picnic to a bed of hay;
She is my beloved bride, Renee.)
And so the two ladies are introduced,
As adorned musicians are slowly produced,
All the guests prepare to dance.
My friend remarks on a genuine lance,
Held by a suit of armor in the hall.
Suddenly, the violins pine with grace,
As everyone bows and ties their place,
Commencing to claim a partner for the ball.

Night

We danced to Bach, Schumann, and Handel.
The ballroom, lit with every chandelier and candle,
Was home to swirling dresses of many dappled hues
Swirling upon the marble, the floor of china blues.
I danced with my Renee, and after we reclined
On a soft divan of tartan, of Scottish design.
We talked by the bay and its ripples were clothed with wine.
(My friend and his fiancée slipped away to dales of pine.)
Other guests began to leave,
Servants retrieved their coats as the moon
Struck through the enormous pane
With a wistful light which set fire to the eve,
Bestowing grace to every smile and swoon
As couples left the hallways, roving into the rain.

Sonnets of Dusk and Dawn

Alone with Renee

I paid the musicians, all the servants retired.
The ballroom was vacant, the lamps were lit low,
All the guests did go, the revelry had expired.
Two candles in the corner, by the curtains did glow.

Yet fair Renee stayed, sleeping in my arms.
I carried her to the northern wing,
Where a chamber's bed received her charms.

She awoke as I laid her down on the pillow,
And whispered "love me" as the spring
Outside caressed a scented willow.

I gazed into her hazel eyes as I felt my streams,
From velvet sighs to velvet dreams,
Find one between us two,
As stars alighted to her pregnant gaze, of a sea's beatific blue.

Claudia

The benevolent queen with long, dark hair
Walks as a goddess in the autumn air,
Through tall blades of grass, and russet reeds,
Portraying only beauty, aware of all she needs.
She wanders slowly, as Iris, though a rainbow:
Her lips promise solace as she sings of fair love.
She reaches out, in the moonlight, to swallows above.
She collects her Spanish locks in a long, dusky bow.
While she sleeps, all the angels laud her face.
She appears as a starlet, content in her slumber;
She peruses her dreams with a wise, ancient pace,
And with ease she commands, with a lily or with thunder.
In tune with her desires, all waterfalls which flow,
And her prince remains her servant, wherever she may go.

Sonnets of Dusk and Dawn

Belgium

The streets of Brussels awake to the summer.
Its grand, bright square, to tourists unaware,
Still reveres the old, in the languorous air.
My thoughts are with the gardens—and her.

For I rove amidst violets where the soft wind sways
My lady's scented, dusky airs, clad in her evening dress.
She lives for the romantic pairs, and a moonlit caress.
In the majesty of the shade, her eyes are crystal, dark bouquets.

And when the lamplights are lit with candescence,
I inhale her radiant, elysian quintessence,
Among the wooden branches, in the breezy, ancient park.

We pass like angels upon the lawn, in the still and solemn dark,
Privy to only beauty, the shade, the scents, the dark bouquets,
For we rove amidst the violets, where Bach's piano plays.

Reflections

The dawning sky of deep damask,
In soft solemnity,
Reflects bright branches in my flask,
Bestowing a rapturous souvenir
Of embraces which ring with rhapsody
In our misty, youthful, united mind
Which the billows revere
As they always do in kind
With lovers who are struck by twilight.
The waves with their scarlet, symphonic night,
Carry through boughs to the frothy piers,
Leaving traces of ecstasy
In your dusky eyes shaded like the sky,
Gazing at me, with their starry chandeliers.

Sonnets of Dusk and Dawn

Azure Heights

Pray for him. Beneath wandering skies,
He passes, forming verse in the meadow,
Using alchemy to tinge every starlit furrow,
With gold and a lady's heartfelt sighs.

In garments woven on jacquard looms,
He appraises bowers and drinks his ale,
Watching every windblown ship and sail,
As he roves amid bright, lavender blooms.

And when twilight finds him beside the lane,
Lost in the empyrean of a mystic mane,
He sleeps in a reverie beneath the stars,
Beside the embers of a campfire's bars.
And when the night's refrain alights in a mystic way,
From his balcony's bay, his soul ascends to heights of pain.

The Visitor

Candles frame the rectangle hall.
In the center of the room sits a grand piano.
Within it can be heard a portamento,
Rising to the windows, addressing each wall.

A ghost wanders in, with a pale, white face,
Gliding across the marble floor,
With an eerie, Orphic, awful pace;
Her home is in the graveyard, beside the moor.

She wears a white shroud, and her gaze is red.
No reflections are cast, no words are said.
Her countenance is hazy, of vapor, of fog.

Shadows of the night steal in through the curtain.
The purpose of her presence is nebulous, uncertain.
And she passes through the sashes, disappearing in the bog.

Sonnets of Dusk and Dawn

Central Park (2012)

The damask of the sky, over the city cleaves,
As families walk by, to boughs of yellow leaves.
Chestnuts sold, by a lake of toys sails,
Add a fragrance to New York, as daylight pales.

The noises blaring from speeding cars
Are distant in the park, where one can listen
To the coo of pigeons, as skyscrapers glisten:
To the south they rise, to the urban stars.

A Republican reads The Journal, as a Democrat walks by,
In the circus-like fanfare, they see eye to eye,
If only for a moment, by a strawberry field.

They are dizzy in the potions that musicians yield.
Children, at the zoo, feed ponies, licking ice cream,
As lovers walk the promenades, drunken gypsies dream.

Ode to Lord Byron

Vibrant are the colors that grace the mignonettes
Which flower on the entrance ways
Of sunlit bowers, beneath a balcony's bays.
In the shade of statues' slender silhouettes.
A poet writes of autumn eves, where towering trees
Speak to him of swirling, summer symphonies
Which enrapture his carafe in the scented breeze.
He bows to an English lady of ducal airs,
And sits on a bench beside the gardens' hedgerows,
In an aesthetic stupor, when every chardonnay flows
From freshets, by florid, flowery boughs married in pairs.
They scintillate his mind, in the dulcet, Hampshire clime.
As a lyricist, his lines are composed in standard time,
As he drinks in the moon, weaving meaning with metered rhyme.

Sonnets of Dusk and Dawn

The Mansion by the Sea

My lady's eye catches the bending willows,
Which thrust against the windowpanes,
Of the gleaming terrace, as July's dulcet rains
Water the ocean's teeming billows.

She looks pretty in her white redingote.
In the drizzle we shiver, dreaming in the scattered shade.
Her hazel gaze wanders to the blue, sloping glade,
Where reeds are aquiver, and virid lilies float.

The winds marry the willows to the watery dell,
As heaven's cloudy sphere becomes a wishing well
For lovers who dream in aromatic gales.

We are taken in our minds to paradisaical vales,
As the colors of summer blend upon the gallery,
Made of old, stately marble, sprayed by the sea.

Switzerland

The evening stars of glory
Are lit like fireflies,
Swirling above the wintry house,
In the forest of the skies.
On the second story,
Candles douse
The darkness of the night.
In our bedroom, the moonlight
Silver, soft, and sad
Sifts in through the window,
As you unloosen your bow.
Yet your gaze is glad,
Where angels show
The distant mountains' falling snow.

Kissing in the Woods

We walk along beneath whited trees,
By snow-clad hedges of frozen grass,
Caressed by the frosty breeze.
The romantic hours pass
With a delicacy of sweet delight.
How lovely you look tonight!—
In your furs you receive the cold with ease.
Let me kiss you until the seas of your eyes
Are released in an ecstasy of bating sighs.
Let me ravish your lips with heat,
And feel your heartbeat
Go wild in the cold.
And then let me but repeat
Those kisses of sapphire, rubies, and gold!

Wines I

The summer sun, descending
Over the horizon, never ending
Touches upon the ascending
Moonlight of tears, rending
Hearts and minds where gales
Over meadows of green
In reveries serene
Make waves as daylight pales.
The bench by the sea
Holds you and me,
As winds stir the pines.
Let us drink the evening's wines
Until all around are starlit skies—
And paradise falls into our eyes.

Ode to Baudelaire

An ivory castle is painted black
By the poet's mind
Finding nothing kind
In the beauty of a lady's voluptuous back.
The canvass is painted with gold,
Of flowers which do not hold
The clemency of the benevolent sun.
They wither, one by one,
Becoming more lovely as glorious death
Breathes banefully, a languid breath
Over ships and moors, meads and fields—
Let all be extinguished in the poison that yields
Cancers and limping, mad, old men—
Let fire consume us, time and again!

Sonnets of Dusk and Dawn

The Hurricane

The bedrock, shaken by furious waves
Thrusting upward, foaming, receding to the graves
Of sailors, skeletal, weeping in the night,
Is falling, stone by stone into the sea.
The ominous stars scream to the moonlight,
As a mad horse wails in a distant farm.
The hurricane assails with a wild sonority,
Amassing all music, rising with the curtain.
All trees upon the plain shall meet with harm,
For malevolent whirlpools are certain.
We shall need to retreat to the highest tower.
The crypts are flooded, the fields are lakes.
Alas!—Do you hear?—the window breaks!—
Upon your knees, it is the hour!

Calm

Calm, calm, be calm my dear.
The hurricane will pass—
My frightened, lovely lass.
Let us drink our wine
In the ballroom, beneath
The gold chandelier,
And await the glorious sunshine
Which shall rise like a sword from a noble sheathe!
What do we care if we have to swim?—
For the first to fall may be this tower!
Let us take no heed of him,
This small breeze that makes your hair stand on end.
Let us dive for adventure into the bower,
For a life truly lived, such madness is a friend.

Sonnets of Dusk and Dawn

Buried

Like Poe, he has sealed his sister in the wall.
Stone by stone, the castle on the hill
Decays in the black and vaporous still.
He drinks from his carafe, and does not mind at all
The pleading of his sister
To release her from the grave.
He adds an olive to his cocktail,
"Be silent!" he says to her.
In the wild night he hears her wail,
Then all becomes silent.
These habits which deprave
His oily soul are prescient.
For she shatters the bricks, angry and dead—
Just like the maddened poet said.

The Crypt

The seer can penetrate
His lover who met her fate
Hanging from a tree.
There is not much for the mind to see:
The coffin is green, of an awful dread.
The flowers are dead,
Yet her body is still as charming
As her lips are disarming:
"I am still in love," she said.
What wondrous words from the corpse of charms,
As the madman yearns to hold her,
Once more in his loving arms.
He becomes a witness to her walk,
Though her pallor is deathly, and one of chalk.

Sonnets of Dusk and Dawn

The Chameleon

She is a teacher in the day.
And a lover in the rustic hay,
Whence comes the night of passion.
On a cruise she sips
Her Chardonnay,
And paints her lips
With a proud precision
To enjoy with the captain
The stars upon the sea.
Yet when she calls on me
In the scintillating night,
She pretends her studies never die,
And consume her every sight—
And she never tells a lie.

My Host

The castle is addled upon a mount.
I am the guest of an ancient, Romanian count.
He betrays protuberant teeth!—
He is something from Stoker,
A latecomer, a graveyard walker.
All the shadows and shades bequeath
Dread, for here the dead for blood still pine.
He covers my meats with vinaigrette, as I quiver as I dine.
He sees my regret, and pours old wine.
I do not believe in vampires,
Though his eyes seem set with fires.
Woe to me here within these blackened spires!—
How I loathe to hear his frightful talk
Of barrows below where witches walk.

The Dance

That mystic, crystal lights
I behold today!
Heaven is all around us!—
From mellifluous heights,
Banishing every gray!
God descends with a loving buss,
Kissing every cheek at play
In the giant dance which makes us.
Our lives are lived within a ball,
For despite our pains love does reign
In one, as in all.
I welcome these dour days of disconsolate rhyme!
I welcome you, my sorrow, my anguish, my rain,
For all, save love, shall perish in time.

Advice to Young Poets

Let your verse be of the breeze,
Scented and terse, of ecstasies.
Carry your poetic mind
Wherever you go, whether or not you write.
Never compose for profit or renown,
It is far more important to be kind.
And when you receive the insight
Which is a blessing to own,
Do not reject it out of fright,
For into darkness you must go
To find ineffable light.
Rove where the currents rarely flow,
Make your home in the homeless night,
To awake, to feel, to find, to know.

The Carriage I

The mahogany bar sells liquor and ale.
I finished a belt and summoned my carriage
To ferry me over the emerald dales
Homeward to the call of marriage.

The brooks are frozen, the trees are white.
Canticles play in the gleam of the woodlands.
I dream of my woman's tender hands,
As the coach is tossed in the windy night.

On a precipice we travel as snow begins to fall.
My driver is a veteran, and used to it all,
Though the coach sways madly in the bitter cold.

He tells me we should rest on the side
Of the rocky, whited road, for the wheels begin to slide.
But my bride awaits with lips of gold.

On Betrothal

Choose for your wedding strain
A sacred melody;
Come sunshine or rain,
Restraint is the key.
For intimacy in the flesh
Prior to the marriage feast
Defaces one's dignity,
Even though your hearts may mesh,
It is loving in the least.
Many words can be read
Within your lover's eyes,
Without a syllable said.
For reality and romanticism share the same skies.
For two are one forever for the holy, blessed dead.

Ode to Henry David Thoreau

He fed a horse by Walden Pond,
In Concord, where dreaming
Was conducive near the gleaming
Of rippling emeralds which were seen beyond
The shores of the lake, among golden trees.
Civilization and greens must correspond
Like moonlit sonatas and symphonies
Played on the same grand piano,
By a hand which agrees
That solitude is not the purpose of the morrow.
For I am sure many tears were shed
In the small, lonely cabin of sorrow
Where so many books were written and read
Graced amid the grass of Sleepy Hallow.

An Irish Garden

The transparent rains in the temples of your eyes,
Where strophic modes of strains arise
Course through my heart, as we walk hand in hand,
Upon a holly-green path in Ireland.

We spoke of Yeats at the roadside bar,
Where he sat and watched the sun descend,
Having beautifully penned
The eloquent scenery, near, below, above and far.

A castle of old sits upon a hill,
Above us as we rove in a garden's still.
There are verses to be written yet,
Of your flesh, white face,
Scented with mignonette,
Commanding all my love in this shaded place.

Raptures of White

Persian carpets and tapestries of old
Grace my mansion where a stray breeze enters,
In between the curtains, gilded with gold.
It veers through the halls and Victorian chambers.
For the windows of the gallery
Are open to the pelagic hymns of the sea,
Where every pause and harmony
Bequeaths to my dreamy psyche
A redolent rose, of charming airs.
A blessed countess awaits upstairs,
To be caressed by loving hands.
Immaculate nuptials and wedding bands
Soon to be tied in raptures of white
Beckon like heaven in the diamond night.

Sonnets of Dusk and Dawn

My Lady I

I am taken in my reverie to a soft and wondrous air,
Where a lady passes, by a summery cove,
In the warm afternoon, where breezes rove,
Over sandy, sunlit dunes, releasing wine upon her hair.

Free of thought, she wanders through bowers,
Bathing in florid rainbows which send
Her longings to where the lindens bend,
By the redolent sea, amid the flowers.

She is clad in a night gown, silken and white,
Lost in a vale of amber hued, tender light,
As her feet grace a path by the frothy, blue ocean.

She ponders on only ardor and emotion,
As the billows rise and fall—
And my dream is not a dream at all.

The Fountain

I sat by the fountain writing effulgent rhyme,
On the college campus, when my heart was young.
A Jewish beauty from Palestine
Placed her hand into mine
In a timeless time,
When ale was drunk, and songs were sung.
To the west, Manhattan's skyline
Seemed always doused with an empyrean's wine.
And in the evening, when fireflies
Sail over the grass, beneath clear skies,
I held her in umbrageous, scented stills.
Her eyes were starry, and free from fears.
And as the stars did rise, amid the fountain's tears,
Where poetry reigned on buildings, on exalted flowerbeds.
We wandered to the meadows, with quatrains in our heads.

Sonnets of Dusk and Dawn

Dusk I

When the carafe of absinthe has been filled,
And every hill is dressed with dew,
I shall glance with love at you,
In your dress of white, befrilled
With tender stars that softly rise
Over shaded lanes, scented with the rose.
We shall walk in the little garden-close,
Among the statues, where a fountain sighs.
And as the diamond, dusky gazes of your eyes
Sweep through God's canvass to the gilded shore,
I shall praise your name in the sanctified night,
And write of your glances in the stupendous moonlight.
As the dusk, nascent with the reticent hours,
Graces your mane, with redolent showers.

V

Eternal Verse

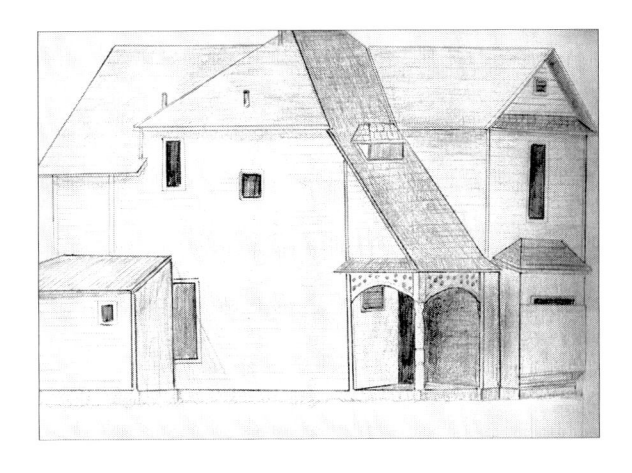

Eternal Verse

Preface

What I have attempted to accomplish with this book on heaven is to poetically out-duel Dante's Paradiso, his poetic treatise on paradise which makes up the third and final part of his famed Divine Comedy. I have always thought that his depiction of heaven, although fantastic and possessing merits which time can not efface, was too generic in description, and I tried very hard while writing this volume to be more specific and vivid descriptively than he was in his trilogy. John Milton's *Paradise Lost* in his presentation of Eden, and John Keats' *Ode to a Grecian Urn* are the two other works which I attempted to surpass in their poetic descriptions of the celestial and the infinite. In my descriptions of the celestial paradise I remained faithful to the teachings of The Magisterium of The Holy Roman Catholic Church. And if one wishes to doubt this face, lest one does not believe in eternal romances, (and I use this one topic as an example) one need only to read the works of Saint John Chrysostom, the most profound of which are included in The Catechism of the Catholic Church. When I write in his book of "marriage," "husband," and "wife," I am not referring to the earthly marriage state, but to the heavenly fruition of it. When the Pharisees asked Christ about marriage in heaven, His response was, "They shall be as angels."

For the things of this world shall pass away. Yet love between a man and a woman shall not pass away, neither will the love of virginity pass away.

"As Saint John Chrysostom suggests, young husbands should say to their wives: I have taken you in my arms, and I love you, and I prefer you to my life itself. **For the present life is nothing**, and my most ardent dream is to spend it with you in such a way that we may be assured of not being separated in **the life reserved for us… I place your love above all things**, and nothing would be more bitter or painful than to be of a different mind than you." (The Catechism of the Catholic Church, section 2365, page 628).

And I attest, in agreement with The Church, beyond the shadow of any doubt, that every tear shed here on earth is transformed into gold in that happy kingdom which shall find us all together one day, reunited with the ones who went before us. I believe in one God, One Holy Catholic and Apostolic Church, and in all of her teachings, including the existence of Hell, Purgatory, and Heaven. And I do affirm that there is an extreme irony whoever we doubt in the existence of heaven, no matter what personal beliefs we may possess, atheistic, agnostic, or religious, for then we become depressed, and the joke is on us.

Having years ago been a quasi-agnostic/atheist myself, and a veteran reader of all the works of those famous atheists, Victor Hugo, Schopenhauer and Nietzsche, have in my youth flirted with their godless theories, have I died back then, alas!— What a surprise I would have been met with beyond the grave! For I know after years of many profound personal experiences which gave birth to and established my faith, that heaven is more of a solid, objective reality than this temporary veil of changes that we call "life."

In truth this life, ever since the exile of our first parents, whether you believe in Biblical accounts or not, whether you believe in the teachings of Catholic Christendom or whether you believe that existence came from nothingness, whether you are a deist, a philosopher, or whether you reject all religion, whether you realize, acknowledge or reject the fact that the Cross is our only way to our personal and collective salvation, this

Eternal Verse

life is more akin to the shadow of death, because of our inclination to suffer here, and due to the reality that our earthly bodies die and disintegrate. We cannot escape these facts, no matter how pious, pure, or holy we may be or become as individuals. We are all in misery and trepidation down here when compared to those happen citizens of heaven, even in our most animated and joyous moments. And while we doubt and fear that human life is finite and is devoid of any purpose, the Saints are pitying us and our absurd doubts, at our lack of knowledge and disbelief. And while we doubt and fear that all life is finite and is devoid of a sound purpose, the Saints are laughing at us as well, at our lack of knowledge and disbelief. And so, I have chosen by writing this book and by making this book public to give as I have received from so many poets and their poems written by sages, Saints and seers which have held out a candle to me in the midst of my darkest nights.

~John Lars Zwerenz

Of Two in Paradise

When the silver fountains sigh
To the paradisial sky
Eloquently, majestically,
I shall gaze into your ebony eyes
As the snow descends upon your jet-black hair
And your face so astonishing,
Astonishingly fair.

The castle by the sea
Where the azure currents rise
With the grace of an angel's wing
Is a witness to our ardor there.

And as the pines, wrapped in a breeze
Of blue and velvet rhapsodies
Shake their perfumes upon your dress,
I shall find ecstasy in your feminine caress
And our kiss shall recite The Angelus.

Moonlight II

When the purple veils of night
Are opened by the wings of angels,
And all of heaven's citadels
Are revealed in diamond-hued light.
The lilies of the bower
Find their splendid, majestic hour
In the umbrage of the vine-clad tower.

And the grasses which sway
Beneath our naked knees
Find refuge in the fallen leaves,
Surrounded by the starlit bay,
And the lapping play of azure seas.
Their billows rise and rove in a splendid, soft array
Where the rose of the nascent moonlight weaves
Its solemn, scarlet ecstasies.

The Courtyard I

Our love is like the fount
Which rises from the eternal courtyard,
By the green, majestic mount.

These verses from your bard
Exist beyond the earthly sun.

Let us wander on the mead
Where the beatific currents run.
Let our every lovely deed
Be of rapture as we, as one
Know peace in the diamond of the second sun.
The Father's smile, Mary's adorable Son,
And The Holy Spirit dwell within our kiss,
Where statues and carriages
Gleam in our midst,
To gild our eternal, ecstatic tryst
Of flowing, ineffable, sacred bliss.
Ah!—The wind speaks of marriages!

There is no eternal burden nor weight
Such as others have said
In those dusty verses I have read
Once one passes through the golden gate.

Love reigns, and God alone
Shines in your tresses
Which glisten among the silver-struck stone,
Where the diamond beads of waterfalls
Grace your wedding dresses,
As we dance in gilded balls,
Enraptured in caresses.

Eternal Verse

The Garden I

I took her hand beneath the quivering trees
Which shook their hymns upon us in the warm October sun.
Flute and horn, wistful and fantastic
Swept through the lavender breeze,
Near nature's brooks which forever run
Through valley and dale, mellifluous and majestic,
Gracing reeds with currents that shine in gilded rays.
I love my bride, and her angelic ways.
The ocean nearby, beyond the statuary,
Rises with the tide and caresses the rocks,
As she reclines on a marble bench with gracility,
Dreaming in her trances, caressing her raven locks.
And the sunset sighs as the fountains rise
To the nascent stars in the vast and silent courtyard,
As she speaks of things with her sanctified eyes,
To her handsome, young lover, to her passionate bard.
And our kisses are of ivory nights,
When the moonlight sobs, when candlelights
Illuminate the astonishing bower.
Come walk with me, my love, it is the hour
When all holy seraphim sing their hymns from heights above.
Come walk with me, my lover, my love.

A Rhapsody

We paced upon the reeds of wine,
In the infinite boons of the moonlight,
Among a stream which passed through the sacred night,
Among the glistening star struck vine.

The languorous cadences of rhapsodies rising
Blends with the cherubim, appraising
The mysteries of your bated sigh,
Beholding with gazes of sapphire, diamonds and gold,
As the lindens waver, older than old,
In the splendor of the charming cold,
Where the rose of your lips of crimson, open on high
Leaves me utterly speechless, and overcome.
The miraculous fountains flow and drum,
As the carriages circle around the statues which gleam
In the marble square, in this realized dream.

Eternal Verse

The Sea Below the Forest of Pines

I walk beneath the Holy Father's sun,
Hand in hand, with my beloved one.
Among the teeming, bright, holly-green pines
Which carry on the breezes perfumed wines,
On the gentle slope which runs to the sea,
From which all the blessed enter victoriously
The Kingdom of God to the applause of the saints.
There where the earth and purgatory faints
Behind the new arrivals who pace upon the waves
As the ones they left behind still weep,
Still weep upon their graves,
Disillusioned with thoughts that they forever sleep.
Yet these beings no longer know shadow nor shade—
Only Mary's smile greeting them.
Beneath the diamond sky lit by He
Who gave us His Son to set us free.
For the sea is the gated, golden gem
Which Saint Peer covets so adamantly.
O, glorious glory—Gaze at them!—
These victors who enter so joyfully.
And the pines sway above them silently,
Beneath the sun that never sets in these regions,
Of eternal day, among God's legions.

Let Us Rove

As the astonishing, white stars glitter and shine,
Like pouring, exquisite, eternal wine,
A charming, sweet song,
Languorous and long,
Wafts through the warmth of our candlelit cottage.

Let love unite us
In this ageless age.

Above and around us,
A sea of blue and beige
Is of the wintry breeze.

Let us rove outside, among the whited trees,
And walk without speaking.
Let our thoughts be of the wondrous gale,
Where our footsteps break the cover of snow,
Among the hush of the flow
Of the silent gleam seeping

From the immaculate dale
There bubbling in the stream of ale below.

Eternal Verse

In the Evening II

In the evening, of saffron air,
Devoid of all shade, sadness and despair,
We wander on the glade
Clad with lilacs, daisies, roses and wine,
Where the scented breezes wade,
Engulfing us in the quintessence of the Divine,
As the white, misty moonlight clothes the promenade.
There, in sumptuous gardens, where the towers
Of the grand, Elysian bowers
Sanctify and shine
Our love which fills the angels with wonder
And ignites all the lights of the nocturnal ardor
Which pass through those starlit rivers of blue
As a sacred stream,
I shall ponder you,
And possess your every thought, your every movement,
Your every mystic dream,
As the glistening firmament
Reflects its majestic glory in your sable gaze's gleam.

On Entering Heaven

I ventured out among crystals,
Invisible to all but God.
Passing through thoughts neither prosaic nor odd,
But feeling every good emotion,
I traversed beyond the sea of stars,
Beyond the firmament's fantastic ocean.
I ascended beyond the russets of Mars,
Beyond the gilded rings of Saturn,
Above the coveted curve of space,
I gazed down upon the innumerable beams,
And their roving planets
Which seemed as small as stones
Glistening in streams
To my widely enlightened eyes.
I met flowers in bowers among a wreath of musical sighs.
I met Saints and angels, one by one,
In a new, incredible diamond sun.
I heard harpsichords play
In the amber light of their melodic sway,
And I took delight reclining in the furrows of gilded hay,
In those wavering dales of boundless day.
I rejoiced to see a cloister filled
With blooms of summer over-brimming
With every hue of the dreamer swimming
Through every petal, swaying yet stilled,
In a photograph of becoming
Which became.
And I found my queen by the laughing, white brook
Where she told me her beatific name,
And I undertook
Loving.
And I loved her just the same
As I did upon the earth.
And in her gleaming gaze's birth
She sang to me

Eternal Verse

A soft, delicious melody
Which flowed from the mountains
To the courtyard and its slender, white fountains
As the carriage of The King came to take us away
Into a higher, brighter light
Devoid of stars, devoid of night,
Of purity, bliss and eternal day.

Eternal Verse

Snow

Close Homer's new book
With your adoring, ebony, liquid look,
And come with me, by beloved, by dear,
On a walk to the square,
To the gold, immaculate shrine,
To the ornate and spacious belvedere.
We can pluck the many roses there
Which gleam in the snow,
Falling like flakes of alabaster wine.
Come, my beloved, and let us go
Into the village where the white brooks flow.
We can meet the other lovers whose bliss
Is touched by the grace of heaven's fleecy downs,
Settling on store-front windows,
On their roofs of amber-browns,
As they rejoice in the warmth of a wintry kiss.
Let us run to the water of the shaded, sweet lake
Covered with a cheerful, diamond sheet
Of ice and froth where the bending boughs meet.
Come, my beloved, for the loving's sake!
Your coat will be black,
A pea jacket that receives
The descending crystals blown by the breeze
To bless your woolly, sable-covered back,
Among the glistening Christmas trees.
For the perfumed wind no longer grieves—
And harbors only ecstasies!

The Rain

We met Bach, Beethoven, Mozart and Twain
And spoke in canticles in the mist of the rain.
Lamplights led the musical plain
Down the effulgent path where the briars sway.
Remind me, o my love,
Of their poetic words devoid of all darkness
Spoken from their hearts which nevermore know pain.
Remind me of those charming drops which fell from above,
And of the ethereal roses, the chrysanthemum, their eternal power,
The breeze-blown daisies, the lilacs.
Let us rove and wander with the rain upon our backs,
And rejoice in our ardor. It is the majestic hour!
Behold, my dear, behold
How their pianos and verse
Of ineffable gold
Gently disperse
The gleeful clouds which surround the heights of the universe,
Above our regal garden bower.

I Hold You on a Bed of Gold

I hold you on a bed of gold.
Your fair, white neck, half-covered with your longish mane
Is held by my passionate hands as your feminine petals gently unfold.
In the languorous ecstasy of a fountain's rain
I see God within your eyes of glistening, tender, sable-tinted ebonies.
The sanctified temple of your beating heart
Is a house of rapturous rhapsodies.
As we peak beyond the heights of the diamond skies,
Our symphonic ardor does not depart.
For you set my blood afire with the profound, delicious art
Of your astonishing face and hair, and your body's wondrous, enveloping sighs
Which emanate like stars from your soul into my eyes.

Eternal Verse

After Our Walk Amid the Reeds

The breeze is cool,
But does not bite.
The world regarded us each a fool,
But there is no longer a reason to be contrite.
Let us stroll beneath the crimson blooms
Which laugh above the brooks of white.
And after our walk amid the reeds,
Let us retire to our palatial rooms,
Among our busts and vases;
Let us look out our grand bay window,
To where siroccos blow,
Out upon the meads.
And there, surrounded by fine tapestries,
And the most majestic, eternal art,
In between our lips' bated pauses,
We shall witness blue jays ascend in ecstasies,
As they flutter and dart
To the immaculate seas.
I have waited for this moment all of my life
To posses you as a woman, more than a wife.
For as angels in a palace we dwell—
In heaven's crystal citadel!

By the Lake

Modest in your evening dress,
You sit among the grasses of gold,
Amid the wavering watercress,
Lost in sumptuous raptures of old.
And in your sunlit reveries
While a symphony sighs on the balconies,
The mountains in the distant, violet light
Gleam beyond the courtyard's statues of white
Where the first diamond orbs of night
Approach in veils of purples shining and bright.
How I long to touch you in those reeds by the lake,
And inhale the many perfumes that your sable tresses make,
Which, carried on the wind leads me to dream,
Of a silent wood, and a flowing stream.

Eternal Verse

The Gilded Ball

Dante and Beatrice, Shelley and his lovely Mary,
Robert and Elizabeth, William and his Juliet,
Herr Schumann and his dignified Clara once met
In the mist of love, in cupidity's airy
Romantic ball.
They live on, they live on, everyone and all!
Welcome to the palatial hall!
The vassals will take your furs and coats,
And usher you into the drawing room,
After your excursion by the lake on the soft, sunlit, wavering oats
Glistening in the light of the alabaster moon.
Each bride has her groom,
Each man has his mate.
Rejoice, for earthly gloom
Is forever gone, beyond our fate!
The trumpets soon
Shall trumpet. All silence shall abate.
Leave your worldly life behind you in the hall.
Welcome one and all, to the dance, to the ball.
The marble floors await your paces.
All of us saints are gleaming with enraptured faces.
And all the places we have seen,
Through beautiful beyond all worldly expression,
Are but the beginnings of sacred delights,
Always new in our eternal possession!

The pleasures here are potent yet serene.
Let the astonished angels light the lights!
The ballroom awaits with views of the majestic heights,
Seen through the grand bay windows.
I shall take your fair hand and kiss your braided bows,
In the gilded corner where the candlelight glows,
Aside the piano, next to the books,
Where Sappho traces her adoring looks
Over her new poetic volume
Which speaks of ruddy roses in summer, in everlasting bloom.

Eternal Verse

Let the dresses swirl across the room!
The piano plays, the trumpets blare
Melodiously amid the fantastic fanfare,
And the silver stars within your eyes
Beckon me: "Take me dancing until the fantastic skies
Are lit with the glistening of a thousand sighs,
Shaken with the thunder of harmonies,
Of ecstasies,
Of flowing, white wine descending from flasks
Pried open by the cherubim, by their fluttering, adamantine wings."
(Such glorious tasks
Are ineffable things.)
And the band serenaded the musicians and the other saints,
Until the dawn rose upon the meadow,
With glorious, wondrous, purple paints.
And every scented shadow
Sent a shudder through me
Of happiness without an end,
Of light without a pall.

O, take me, take me
To where the willow trees bend,
With a carafe in your hand,
To the boundless fields over the dew-clad land,
After the wonderful, gilded ball
We shall lie as dreamers do, yet wide awake,
And with gratitude we shall take
The kisses which make
The things of folklore,
Especially here!
Let us wander by the belvedere,
And caress among the glistening fountains,
Beneath the breeze-blown trees, green, slender and tall,
As the revelers depart from the opulent hall,
In the dance of the dawn, in the cradle of the mountains.

Eternal Verse

I Met You in a Dream

I met you in a dream.
Your lovely eyes
Commanded my sighs,
And let me to a mystic stream.
There butterflies
And the roving breeze
Possessed rare, redolent symphonies.
And I witnessed your graceful mane
In a rapturous, misty moonbeam.
My spirit shall never to be the same.
For when I met you in the flesh
Our eyes did blend,
And our hearts did mesh.
And all that was holy, of romance, of love,
Permeated our passion from above,
And instilled in our first kiss
A sanctified, sacred, sacramental bliss.
The things of heaven are made of this!
And because you entered this Kingdom first,
You protected me from hunger, from want, from thirst,
From all other eyes,
And worldly skies.
And when I ascended
Our spirits once more blended,
Yet this time it was forevermore.

You are the only I adore—
And now all sorrow and pain has forever ended—
Ended! It is over. And the old earth's feverish, tearful door
Is eternally closed behind you.
Your brown eyes now rejoice
And mingle with the Sahara-blue
Of the radiant sea,
As your heart beats beside me,
Waiting with an enraptured, bated breath

Eternal Verse

For the loving whispers of your poet's voice,
And for his soft and tender, masculine caress.
I behold your cherry lips upon your face,
Of your royal countenance, your regal grace,
And your long and ivory, gleaming dress.

Eternal Verse

My Mansion by the Sea

In my Father's House There are Many Mansions.

John 14:2

I spoke with Keats, and we, immersed in his urn,
Walked upon a stone-paved trail,
Lined with lilacs, and bright, green fern.
We wandered to the field where the breezes softly sail.
Beneath the happy, leafy boughs that cannot shed,
We pondered true love between our brethren and God.
Strolling in our robes, each with a rod,
His thoughts turned to Fanny, and mine to my maiden.
So we agreed to meet that night,
There in the glistening, glowing, gleaming light,
In my mansion by the sea, strewn with ivy and laden
With climbing roses which cradle each tower.
Come the moon I receive him, in my little garden bower.
He introduced his lady to my dear, beloved one,
As the stars ascended brightly in the red, descending sun.
And we spoke of things,
Of ethereal rings,
Of chaste and tender whispers, which like tapestries were knit
In our mutual gazes, candlelit.

Mary

Her majesty emits a soft perfume,
Which makes the poet weak.
Her feminine power commands his will,
And makes him humble—meek.
Her beauty is one with the blooms on the hill.
And when her petals unclose,
Like a starlit rose,
She captures him with a charming ease,
As he surrenders to her gleaming might which flows
In the tranquil, sacred breeze.
She shall be adorned with many costly jewels,
And with diamond rings around her fingers,
Precious pearls around her neck,
For her immaculate scent which forever lingers.

Eternal Verse

The Castle II

In the silence of the round, majestic square,
Of a rosy, mellifluous, pacifying air,
Where deep blues cascade with their glimmering hues
From the star-bejeweled firmament—
The beauty here is permanent.
I walk there in the breeze, on the marble with my muse.
Gazing up at the towers
Of our castle by the sea,
I inhale the springtime cacophony
Of a thousand redolent, sun-kissed flowers.
And as you wave to me
From the bastions' highest balcony,
I can see in your eyes
Beneath the tranquil, azure skies
A longing for my lips.
I love you, my darling, I love you!
For our mouths take sanctified, delicious sips
From the golden carafes in the ballroom by the lake,
And in our ecstatic fever let us gratefully make
Vows in the fire of our passion's wake!

The Cloisters

The wide, golden portal led to the diamond sun.
I witnessed rosy petals open, one by one,
In the umbrage of a cloister, free form all lament.
Like breezes stirring in a vase, emitting every lovely scent,
The wells of the enclosure, so very redolent,
Left me dazed in wonder as I met a lady fair,
With cherry blossoms dancing in the tresses of her hair.
We strolled as a god and goddess through the garden alive with vines,
And we drank from the matin dew
A manifold array of mystical wines.
We fell asleep in rapture beneath a willowy yew.
As we reclined amid the eglantines,
Beside the vast and somnolent, silver sea,
My thoughts were of you.
Your thoughts were of me.
How I wonder where went the spring
In the bright summer's saffron echoing
We heard carillons play from harpsichords of white.
Then Venus ascended with an angel's wing,
And she brought with her the night.

Paradise II

We wandered in the sand by the sloping, frothy ocean,
Pondering on naught but freedom and devotion,
In the afternoon sun which resembled ancient Greece,
Exalted beyond all comparison.
Apollo has been amassed by The Holy Catholic Church of peace,
And among the glistening, ivory colonnades,
The scented winds release
A serenading perfume upon the willow and the birch,
Where the dappled shadow fades,
Possessing ambers, golds, china blues and grays.
We walked still further to behold Doric columns which stood
Among squares of alabaster verandas, gondolas and the boundless wood,
And we kissed amid the daisies, fragrant with the spring.
We heard the triumphant voices of many angels sing,
As you capriciously took my masculine hand,
And led me to the fields which play beneath the cloudless sky.
A breeze scattered gold upon the lakes of the land,
As we kissed once more, and fell into a sigh.
Then the night ascended with its marigold reeds,
As we wandered further into the moonlight,
Barefoot upon the dew of the bright, eternal meads.
There radiant winds carried your perfume,
As we walked among the colonnades of white,
I became betrothed to every floret, to every bloom.
We beheld the spirit of Iris,
And tasted her rainbows beneath the boughs of a marvelous cypress.
Then, infinitely more glorious than the myths of Zeus,
In that splendid, astonishing, Ossianic moon
Christ blessed our love, and leaving your tresses loose,
A summery zephyr parted your mane.
We walked nude on the beach in the silver rain
Beside the massive, swelling lavender brine.
We sipped each delicious, intoxicating wine
Which flowed mellifluously from the stream,
Through the glistening, starry, amber sands.

Eternal Verse

Then tall, ornate Corinthian towers,
Situated among the spacious bowers,
Redolently crafted by God's omnipotent hands,
And gilded with azure hues of Catholic arts,
Led our minds to dream
Of a troubadour's song.
How we loved in those gardens with all our hearts!
Then we fell into a symphony, languorous and long,
Of ecstatic beatitude, of a pearl-bedecked beauty,
Which illuminated every orb fantastically,
Until diamonds rose from the rapturous ocean,
To the scarlet skies where the blossoming dawn
Fed us every scarlet potion.
And as we lay upon the emerald lawn,
In the great, green garden, in that wondrous dawn
With the sun behind it—to the sun's delight,
Your lips became as wine, delicious to behold,
As they inhaled the stars and the sunlight's gold
Our passion rose like a furious fire
In that good, majestic, mighty and gold
Sun of the morning's bright desire.
And your sunlit, sable, liquid eyes
Gazed up at the blue, paradisal skies,
Overwhelmed with gratitude, ecstasy and bliss,
As a sanctified breeze swayed the singing cypress
We beheld The Blessed Trinity and fell into The Father's kiss.
And our sprints ascended above the wide palms
Of the wavering, emerald tree,
To the golden realm of King David's psalms,
To the wedding feast above the sea.
And we passed through veils,
Brighter than all suns, in a radiant, blue glory,
Where The Virgin hails
Her Son with regal praises of an alabaster sanctity.
And at the height of heaven The Father took our hands,
As his Son bound us in eternal bands,

Eternal Verse

And His Spirit roved around us gleefully,
Pouring me into you,
And you into me.

Now we behold our mansion beside a throng of willows
Beneath a woolen blanket of diamond billows,
O, my lover, come to me!
Let us drink from the carafe this Kingdom's wine,
In the foyer of the library, in its verse flooded study,
In the courtyard strewn with the carmine rose,
In the cloister with its glistering vine.
And when your dusky eyes shall close,
In that tower which overlooks the shore,
In the sacred night
I shall kiss you evermore,
There where you lie
In our chamber where the light
Shall nevermore die.
Come, my love, my lover, my friend,
Our happiness is our perpetual end,
The infinite our delight!

Eternal Verse

The Way to Heaven

The way to heaven is paved
By suffering and sacrifice,
By a spirit laved
By fire and by ice,
By true fidelity to truths unseen,
By the mortification of all the senses,
And not by visions on the English green,
But by doing good in the realm that is lit,
By living in the realm of the spirit.
For the lenses
Of the eye
Can lie,
And the touch can confuse.
One must rightly use
One's power to choose
Only and always what is right.
Then the silent, destined night
Shall gently infuse
The balm of sincerity, of God's loving light.

Eternal Verse

In the Hush of the Morning

Now that we have attained our eternal reward,
Let us walk beneath the orange trees,
In heaven's pregnant rapture,
In the hush of the morning.
For upon the earth it was you I adored.
Let the somnolent, calming, soporific breeze
Softly capture
The majestic dawning
Which glows in your glances.
The swirling leaves in the autumn gale dances,
Around the statues of the court, in the boundless sun.
I chose you in Paris as my sacred, only beloved one,
Upon the old earth, well behind us in time.
Alas! We know now only infinity and wine!
Let us lose ourselves in a flurry of exquisite rhyme,
And enter the enclosure clad with columns strewn with vine.
Immersed in the gleaming jewels of the charming melody
Which descends from the golden balcony,
We shall love in our bastion by the tranquil sea.
And I shall take your face into my hands,
And kiss your dark, pink mouth intensely so.
I shall undo your every braided bow.
On the radiant beach, on the gleaming, starry sands.
And I shall kiss your parted lips fervently until
Your eyes betray their dusky daffodil,
And your feminine passion is betrayed with a sigh,
With a blissful moan of sacred, chaste pleasure,
Beyond the realm of all earthy measure.
We shall incur the envy of the angelic court,
As they gaze upon our ardor confounded.
And our love of a fevered, portent sort
Shall leave them all in awe—astounded.

My Fair Love

I refused to pursue some Helen of Troy,
Nor to take the hand of some convenient Beatrice.
Neither did I yearn at some foolish balcony
Waiting on the likes of Juliet—No.
For my true love waited beneath a moonlit cornice,
In a bower below
The colonnades which surrounded her there,
Where she sat upon a marble chair,
Her black, parted mane
Gleaming in the sunlit rain.
All the garden knew in its florid, summery mind
Was to cradle her glistening feet,
Among the flowers of red and white,
Where the somnolent violets meet,
In the streams which glide by her kind
Reveries which glimmered in the tender, morning light.
For I found my fair love
In a cloister by the sea,
Where the astonishing skies sighed above
A rapturous, radiant melody.
For I listened to my romantic dreams,
And O, my muse, I was faithful to you!
Now the tender forest beams
Near the garden, near the glade,
Glorious strains of sapphire and blue,
Upon us as we walk in the shade,
In the scented silhouettes, of the azure avenue.

Eternal Verse

The Chaste Wood

The Cyprian corianders
Held no laurel wreaths for me.
Aphrodite's oleanders
Perished by the salty sea.
And for you, the handsome chest of Dionysus
Failed to intoxicate your pristine eyes.
Nor did his gleaming, gold face
Lure you to drink from the Grecian skies.
For we turned our back on specious beauties.
And your eyes, victorious over the sculpted sigh
Of beauteous men with external might
Gave yourself chastely to only one;
A visionary poet who roved in the sun.
Now the burgeoning murmur of the lofty dawn,
Which marvels at our celestial brows,
Finds us as god and goddess,
Exalted in a wood on an emerald lawn.
Here and there a rushing brook plays.
A tree shakes its leaves upon you and me.
The light of heaven fills the sky with sanctity,
And awakes the daisies in the wavering hays.
We intercede for sinners and gladly pray
As the glorious blandishments
Of the florid horizon
Carry on a breeze
The kisses of Christ and Mary
As we sit beneath the pines
In languishments
Of ecstasies.

Her Kiss

Order and measure, meter, words and rhyme
Are what I hear when cathedral bells chime.
My verse is born in the soft, scented breeze,
And ferries to the blue, splendid ocean,
Near the rapture of the willow trees
Immersed in Our Triune God's emotion.
It wavers like my girl whose love is fair and true,
Whose passion is soft, and then a violent hue
Possesses her heart; she becomes all aflame.
Her kiss is of melodic gales—*the harmonic cadence of her name.*

Eternal Verse

Le Chateau

Nous sommes montés la turquoise l'escalier tapissé,
Avec la grâce aromatique
De vraie félicité dans l'air.
Le soleil a brillé par les rideaux sur votre visage.
Dehors, les peupliers on melt avec la rosée.
Its ont été oscillé par les vents de
l'ouest, de même qu'étient les tamarins
Les myrtles et le lindens,
Les roses de la tonnelle.
Nous sommes reposés dans les repaires somptueux et dorés
Et aimer de l'amour doux a pénétré chaque fleur rayonnante
Qui a revêtu la vanité ornée
Dans les vases faits de tiffany.
Nous avons embarrassé pour une heure langoureuse et rayonnante
Dans le petit salon après notre promenade dans le jardin
Oú les fleurs on caressé votre crinière d'ébène
Avec leurs pétales rappelants, leur violet, rose et blue.
La surface des étangs a commencé à durcir
Comme quelque neige est tombée dans la lumière du soleil,
avec une tension glorieuse
D'une teinte en albâtre.
Je vous ai pris et vous a embrassé là en dessous du frémir,
l'if sanctifié Parmi les colonnades qui on réfléchi à vos cheveux
Une teinte romaine de tacheté allume.
Nous avons pris la retraite au chateau pour la nuit solennelle
Et se sommes perdus dans un rêve mystique
Dans la cour de marbre oú un ruisseau d'azur
A Couru par les statues et à côté de la calèche noire.
Dans la lueur de la lune j'ai demandé votre main dans le marriage
Et votre fiévreux «oui»! était une faveur en extase.
Le Chablis de vos lèvres que je peut goûter toujours à la suite de l'aube qui a tenu
Chaque roseau
Avec l'ambre et le jaspe, sur la tonnelle, sur le mead,
Sur les étangs vent-motivés, le virginal, le blanc et chase.
Alors nous sommes augmentés à la deuxième historie

Eternal Verse

Et aux cigarettes allumées parmi la cheminée.
Nous sommes délectés de notre gloire nuptiale, hors due royaume de temps et d'espace.
Et j'ai tenu votre tête intensément, avec la passion,
Et j'ai embrassé une fois plus votre visage immaculé,
Et nous avons allumé chambre dans le bastion
Comme le soleil fleurissant est monté avec la grace.

Eternal Verse

The Chateau

We ascended the long, turquoise carpeted stair,
Which possessed the rich, aromatic grace
Of true felicity in the English Tudor's glowing air.
The sun shone through the curtains, upon your lovely, pristine face.
Outside, the poplars mingled with the dew.
They were swayed by the western winds,
As well as were the tamarinds,
The myrtles and the linden,
The roses of the bower.
We reclined in the sumptuous, golden dens
And love's sweet loving permeated each radiant flower,
Which lines the ornate vanity,
In vases made of tiffany.
We embraced for a languorous, radiant hour,
In the drawing room after our stroll in the garden,
Where the blooms caressed your ebony mane,
With their redolent petals, purple, pink, and blue.
The surface of the ponds began to harden,
As the snow fell in the sunlight, with a glorious strain
Of an alabaster hue.
I took your hands and kissed you there,
Amid the Archangels' sacred retinue,
Among the colonnades which reflected on your hair
A Roman tinge of dappled light.
We retired to the chateau for the solemn night.
And lost ourselves in a mystic dream,
In the marbled courtyard, where an azure stream
Ran through the statues, beside the black carriage.
In the glow of the moon,
I asked for your hand in marriage,
And your fevered "yes!" was an ecstatic boon.
The Chablis of your lips I still can taste
In the wake of the dawn which cradles each reed
With amber and jasper, upon the bower, upon the mead,
Upon the wind-driven ponds, virginal, white and chaste.

Eternal Verse

Then we rose to the second story,
And lit cigarettes among the fireplace.
We reveled in our nuptial glory,
Outside the realm of time and space.
And I held your head intensely, with passion,
And I kissed once more your immaculate face,
And we lit a fire the chamber in the gold regal bastion,
As the burgeoning sun ascended with grace.

Eternal Verse

I Lay Down with Christ

When I first arrived in paradise,
After my journey through the fire and ice
Of my earthy life,
Of bitterness and strife
I lay down with Christ beside the massive, blue sea,
Where he welcomed me,
And anointed my brow
With a laurel crown of victory.
The palms in the glow of the diamond sun
Rejoiced in my baptismal vow,
As a Catholic Christian now
Received by The One
Who contains the universe in the smallest atom
Of His omnipresent, Kingly hand.
And now I rightly understand
Why because of Adam
He descended to our wasteland,
And gave Himself up as a ransom for all.
We spoke as friends, and the briars, tall,
Swayed in the salty, mellifluous breeze.
I thanked him for my ecstasies,
For creating me, and saving us.
Then he kissed me with a tender buss,
Upon my blessed cheek.
I thanked Him once more,
Upon that sunlit shore,
For living beyond the burden of the day, the month, the wild week.
And we walked as God and god upon the gleaming sand,
In a unity of love, inexpressible and grand.

Eternal Verse

Une Promendade dans la Ville

La ville est immergée
Dans un doré, en or allumer.
Ma jeune fille est versée
Dans les arts de plaisir.
Avec chaque fenêtre recouverte de neige

Nous passons dans le carré de village
Elle me désire à unloosen son arc
Et l'embrasser dans l'air parfumé.

A Walk in the Town

The town is immersed
In a gilded, gold light.
My lady is versed
In the arts of delight.

With each snow-clad window
We pass by in the village square,
She desires me to unloosen her bow,
And to kiss her in the fragrant air.

Eternal Verse

Je Vous ai Recontré à Paris

Je vous i recontré â Paris
Dans un tonnelle par La Seine.
Entouré par la rose, le souci, l'iris,
Vous avez souri à moi dans
La coupe, à la pluie d'automne.
Et oscillant au-dessus de votre crinière brune
Etaient les branches aromatiques de vert Qui a
Frémi dans la lumière du soleil, tendrement, tranquille,
Comme j'ai appartenu au charme visuel! Do votre esprit
Merveilleux comme
Nous, bras dessus bras dessous,
A Traversé les brises mystiques inaperçues.
Maintenance nous fixons hours sur l'obscurité, le lac
Bleu au-delå de notre château, de val plus grade tour
Increstée de joyaux avec chaque gemme, béni avec chaque fleur
Dans le diadème du ciel, dns la suite passionnée
De l'amour heure majestueux et tendre.

I Met You in Paris

I met you in Paris,
In a bower by The Seine.
Surrounded by the rose, the marigold, the iris,
You smiled at me in the soft, autumn rain.
And swaying above your brunette mane
Were the aromatic boughs of green
Which quivered in the sunlight, tenderly, serene,
As I fell into the visual charm
Of your wondrous spirit as we, arm in arm,
Walked through the mystical breezes unseen.
Now we gaze out upon the dark, blue lake,
Beyond our castle, from its tallest tower,
Bejeweled with every gem, blessed with every flower,
In heaven's diadem, in the passionate wake
Of love's majestic, loving hour.

Eternal Verse

The Priest

I behold the priest
In the cloister near the cathedral,
In his passionless passion,
Enjoying the gold of his marriage feast.
With Christ as his Bridge groom, the chiming bell
Did grandly knell from the heights of that holy bastion.
He walked with God in the tender wood,
Completely in love with The Trinity and brotherhood.
He wore a majestic, holy vestment,
Of purple, gold, and white
Imbued with the words: "In persona Christi".
And the turquoise firmament,
Cloudless yet misty,
Immaculately vibrant,
Was lit with a gleaming, celestial light.
He gazed up at diamonds, surrounded by blooms,
Comprised of chaste petals.
He was well acquainted with the mysteries
Of heaven's countless citadels,
And his spirit sailed across the seas,
Which sighed with rapture to the astonishing sun.
He bowed respectfully to a devoted nun
Who was a Carmelite from Lisieux, lost in the deepest prayer.
She passed him slowly with reverence,
In the incense
Scented air.
Wide streams fell from a lofty mountain.
From the Court of Mary rose a fountain.
The Spirit of gold struck me from a hill,
As the priest gathered roses and gave to Thérèse a daffodil.
Then I ran to him with a beating heart,
As the sun's sparkling rays did descend and depart,
Silver-winged finches flew around him with a passionate flame.
I asked for his mysterious name:
Then, in the solemnity of that reverent night,

Eternal Verse

As the moon arose and gave its light,
Over the hill, kissing every dahlia, lilac, rose and iris,
I heard him whisper with a tone of might:
"I am from Assisi and my name is Francis."

Eternal Verse

The Flowers by the Ocean

We sat by the rolling, exuberant sea.
Among the florid gardens which surrounded us there
There were tall, ivory columns which stood in majesty,
Above the sprawling enclosures which were radiantly fair,
Framed by vine-clad, teeming walls,
Where the ogives led to mystery.
After drinking our fill in celestial balls,
We heard carillons play in a charming wise.
Their rapturous strains of lullabies
Lulled us into dreaming
Of soporific sapphires, jades and ambers, paradisal blues.
The sky was cloudless,
And we roved among the Fleur-de-lis, the blissful, summery, gleaming hues.
We ran down to the meadow,
In the cradle of the moon.
And we wandered barefoot in the meads where every sacred, sanctified bloom
Told me its name in the warmth of your kiss.
The heavens remained cloudless,
And the grasses in the field
Intoxicated our enlightened minds
With the effulgent potions that they yield.
The bands which bound us were of eternal kinds.
I watched you as you slept, after our stroll,
In the chamber by the study,
Ornate with silver, diamonds, and gold.
And in the distance the cathedral bells tolled.
As you reclined, your raven mane, which framed your fair face,
Upon your white pillow, dressed with the dew,
Fell like stars with an astonishing grace.
Outside the polars called to you,
Swaying by the ponds, beyond the alabaster, marble square,
Where a carriage awaits to take us tomorrow into the florid countryside,
With me as your husband, and you as my bride.
Our bedroom where the fire glows
Is of only peace, and soft repose.

Eternal Verse

Your fair cheeks blossom with the tint of a blushing rose,
As you dream of my embrace, you remove your dress,
Your wedding clothes.
And you bathe in the warmth of my tender caress,
Swooning in your chamber of a regal, pearly white,
As the moon appears through the curtained glass pane,
Announcing the arrival of the nascent night,
As I place my lips upon your face and mane.
The firmament is painted with a canopy of light.
As the windows in our tower receive the laughing rain,
Speaking of love and its reticent hour,
We shall awake from our ardor, and walk into the shower,
Looking up at the fountains, and the statues of terra-cotta.
We shall mingle with the moonlight ryes, ports, and burgundies.
And drink them in the narrow archway,
Studded with blossoms, red like the dawn.
There the fragrance of heaven shall make its descent
From the exalted boughs which hover above,
Of emeralds, of violets, of coriander-like flowers.
We shall take our union to the seas,
Beneath the ascending, china-blue stars,
In those sacred, silent, boundless bowers,
To the wistful, haunting harmonies,
Of mystical, white guitars.

The Colossal Wood

Dear Saint Dymphna was widely misunderstood.
I recline insane on a purple divan, overlooking the colossal wood,
In my elegant mansion, more grand
Than the Crystal Palace and Hampton Court;
I look out mad upon the dappled, green land,
Upon spectacular blandishments
More bejeweled than Baghdad;
I was doused in my visionary mind
With the bright, Baroque canopies
Of an immaculate, eternal kind,
And I lingered there in fevered ecstasies,
In bated languishments,
As the terraces below my room
Caught the blue, Gregorian sunlight,
Clad with every marvelous bloom.
I dove into the depths of the most majestic expositions,
Of the finest paintings of Van Gogh.
And in those deranged, diamond galleries,
I found there, high and low,
The visuals dyes of symphonies,
Which carried on the hallucinatory breeze,
Cradling squalls of joyful, white snow.
And as the radiant chapels took on a mystic glow,
I was struck with more visions of still more ecstasies,
As my bride returned,
In a long, white dress,
Her exquisite, sable tress,
Clad in a pearly, braided bow.
God bless the mad bards and the things we know!

Eternal Verse

The Zephyrs of the Paradisal Sea

The zephyrs born from far away
Raise the bramble, the reeds and the hay.
With a soft, scented, loving approach,
They gild the beaches where I lie, reclined,
Forever beyond divine reproach,
Blessed with the muse, and thoroughly wined.

In Love's Eternal Realm

In the realm of love
Every woman should confess
That men possess
Every key of power.
And men likewise must admit
In their truthful hour
That woman, in the realm of love, also possess every key of power.
For they posses the same tender might.
(The man appears as a god to her eyes,
The woman is a goddess in his sight.)
They are equal in every manner.
For in their difference, lo!—they are the same,
As blooms are of a turquoise-blue (the man) the other (the woman) are of a light-red flower.
And a bright, regal purple shall be added to their power!
They form a perfect match in God's loving sight.
(Such is a pair
Wedded in this elysian air.)
The ballrooms where they will find themselves
Are grand and graced with jewels,
With the finest gold, and silver dishes.
Each exits as a faithful vassal,
Merely to render
To the other's sweet commands, to the other's wondrous wishes.

Mary, The Mother of God

The scenery of Mary's Court is green, white and gold.
Green are her trees, white is the sun,
And gold is of The Spirit, containing every other hue.
There are brooks which run, of azure blue
Through her forests and her gardens, framed by regal eglantines
And gilded, holy, gleaming moss.
The brooks are of wines,
And gently toss
The reeds which play beneath the cloudless sky.
The Palace of The Virgin
Is heaven to the eye.
Her Kingdom is devoid of everything old,
And pertains to only that which is new.
The glistening gloss
Of the morning dew
Is found in her palatial field
Where her rosy bowers yield
Perfumes of marigolds, daisies and gems.
I met The Mother Of God donning diadems.
Her long, black hair
Is astonishing to behold,
As if all gold
Finds its temple there.
Her crown is studded with immaculate jewels,
Each the reward of a Saint's fidelity.
With a tender love she commands all citadels,
And all the angels glory in her beauty.
All the Saints are in awe of her dusky, Jewish eyes.
Her gazes outshine the bright, celestial skies.
And her skin is fairer than all of heaven's blooms combined.
Her song is that of such a charming sound
That it leaves a man blind
To what is all around.
Her fingertips are of a pearly-white,
And when she roves in her Court, beneath the purple stars of the gleaming night

Eternal Verse

She smiles at her sons and daughters in that vast and holy square,
Majestic and massive, made of marble and stone.
Her perfumes are of honey, and permeate the midnight air.
She rarely wishes to be alone,
Except for the times she converses with Her Son,
Pacing on the hallowed beach, where the streams
Of violets swirl around her feet
And run
To the tranquil sea, beneath the terrace where the vines meet.
She is often inclined
To find
Her desires
In sacred dreams.
Her passions are those of chaste, refreshing, cooling fires,
Guided by her reason
Endowed beyond the wisdom of every time and place,
Of every world, of every season.
Nothing, no one, save
For God Himself
Possesses such a lovely face
Whose expressions are light, yet sometimes grave,
Grave as in solemn,
For there are many souls she wishes to save.
She frequents earth and purgatory,
And in the latter, where the flames torment and lave
She wipes the sweaty brows
Of the suffering Saints.
And she often allows
Their punishments to cease,
Long before their time,
Ages before their due release.
She often graces the dawn with celestial paints
When cathedral bells chime in the western wood.
And she loves to say
When the consecrated pray

Eternal Verse

In their cloisters of rapture,
Clad with lindens, willows, yews and birch:
'God Bless The Holy Roman Catholic Church!—
Its eternal truths be praised!
She cares very much for Jerusalem,
Where she was born and raised,
And she is anxious for Israel to acknowledge her Son.
She opens petals, one by one,
Merely by caressing them in her little garden-close,
In the corner of her spacious Court.
The scent of her beauteous body
Is of an immaculate, dark-red rose.
And the rhapsody of her flowing voice
Is bestowed to transport
The hearts of all the blessed,
Enraptured without a choice,
To the highest realm in heaven, of music, art and rhyme
Where The Magnificat is sung
Beneath the dome of God's Cathedral,
Far beyond the realm of time.

A Wandering II

We wandered hand in hand beside
The vast, blond horizon
Of the princely Hesperidean sea.
Among the thickets and the scented tide,
We beheld our enormous bastion
Surrounded by groves of mulberry.
And your face's elegant blush
Was one with the hydra,
The constellation's rush,
As we gazed up at the astral umbra,
The stars expanded mystically.
Then we strolled to the Shepherd's countryside,
Where the summery, languorous, redolent shade
Declared you as my eternal bride,
In the sunlit garden, on the wide promenade,
In the teeming shadows of the vine-clad colonnade.
In the diamond day we scrambled,
Down the purple hill we ambled,
And found in the landscape a wafting shrine,
Not far from the wells where the cherubs in their mystery
Bequeathed into our souls a nocturnal wine.
And we drank delicious ciders,
In the cool, enchanting cellars
Of our castle by the sea.

Eternal Verse

Your Face in the Garden

Lost in the somnolent trances
Of your soporific glances,
Where iridescent rainbows grace
The cloisters near a lutescent dome,
The blooms sway gently in the sonorous breeze,
More precious than the satins of Rome.
Your soft, angelic, holy face
Beneath the briny, foam
Kissed trees
Is like a statue's, solemn and grave.
As the western zephyrs softly lave
The marigolds and lilacs, the scented rubies, the carmine rose,
The angles sit among us,
Within our little garden-close.

The Holy Trinity

I ascended to a majestic mountain,
Above the radiant gold of a Cathedral's Dome,
Where at its gilded height,
There rose a massive, triumphant, wooden cross,
Adorned with a purple shroud,
Which glistened like a diamond in the celestial light.
At the summit of the emerald peak
There was a garden there;
All its dappled blooms swayed like diamonds in the sacred, paradisal air,
Bathed in jasmines, jades, ambers, golds and browns.
In the center of the bower there was a square,
Made of solid marble, where rose a fountain.
A violent breeze gently did toss
The quivering lilies, which to my eye seemed bright,
And precious to behold.
And from the zenith of that Court,
The Father sat on a throne of humility
And to His right, eternally begotten,
From the light
Of a clear blue stream,
His Son rejoiced, sharing in His Divinity,
Wearing a simple robe of white,
Adorable beyond all beauty.
And preceding from The Father and His Son,
One with The Godhead, as God is One,
The Holy Spirit received their love
In the form of a well,
In the spirit of a dove.
He reciprocated in kind
To the Father, and through Him, to the Son,
In a wonderful wise.
For He ascended the mount in the form of a rising stream,
Returning to The Father's bosom,
As the cherubs circled them,
Each one's wings glimmering in a diamond beam.

Eternal Verse

And so goes the infinite merry-go-round,
Made of love alone,
And only love.
I walked upon the courtyard beneath cedar trees above,
In a cloister made of stone,
Clad with gleaming, verdant vine.
And I knelt in praise,
As the Heavenly Host
Anointed my brow, with unspeakable wine.

The Little Flower

I ventured out eastward,
Leaving my bride at home
In our mansion by the grotto,
More magnificent than Rome.
Only to find a little cottage,
A thousand times
More beauteous than my own.
Along the way
I met golden furrows,
Which glimmered and glistened in the sun.
Upon the meadows
I encountered brooks,
Where silvery, swirling currents run.
There in those woods rose lindens tall,
And sanctified nooks
Bathed by a teeming waterfall.
And so I ferried beyond the vast sea,
On a ship to an isle lit by a rhapsody,
Which sailed on the pleasant breeze.
Beneath the boughs of willow trees
I encountered a little cottage,
Fragrant with the blooms of summer.
And behind the little, wooden house,
There was situated a garden, small and paved,
With a little path, made of humble stones.
The roses of the zephyrs softly laved
My curious brow; as I beheld a nun
Walking serenely in the eternal, bright sun.
Her hair was dark, half-covered with a veil.
She wore a habit, and her countenance was lovely.
She owned every flower,
And every flower owned her.
I bowed chivalrously,
And she beckoned me to enter
Her cloistered, little bower.

Eternal Verse

She spoke with a voice the angels envy,
So charming to hear,
Her radiant inflection,
Very French in its delectation,
Said to my chiming, enraptured ear:
"My ideal was to be another Christ.
Yet your ideals and idols
Were a beauteous woman, poetry and song—
It is a wonder that you made it here.
For without a prayer—
You had no prayer."
I stood transfixed in the garden there,
And I felt a delicious briskness in the weather.
Her face became immaculate, and fairer than fair.
"You know me?" I with bated breath did ask.
"Yes," she said. "You are the poet who donned yourself in leather,
Who drank until drunk from every flask.
While no sacrifice astonished me,
You swallowed visions gluttonously;
You were the Les Buissonnets,
Grand on the outside,
Yet in the inner, prodigious with wine;
And you lived like a Pagan,
Having walked with Dionysus,
You reveled in the sunshine;
You slept intoxicated
In the field of the fall.
Verily I say:
It is a wonder you are here at all!
Yet The Virgin only has to pray once to her
Beloved Son.
And still you are aflame with the vine!
John, you are a funny one!
Welcome to this cottage of mine;
For you are my bother,

Eternal Verse

Never mind the wine."
Her beauty was such that I knew no other,
Except for my brunette bride.
And then to my astonishment,
She offered me
A fine carafe filled with burgundy.
I respectfully asked her:
"What is this?"
"Ah," she replied
"The quintessence of a Saint is sweetness!"
I drank from the flask and she said as she sighed:
"My mother was a lace maker.
Just like your bride!"
"How do you know all?" I asked.
She answered:
"Where do you think we are?—
All glory varies from star to star
My name is Saint Thérèse. I am the little flower.
See me here in my soul anew,
Blooming forever
For the glorious pleasure
Of a King, *A Catholic Jew*."
"Perhaps you know of my sisters?—
Marie, Pauline,
Leonie, Celine?—"
"All I knew, my holy lady fair,
Was weaving verse and sipping Chablis,
Kissing my lover in the bright lights of Paris,
Where lilacs swayed in the aromatic air,
And that you were cloistered as a Carmelite, in Normandy."
"Yes, my brother John,
Although the night at times took hold of me,
I chose to carry on.
I forgot myself in making others happy,
And my empty shoes were filled."

Eternal Verse

She gazed at a rose,
And it wavered as she willed.
And as I left her garden-close,
As the sun's diamonds shed,
She gave me a note, a poem, it read
Wonderfully and discretely said
As a sacred, solemn gift:
"A little soul is easier for the breeze of love to lift!"

A Tuft of Daisies

Behold the brilliant tuft of daisies,
And the breeze
Kissed trees.
Let us wander amid the posies,
To the strains of tender melodies.
Let us venture out, beneath the moon,
And immerse our hearts in a timeless June!
Let us walk among the statues in the vast, marble square,
By the languishing tide
Of a roving sea of white,
In the rosy, scented, majestic air!
Let us stroll through the groves,
Which in the purple umbrage hide.
Let us drown our souls in the soft, sacred night,
In these gardens of many manifold loves.
And there beneath the diamond-studded stars,
Which ascend in the warmth of a campfire's bars,
Let us love in the dawn, cabalic and bright!

Eternal Verse

The Hallowed Beach

Let us sleep upon the hallowed beach,
In trances of ecstasy,
Each to each,
A spouse and a lover.
There, in the wine-laced, marvelous air,
We shall inhale every symphony,
And depart for the teeming, vine-clad towers,
Of our eternally lit, majestic lair.
And from our bastion's glorious heights
We shall gaze down at the rose-filled bowers,
At peace with the days, at peace with the nights.

Night in Paradise

The night is veiled in a romantic purple.
My lady walks with her long, black mane,
Upon dew-clad reeds, tall, smooth and supple,
To the wooden gazebo, in the moonlit rain.
She smiles at the slender, sallow grass,
As soft, sweet zephyrs gently pass
The greenery by the gondola, where she longs for a kiss.
Such is of the sacred night, such things as only this.

Eternal Verse

The Study

You lay asleep in our study among the books,
My black-haired belladonna,
On the cozy soft divan, your astounding looks
Reflect with a rare humility the beauty of The Madonna.
Outside, the summer rain
Trails softly down the windowpane.
I am reading Shakespeare's new play
With bated breath.
(It its far superior to his old Macbeth.)
And as you in your trances dream
Of a wavering wood and a sunlit stream,
I hear in the distance, on the meadow, by the bay,
The whistle of the wind make its playful way
Through the sycamores and lindens, bending their leaves,
Upon the belvederes, beyond the eaves
Of our castle by the sea.
Now the rain turned to diamonds, and rapturously
A flock of blue jays ascend from the trees
As you opened your brown, raven eyes anew
To the clouds dispersing in the blue,
At one with the nascent, nocturnal breeze,
And its scent of mignonette, of eternal ecstasies.

The Balcony

The gold, gilded wooden stairs
Ascended to the English airs
Of the palatial rooms,
Overlooking the sea.
There we found Keats in urns made of tiffany,
Filled with luminous, russet blooms.
We walked out upon the balcony,
Beyond the tall curtains of alabaster-white,
And the angels filled our carafes with wine,
In the cradle of the gilded terrace,
Of infinite, pearly, luminous light.
Then there rose from the trees a fair, divine,
Melodious breeze which caressed your hair and face.
Your gaze then settled upon the widely graced, purple stream
Which flowed through the yard like holy, hallowed dream.

The Carmine Hill

We strolled down the side of the carmine hill,
On a grassy path, down its florid slope.
Nevermore needing faith nor hope,
We encountered with a starlit daffodil,
Every lilac, dahlia, daisy and rose.
We found ourselves surrounded by marble,
In a vast and sunlit garden-close.
I ran my fingers through your tresses of sable.
And we reclined among the vines,
The marigolds and the lofty pines,
Next to a brook of azure wines.

A Walk in the Dawn I

On a trail lined with emerald gauze,
At one with the dawn,
I met a giddy, drunken faun
In an ethereal pause
Beneath pillars of gray.
The new, astonishing, carmine day
Wrapped around the purple trees,
And their leafy, sunlit filigrees.
(Last night I was one with the hunter's moon,
In a vast, glowing bower,
Awaiting the noon,
In the somnolent boon
Of the Shepherd's hour.)
I continued down my path of bliss,
Seeking out a princess and her tender kiss,
As the waves rolled in from the pining sea.
I found her among the darnel and the reeds,
Where she gazed upon me,
Fulfilling all my needs.

And I proposed to her there,
Upon my knees,
In the soft, redolent, oceanic air,
In a rapturous glee—
Of ecstasies.

Eternal Verse

Your Eyes

What tender colloquies
Arise
From your eyes,
As you gaze
At the haze
Of the seas,
Where they laze,
Beneath the arch of the turquoise skies?
What opaque rivulets

Frolic in your mane,
Of sable wool,
Where blue coquettes
Are sable still,
Whirling in the rain
Of your unsullied glances?

What translucent dances
Of ravishing clover
Scent the whimsical breeze,
And ramble over
The pine trees' tender
Tapestries?

A Lady Most Lovely

There is a castle which stands
Over green-clad stones,
Of ancient, gray and brownish tones.
It is perched like a rock on the cliff it commands.

On a terrace, in its tallest spire,
A lady most lovely, a lady most fair,
Walks as a goddess in the salty air,
Gazing down at the red sea of tranquil fire.

Her eyes are dark,
And her dress is long and white.
Happy is her lover who receives her at night,
Where she wanders in the courtyard, where the dreaming blue lark
Awaits her splendid carriage, beside the gleaming torch light,
In the spacious, silent, silver park.

Eternal Verse

Serenity

The amber murmur of the afternoon breeze
Cradles the tall, slender, sallow reeds
Which waver on the billowing beach, beyond the meadows, beyond the meads,
Beyond those dew-dressed dales, of translucent, bending, weeping trees.

With each lustrous wave that brushes the sand
Made of liquid jade, gold and other rare and pristine gems,
You are kissed, half-dreaming of diadems,
As I tenderly take your fair, white hand.

And all of the paradisal billows that are swirling
Fill your azure mind, languished and whirling
As they grace the briars upon the shore.

God approves of your serenity forevermore,
As He raises the sun over the sea,
With His own illustrious majesty.

Adam and Eve

I sat upon an emerald lawn,
When Adam and Eve did pass me by.
I then asked of Adam in the dawn:
"Are you once more exact in the art of taste?"
Such was his reply:
"Well, now that I can no longer lie,
Yes, by the merits of Christ,
Although differently, in a spiritual wise,"
Eve then did insist:
"O, happy fault!
Of this do not despise.
For Christ hath had us enter into a greater paradise
Than we had known in the first!"
Than Adam said to me:
"We learned from our mistake, my good man,
And for the love of all of us
God saw fit that we nevermore thirst."

They walked away, hand in hand, and all was understood,
As their Redeemer blessed with gold the pines of laughing wood.

A Journey

We ascend to the base of a circular colonnade.
Its roof was arched and lit with the sun,
Of carmine, saffron, jasmine, and jade.
There where vines aside the brooklet that did run
Beside the huge veranda which captivated our sight.
The Saints upon the earth
Aspire to such height,
And their dreams give birth
To the garden's glow
Which ravished our hearts,
Situated next to the temple where darts
The angels which alight there as they kindly bestow
Wines of a wondrous kind,
To inebriate our regal minds
With visions of a wintry snow.
Now take my hand, my maiden fair,
Let us ascent to towering loves in other skies!
The ruby fairies have sprinkled gold into your eyes,
Among a hush of lullabies,
In the sanguine, foamy air.

Hello, garden bower,
Good day to you!
Your teeming garments of a china-blue
And every other marvelous hue
Color each flower
With Noel anew.
We have come to greet the Lady of Palestine,
Who grants to all Saints the Kingdom's Wine.
Behold, my love, the ornate ogive
Is made of bronze and is clad with roses.
Let us give
To one another kisses true,
Before the spray of the sumptuous evening closes
Our star-enlightened eyes
To the well-favored, comely skies,

Eternal Verse

Of a royal, turquoise blue,
Above in the radiant, cloudless sea.
Let us rove on the sand,
And gaze into one another's glances
Where colloquies are fashioned,
Scriptural and grand,
Of sunlit trances,
Of ecstasy
Of impassioned
Flavors of sweet grasses stirred gently.
Let us lie in the fields of intoxicating dew,
In the vacillating poppies of the greenery,
And loose ourselves in the mountainous scenery,
Beneath the bright, laughing blue
Of the brooks that trail
As a silvery cascade,
Among the rocks of the enormous glade.
Alas!—The breeze that does sail
Is paradise enough alone!
It is perfumed on a flowerbed,
Next to a vine-clad wall of stone.
And above these glittering belvederes,
Above the cupolas, the gardens and the brooks,
The sea and its lofty, ethereal tiers
Beckons our mansion of white and gray.
I shall take you today
With your voluptuous looks
To starry nooks
By the boundless bay!

In our study by the sea, our divans made of leather
Are so cozy to recline on in such fair weather.
Let us drown in a rapturous rhapsody
As it begins to gently rain
Upon our crystal, azure pane,
In the soft embrace of the drizzling melody.

Eternal Verse

I wonder how in France below
The lamplights must be gleaming
With all the sleeping children dreaming.
I shall lay you down beside the many fine books
And let you sleep as I choose for you
Some poems to recite.
(In such dappled nooks
It is a sure and true, profound delight!)

Outside the poplars tap against the towers
As the evening dew,
Fresh for endless hours,
Awaits our romantic rendezvous.
Then as king and queen,
We shall inhale all the radiant flowers.
The sun is descending upon the florid green,
And as its fingers touch the tops of the trees,
Of oaks, willows and lindens, caressed by a wistful breeze,
The statues become translucent in the courtyard below.
There sunlight and statuary glow,
Blending as the soft, serene green of a mount
Are framed by torch lights, by a splendid carriage,
Which circles around the fount,
Like the infinity of Christian marriage.

The Arbor

The white, charming clouds
Shed their drops of silver upon the plain.
We kneel before a shrine of shrouds,
In the warm and misty, summer rain.

In the humble morning, where all is wondrous,
Yet nothing mystifying, we tour
The drizzling paths secure,
In the arbor, beneath the cypress,
Pure.

Eternal Verse

Amour

Our pilgrimage is over.
Behold the lapping rain upon the clover,
Which paints the gray of our castle's tower
With water from the colossal bay,
Among the garden bower.
Our spirits converge anew.
I kiss you
As you lay.
Let our kisses speak of the morning dew,
Let them softly allay
Our last ecstatic rapture of the blue,
As the clouds cover the Victorian eaves.
There are Carmine leaves
Which speak of lovers, faithful and true,
In the forest where the linden grieves,
With sobs of felicities,
Pondering you.
I shall take your delicious head in my hand,
As the showers grace the majestic square,
And the blond horizon of the dappled land.
We shall inhale every wine which flows
From the rain which glows in the autumn air.
And I shall kiss your lips forevermore.
Let our love rattle thunder upon the oceans' floor.
Let the diamond heights
Of our nuptial night
Pace like ghosts who only speak of their love
To one another, upon splendid dales of saffron grass,
All clothed with glistening dew.
We have achieved the pinnacle of heaven, no less!
And when the night does pass
I shall truly confess—
Everything and all of beauty is you.

Eternal Verse

Golden Shores

I beckon you, dear reader, to arrive
Upon these golden shores,
More beautiful than Aphrodite;
That Cyprian queen has been exalted
Here where the angles sing.
O, Death, where is thy sting?—
Behold—Ariadne was but shadow and shade
Upon the Grecian moors.
Now she sleeps in rosy grottos which thrive,
By the bright lagoons of the emerald glade.
Leda is wreathed with water flowers,
And Theseus has ascended with the glorious Athenian bowers.
Endymion plays in a whirlpool of gleaming wells,
And Aphrodite, dreaming,
Makes love to the chime of cathedral bells.
And all of mankind's citadels
Have been transformed to higher realms.
All the gold of America, Europe, and Asia
Have been painted anew upon the sky.

Not that I
Praise the myths of Greece and Rome.
Nor do I laud
The wine-clad brow of Dionysus,
Neither do I wreath with laurel
The lofty head of Egypt's Osiris;
Rather to aspire to Olympus
In the minds of feeble men
Is but a reflection
Of their desire not to die.
Every poor, afflicted peasant shall wear a princely ring.
Hence The Parthenon has been realized
In the cloisters of The King!

Eternal Verse

Our Bastion by the Sea

Let us walk barefoot in the morning dew,
Upon the fresh grass,
As the hours pass.
Let me think of naught but you,
As we stroll upon the path among the greenery.
We shall find flowers bright,
In the celestial scenery.
And your fine, fair neck,
Of an aromatic, alabaster hue,
Shall perfume the wooden deck
Beside the undulating sea.
And you shall think of naught but me,
As the palm trees shiver
Wondrously in the breeze aquiver
Which cradles the blooms by the amber beach.
No blessed boon shall be out of reach.
The meadow is alive with butterflies;
And your dusky, sweet eyes
See only my chest and face.
I shall take you to a sacred place,
Where roses cast a comely spell,
Aside the bubbling, azure-blue well.
And I shall remove my shirt,
To receive your kisses of passion and grace,
As your eyes are enticed by masculine beauty.
We shall be blessed by a tender symphony,
Which comes from the spacious drawing room,
In our palace of white, blue, and gray.
Devoid of all darkness and gloom,
This melody shall have its glorious sway,
Painting purple sunsets at the end of day.
And when your delirious kisses find their way
Into a deeper expression of our love,
The fountains in the courtyard shall rise above
To the glistening firmament, which lends more glory to the dying day.

Eternal Verse

Then the soft ascension of the mystic moonlight
Shall clothe with veils the statues in the square.
And I shall sanctify your lips
With reciprocal kisses in the summery air.
We shall stray to the gilded archway,
Alone with God, in a garden of white,
Where marble seats have been crafted for our delight.
We shall gaze into the shadows of one another's eyes,
And I shall know what it is to be you,
And you shall know the poet's skies.
For our psyches shall blend in spirit and in mind,
In our beauteous bodies,
Of a glorified kind.
And our deep, romantic colloquies
Shall be said without sighs,
Without one word, o, musician of reticence!
No longer plagues by the burden of concupiscence,
We know freedom in our caresses, and bye and bye,
The moonlight dresses the bastion's curtains,
With a tranquility no soul can deny.
There are not rains,
For the heavens are dry,
And bestow only sunlight and moon glow,
To the heights of the spires,
To the gardens below.
I regard your ardor as sacred fires,
Never to be extinguished,
Only to linger, languished.
For here in paradise we only know
Profound repose in between our peaks
Of passionate union—and who can tell
After the end of time
You may indeed become a mother,
And I a father, weaving rhyme.
The brook beside our bastion is lined with moss,

Eternal Verse

Watercress and eglantine.
And the tender breezes gently toss
The roses in the archway, the lilacs and the vine.
Take my soft, manly hand into your own.
Let us lie gazing at the setting sun,
Among the brooks and the marble, amid the walls of stone,
All of heaven softly sleeps
When we bestow our hearts, each to each;
Even The Trinity allows us to be alone in a way.
So we can love in privacy,
In the dewy meads, in the dales, in the tall, slender hay.
And the swan on the lake joyfully leaps,
Next to the oaks which bend their leafy heads into the pool.
(We both were raised in Mary's school.)
And still more beauty, absorbed by your eyes,
Of lofty boughs, of cypress trees,
Stirs within you further symphonies,
As a rainbow paints the clearing skies.
The night, gently rising,
Over us, in the field,
Is a harbinger of rapture
Which the moon is sure to yield.
Let us capture
Each mellifluous song,
Eloquent, majestic, exquisite, and long,
In our ballroom which overlooks the borders of the bay.
We shall dance tonight,
Until the night slips away.
Entranced with your gaze,
And you with mine,
We shall glide across the ivory floor,
Bejeweled with turquoise, swirling in the bright,
Golden, gilded candlelight.
Your long, white dress
Shall swirl in my caress,

Eternal Verse

As we witness
The moon rise and fall.
Our love profits others, one and all.
So Christ has blessed our union most graciously,
As we dance in the evening, into the golden dawn;
Outside the willow trees brush softly against the silvery lawn,
Where we walked without shoes in the morning dew,
By our bastion near the rolling, azure sea.
And I shall think of naught but you.
And you shall think of naught but me.

Eternal Verse

Let Us Drink Our Fill

The tall, swaying apple blossoms
Shed their hymns upon you,
As you dream in the diamond sun,
In your stately, vast, palatial rooms.
In your tall, gray tower,
Over brooks of a diamond hue,
Over every grove and bower,
Where the diamond currents run,
Your reveries ascend to the cloudless blues,
Among a waterfall.
Yet your dream is not a dream at all.

We shall drink our fill in our summer estate,
And kiss with a sigh,
Until the moon rises high;
In the cool of the wine cellar,
We shall indulge in brisk, mellifluous cider,
Until the timeless time is late.

Now we have the mystifying night
To wander heady with wine beneath the fronds that bend.
The lakes are pure, by the moonlit statues, which gleam as stony pearls in the garden light.
(Our love is solemn, sure and bright.)
In this Elysian Kingdom which knows no end.
We shall sanctify our passion where the oaks and roses lend
Enchanting perfumes of thyme, which wafted, wavering, amend
With the sanctified, ornate, opulent breeze.
Struck by the stars of purple, pink, and white,
We walk as god and goddess here,
Beneath the effulgent, flowing trees,
Beside the charming belvedere.
The copulas in the violet sky joyfully ring,
To the cheerful tune of cherubs, as they glorify our love and sing.
Let us stroll into the enclosure where the blossoms speak of Burgundy;
Let us loose ourselves in one another's inner beauty.
We shall recline upon the marble farm,

Eternal Verse

In the cloister, by the fountain which glorified your name,
And utter not a syllable.
Yet I shall kiss every strand of your mane of sable,
And drown myself in the grand pools of ecstasies, of shade.
And we shall love one another in the meadow, on the glade,
And not until the dawn arrives,
Shall we be sated, for our love
In a wonderful, thirsty fount
Which no exalted angel can fathom nor mount.
The skies are aglow with blessings from above.
Even when we walked upon the earth,
Our love gave us life, and eternal birth,
And conquered all sorrow, misery, and sin.
Let us go into town,
To the happy, celestial tavern,
And cherish the songs and the lively din.
And in that felicitous atmosphere,
Beneath the cloudless, azure sky,
We shall drink Port, Chablis, Burgundy, and rye,
Vodka, rum, and beer!

Eternal Verse

Your Name

I used to wander in a daze,
Lulled by the soft cadence of your sonorous name.
Although I did not know the scent of your kiss, the glory of your mane,
I followed my dreams in the morning haze.
But I could not find that blessed name which described you to others, to me.
Was it Susan, Felicia, Renee, Marie?—
Ah! Your scent
Was a charming good wish that lent
Such a symphony to the gold of noon!
And there, in the spring, beneath the lamp-lit, leafy boon
Of the time fragranced linden trees,
Your name arrived with a majestic breeze,
And told me of your soft, sweet, wondrous lips.
You waited for me, by the harbor, overseas,
In a fragrant arbor, seeking new ships,
As they would anchor in the bay, in that lovely breeze!
Now the clouds are gray as they release the snow,
As you gently go,
Clothed in the wool of your black pea coat,
As you wander by the sea,
In love with only me,
Through wild meadows and dales of oat.

Your Wake

You walk as an angel in the soft, summer air,
Wearing a pearl-white braid,
Which clasps a raven tress,
In your long and wavy, ebony hair.
And with each step that is laid
Upon the trail, with your naked feet, below your dress,
A delicious scent is found in your wake,
Meant only for my soul to take.

Beneath the Archway

Beneath the archway, studded with roses,
Your sway is of petals, and each one discloses
Melodies of flowing tones.
You enter the garden, by a wall of ivy
Married to ancient, dark-gray stones.
And your beauty
If of a cadence
Harmonic and complete.
Your gaze is of a radiance
Touching all the water flowers
Where the poplars meet
In the florid, autumn bowers
Which cradle your soft and gleaming feet.

Eternal Verse

Beauty

The strains of Mozart pass
On the blades of amber grass,
In the dawn of mahogany,
Exquisite with beauty.
Your kisses of russet wine,
In concert with the rising vine,
Welcome the lutescent sunshine,
Upon the blissful horizon, wet with dew.
(Last night I dreamt of you.)
Let us wander where
The perfumed air
Leads us to the marble square.
There we shall take languorous sips,
Of the fountain's bliss,
Of its cool, iridescent, silver rain.
And again and again
I shall gladly kiss
The soft refrain
Of your celestial lips.
The strains of Mozart pass
On the blades of amber grass,
In the dawns of mahogany,
Exquisite with beauty.

The Song of Your Love

The song of your love
Is of branches, of leaves,
Of flowery sprays,
Of Victorian eaves.
The Queen of the Heaven
Calls to me
With a sonorous voice
Of felicity.
And I have no choice
But to run to you,
My sable-haired princess
Who hath possessed me so.
Our mutual reverence
Shall take wings and grow,
In the sacred silence
Of the garden-close.
And our kisses shall sanctify
The mystical rose.
The song of your love
Is of branches, of leaves,
Of flowery sprays,
Of Victorian eaves.

God

God cannot create
An entity
Greater than Himself.
And although my love is beautiful,
It is Christ
And Christ
Alone
Who makes her so.
Every wind that does blow
Through paradise,
Through the earth
Is of His origin,
Of His noble birth.
Not even The Virgin
Would rule Heaven and Earth
If it were not for Him
To have Her do so.
All merit comes from Him alone.
For I have seen the astounding, diamond light
Shining on a wall of stone
In a garden immaculate,
Shining bright.
All love is of Him.—
And Him alone.
The fairest dew upon my love's mane in the morn
Is but Christ gleaming from within
The lovely maiden.
And without Him—
There would be no cherished place,
No adoring face,
No sanctified tryst.
She would be nothing:
The nothingness behind the curve of the universe,
A blackness that does not exist!

Peace II

Radiant ebonies
Course through my spirit
As I behold you
Gazing at the sky, waiting hear to it,
Beckoning its firmament of blue
To descend like a drowsy angel, tired of flight
To come home to the cradle of peace and delight.

My Lady II

My lady lives up high,
In a castle by the sea.
She is well-acquainted with majesty,
And she dreams of fair love with a longing sigh.
There is a river that does run
Through her rose garden below
Her balcony and her window,
At one with the summer sun.
She likes to pine in long, white dresses,
And in soporific trances
She ascends to lofty reveries,
As symphonies
Gleam like ethereal dances
In her mind and in her tresses
Of azure blues and ebonies.

Canticles

The lingering fragrance of the tall, florid boughs,
Shake their songs upon us as we wander, strolling
On meadows in heaven where a white brook, rolling
Inspires our ardor and its many sacred vows.
The bright canticles of the gleaming, azure wood
Sing with the souls of harpsichords, burgundies, a flute,
As they cover the snowy dales and softly mute
The din of earthy cities below, as they rightly should.
What starry skies reside in your dark, delicious eyes,
Which inflame my soul with an ascending desire?

We shall clime the heights of the mountains ever higher,
And find only rapture in one another's sighs.
What vases of purple gleam by the fire,
Next to the bookshelf which awaits your mane?
Shall we return to our mansion and walk down the lane?
No. Not until the stars expire.
Behold the classical, sunlit square,
As the carriages circle the majestic fountain.
You walk amid the vines and corianders, debonair,
Inhaling the wines of oleanders, wafting from the mountain.
And in the aromatic garden's yellow border,
We recline on a chair in the gold, gilded light,
Awaiting the moon's arrival, and with her the night,
As we admire a row of daisies, in the Apollonian order.
The blooms reach out to the folds of your dress,
To anoint them by the wavering watercress,
Aside the brook that dreams but for your delight.
The sun is at its zenith, and burns pearly-bright.
All is one beneath the paradisal sunshine.
Do you recall your passing, as I do mine?
What a relief it was to leave our tired bones!
I glory as they turn to ash beneath those cryptic stones!

Fountains

The fountains of silver and diamonds rise
Slowly, majestically, to the diamond skies.
They symbolize love
As they reach above
To the lofty boughs,
To the leafy heights.
(Only love allows
Such sweet delights.)
And a princess is there, among sunlight and fountain,
Wandering unaware, gazing hazily at a distant mountain,
Awaiting my kiss and my soft embrace.
Darling, my darling,
How wondrous are your saintly eyes,
How lovely is your holy face!

Eternal Verse

The Fruit of Iguazú

Day is dawning.
Upon the meadow
It is early in the morning
Alas!—Let us rove
To where the waterfalls flow.
Near the Elysian gardens, the glade, the grove,
We shall see the wondrous fruit of Brazil,
From the heights
Of heaven's pure delights,
In the brisk and lovely winter chill.
Hues of purple, blue, and white
Descend and cascade
Over the eternal mountains,
Merely for our delight!
Let us wander and wade,
In the refreshing pool,
In the rosemary-enchanted, lively cool.
Let our dreamy thoughts of rapture to each embrace,
As we behold the blissful, falling fountains.
All is given from above.
All is majestic, sanctified, and grand.
May Christ bless the tabernacle of our perpetual love,
As I kneel to kiss your fair, white hand.

Eternal Verse

The Rosary

We shall all become as violet:
The color of royalty.
Such was heaven's wondrous design.
In our innocence, our infancy,
The slim rivulet
Shall lead to the Divine.
And to hail Our Mediatrix,
We shall all recite
In the bright, blissful day,
In the comfort of the sacred night,
To Our Lady, our mediator, our lovely matrix,
Our victory and our guiding light,
The decades of her rosary, to glorify her in heaven, as on earth.
(The garden of her clemency
Leads to eternal birth.)
Behold!
Behold all visions of diamond and gold,
There is a ravishing cloister near her immaculate Court.
It is one of a florid, dimorphic sort.
For Christ is one with her majesty.
Lo! Her place is situated near the wide, emerald field,
Close to the vast and turquoise sea.
The blessed with joy joyfully yield
To her beautiful beauty,
To her rhapsody,
And near this palace of blue and white,
There stands a Cathedral of a massive scale.
It dominates the presidium of the highest citadel,
And is The Beatific Vision to all sight.
And rather than rendering all other gems pale,
It is as the sun, and emanates
To every gilded corner of God's kingdom;
It is the glory, the quintessence of all Christendom.
It is the shining rock, the end of human fates.
And in this astonishing silver temple,

Eternal Verse

Where inner blues and scarlet hues
Become a magnificent purple,
The celebration for The Annunciation
Begins with a procession down the carpeted aisle.
And with a perceived fascination,
The blessed walk a radiant mile,
Around The Trinity, praising Mary,
To serve the delight of Christ.
And after the holy procession,
To further laud the virtues of The Queen,
In honor of her sanctity,
Without hunger or thirst,
The universal intention
Rejoices in The Resurrection,
Near to the palace, upon Our lady's dale of green.
And as Mary lead to Him,
So praying to her leads
To this realm of glorious Courts, The Cathedral and the meads,
Of things down below which remain unseen.

Eternal Verse

Epilogue I

Once upon a time, if I remember right,
I knew suffering upon the earth,
And was well-acquainted with the night.
Now every diamond dawn gives birth
To a flurry of redolent, scarlet flowers.
In the courtyard by my bastion
My lady and I rove joyfully in the bowers,
Which are one with the spacious, marble square.
Immersed in the realms of peace and passion,
We hold one another's hand in the aromatic air.
And in our infinity
Every grand, gilded rose
Speaks of only beauty,
As my maiden's petals softly unclose.
In Nomine Patri et Fillet et Spiritus Sancti.
And so I have said to the earth: "Adieu.
Adieu."

VI

A Lady Fair and other Poems

Introduction

    This present volume, may seventh book of poetry, consisting of all new poems, of various forms and themes, was composed in the winter of 2012 to 2013. Published on the heels of Eternal Verse, a volume dedicated to one exclusive theme, that of the afterlife, this book differs in its presentation of manifold subjects matters, and to only a small extent gives reference to that same topic. *A Lady Fair and Other Poems* is comprised of mostly realistic verse, and it deals with the different aspects of this brief, sometimes painful, sometimes colorful life. It was written with the benefit of the reader in mind, not only as a work of art, but as a work of literary interest, and as a vehicle to convey new experiences, thoughts and emotions. The poetry which makes up this book, some of which are sonnets, some of which are considerably longer in form, and some of which are short in length, all have certain things in common, although most of the poems differ in content and style. I have employed the use of classical meter and rhyme in every poem; hence this volume is not one of prose. In this volume you will find the archaic, the timeless, and the contemporary. And in all of these aspects, I write in a very personal way, on a very heartfelt and human level, for I speak as myself. And in this book, as in all of my poetry, there are no fictional aspects. Even the mystical and adventurous poems which you will find in these pages are all based on real, personal experiences.

~John Lars Zwerenz

A Lady Fair II

I ventured out one pristine night,
Beneath blue stars, to a furrow on a hill.
I was one with the rose and the daffodil,
And my steps stirred the grasses in the moonlight.

I came to a garden at the top of the down.
There leafy boughs were scarlet and bent,
In the sweet, summer air, so very redolent,
Over ponds in the umbrage, smooth and brown.

And old, iron archway marked the marble square
Which led to a castle, ancient and grand.
On its tower was a balcony, perched high above the land,
Where stood a lovely maiden, a lady fair.

She looked at me and smiled with a gaze
That left me transfixed in the sun's saffron rays.
Then all became still as our minds did intertwine,
Among the dappled daisies, and the roving of the vine.

Emotions

The russet rubies of the dawn
Course through the swirling leaves
Within my purple heart, a pawn
Compared to autumn eves.
Then, rising with the warm, red wind,
Beneath the airy, green cloak of a tamarind,
Your feminine desires,
Your feminine needs,
Become one with the swallowing, hungry sea,
As you recline in the reeds—
Gazing at me.

Boughs

Two children at play
Open-eyed and both in wonder,
Gaze astonished at the other and ponder
What it is to be alive today.

And the hovering boughs that they go under
Absolve them of the florid plunder,
As they pluck each bloom that meets their eyes,
Beneath the smiling, cloudless skies.

Two-Thirty

I awoke to a song,
A wavering cadence,
Languishing and long,
Of an adamantine dance.
It turned my gaze to the open window
Which looked out upon the garden's greenish boon.
And in that cloister's Orphic glow
It died in the hedgerow, rising to the moon.

A Sailor's Song II

Beer comes in through the mouth,
Like a kiss from a foamy jug.
My vessel travels south,
A tiny little tug.
I ferry down to the dales of Spain
From the chill of a Scottish port.
My mind is of a sailor's sort,
Adventurous and far from plain.
I live aboard the Atlantic's waves,
Young, and tasting sailors' graves,
In a boat which is rocked like a baby carriage,
On the brine which speaks
Of frothy, white peaks—
Calling me to a Spanish marriage.

A Lady Fair and other Poems

The Lake

One quiet eve
By a dark, gloomy lake
The wind did grieve
Pining to take
My soul into that dreadful, dark lake.
And in that nascent eve
The memories of day
Seemed to fade, to pass away
Into the reflection of that grievous, muddy pond.
That same quiet evening
Went far, far beyond
What I knew before of hope and glee.
For hope went leaving,
And left me behind
Crippled by the sight of that small, dour sea.
My once enchanted, charming, charmed mind
Became anxiously engaged by a wavering tree.

A ghastly mast, it wavered at me.
That possessed, flaming, drooping yew
Dripped its toe into the muddy dark-blue
Of the lake which waited, waited for a lifetime
For me to sit among its darnel, its malevolent dew.

My only transgression, my sole mortal crime
Was in loving you and only you.
Yet this pool
Was jealous,
And regarding me a fool,
Became enraged in that reticent, silent night,
Envious
Of any light—
Envious of our amorous play.
Then the wind swept along the baleful lawn
Like a mad-eyed child,
Across the briars and the hay,

A Lady Fair and other Poems

And the many reeds grew wild
As the night grew deeper and cast away
All remnants of the dying day,
The stars and the moon, every orb that shone.

Then the icy surface of that terrible pond,
A presage of hell in the blazing beyond,
Spoke to my soul and to my soul alone,
Whispering in a horrid tone,
As I inhaled a gasping, terrified breath:
"You shall drown, and I am death!"

A Voyage to Cyprus I

I ferried eastward, leaving Cytherea, her wine,
Her temples of ivory, her boundless plains
Far behind me, as Macedonian rains
Filled the vast Aegean's brine.

And in that flowery Ionian wake
I encountered wanton zephyrs of blue,
Where Sirens, Aphrodite's retinue,
Sang solely for my sake.

I arrived on the green of the Cyprian shore,
Whistling as a troubadour,
As the sun rose, burgeoning with gold and carmine,
I came upon a courtyard, and the roving of the vine,
Near the temple of Apollo,
In the diamond cradle of a scented billow.
And there in that square, wandering through dahlias
Strolled Pygmalion's beloved wife,
Enjoying her nuptial, graceful life,
Singing as a statue moonlit sonatas.

In my seafaring boots, I walked to a glade
Where the radiant, fair Adonis drew
From far away, from the Olympian dew,
Lustful Aphrodite.
(And he loved her in the shade.)

Then with a whisper, the Mycenae breeze
Called me back to the port, to the song of the seas,
Where I sat in a garden next to the harbor,
In a wistful arbor
Of ecstasies.

The Billowing Reeds

The folding ivory, Orphic ocean
Sobs as it rises
With shy, azure-blue, somnolent disguises,
Evoking, with its waves, an amorous emotion.

Indistinct, a billow plays
Upon the swept-back reeds,
Which make one dizzy,
In the late afternoon, summery haze.

Upon the sky the sunset bleeds,
With a solemn, silver majesty,
And you, beside me,
Naked in a bed of tall, wavering grasses
Look upon the piers of the jetty,
As the thyme-scented breeze
Sighs as it passes.

Then, the evening with its mysteries
Covers like a velvet veil the hovering, foggy stars,
Along with the moonlight, round and pale,
Amid the florid briars.
Yet I still can see the distant, glowing bars
Of crackling, carmine campfires.

Then rising with the warm, red wind,
Beneath the airy, green cloak of a tamarind,
Your feminine desires,
Your feminine needs,
Become one with the swallowing, hungry sea,
As you recline in the reeds,
Gazing at me.

Wines II

The brisk, wintry gales
Glide sonorously
With the fresh scent of holly
Over frozen dales.

In my lover's dark eyes
There sighs an ebony symphony
Beneath the clouds, of soporific skies.

We walk as pilgrims,
As the gale departs,
In the darkness of the moonlight,
On the meadows of the night,
As our felicity brims,
In the carafe of our hearts,
With delicious wines of white.

It Is the Season

Ah! It is the seasons for a carriage ride!
We shall leave our chambers at noon and go
To where frosty grass meets pearl-white snow.
Our coach shall be warm, with drapes on either side.

We shall glide by gardens and bowers of gold,
And each in a shy way, sitting close, we shall desire
The kiss of the other, the winter's wondrous fire,
Cozy on the cushions, longing to caress and hold.

Then nonchalantly, your lips will open wide,
Like a rose that blushes with petals of pink;
You shall take me in without a thought to think,
As tender emotions will rule by the tide,
In the majesty of night, peacefully sweet and mild,
By the statues, by the grotto, by the oceanic boon.
And you may be with child
Come the vespers and the moon.

To Rebecca

The curtains of white
Look out upon the sunlight,
Regal and gold.
Recall the old.

What was it in your ethereal kiss
That thrilled my soul with a thrilling bliss?
Was it passion alone
And only this?
The sprawling, emerald vines still climb
The teeming tiers of ancient stone.
And the summery nights still hauntingly chime
Their secrets in a wistful tone.

What was it in your dusky eyes
That lulled me with its lullabies
To make a strong man weak?
Why does the rain upon the pavement still speak
Of breeze-blown music in the sacred night?
Could it be I still roam
Through the chambers of your gilded home,
Lost in the fragrance of your tender light?

Why does the refrain
Of the moonlit, misty rain
Still call me to recall your form,
The beauty of your sight
In a swirling storm?

Now that you are gone,
What is this trail I ferry upon,
Strewn with roses
And scarlet dew,
Though garden closes,
Dreaming of you?

A Lady Fair and other Poems

Why does this strain that carries you
Wander though the forest of my mind
With hands that reach out
With gilded rings
And all things kind?

Why do you still stir with ghostly wanderings?
Why are you still about
When sunshine turns to doubt
Of what we were or could have been?
Was there any true love in that cloud of sin?
Why does your song,
Wavering and long,
Still glide through my room to the open sashes,
To the same sunny sun
That finds me with no one
Save the shadows, the remnants of your legacy.
For your flowery ashes

Rise like a Phoenix with a languishing clemency
And whisper the strands of your haunting gaze
Which sail like Homer's Iliad
To the sea, over perfumed waves
In the stunning, saffron, summery haze,
Over your green, frozen myriad
Of wind-swept graves.
Why does each new opening door
Creak like the specter you wrought upon the shore
As heavy tide follows heavy tide?

If with only you I can abide
Will love fashion for us
A reunion in the skies,
Tailor-made for an eternal buss,
Providential as your lullabies?
And why with weeping

A Lady Fair and other Poems

Does your melody rise
With all our secrets silently seeping
Towards the half curtained window
With a love that the world can only despise,
Although it shall never know?

Its notes are of a solemn feeling,
As they caress the piano with invisible fingers,
Sending my tortured spirit reeling
With your modest perfume which lingers and lingers.
The curtains of white
Look out upon the sunlight,
Regal and bold.
Recall the old.

I Shall Call for You, My Love

Free from all cares
I pace upon the grass.
In summery airs,
Where soft breezes pass.
Scented breezes, of merriment and thyme
Taste fresh like the matins' dew,
Or the tangy juice of a dark green lime.
I am one with the marigolds, the willows, and the yew.
All streams flow for the sake of our happiness.
The wind stirs the oaks and the wavering cypress.
(I love the ivory moon
When it's full at the chime of noon.)
Near in the distance, a cathedral's spire
Scrapes the gray clouds,
As I retire
In a farmhouse, clothed in a pea coat,
A woolly cloak of raven shrouds.
I think I'll walk to the misty, blue harbor
And sail my little boat
Over the lake, to the sunlit arbor,
To greet more furrows and fields at play.
And when I find you at the end of day
I shall call or you, my love, my lady fair,
And we shall wander at night
In the hazy, summer air
Purely for delight,
Through the little garden there.

Love II

Love is of diamonds,
Love is light.
The soft, summer rain
Falls upon the window pane,
Custom made for our delight.

What can we give back to this shower, that feeds every open bloom
In our little garden bower,
As we within our cottage sit warmly in our room?

For men are leaving the temples of earth.
Our Creator needs reciprocal rebirth,
Sacrifice and fidelity,
Deeds of lasting beauty.

We shall make no provisions for the flesh,
Save to serve our reason.
Do I speak treason?
No.
For our hearts mesh
Like the slim rivulets that flow
Upon the misty pane of our rain-washed window.
Let us serve our loving Lord perpetually, always.
Throughout the nights, throughout the days.
Let us strive to ever please Him, so we with joy can hear
His laughter among our courts, our humble, little squares.
We shall wander far from servile madness, from needless fear,
Taking comfort in His breezes, of freedom in His graceful airs.
There is music in the downpour,
Amid our nuptial languor.

Our cabin's divans are cozy,
And your cheeks are lovely, rosy.

Behold through the glass the rising lake and its glorious grass,
And its fair, white sand upon the shore.
Let us leave our cabin and stroll in the rain!

A Lady Fair and other Poems

How delicious is a kiss
On the happy, dappled, dancing down,
Of the wild and quivering, prancing grain!
(Our love was made for times like this.)

How majestic are your eyes of brown!
Ah, my love, my only one,
Let us walk beneath the archway of the cloister,
And rove while dreaming in the waking sun.
For the rain has ceased, the storm is over.
See how the currents in the blue brooks run!
Let us recline facing the sky and its wide, azure bounding,
In the tall, wet reeds, aware of all the beauty
In our colorful surrounding.

I shall make a meditative study
Of your raven mane, of your angelic face.
And then, once the sun has reclaimed its rightful place,
We shall love until the stars
Have mastered all of space.

We shall drink our fill in the tavern beyond the down,
In the old, mahogany, wooden bars.
For after we are sated and our gaze
Is one of misty, dappled, astonished haze,
We shall leave come twilight for the town.

And when dawn returns again once more,
We shall wander drunk upon the shore,
Giving thanks to God in the raptures of our amour,
On the soft, white sand of the billowing moor.

The Infinite

I laze on the beach, careless,
Eyes full of the infinite.
Onto faraway places in time!
The white billows, breathless,
Cease to interpret
All nature, her benevolence,
Her malevolence,
Her crime.

I shall be the world's greatest academic,
I shall turn my windy sophistries,
All scented with the dancing muse,
Into a gilded polemic,
Into rubies
In June.
I shall infuse
A new global awareness
Of what is truly holy and good,
And of what is truly evil and bad.
I am Tom Thumb, a dreamer lad,
Who lives in the woods,
Relishing its bareness,
Blinded by the brooks that meander in the sun
Struck with visions staring drunk at the moon.

With all of nature's secrets I am one.
There are no more mysteries to uncover.
In stroll beyond the ogive to where the lindens hover.
And I love myself in every boon.

When You Were Young

On the campus of the college,
In a rainbow by the sea,
I carried your books as you walked with me.
We wandered in your cottage,
After a day of reading Frost and Millay
In the russet nooks of the library.
And when the night ascended with its tender moon,
We strolled upon the grass to the charming, sweet tune
Which wafting on the wind, spoke of true, sacred love.
Its melody still stirs in the reeds now tall and dead.
For our passion is now a song that is sung,
A volume of poetry which sighs to the stars above,
A novel that is closed, a book that is read.
Yet every breeze from the eve that is flung
Renews these thoughts of you
As I walk alone by the fountain's blue,
Pondering you, when you were young.

The Conservatory

Your song is a compelling, melodious flower,
Which wavers gently thought the alabaster parlor,
On autumn afternoons when the piano is caressed
By soft, slender hands, resplendently dressed.
With the liveries of summer, glowing and gold,
The myrtle-scented breezes outside renew the old,
As they swirl around the oak trees with a misty, leafy ring,
Absorbing the pubescent sunlight, amid bending coughs, wavering.

Your fingers of white upon the ebony keys
Breed a manifold delight, a mosaic of rapture,
As your halcyon fragrance reaches out to capture from beneath your pretty knees
A poet and a sage.
What symphonies bleed in this timeless age
Down the wall of vine,
Of stucco, terra-cotta and violet wines!

Your rhapsodies
Are as zephyrs which languishing flee
To the redolent seas
Of ecstasy.

And after your recital in the vast music hall,
We shall wander on the grass,
As the tender hours gently pass,
Like sunlight on the vine-clad wall.

We shall picnic on the verdant lawn,
And your hair, of a dreamy, summer dawn,
Parted in the middle, shall on your shoulders lay,
Long, straight and raven, darker than the night.
And beholding such a beauteous sight,
I shall be rendered mute as a word of clay.
And I shall love you there beneath that Kendal green tree,
As you gaze upon the conservatory,
And its lily-white chasm
With liquid-filled eyes,

A Lady Fair and other Poems

Struck with a fair, delicious spasm
Beneath the absinthe-tinted skies.

Southern California, 1966

Sounds of treble, brass, and tremolo,
Sailing in the sun or rain,
Soothe me of my languor,
Soothe me of my pain.

Beyond where the roses marry the trellis,
Upon the white fence gleaming with indigo,
A princess lives in that suburbia's arbor.
And in her bedroom she combs her long, black hair,
While smoking with her windows open wide,
Overlooking the ocean, the cars and the tide,
In the sacred perfume of the summery air.

It is Southern California. It is 1966.
She turns on her transistor and walks to the sea.
She hungers for her nightly fix,
To go crazy in the back of a Chevy,
Parked by the pier, just for kicks,
To love her boyfriend wildly,
To kiss until she cannot see.

And the surfers come in
Along with the nascent night,
Among the campfires' din,
As the gilded, descending, western light
Sinks over the rim
Over the massive Pacific to torch lights dim,
To rock and roll salvific.

The Hallowed Eve

The gray clouds race,
Thrown forth by the winds in the skies,
To amber, southern fields,
Over the hills where angels pace.
I am one with your dusky, raven eyes.
The perfume that your body yields
Blends with the breeze
Which ferries through the linden trees
In the silence of the hallowed eve.
All dappled boughs begin to grieve.
And winter shall soon take the summer's place.
In nights such as these
I find your face
To be at one with ecstasies.

I Came Upon a Castle...

I came upon the castle where my princess resides,
Perched high upon a fleecy,
Wind-swept down.
She saw me from the ornate balcony,
With her dusky eyes of sunlit brown.

She swooned among the long silhouettes of the boxwood trees,
Where soft Baroque symphonies
Glide to the seas,
And to the sunlit tides.
(Her radiant, perfumed tresses are of rare modesties.)

I entered the foyer of stony gray
Where an ancient row of knights stood in array
Against the pale wall,
A wall of ancient gray.
I walked up the circular stairs
To her father's reticent study,
Of aristocratic, stately airs
Amid mahogany, cushioned chairs.

Then a lovely servant did call.
"I am here to see the princess," I said.
And curtsying, she left me in the stately hall.
Outside the rays of the sun did fall,
With scarlet, saffron, and carmine-red.
Its beams flashed languidly through the stained glass panes
Before they set beyond the peaks of a distant mountain,
Before they turned purple, before they were dead.
In the courtyard below rose a solitary fountain,
Next to a carriage which circled in the square.

My love entered the chamber,
As in through the sashes
Came the sweet and fragrant summer air.
I bequeathed to her
A new bouquet, and the dew of my sailor's coat;

A Lady Fair and other Poems

I hugged and embraced her,
And her lovely, black lashes
Opened to the evening.
"Can we walk about to your comely, little boat?"
I heard her sweetly say.

So we left the castle happily,
And strolled to the grotto, by the frothy, vast sea.
And when she took my hand
Into her own,
Her tender heart went through me,
Beyond all softness that I had ever known.

We sailed to the shores of Venice, to Italy,
To the mainland, north of Palmyra in Sicily,
On the Mediterranean's breezy brine.
And after some days of travel,
Venturing further north,
To where the breezes are brisk carrying forth,
We immersed ourselves in Florentine wine.
And with each new star that silently rose
We were greeted with a mystic marvel,
An ineffable brew of the true divine!

Autumn

In the death of my gladness
There are no pleasures at all.
My profound, dire sadness
Arrives and does pry
Along with the autumn,
A bottle of burgundy intended for me to die,
Within the gales of the mortal fall.
And as the daylight does call,
Languorously and solemn,
With a soporific haze,
Which ferries through the silhouettes of the oak trees
Scented with a baleful rue,
Beneath a sky of turquoise-blue,
I am left with naught but a tristful pall.
I am shaken by the chill
Of the meandering, wayward, wanton breeze.

Yet in spite of all of this,
I still yearn for my lover's diamond kiss.
And all of my will,
Pining in the autumnal haze,
Is plaintive to the call of ecstasies.
For the yearnings of my leafy gaze
Are the lips of my princess,
Who roves, dreaming of fair love,
In her bower below the mansion on the hill.

She sings to the swallow sighing above.
Her flesh is of the daffodil.
Her kiss is precious,
Her fingertips glow.
And her eyes, dark and bright,
Bright solace to the autumn gales,
As the daylight pales.
Behold, the night.

We Shall Wander

We shall wander as children beneath the multicolored leaves.
Beneath their boughs of indigo, beneath Colonial eaves,
We shall rove where the zephyrs flow, in the silence of the night.
And sitting in a tuft of daisies we shall pine in sweet delight.
You shall ponder only me,
Beneath a blossoming myrtle tree,
And I shall ponder only you.
We shall fell the cool breath of the sanctified dew,
Barefoot and dreaming, among the fireflies
Of the summery glen,
Where they flutter
As the massive sky rumbles with thunder,
And purple dragonflies
Hover over the pond, and then
We shall recline
In the wind,
In the vodka of the grass,
As the shooting stars like lightening pass.

And when the dawn ascends, majestic and gold,
You shall give me your fair, white hand to hold,
As the hedgerows awake
With a gleaming, exquisite, summery sheen.
We shall wade by the pond,
By the violet, little lake,
Gratefully humble, gratified, serene.
And gazing at the great, gilded beyond,
We shall sigh as the sun
Upon the sacred land,
Unites us as one,
To the weary world unseen,
Beneath the moon, full, white, and grand,
Enraptured in its comely veil
Upon the pleasant, dew clad dale
Of effervescent, holly green.

We Shall Rove

Let us dance and let us sing.
We shall rove,
And we shall wander to the meadows over yonder,
Among the grape-scented immaculate vines,
Among the fragrant, dappled watercress,
Among the jade of the dewy clove
Of the brook-kissed eglantines,
In my sailor's coat,
In your long, white dress.
Where the wavering greens of the tepid lilies float.

Where the soft, amber light
Sifts through the boughs, all clad with emerald leaves,
We shall walk as lofty divinities
Happily, as the sunset grieves,
Lost in our felicities.

And when the angels descend
Upon the starlight moor,
Next to the lighthouse, on the luminous shore,
Our day shall end
There by the sea,
Where the palm trees bend.
And we shall love eternally,
Indeed forevermore!

Dreaming

Walking through meadows I shall dream,
Wearing a sailor's coat, of soft, raven wool.
I shall bathe in summer breezes, scented and cool,
Sprayed by the happy froth of a stream.

I shall meditate on only love,
And make my way to the church by the sea,
To kneel by a shrine, dedicated to her majesty,
Beneath the radiant sky above.

And when the evening comes, docile with the pace
Of the silent shoe of a vagabond,
My dream shall ferry to the grand beyond,
Above the realm of time and space.

A Lady Fair and other Poems

Spring

It is blue-butterfly day here in spring.

Robert Lee Frost

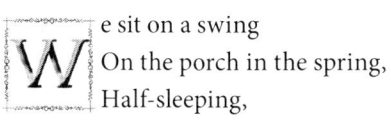

We sit on a swing
On the porch in the spring,
Half-sleeping,
Just resting,
As butterflies of blue
Go flittering and fluttering
Beside the holy grace of you.

Looking out upon a tuft of grass,
The summer breezes gently pass.
How I love your eyes, my lovely lass;
They take in the skies, like old, red wine.
Around the old, Colonial post
Which climbs the heights of the holly green vine.
(It is you, my dear, I love the most.)
Let us laze in the yellow, saffron sunshine,
As siroccos from the Caribbean blow,
Upon the brook and its dewy eglantine.
We shall find a warm rapture in every carmine billow,
As you place your tender hand in mine.

We sit on a swing
On the porch in the spring,
Half-sleeping,
Just resting,
As butterflies of blue
Go flittering and fluttering
Beside the holy grace of you.

A Lady Fair and other Poems

A Voyage to Spain

My boots are of leather.
I am a buccaneer.
My spirit is devoid of fear,
I sail on furious, thankless brine,
In dangerous, windy, wild weather.
I am always drunk with holy wine.
I worship neither Poseidon nor Pan.
None but God do I adore.
I seek a woman from the sacred shore.
I am glad that I was made a male, a man,
Masculine to my very core.

I ferry on a schooner over the raging North Atlantic.
I manage the wheel, every tackle and mast.
I am destined for the verdant meadows of Spain.
My dreams are blissful, ethereal and fantastic.
I welcome the sound of the thunder blast,
The jagged lightning, and the down pouring rain.

I possess secret ales
Within a silver flask.
I have met the rocky port,
And collapsed are all my sails.
I have roving as my only task.
(My mind is of a wandering sort.)

My ship is ruined, so be it—good.
I shall pick my teeth with is splintered wood,
And walk to a tavern near the town of Seville.
My state of affairs shall be one with the skies
Of a young señorita, of brown and dusky eyes.
In Andalusia all is tranquil.

I sit in the back, in a wooden booth
Of piny, stained mahogany,
Removing the bark
From my pirate's tooth.

A Lady Fair and other Poems

And with the rain-swept, morning lark
I hum an ancient sailor's tune:
A vagabond's joyful rhapsody.
(It is the joy of the moon,
It is the song of the sea.)
I leave the din
Of the rustic bar, finishing my frothy beer.
Unable to find an inn,
I travel south in a horse-drawn car.
And I stroll to a boundless, amber field,
To where ancient potions
Wistfully yield
Immaculate furrows, grassy oceans!

I sleep in the hay
In a farmhouse not far
From the moonlit pier,
By the sea, in the bay.

I awake to a voice, youthful and dear:
¿"Qurría usted que algún vino para comenzar su día"?
She was a peasant girl from the south,
Her melodic name was fair Maria.

I kissed the slopes of her red, lovely mouth,
And I loved her in the umbrage,
In a corner of the stable.
(She was very young, of a tender age.)
Her legs were ravishing, smooth, and fair,
And the curly tresses of her hair
Were scented, long, and sable.
Her eyebrows were black,
And the fair, white lily of her soft, Latin back
Struck me with its flowery beauty.
Her fingertips and toes were of a glistening hue.
And her Spanish gaze of majesty
Was written in the dew.

A Lady Fair and other Poems

We sipped from her carafe a heavenly brew
Of burgundy, flowing, mellifluous, chilled.
Her embrace
Was angelic, her bosom thrilled.
And her face
Was flushed with satiation.
I left her half-asleep, as she begged me to go.
I escaped her father's certain blow
In a haze of elation,
Wandering to the florid bounding
Of the vast and grassy, beauteous plain.

In my luminous surrounding,
Wet with redolent rain,
I walked to the mountains,
To the whistling tune of a troubadour's strain.
And I rested, rhyming quatrains
And the other verse, some prose here and there,
In the wondrous winds of the Spanish air.

I ascended a down which gleamed like sand
In the bold, summer sun where towering and grand
Stood a vast, stony bastion,
Massive and Castilian.

Its king owned a prince
Far to the north,
And in it was a princess
Whose name was fair Maria.
And the blade like gold
Came down,
Pouring forth
My blood on the scaffold
Like sunny sangria.

The Music Room

Astrophic cadence flows,
Of meandering verse and prose,
Touching my heart,
In the conservatory, in the chamber,
Where gales glide in from the large, open windows
Before they depart
With thoughts of her.

A piano is kissed by fair, white fingers.
From its keys arise a wistful song,
In the hazy music room,
Where the bloom of her perfume
Conquers me as it lingers,
In the sunny afternoon, wavering and long.

What is it in her mane's bouquet
That renders my spirit weak and trembling,
As the moon ascends
Above the hemlock which bends,
In the twilit gray,
Dispersing the billows,
Dissembling
The day?
What is it in her face's unspeakable rose
That weeps in languish a haunting mode
Veering to the window with a solemn, mysterious ode,
Dying in the greens of the cloistered close?

It is Snowing in the Town

I have come from the village, it is snowing, my dear.
Let us walk to the inn, let us have some beer.
And after we leave the din of the tavern,
We shall walk among the frozen brooks,
In voluptuous nooks,
Beneath the full, wintry lantern.

It is snowing in the town.
Let me gaze astonished
Into your liquid eyes
Of a midnight dusky, ebony-brown.
And when I am finished,
Beneath the cold, dark skies
In the excitement of the wintry chill,
We shall wade through snowy piles deep,
And I shall kiss your crimson lips until
All the townsfolk are asleep.

My Poetry

I, a martyr, give to you, the world, my poetry,
Written to release you from the burden of time.
And if my stanzas instill in you a dream with rhyme
I have sacrificed rightfully my life for beauty.

For I paint many landscapes with an architect's flare;
Statuaries, courtyards, and castellated bastions,
Teeming high and clad with vine, gleaming in the fragrant air.
Onto faraway places and new-born passions!

Tell me, what is your need for Homer and Shakespeare?
It will not be long before I cease to serve you here;
And who among our day can out-duel me with the pen?

After my death, do you know, what then?—
Will there be burgeoning, gifted bards to follow?—
Or will their poor prose and rhyme still render you hallow?

Beauty is Her Name

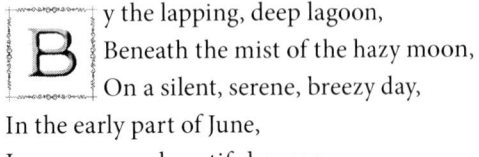

By the lapping, deep lagoon,
Beneath the mist of the hazy moon,
On a silent, serene, breezy day,
In the early part of June,
I came upon a beautiful queen,
Lazing in the starlit hay.

On a soft, scented patch of turquoise-green,
She dipped her raven head
In a dappled, grassy flowerbed,
Amid the sunlight's setting violets,
And its descending, swirling, azure-red.

There, among fragrant inlets,
Purple and streaming,
She pondered many sanctified things;
For in her reveries were wanderings.
She beheld a castle, and a gold, cushioned carriage,
Dreaming of silver wedding rings,
Calling her to a sacred marriage.

She awoke to the night,
Gazing out to sea,
Next to the mansion and marble
Of the square.
And when she did alight
In the sweet, summer air,
Her mane of sable
Gracefully
Blended with the scent of mint and rosemary,
In the vast garden-closes,
Among a throng of roses,
Next to the solemn statuary.

Recollection II

The soft, tepid breeze above the rippling ponds
Wanders through the trees and their bright, fragrant fronds,
As the reeds, blown back, scent the morning dew.
I walk in the bower, thinking of you.

Your gaze, of hazel, an astonishing hue,
Captures my recollections
With rapturous, tristful reflections,
As I pass on the grass beneath the myrtles and the yew.
Yet what if we married, what then, my dear?
Our hearts would go wild
As a swinging chandelier,
With or without a child.
The gilded sea and its sky are blue,
Blue as in eternity. (I shall forget you.)

Onto the mansion, where my memories revive
Other things and people, my friends here and now.
We sip wine upon the balcony, among a leafy bough,
Glad to simply be alive,
After all we have been through.

Our Chambers

The splendorous ocean, the broad, vast sea
Billowing beneath the arch of the sky,
Enraptures our souls, as we sleep and sigh
Engulfed in a radiant harmony.

The courtyard by the grotto, clad with vines,
Where the white statues made of marble rise
With slender fountains, in a solemn wise,
Serenades the mountains, laden with pines.

The pleasure of the peaks, in somnolent array
Refreshes our gazes, and our hearts which pray
For bliss come the vespers, the stars and their plumes.

Now that the rivers swoon with rosy blooms,
(Below the bright terrace, they flow in the light)
We shall kiss in our rooms, in the moon glow of night.

A Lady Fair and other Poems

An American Montage

Vegetarians are plentiful in Beverly Hills
The lens of their cameras like to keep themselves lean.
Flying down the highway kills,
As do hotel rooms with many pills—
Just ask Monroe and Dean.
From a book depository came
The oblivion of Vietnam;
A bullet through the temple
Wrought the day's present reign.

So Oswald can claim
The death of a Republic's calm,
Having ended the innocence
After making a decision,
To fire a bull's-eye aim
With demonic precision,
Firing thrice on a plaza with awe.

And the orphaned world was set all aflame,
When the British, long haired Beatles came,
After Johnson swore in his day of infamous fame,
On a blue and white American plane.

Now men lurk the alleyways, and rich women pay.
The pyramid is off its head.
How hazy are these present days,
When our leaders laze,
Grazing by the laughing Potomac,
Drunken near a flowerbed,
And all the nations of the world,
Including the few,
Remaining red,
Present to you a circus-like fanfare.
Some Elysian, strange, Utopian world
Is setting off fireworks in the eastern skies.
(In a very clever, specious wise.)

A Lady Fair and other Poems

The western hemisphere
Has relinquished its once authoritative air,
And with many tears has unfurled
Its flag of old presbyters with somnolent sighs.

The wild winds whip up a fit
Ruining cities with their terrible tide
From furious gulfs at night.
O, lamenting American,
When will you admit
That neither side
Was right?

In the now and here
I listen to the tomb of Lincoln,
Pining with a plaintive cry.

I wander into a rustic, old tavern
In Baltimore, to drink a toast to Poe.
Yet I become nervous, for an ominous fluttering
Is heard in his raven's descending wings.
For broad, hungry, craven wings
Are waiting for the moment to cast into perdition
Our mantles of freedom, of speech, of the press,
For assembling on the left, in dire distress,
Is a firm and deadly, liberal resolution
To betray our sacred honor, our glorious constitution.
Our morals are being slain by Satan's revolution!

And I visited the cherry blooms,
Where Jefferson still looms,
Patrolling in his wanderings,
Among a throng of temples and tombs,
White—with violent stirrings!

Terror

Baudelaire terrified me to the very bone
When he wrote of hell's complete despair.
Beyond the horror of any fiery dream,
The prisoners of Hades, are unable to scream,
As they walk very slowly,
Silently on the grass
Of the eternal, fallen graveyard.
They, creeping, pass,
Wearing burial shrouds, all tattered.
There resides nothing holy
In that netherworld of gray.
Please pray
For me solely,
Dear reader, now—**today!**

A Carolingian Ride

Bright, flushed-faced equestrian,
Welcome the sun in your saddled stride,
And the soft, romantic strain
Which flows from the river as you ride.
My princess and my youthful, young bride,
We shall as Carolingian invaders take the reedy sands,
Which gleam as gold next to the flaming tide;
We shall conquer every sea as well, all the European lands.
And when we retire,
We shall climb the carpeted, Persian stairs,
In milky, Zoroastrian airs.
And in the chambers aglow with the balconies' fires,
Lit by the streaming, summery moon,
We shall fall into dreaming, in the dazzling boon
Of raptures gleaming, of passion, desire.

Let Us Cross the River

Let us cross the river and walk to the Louvre,
You as my lady, I as your bard.
In its terraced bower we shall be in love.
And after leaving its sunny, old, vine-clothed yard,
We shall admire the canvass of Fragonard,
And pace the corridors, the artistic halls,
Of white and gray,
Among the drapes alike to a lover's buss,
Where Watteau
And Leonardo
Grace the endless walls,
As the likes of us,
Our naiveté.

A Lady Fair and other Poems

The Lady of the Garden

In the summer she paces on the promenade,
Among the blooms of the enclave, of the garden.
She gazes on the distant grasses of the glen,
Walking in the breezes of the cool, fragrant shade.

And when the perfumes of the park flow through her hair,
She pines for the dark and a kiss beneath the fronds.
In the sanctuary of the vast, elegant square,
She roves among the lilacs, and the blue, scented ponds.

Her heart is liberal, she is courteous and kind.
The garden's blooms entrance her eyes, and fill her humble mind
With dreamy thoughts of night, and boons of the season.

She strolls in the moonlight, consumed with only love.
She sings to the blue jays in the tall trees above.
And she lauds God alone, the crown of her reason.

My Irish Love

I sailed to a port near the ancient rock of Hags Head,
Where I met by the rolling billows, you, my lovely lass.
We walked among the shells of the gold, breezy beach,
And we sat beneath the willows, upon a soft, grassy bed.

We roved through splendid bowers as the hours did pass.
Your lips were of the Gallic rose and of the blossoming peach.
I produced from my pocket some old, romantic rhyme,
And I read some lines from Yeats as the day began to die.

We beheld purple finches, leaving their nooks to fly
Over white, wandering brooks, in the brisk, Celtic clime.
We waded in the waves and sipped the crested brine.

Then we walked into town, and sat at a mahogany bar,
Of an old, wooden inn, where hidden from every orb and star,
Your wedding ring glowed, gleaming among the flowing wine.

The Lost Art of Poetry

What of a castle?
What of this?—
Expressing through words such verse that lauds
The pursuit and attainment
Of noble bliss,
Of timeless ages,
When courtships and chivalry
Composed the best of pages.

Truly there have been
And shall be better ages!
Yet of what do my contemporaries
Wish me to write?—
Of this day and age?
Of what Indeed!—

Hedonism and perversity
That reverberates, unfurls;
Do they desire that I set these things to rhyme?—
The tragic constant news of monotonous crime;
Of madness and murder,
In the severed, sordid, urban night?—

Yes, I believe indeed they do.
Yet which of these worlds
Would most edify you?

A Nocturne Song

I slept upon white pillows
In the lonely, old carriage,
Aside the haunting willows
Which in their gloomy dew
Spoke of you,
So far away,
With the promise of day,
And a happy marriage.

A Soul in Purgatory

Haunted in my study,
I turn from drink to drink.
In a dour attack of madness,
I am only compelled to write
Things of sordid infamy.
I cannot reason with clarity
Nor can I think
Of anything but the mire of sadness,
Of the pools within my terrified sight
Where drooling from the walls
Are paintings in the candled halls.
I am Schumann, Mozart, Byron, and Baudelaire.
There are specters which seek my very soul
In the icy chill of the midnight air.
God help me if I fall into despair!—
For I hear the bells of a chapel knoll,
In the blackness of the unforgiving night.
Shall we dance, you terrible wrath and I
Until the hazy, Orphic moon
Swallows me soon,
Long before I see the dawn's golden light?
I shall be taken by the nymphs of the sea,
Where my washed, floating body will lay.
There shall be nothing left of me.
Until I am kidnapped by my omnipresent ghost,
I shall remove the candle from the wall,
And dance like a gypsy down the deathly, cold hall,
Suffering as a saint,
Without complaint,
For the Virgin, my dear, the most,
And for you my readers, one and all.

A Walk in the Dawn II

On a trail lined with emerald gauze,
At one with the dawn,
I met a giddy, drunken faun
In an ethereal pause
Beneath pillars of gray.
The new, astonishing, carmine day
Wrapped its rays along around the purple trees,
And their leafy, sunlit filigrees.
(Last night I was one with the hunter's moon,
In a vast, glowing bower,
Awaiting the noon,
In the somnolent boon
Of the Shepherd's hour.)
I continued down my path of bliss,
Seeking out a princess and her tender kiss,
As the waves rolled in from the pining sea.
I found her among the darnel and the reeds,
Where she gazed upon me,
Fulfilling all my needs.

And I proposed to her there,
Upon my knees,
In the soft, redolent, oceanic air,
In a rapturous glee—
Of ecstasies.

La Villa au Bord de la Mer

Ah!—The villa by the sea,
It was an enchanting stay.
Although it was the summer of 1933,
It seems I was there only yesterday.

With the tall, gray mountains as a backdrop,
And the Mediterranean lapping below
Every white-sashed, long, open window,
Every night and day the bottles would pop,
Flowing with bright champagne and Chardonnay.

You wore a short dress of carmine-red,
And danced to every song until the moon went dead.
I kissed you that summer endlessly,
Upon the many terraces, upon each breezy balcony.

Ah!—Drinks were of plenty, plenty.
And when the ballroom lights went dim,
We followed the pipers, the many seraphim
Down to the shores of the blue Rivera.
We were surrounded there by many marigold blooms.
And when we were sated with the fresh sangria,
We would return to the joyful, airy dance rooms.
I was your drunken Byron, your Poe,
And you were my girl.
How the wine did flow,
With a wish and a whirl!—

Remember riding
In your sister's black car?
What fantastic orb or beaming star
Did we not see go gliding?

We rode through the hills
With the radio streaming.
Your breasts were pointed daffodils.
Am I still there, or am I dreaming?

Down the mount, over the glen
Our wheels did roar.
Our days were the things of dreams.
Such folly now it seems?—
O, tell me, then,
What was life made for?

Hyde Park

I walked among the spacious villas of Sydenham Hill,
Before I came upon the grand entrance of the park.
I met with the scent of many a lily and daffodil,
In the gold, gilded dawn which effaced the purple dark.

I strolled beneath the pillars and arches of gray,
And soon, as I paced on the long, regal Rotten Row,
I sang a sailor's song, and met a girl with a scarlet bow,
Clipping black, braided tresses which gleamed in the day.

We wandered in the wafting wind, fragrant with the peach,
To the tall, glassy walls of the grand Crystal Palace.
She asked for a sip of port from my gilded chalice,
And we swing like monkeys from the Weeping Beech.

The Drinking Horse found us drunk and in love.
We found the Italian courtyards, and kissed in its rocky dens.
As the old moon arose, we left for Kensington Gardens,
By way of a florid close, beneath gold fronds above.

We were married in Knightsbridge, there in London Town,
And stayed at The Lanesborough, opposite the park.
The starry, English skies filled her liquid eyes of brown,
As French champagne arrived with strains of the morning lark.

Morning

Dawn's romantic overture
Scrapes the scarlet from my eyes,
Ever expanding,
Like a jeweled, mellifluous cloak,
Of ascending, regal diamonds
Thrown upon the dismal tenements
Of ashy lamentations,
Echoing in the dusky streets
Like sacred, sobbing cathedral bells
Met with indifference—
Unheard and forsaken.

A Lady Fair and other Poems

An Elopement

From the tower's height,
To the sun's delight,
A gypsy-blue,
The courtly hue
Of the queen's
Noble retinue,
Reflects on the greens,
On the cloistered sheens,
On the silhouettes of the avenue.

This majestic palace of china blue and white
Shall find me below the terrace tonight,
Awaiting the gaze of a young lady fair.
We shall elope, we shall run
Before the arrival of the summer sun
To the port of the sea, in the brisk, cool air.
And before her Mother finds us there,
We shall cross the Channel and sail to France,
Where poets write and lovers dance.

Dante's Saloon

I wandered out beneath the full, white moon
Near Denver, Colorado,
As a desperate desperado,
To a mysterious inn,
To a cryptic saloon.
I sat in a booth among the lively din,
And refusing to drink from the ales of God's ire,
I avoided the wines of Purgatorial sin,
Along with the Stygian tide,
That place of ephemeral regret.
I merely requested water with ice,
And I repented and sought naught but Paradise,
Where I now reside—
Along with my desire,
For my belly met
With a rifle's fire.

Cafés

Tambourines in the city street
Blend
With joy and sorrow's end,
Where musicians and Parisian poets meet
In sunlit cafés,
In loquacious ways.
They are charmed by the trees
Which ferment the perfumed breeze.
Conjuring up rare harmonies,
They take up bass and fiddle within their minds,
They are mad as adders, drunk with wines,
Lost in all the sunny pageantries
Of the mystic season's liveries,
Polishing their perfect lines.

What literary school
Of yours, dear professor,
Shall we place them in today?—
As a rule,
As their confessor,
I will certainly have to say,
They are Symbolists,
Romanticists,
Decadents at play.

A Lady Fair and other Poems

My Politics

I walk in my sailor's coat,
Upon a cemetery mound.
Sober and sound,
Acutely aware of my imminent death.
The brevity of this life,
And the assurance of my final breath.
Such is my political foundation.
Whether of a liberal or a conservative persuasion,
We either love one another,
Or else we shall perish,
From ocean to ocean, from sea to sea,
Along with our dimorphism of our dying society.
And so now it has been said.

From the falls of Niagara to the Mississippi's mouth,
New York and California
Vote blue unlike the south.
(For Hamilton or Jefferson
Still duel for our nation's head.)

Nevertheless, we shall all see eye to eye
From San Francisco to the Texas sky,
When come our final days.
Meanwhile in the Federal laze,
Republican powers are rapidly declining,
The Democrats are spending whilst dining;
Discotheques
And the torrid ghettos' pall
Still dance a jig to the left,
As Wall Street jives
To the vanishing right.
Congress is in a haze.
And America is bereft
Of reason, of a visionary gaze.

Children weep in the streets today.
The western world is wild.

A Lady Fair and other Poems

You!—Young, male seducers,
Without thought you conceive a child,
The woman is but your easy prey,
With whom you casually mesh.
And after these women surrender to the weakness of their flesh,
To your bold enticements, to your beauty, to your seed,
To your words, to your looks, to your natural charms,
You trade yourself in for what the government renders
In place of the basic need
Of a loving father's tender arms.

And you!—Spineless statesmen,
Intolerant of all other ideas,
Save your own, small, tiny, microscopic specks,
Hypocrites, all!

You shall spend our every dollar
Until we are all in abject poverty.
Wait come soon some terrific summer,
Come some horrid autumn,
Come some miserable, terrifying fall,
The crash of '29 will seem like a sunny Saturday.
The dollar will cease to hold a penny's sway.
It will be a colossal, collective ruin,
This savage bruin,
This future rue,
This approaching monster from out of the blue.
(Just add, my dear economist,
The sum of two and two.)

For what happens when the tide of debt
Reaches those with gold,
The aristocrats, the young who are privileged,
The poor, the sick, the afflicted and the old,
The poet who scribbles verse in the air,
The pilot of a jet?—

A Lady Fair and other Poems

Now no one seems to care.
(Because it has not happened yet.)

But then, too late,
All factions will abate
Upon rocky, tragic shores.
Even Presidents,
Senators,
And Congressmen
Will become outright mendicants
Wandering on a homeless glen,
Begging for dimes in corridors;

Suburbs and cities
Will join their disaster, their downfall, their fate;
For they shall resemble broken caves
Crushed like sand,
Beneath a storm of tidal waves,
With their greed and contraband.

And the farmer
With his fiddle,
Brown, with a bow,
Mahogany and long,
Shall serenade our wavering grain
With the pain
Of a sorrowful swan song,
Beneath our once brave, noble skies
Of a rich, dark, dour blue.

Yet after all that I have been through,
Knowing that to give is to save,
If our final fate shall be as Greece and Rome,
At least I shall have a home
In the silence of my grave.

Romance in Town

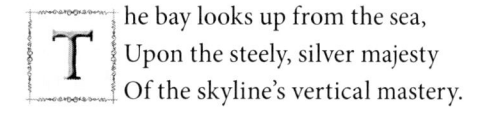

The bay looks up from the sea,
Upon the steely, silver majesty
Of the skyline's vertical mastery.

The red, green, and gold
Of the sky high casements
Of the Empire State Building are exquisite to see
At Christmastime.
Yet traditional sentiments
Are but a tale that is told;
Although the birds in Central Park still sing,
Their song withers in the urban cold;
For the old New York is fading.

Still, Cathedral bells chime
From the gray of Saint Patrick's ornate towers.
Yellow taxis dart throughout the hours,
As horse drawn carriages
Clip clop up and down Fifth Avenue,
Celebrating wine,
Romance and marriages.
(In a black one we recline,
Drunk with our passions,
Enraptured on cushions
Of white and blue.)

From tiny, metal carts
Hot dogs steam;
Many chestnuts and pretzels are bought.
We shall be brought
Uptown.
To where the poets dream,
Beside the boughs and branches of tawny brown,
To the fine museums of the arts;
We shall gaze at Rembrandt and Monet,
Until the gates are closed for the day.

And when the night is over,
We shall wander by the Hudson to the west,
Where you shall sleep upon my breast
Beneath the fronds which hover.

And underneath that wavering tree
All of the city's majesty
Can see
I love you best,
My dear, my bride, my lover.

South of Florence

I left my home, with my satchel, full of books,
In the bronze, bright light of the burgeoning day.
Among the enchanting, holly green brooks,
The purple orchids of a blossoming prairie
Sway with amber hay;

I scuffled carefree down a reedy, boundless lawn,
To the flowery outskirts of an ancient city.
And I dreamed of a lady by a river in the dawn,
Seeking a princess, more than merely pretty.

I approached spacious brick houses of brown,
Framed with black, iron gates,
Where gargoyles appeared as dour gates.
The sky, iridescent, reigned like Rembrandt's fair renown
Over the ancient, noble town.
In my cowboy boots there were two holes.
I was weary of walking through the groves,
In search of adventure and immaculate loves.

I hailed a postilion
On a broad, Patrician avenue.
And soon I beheld a castellated partition,
As we rode to the north,
Beneath the wide, opalescent sky
Of flowing white and china blue.
The coach went forth,
And there came into view
A lovely, young lady,
Along with a sigh.
She lived in a tower,
Up high
Above a bower.

I left the carriage,
And ran to the bastion
In the saffron light
Of the glittering sun.

My thoughts were of marriage,
As I beheld her wearing a bright,
Redingote of regal, medieval fashion.
And before the summer's soft, lutescent end,
Our souls were married, and our spirits were one.

Now, beneath wavering boughs that blend
Their perfumes with the fallen leaves,
We walk on the green
In rapturous, autumnal eves,
Unseen,
In a little garden close,
Passing by the water rose.

A Morning Song

The furrows are alive with crystal and jade.
I wander as a troubadour through cloisters by the sea;
Near oceanic orchards, I dine on oysters blissfully.
Come the night I sleep in reeds, in grasses, on the glade.

I have within my pocket a volume of romantic rhyme,
Snug within my sailor's coat, I write of love and travel.
Roving on the beach, carefree, I kick the sandy gravel.
I am free from the weight of every place and the heavy myth of time.

There is a lady who lives in a castle high.
I behold her now, along with a sigh.
She is clad in a long, alabaster dress.
Her lips are of wine, of bliss; enchanting;
She sings of fair love in the warmth of spring,
As I pine for her kiss and her soft caress.

The Meadows

The cool wine cellar, furnished with your sighs,
Shall leave us drunk and dreaming
In the summerhouse at night.
After our kisses, our loving hearts beaming,
Into the gold-tined meadows, alight
With daisies, grass, and fireflies
We shall go, hand in hand,
Among the radiant and grand
Warm, scented, southern gales.

We shall rove like poets on the dales,
And refraining from all thought,
We shall glide among the rose-colored vales,
On the boundless field by the rising ocean,
Immersed in naught
But love and emotion.

A Troubadour's Song

When the moon is full and round and fair,
I saunter through the breezes of blue
Whistling with love a troubadour's air,
To my lovely, charming thoughts of you.

Rain

The lamppost, sad,
Somnolent, and wistful,
Can drive a poet mad
And tristful.
Receiving the misty rain,
It kisses every bough with tears,
As it has done now for countless years,
Under the long, gray curtain
Of billowing, heavy skies.
Such painful tears
Are certain.

For the gaze of my eyes,
Sadly and full of pain,
Wanders madly like a breeze,
Wayward and winding,
Beneath the wet
Silhouette
Of tall and sprawling orange trees.

And yet,
With nothing apparently binding,
I call to mind my reveries
To render some portion of the day
To the realm of joy,
As I would do as a boy,
Dreaming of light in spite of my sorrow,
Hoping for a bright, golden tomorrow,
Lost in an amber bed of hay.

Inebriation

The jetty overlooked the anchored, white ships
Which sailed like ghosts into the wide, blue harbor.
My friend and I took fermented sips
From a cold carafe in a bay side arbor.

Music rang from speakers to the hazy, briny bars.
Tears from the moonlight rained on the reticent sea,
Which glittered beneath the violet sky, soft, majestically.
Our ears were immersed in the strains of guitars.

I asked the pretty maid for another frothy round.
We toasted the end of summer which found
Us lazing, dazed, by the swaying, old piers.

We raised our mugs and downed our beers.
Then the stars arose, purple, lofty, and bright,
As Jupiter ascended, along with the night.

I Once Lived in Luxury

I once lived in luxury,
A king, I reveled, below the ornate porticoes.
Drinking from the royal ponds,
A plaything of the emerald fronds,
Of the teeming trees,
I lazed beside fantastic seas.
All seasons were my ecstasies.

My loves were all sated,
All kisses were fine.
My every emotion was elated,
Every vineyard yielded flowing wine.

Then came one winter,
Which possessed a chilling breeze.
It froze my throne,
And my kingdom fell.
The death bells did knell,
And I found myself alone.

Now I rove as a pauper goes,
Amid the harrowing wind
That freezes as it blows,
Below those teeming porticoes.

Landscapes

The commencement of voyages,
Florid, marvelous landscapes,
Beautiful maidens in gleaming towers,
These are the things
Which sanctify my hours.

I know of many mystic misty rings.
A tree immersed in flowers
Is clothed in a cloud, where
Indigos and alabasters
Seen in a marble square bequeaths,
A sweet, angelic air
Into my ears, with silver wreaths.

October Nights

Haunted dwellings,
Flickering candles,
Whispering in long, endless corridors,
Accentuate the horrid mantles.

Derelicts rising from their graves,
Moonlit caves,
Are strange and morose.
A ghastly host
Welcomes me to his ancient house.

I stroll beneath the cryptic clouds,
Conversing with wraths,
In burial shorts.

And when the fingers of the dawn
Rise in the east,
I am but a meal
For a zombie's feast.

Madness

The chandelier sways
Ominously.
The moonlight plays
Mysteriously
Upon the boughs of the cryptic, weeping birch;
On the panes of my chamber,
Its baleful branches pat and lurch
With frightening hues of dark, blackened amber.
The hallway is ghastly
And uninviting.
I could swear I saw a specter hiding
Outside on the furrow,
On the grave-like meadow;
The light on my candlestick is dying.
In the abysmal wind I hear howling and crying.
I believe that ghosts from their crypts are rising.
My wooden desk is far from bright.
My verse is poisoned in the hellish night.
And all my soul is sighing.
Hallucinations are abounding.
The bell of death is suddenly sounding.
I fall faint with terror on the hard, marble ground.
All is madness, as I hear the sound
Of mortal waves of dire sadness.
I shall nevermore know sunshine nor gladness!
In the dour evening, heavy with fog
My tortured mind is carried to the bog,
Where every tree is clothed in misery.
The night is darker than grimy coal.
There is no place to run;
Damnation has killed every remnant of the sun.
And the cryptic crypt awaits my soul!

My Lady III

I scurry carefree on the emerald down,
To purchase Chablis in the rustic town.
The winds are from the north today.
I am in love with a lovely, regal lady.

Her face is angelic, her eyes are dark.
Her hair of moon glow, her mane is black;
Her tresses recline like fleece upon her back.
At peace with all nature, she sings with the lark.

She resides in a bastion by the tranquil sea.
Her gaze is of silver, at one with the moon.
She sings to the stars a blissful tune,
With a radiant voice of harmony.

A Lady Fair and other Poems

London, 1969

Smoking a cigarette on Abbey Road,
As a gorgeous blond goes walking by,
She is the apple of my dreamy eye,
Passing by a wall of brick and brown.
The sunlight permeates the famed, vast town.

The morning after,
In our college abode,
There are ashtrays full,
Situated next to the revolving record
Which spins on the stereo.
The summer's golden light
Comes in through the window,
Shining bright.

Felicia, Angela, Laura, Brian, and John
Sleep after the party,
As the music plays on:
Led Zeppelin, side one;
The glistening, gleaming sun
Finds my beauty
On the soft, leather divan.

I shall kiss her lips
To waken her
Just in time for English class.
From the good, British air
I take a splendid, long sip
As Laura leaves for the academic grass.

We awake one and all, thinking of our youthful past,
As down the road four famed musicians record their very last.
Laura must you be so pretty?
I'll smoke another fag.
All classes are a drag.
I think I'll take a walk through the city.

A Lady Fair and other Poems

In the summer there are various hues and tones.
Motor cars are parked by the brownstones.
The chords of I Want You stir the green leaves.
Two girls are smoking cannabis hiding in the shade.
Beneath wide, Victorian eaves.
And their problems that seem to fade
Fly into the clear, blue sky.

A taxi passed by.
Off to the University:
I shall take Laura's hand in mine.
Prior to our studies we shall buy some ale and wine.
Life is short, do you see?—

After lectures on Shakespeare, Hugo and Schopenhauer,
We pass through the heat of the hot, summer hour
With the sweet taste of Port and beer.

Golden Slumbers pour forth from a building nearby;
Laura wants an autograph.
I gaze up at the sky
And I cannot help but begin to laugh.

Two black limousines arrive.
Four men enter from a gated, white enclosure.
They hide from exposure.
They are finished too.
Although their careers still thrive.
(Laura wants to marry two.)

We return to the cozy, spacious, flat
Where we loose our minds in thought
As Brian sleeps like a gypsy on the floor,
Upon a new bought Persian mat.
Outside the billows being to rain,
Throwing silver at our windowpane.
Laura, my love—
We shall meet once more.

Juliet

Black-haired beauty,
Touched my the moon,
Upon your vine-strewn
Balcony,
You inhale the soft, summer perfume
With a languorous swoon,
On your gilded terrace
Near the boundless, Roman sea.
Your lovely, white face
Does blush and bloom,
As the stars revolve with majesty.
And far below your luxurious room,
Romeo pines, longing for you,
As you gaze beyond him, to the moon,
As though he was but a mere statue.

On Poets

Some write copious volumes
Of prosaic verse and prose.
Yet they know not the poet's life.
They are blind to the rose,
And they are free from ecstasy
And dire strife
When the carmine reds of sunsets
Mystically close.
They refuse to shed their blood
For golden pages
That transcend every place and time.

Their rhyme when used rings falsely.
They fail to revere sanctified things.
Their writings are a mere hobby—
The dim flirtation of flighty birds.
And such ephemeral infatuations
Never grow wings—unlike sublime, angelic words.

The Lane I

I wandered along down the sleeping lane,
Which descended to a rushing, blue rivulet;
The breezes were scented with mignonette,
And with the bright, lapping stream's morning refrain.
You walked beside me, with your long, black hair,
Tossed by those sweet gales in the autumn sun;
You inhaled the majestic wines of the redolent air,
Of roses, of grasses, of carmines and saffron.
We went to a picnic in a garden there,
Aside the brook, beneath the leafy, old trees,
Tall reeds wavered around your smooth, white knees,
As the ivory moon arose, full, round, and fair.
Then you tuned to me, ablaze, dreamy yet aware,
Of your love in a haze of ecstasies.

Your Mane, Your Eyes

Your ebony mane,
Surrounded by roses,
Touched by the rain,
In garden closes,
Wafting through red leaves
Bequeaths a sweet refrain,
To the cool and magical, brisk, autumn eves.

Your dark, brown eyes,
Surrounded by the ocean,
Touched by the skies,
Filled with emotion,
Gazing, foster mystic shrines,
A charming strain of bating sighs,
More sanctified than sacred wines.

Silhouettes

In the evening, the opaque rivulets
That sigh to the moonlight in scented flower beds
Produce a thick mist of grays and violets,
Amid silhouettes of leafy, dark reds.
The courses which they flow through are of slender grasses,
Ending in the starlit bay, not far from the statue's enchanting song,
Which grace the regal courts above,
Of deep, starry blues, of infinite love.

My Lady is Lovely

My lady is lovely, my lady is fair;
She walks in the noonday, glistening light
To the square, to the veranda, dreaming of the night,
In soft, saline breezes which sail through her hair,
Perfuming her tresses, gleaming in the sun.
She wanders amid the statuary,
Gathering blooms with delicacy,
Where slender, lavender brooklets run.
They are sweet and of the evening, gently do they glow,
Like rain upon the streams, which glitter as they flow;
She meditates on love alone, pining with a sigh.
And when the alabaster moon ascends, she strolls amid the ponds,
Beneath the fragrant boughs, beneath the minty-scented fronds.

Summer

When summer's emerald liveries
Are astounding in bloom,
And the forest's florid filigrees
Gleam beneath our balcony,
Below and beyond our palatial room,
We shall ride in a luxurious carriage,
Down the lane, into the country.
We shall rejoice within our band of marriage,

As we ferry past the breezes which swirl
Around leafy throngs of the lindens' silhouettes,
With a circular, scented whirl;
We shall inhale the gold of a red sunsets.

And when we reach the expansive, azure sea,
Beneath the turquoise arch of the splendid skies,
We shall love one another rapturously,
And I shall drown in the pendulous ocean
Of your dusky, delicious, Elysian eyes.

We shall abandon our united mind
And savor only profound emotion,
Immersed in our fiery passion
Of a lasting, tender kind.
Then, returning to our bastion,
The moon, of a liquid, pristine light,
Shall fall upon our balcony,
Beneath the lindens' emerald, soft sway,
With a wistful cadence, a wavering melody,
As it does in the sacred night,
As it does in the boons of the gleaming day.

A Walk After Painting

Our passion, tempered by the daylight,
Of the art room, where skins, wet with paint,
Scent the breeze from the window,
Pungent yet faint,
Awaits the raptures of the lovely night.
I shall undo your long, sweet, braided bows,
As we drink champagne where the sunlight glows.

Coloring like Van Gogh,
In the zenith of the summertime.

After we are done, we shall rove amid the purple vine,
Your soft, tender hand, gleaming, holding mine.
And as the slender, sobbing fountains ascend
Above the scented, green fronds that waver and bend,
We shall be caught in their pearly, silvery spray.
When the somnolent evening shall gently arrive,
Along with the bees and their buzzing hive,
We shall kiss in the dusk, as the fireflies stray.

An American Girl

She awakens on her bed
Of gold-rimmed pillows,
With fresh, scented, summery bows;
She showers and applies some delicate perfume
To the delicious nape
Of her fair, white neck.

Then, smoking in her bedroom,
She combs her long, black hair,
As the swimming pool outside her window
Receives the sweet, suburban air.

An Autumn Sunset II

Teeming, grand, vermilion waves,
Roll and ascend, descend and sigh,
Beneath the amber jades and blossoms,
Brushed against the twilit sky.
Each billow paves
A river in the sands,
Where little children wade,
Splashing at the brine,
With their tiny, little hands.

Like a princess you recline,
Beside me on the beach,
Grasping every star of silver and silk,
Within your tender, feminine reach.

The sunlight streams like mother's milk,
Iridescent, lutescent, beaming and gold,
As you close your gaze,
Slowly as you laze,
In the tender hold
Of the late summer haze.

Candles

The candles in our silent room,
Flicker like gold,
And lights from the past.
They celebrate the new, the present, the old,
And our soft affections which shall always last.
Your cheeks in bloom
Are of a lovely cast,
As I kiss you as the sun descends,
Outside our mansion, where the fleeced bough bends,
Sending us into raptures, timeless, and true.
The moon ascends majestically, into the endless, Orphic blue.

Epilogue II

And now, dear reader,
I have written my rhyme,
In a cloistered yard,
Beneath a redolent, leafy, summery cedar;
I have fulfilled in my time
The duties of a lifelong bard.

Enough of fair poetry,
Enough of chiseled verse,
Enough of the word, our mystic ruby,
Enough of the traveling high and low,
Throughout the varied realms of the universe;
Enough of sun, the rains, the snow.

Now I am free to freely go
Into a reticence called wisdom.

I shall laze by the sea,
In the solemn glory
Of another celestial kingdom.
And so I end my soliloquy.
Fini, fini, au revoir, fini.

VII

Ecstasy

Ecstasy

In the lavender glow of the nascent dawn,
When ecstasy reigns in the boughs of the square,
I shall bury my mouth in your raven hair,
As your fair, naked back sheds grace upon the lawn.

And in the dew, beside the silver fountain,
Among the statues in the autumnal rain,
I shall kiss your gleaming lips, again and again,
As thunderous billows crown the courtyard's mountain.

And as the sun peers through the elysian clouds,
Bequeathing to the colonnades a ravishing rose,
We shall behold paradise in our little garden close,
Beyond all earthy veils and worldly shrouds,
And when moonlight finds us—twain yet one,
Our souls shall have attained the bliss of the second sun.

An Angel's Song

We ventured out in the gray of night,
On amber furrows beneath the linden trees,
Where the breeze caressed your naked knees,
Smooth as a stream, kissed by the moonlight.
The fountains which sobbed in the marble square
Bequeathed to the brisk, aromatic air
A somnolence of grace, repose and song,
As I worshiped your black and braided hair,
Which sighed to the stars, mellifluous and long.

The Rose Garden

Where can we find a cove where love and lute
Are married to the strains of cello and flute,
Sheltered from the rains in our garments of white?
Let us walk to the courtyard basked in the moonlight!

And there, amid Cupid's statues of the square,
Where cormorants gleam in the sweet, summer air,
We shall encounter blooms of the redolent rose,
In the bliss of our secluded garden close.

And there, in our sanctuary of amorous play,
In a sanctified nook which no one else knows,
We shall love one another in the hazy day,
And wander through the dappled stream which glows
Like the tropical glimmer of a soft, sunny ray.
O, lead me astray where the lovely, fragrant zephyr goes!
And there, beneath the sobbing sculpture, struck by silver stars,
Which rise above the fountains, weeping to the sky,
I will hold you to my bosom, and kiss you as you sigh,
Surrounded by emerald mountains, and mellifluous guitars!

Love III

The morn is giving birth
To the dawn—yet to reign, still budding, undone.
Shall you play the earth,
And me the sun?—
Why not?—
Let us go, let us go
Where the blue currents run,
Now hither, now there, now high, now low,
Upon the lot
Of the breeze-caressed hill.
Let me kiss your sweet flesh of the daffodil,
And embrace you in the wakening glen.
And then, let me love you
In the succulent vineyards,
In the blooms of the hazy, yawning garden.
And there, beneath the greenish hue,
Of the quickening firmament,
Astonishing and bright,
Where lovers and bards
Succor in the sunlight
Nipples of crimson, lips of wine,
Beneath the fleecy willows bent,
Let our bodies unite
In the rapture of the sunshine,
Where sure delight
In yours and mine.

And the approaching rain
Shall find us—twain
In spirit and in flesh,
Indeed as one—
As the gray clouds mesh
With the scarlet sun.

Ladies and Men

The window box looks down below
To the avenue where young ladies pass
On concrete lands, next to patches of grass,
In the gilded gold of the summer's glow.

The apple cart, upon the street dips,
Topples over, and a crimson scent
Of fresh, ripe fruit, so very redolent,
Makes the young ladies pucker their lips.

The shopkeepers, the salesmen and the cops
Pretend not to notice when a neckline drops,
Nor to admire the softness of a lady's arms—
Just as women fake indifference each day
To the sight of muscular charms—
That masculine display.

For the female eye is always hungrier
Than any manly or bestial gaze;
With insatiable lust, they make sure to appear
To ascribe to proper ways
(While they secretly leer
At the menfolk all the nights and days.)

One blond coquette
With her parasol
Looks like a doll
In the luncheonette,
Smiling at a princely squire
Who as a gentleman
Must return the grin,
Whole, entire.

The Grave of Charles Baudelaire

Snug within your rainy cave,
There are stanzas which rise
From the grass of your grave.
Beneath the languid moon you hypnotize
The rare passersby
Who lay their fresh bouquets
Over six feet of earth,
Over the wooden casket in which you lie.
The lawn plays above you in the sunlight's summer rays.
And when no one is near your mouth gives birth
To a new protest, in spoken verse to the starry sky.
And when the stars are eclipsed by the darkness of the clouds,
You ascend from your crypt, strolling amid the burial shrouds,
Among the tombstones devoid of light,
Alive once more in this world you thought to be banal.
And you recite as a specter in the cryptic night,
Below the mysterious, haunting trees.

Les Fleur du mal
In the ghostly breeze.

Our Love

Our love was an ivory boon,
Which reigned with the angels in the night.
We would kiss beneath the moon,
Among the statues in the light.
But your death arrived too soon,
And so soared our felicity out of sight,
Which was once so gold, which was once so bright.

Now all that I can ponder,
All that I can see,
Is your fair face over yonder,
In a court of majesty,
Surrounded by slender, radiant fountains,
Where in a haze, you dream,
In the square beyond the mountains,
Lazing by a falling stream.

Scarlet Breezes II

Scarlet breezes swirl through the square,
Beckoning us to come
In bright, elysian fare.
A cello and a drum,
Clarinets and trumpets
Arise and stir and glitter in the fountain,
Around your sable ringlets,
In the cloister on the mountain.

There are diamond drops of rain
In your long and raven, perfumed mane.
Let us wander to the amorous refrain
Of violins by the ivory colonnade.
And there in there somnolent, redolent shade
I shall take your tender, fair, white hands,
Where only rapturous love commands,
As we rove among the blooms,
In the garden by the ocean,
Reveling in the deep emotion
Beneath our gilded palace,
And its grand, palatial rooms.

And I shall kiss your lovely face,
In a state of imperial, gracious grace,
To the chime of harps and wedding strains
Which will emanate from daisies, dahlias and the breeze,
From the chapels by the rustic lanes,
Beneath the golden linden trees.

The Bower

Beneath the rarefied glow of our castle's tallest tower,
As the burgeoning dawn was dawning,
In the soft and tender cradle
Of the spacious, florid bower.
Your repose was sweet,
As if your mind was drenched with wine,
Poured from The Shepherd's golden ladle.
You dreamt beside the white, wooden lattice
Where the sprawling vines meet,
Beside the stone wall, strewn with vine.
Your beauteous soul ascended twice:
Once to the massive, wavering oak trees;
And once, with rapture, over the crystal ice
Of the cozy, wintry pond,
Carried on the brisk, matin breeze.
And then for a third time,
Your spirit went beyond,
To the Cathedral's dome
As its bells did chime,
In the cloudless, hesperidia sky.
You transcended the aesthetic heights
Of Greece in its golden age, of Imperial Rome,
Before the coming of Germanic knights.
And your precious lips of red did sigh
With a languorous, emotive, plaintive cry,
Of ecstasy and passion. And bye and bye,
You longed for my kiss and the caress of my hand.
Your hair lay like diamonds upon the marble divan,
And its scented tresses released a rapturous command,
Over the corners of the florid bower,
Over every bloom on the snowy, gilded lawn.
And as midday ascended, leaving behind the gold celestial dawn,
The slender, blue brooks, with a sacred harmony
Burst through their icy borders,
And overflowed upon the drowsy reeds,

Ecstasy and other Poems

The dahlias and the corianders,
Rushing to the feathery meads
Glistening like jewelry in the fantastic, pearl-white sun.
Then your sable gaze and the light became one,
As you awoke like an angel from your soft, sweet slumber.
You drank in the diamond stars of the hydra,
Of an innumerable number,
And every other blessed gift which the noonday umbra
Was pleased to bestow
To your lovely gaze,
Surrounded by the oaks and the oleanders,
Which glimmered in the cloister's glittering glow.
And in the wistful dusky gems of your waking haze,
More magnificent than each of the world's Cassandras,
And filled with silvery-blue cascades,
You took my hand and bequeathed to me
In your state of beauteous, blinding bliss
A wonderful, warm, womanly kiss
As I raised you, embracing, from the marble divan.
The saffron reeds awoke, half-dreaming and wan,
Stretching their heads, indolently pale,
Releasing Burgundies, Port and ale.

We strolled slowly down the stone-paved trail,
In a soporific, languishing, alabaster mist,
At one with the velvet veil
Which is the essence of heaven, the crown of our tryst.
And in that Cupid's halcyon, Cyprian breeze
We fell into another well,
Lost in our felicitous, romantic spell,
Of sanctified, sacred ecstasies.
And as the cherubim sang,
In the northern distance
A church bell rang,
Clad with soft, auriferous snow.
It chimed high and low,

Ecstasy and other Poems

To the glories of the mountains,
To the glistening, sunlit fountains,
To our reticent cloister, here below.
And we passed as god and goddess
Beneath a towering colonnade,
As we walked to the bower's rosy edge,
Upon the sunlit promenade,
To the heights of the florid ledge
Of the flowery cornice,
More beautiful than dreams,
Adorned with wines,
Cool to the taste, melting from the streams
Of mellifluous, floating, delicious ice
Descending over the cliff to the sea,
Beneath the massive, swaying pines,
Which rumble so majestically.

To My Future Bride

I am faint with love.

                                                                                 The Song of Songs

Come, my lover, come to me!—
To the sandy glade beside the rose-clad sea,
Where the blossoms of my perfumes master thee!—
Come, my lover, come to me!

Let our sighing hearts be of one accord.
Let our kisses be of fire!
Let us give ourselves, each to the other,
With the solemn blessing of The Lord.
And before we are breathless, ablaze in desire,
Let us thank sweet Jesus and His Blessed Mother,
For gracing our embraces
With ecstasy in the realm of the dove,
As the sun upon our faces
Instills within our eyes
Elysian visions from the highest realm above.

Come to me, my lover, my love!
We have raised the sea and have vanquished the skies!

Ecstasy and other Poems

My Eternal Beloved

I cannot let go
Of the woman I have seen,
With long, black, wavy hair,
In sanctified visions, soft, serene.

I cannot walk away
From her dark, brown, raven eyes
Where mystic courtyards dwell,
Where slender, silver fountains rise.

A blond hair beauty
Would not be her.
Nor would be a red haired queen.
I know the very spirit of my only, cherished love.
It is of cinnamon, vanillin dreams and eglantine.
It is of rapturous streams of shaded, purple wine,
Of paradise above.

Her hands are of ivory,
Her face is white and fair.
I am destined to deny
All other angels who breeze blown rove
In the worldly mosaic of the summery air.
My God, my God, how I shall sob and cry
Until I have kissed her in a sovereign, majestic, sacred lair.

My God, my God, deliver to me soon,
This ineffable radiant saint of the skies,
Who possesses the rain, the sun, the moon
Sable symphonies of dew,
Holy rhapsodies of sighs.

I cannot let go
Of the woman I have seen,
With long, black, wavy hair,
In sanctified visions, soft, serene.

I cannot walk away
From her dark, brown, raven eyes
Where mystic courtyards dwell,
Where slender, silver fountains rise.

Romance II

I love the heart of all romance,
It must be of the sacred brook,
It must be of the eternal dance.
It must be of her sable, raven look,
And of mine returning purity for purity.
Romance is love and love is romance.
It is of the azure, gleaming stream,
It is glory beyond all ecstasy.
It transcends all pines, all wines, all loftiness,
It is not a fabled, windy dream.
And when one is immersed in its ineffable caress,
When diamonds are donning her wedding dress,
The sun and the stars rise merely to greet
Yet another night where lips do meet.

A Garden in Paradise

I took her hand beneath the quivering diamond trees
Which shook their humans upon us in the warm, October sun.
We found paradise in the glades beneath our naked knees
As flute and horn, wistful and fantastic
Swept through the redolent, scarlet breeze,
Near azure brooks which forever run
Through valley and dale, mellifluous and majestic
Gracing reeds with currents that shine in gilded, diamond rays.
(I love my bride, and her angelic ways.)
The ocean nearby, beyond the alabaster statuary,
Rises with the tide and caresses the purple rocks,
As she reclines on a marble bench with gracility,
Dreaming in her mystic trances, caressing her raven locks.
And the sunset sighs as the fountains rise
To the nascent stars which languishing, hover,
Over the vast and silent courtyards,
As she speaks of things with her sanctified eyes,
To her handsome, young lover,
To her passionate bard.
And our kisses are of ivory nights,
When moonlight sobs, when candle lights
Illuminate the astonishing bower.
Come walk with me, my love, it is the hour
When all seraphs sing their hymns from above.
Come walk with me, my lover, my love!

Ecstasy and other Poems

I Ventured Out Beneath the Moon

I ventured out beneath the moon, full, white and round.
My boots broke the sheets of snow as I walked with the muse, my guide.
I approached the ocean and its starry, azure tide.
The breeze blew through my mind, yet I heard not a sound.

Then an angel arose, like a Siren on the waves.
Like a beautiful Phoenix, she came to me,
To take my soul beyond the skies, beyond the wild sea,
To eternal vistas, to shimmering, diamond enclaves.

I ascended to a rushing stream,
Beyond the realm of time, beyond the illusion of a dream.
There I was welcomed by a gilded ball.

My love stood in a vestibule, and I heard the voice of God.
I had passed beyond the prison of earth, and though it might seem odd,
I found myself at home, loved by one and all.

Ode to Edgar Allan Poe I

The tall, rained tower, by the sea of sable wine,
Where silver stars alight, in the moonless night,
Is the seat of a raven which rarely takes flight;
Its dark eyes look down on the scorpions of the brine.

With each chilling breeze that poison billows carry
From dusky, northern currents of the half-swallowed pier,
Heard in the dreadful hall, where heads and horror marry,
Are whispers of the dead beneath a swinging chandelier.

A skeletal sister clutches for a face
In the blackness of the castle's most deserted place,
Wrought by the hand of madness, not ended.

In the screaming, wild wind, from splintered coffins wail the damned;
The raven wraps his talon around the weird sister's hand.
All this is Poe—his hells have all ascended!

On My Way to Boston

Marigolds sway behind the vine-clad lattice.
I stroll on my way to Boston, drinking from a chalice.
The winds are from the north, and my lady awaits
For the gift of my verse, and a new bouquet.
There are many white sails drifting in the bay.
Some ferry up the river as the sunlight abates.
I shall call for my love at the end of the day,
And take her to my wooden carriage.
We shall kiss among its cushions of white,
And speak of love and sanctified marriage.
And when arrives the violet skies of night
We shall ride through Harvard and Beacon Hill,
And every poem she reads of mine
Shall fill her bosom with a redolent sunshine,
More tender than the daffodil.

The Outer Darkness

I ventured out one Godless, bitter night,
And looked up, astonished, to see no stars on high.
Winds rose and froze ponds and wells, and without a cloud in sight,
I fell into the firmament, into the cold, abysmal sky.

Despair in the air of damnation reined with might.
I saw tombs and caskets filled with cobwebs and bones.
The reeds I found were dry, of deathly pale tones.
And I was alone, abandoned, devoid of hope, all light!
My feet wreathed with thorns rustled in those prickly vines,
Where waves of blood like poison brines
Swept the coal-black grass bereft of all love.
Horror governed all below me and terror reigned above.

Beyond reconciliation, I broke a sepulcher with my head.
Now forever do I weep, gnashing my jaw,
For to my pitiable anguish, in an ecstasy of awe,
I am in the outer darkness—dead!

The Acropolis

Colonnades of white, erected by the sea,
Clad with many towering vines,
Cradle the arched temple splendidly,
Where one breathes in the wind of wines.

Athena walks with golden hair,
By hedgerows of green,
In the summer air,
Passing through the world unseen.

And with every path she paces on,
A redolent, wafting, delicious scent
Is rendered to the Parthenon,
And to every fragrant bough that is bent.
As her servants, invisible, duly rise
To the realm of Zeus, in the azure skies.

Of a Dark-Eyed Lady

I ventured out in the dew at dawn,
To the florid countryside,
Walking on an emerald lawn,
Dreaming of a youthful bride.

There brooks of blue,
Lit by the sun,
Ran flowing through
Gardens and glades, one by one,
In the scented boon
Of amaranthine shades,
I discovered at noon:—
Forested promenades!

I came upon a marble square,
Where a princess roved, with sable hair!
(She was dressed in a lovely, ancient style.)
There were rhapsodies in her diamond eyes,
And moonbeams in her smile.

Then the rays of amber sunlight,
Ascended with a redolent breeze,
As our impassioned sighs
Reached their flowery height
In the canticles of the turquoise skies,
In the cello of our ecstasies.

Of She Whom I Love

Her hair is wavy, black and long;
Her gazes are of wine, and of a sailor's song.
She prays to the Virgin, in the courtyard of the church,
And petitions eternal love, before a shrine below the birch.

She praises what is holy; she is faithful and secure.
Of lovely things she muses on; she is humble in her dress.
She awaits a man of virtue; she dreams of his caress,
As she walks among the statues; her thoughts are sacred—pure.

Her countenance is double fair;
It is of an angelic, pristine white;
She hides from the world, with a regal air.
Her heart and mind are filled with vespers of delight.
She keeps to herself; she is sparing in speech.
Her scent is of a queen, and of the blossoming peach.

Her Melody

I can hear it still.—
Languorously sighing, wistful and fair,
Her melody, through the autumnal air,
Carried over vases and vines,
Sprawling over the window sill,
Down the wall—to eglantines.
Melodically, it summons my will.

I can see her still.—
Caressing whites and ebonies,
In rhythmic time,
Gazing on the daffodil,
Atop her piano's flowing keys.
Her strain still sails like mint and thyme—
And whispers only ecstasies.

A Melody

What wafting mist over the meadow plays?
What tune arises from the greenery?—
It is soft and sweet, of a rhapsody,
And lends such feeling in the morning haze.
It is tempered by love, a calm desire.
It glides along the moss, ethereal,
Approaching the house, and its portico,
Taking on the hues of a tepid fire.
Why seeks it my heart from its matin dew?—
Why does it come through the curtains with grace,
Painting a vision of your lovely face,
When I pondered I saw the last of you?—
Why this melody that wavering arose
From the gentle sway of the grassy glen
Brings forth a bouquet of a scented rose
That lingers around the colonnade, and then
Enters through the long, sunlit sashes
To rest among the busts of statues
As the sky above the meadow, of china blues,
Also enters, along with the ashes
Of my memories of you, angelic and young.
Your black mane parted, your brown eyes gleaming
Has wrought this rapture, this song that is sung.
And all the rays of the sun are beaming,
All the flowers below the terrace are in bloom
In this symphony which engulfs the room
And speaks of your name as the golden light
Strikes the spires above, as it does at night.

The Black Baby Grand

The black baby grand,
Caressed by a slender fingers,
By a young, red-haired's fair, small hand,
(With her russet curlicues in a bow.)
Emits cadences that languishing, lingers
From the royal nook of the lady's parlor,
Where she gazes through the stained-glass window
Upon the florid, turquoise harbor;
(A wave ascends, then reels,
Circling down to the watercress.)
Her patrician dress
(One might confess.)
While modest, reveals
Her soft, lavish knees,
Where lilac-scented harmonies
Ring from that medieval chamber,
Out into the garden below,
Through the half-open, blueish panes,
Where the daisies, slumbering, waver
Now to and fro, now high, now low,
Kissed by those amber, ghostly strains.

A Walk in the Square

On a stone-paved path, obscured by mist,
Your flesh smells of roses, dew and thyme,
As your cherry-hued lips are softly kissed.—
The breezes here are redolent with rhyme.

Let us bask in the shade,
Where canticles weave
Among an ivory colonnade,
New, matin hymns of you.
In the vast, marble square,
By a gleaming brook of Sahara blue,
We shall take sweet breaths in the soft, spring air
Where bending boughs conceive
Slender silhouettes on the sallow field
In the fair, ethereal, solemn eve
Where your succulent perfections yield
The redolent shades of heavenly gold—
And the visual paradise I behold:
Your pristine face, touched by the sun,
And your raven tresses, clasped as one,
In braids which make me tremble and sigh,
Beneath the boundless, russet sky.

A Walk With My Love

Come, my love, let us kiss, and let us take
A walk in the wood, beneath the emerald pines.
Let us inhale the good, heady, wintry wines,
Under white, misty boughs which the larks' wings shake.

Come, my lover, let us dream and let us go
On frozen paths of silence, lined with stone,
To the alabaster court, where we can rove alone,
Through chilly, brisk gales which toss the snow.

And when the nascent moon grieves
Upon the smooth, bright, glistening land,
I shall collect your tresses and its braids in the palm of my hand,
And inhale their perfumes among the fallen leaves.

The Muse

I shall leave the city, the bustling town.
I shall walk to the outskirts of the wild plains,
And drink from heaven mystic rains,
Lying in the reeds, drunk upon the down.

My shoes are worn, of coats I have one.
I am a martyr of the furrows and the fields at play.
I live for adventure and the brilliant, gilded, golden day,
Come the weeping moon, or the soporific, gleaming sun.

I have in my pocket a notebook I keep.
I wield it come the dawn, along with my flask.
I compose florid verse, a vagabond's task,
Beneath the blue sky where the angels sleep.
I drink my wine after rhyme and prose,
In the flowery cradle of a garden-close.
I am struck by visions beside the lane,
On warm, autumn nights, at one with the rain.

I take my dreams for what they are:
The flow of ethereal, lavender seas,
Which rise to every astonishing star,
Swallowing their ecstasies.

I hallucinate when rainbows pass.
I am a symbolic, a saint.
My pages are my canvass.
My stanzas are my paint.

O, muse, I have been faithful to you!—
On trains, on foot, in poverty,
I have brought down the sky and raised the sea!
I have resurrected gold to its rightful hue!

As an alchemist I have perceived the wondrous blending
Of blue and red gems in unions never-ending.
I am the world's greatest scholar:

Ecstasy and other Poems

All mysteries are known to me.
The forest is my exquisite parlor;
The firmament: Infinity!

Every brook is romantic; all my kisses are of fire.
My lover's name is Mary; there is music in the marvelous sun!
To paradise I aspire,
To the bliss of everyone!

Ecstasy and other Poems

I Walked with Byron

I walked with Byron in the regal sun,
To the chime of his lordly laughter.
We spoke of our time on earth as the sea
Kissed our ruddy faces with delicious brine.
Then soon after
He softly said to me:
"Let us drink our fill of mystic wine!"
So we went to the garden, ornate with the vine,
And besides a charming trellis of white,
We dipped our carafes into the glistening well,
And our minds became enlightened with light.
He was in a poetic mood, and I could tell
That he wished to recite
Some verse from his books.
We reclined among the silver brooks,
And O, with what rhapsodies his lines did sail!
She walks in beauty was fine, but alas!
He spoke with the voice of Christ as a breeze did pass,
And his rhyme was like the rapture
Of the bright, midday moon's marvelous, misty veil
Which enclosed us there and did softly capture
My heart and my soul as I heard his song.
His words dripped like honey,
And my heart did long
For the beauty
Of the maiden which graced his every line,
Which was carried on scented zephyrs of blue.
For he praised my love, and her soft, sable eyes.
He praised her parted mane, and its raven hue.
And as we sipped our wine
His verse ascended to the celestial skies,
With the broad, bright wings of an angelic flight.
Then came the eglantine,
The spell of the radiant rose,
And the fresh mignonettes of the nascent night.

Ecstasy and other Poems

And after he was done,
His violet book did softly close
As the setting, saffron, splendid sun
Left me in awe of his rhyme and his prose.

He anointed my brow with still more wine,
And we walked amidst the flowing, slender streams,
Each living for the other.
And we lost ourselves in splendid dreams,
As friend and brother,
Amid the dappled, succulent shade,
Beneath the brilliant, English ivory
Of an English colonnade.
And in that majestic umbrage
Of purple boundless beauty,
Of beatitude and silent light,
We felt the youth of our eternal age
Blend softly with the canticles
Of the beauteous, blossoming, silvery night.
And we rejoiced over our former manacles
Which once possessed our heart and mind
With darkness and moments of a lasting kind.
For every tear that was shed upon that weary orb of blue
Has become a wreath of laurel!
(And the same, dear reader, shall be for you!)
Then we gave thanks beneath the emerald, sorrel
Trees of willows, dappled oranges and yew.
And before he left me, he whispered into my ear,
With the inflection of a sigh,
Which the night alone did hear:
"When poverty had you, it was I my friend, yes I
Who came in disguise and bought you that beer."

Epilogue III

Once upon a time, if I remember right,
I knew suffering upon the earth,
And was well acquainted with the night.
Now every diamond dawn gives birth
To a flurry of radiant, scarlet flowers.
In the courtyard by my bastion,
My lady and I rove joyfully through the bowers,
Which are one with the spacious, marble square.
Immersed in the realms of peace and passion,
We hold one another's hand in the aromatic air.
And in our infinity
Every grand, gilded rose
Speaks of only beauty,
As my maiden's petals softly unclose.
In Nomine Patris et Filii et Spiritus Sancti
Amen.

XIII

Elysian Meadows

Introduction

It is profoundly imperative to live a poet's life in order to compose true verse. One must embrace a poverty of spirit, combined with a sense of never being nor feeling quite at home in this world of ours. As a lifelong poet, I speak from empirical knowledge, and if one would ask me which intangible ingredient is the most important to possess in order to live out the poet's vocation, that would be the love of service.

For the poet's calling is to that of serving his fellow men and women in a manner in which he expects nothing in return, save the knowledge that his art is beneficial to his readers; beneficial in the sense that the poet is able to relate through words the common joys and sorrows of humanity in a way that confirms to the reader that he or she is not alone; that definitive happiness is our eternal end, that all our lives have a special meaning, and that we did not evolve from a soulless void.

~John Lars Zwerenz

Elysian Meadows

The First Sonnet

She is from France, there are roses in her hair.
She leans calm, pristine, against the wall of the church,
Beneath soft, white willows and chestnut colored birch.
Her lips glisten in the sun, russet, warm and fair.

She arrived from stony chambers, over the sea,
Where she was raised a princess in her father's court.
Who taught her reverence from hardship and majesty.
She is angelic in her ways, a dreamy sort.

And when the sky turns sad, gleaming with gray and blue,
She is clad in a pea coat, lost in reverie.
And she turns her sable head, graceful towards me.
(The stars sob with light, tender, filled with rue.)
And she alights like a ghost from the marble divan,
To walk upon the fields, so hopeful, old and wan.

Elysian Meadows

The Autumn Lane

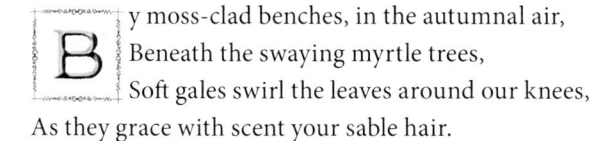

By moss-clad benches, in the autumnal air,
Beneath the swaying myrtle trees,
Soft gales swirl the leaves around our knees,
As they grace with scent your sable hair.

And as we trod upon the wooded lane,
At one with the rising, sallow sun,
Harpsichords play, uniting us as one,
In the lush, sweet song of the misty rain.

And as I lavish upon your russet lips
A buss of passion, laced with thyme,
We compose a flowing sonnet of rhyme.

And the moon, half hidden from our gaze,
Transforms into radiant rays as it dips,
Lauding our love and its sacred ways.

Elysian Meadows

Billowing Reeds

The folding ivory, Orphic ocean
Sobs as it rises
With shy, azure-blue, somnolent disguises,
Evoking, with its waves, an amorous emotion.

Indistinct, a billow plays
Upon the swept-back reeds,
Which makes one dizzy,
In the late afternoon, summery haze.

Below the sky the sun sets through the trees,
With a solemn, silver majesty.
And you, beside me, on beds of hay,
Of tall, wavering grasses
Look upon the piers of the jetty,
As the thyme-scented breeze
Sighs as it passes,
In the dying reds of the summer's day.

Then the evening with its mysteries
Covers like a velvet veil
The hovering, foggy stars, the moonlight, pale,
And the distant, glowing bars of campfires.

Then, rising with the warm, carmine winds,
Beneath the airy, green cloaks of tamarinds,
Your feminine desires,
Your feminine needs,
Become one with the swallowing, hungry sea,
As you recline in the reeds,
Gazing at me.

Elysian Meadows

The Black Concerto

The dark keys resigned
Upon the torrid harpsichord,
Determined to destroy—disdained
By the composer who begged The Lord
To be free from the horror; Devoid of light,
The firmament sobbed in the Godless night,
And wept upon the face of the tortured bard
Who beckoned as he played,
Revolted at the sight
Of the crypt in his yard,
To where his black mind strayed.

He pleaded and pined,
As the demons dined,
For his love, for his wife,
For a dim, dying star
From his happy, former life—
As the last pyre expired from the final bar.

Then the curtains met with snow
In the solitary room,
Revealing as they wavered in the horrid glow
Of his destiny captured
In his funeral's gloom;

And the player fell, enraptured,
In an ecstasy of pain—
And the night consumed his psyche, utterly insane,
As a demon laughed at his soul—forever undone.

And no sympathetic bell
From a church saw the sun,
As the sunless sun fell
Through the leafless trees,
To the tune of a deadly, baleful breeze.

Elysian Meadows

The Cloister II

Scented with myrrh, emerald and moonlit,
The silent temple of the cloister's blooms
Enraptures us as one, solitary spirit,
Outside of our mansion's curtained rooms.
Amid white statues and sprawling eglantines,
How sweet all life does seem.
The evening's hues upon the vines
Instill within our minds a dream.
And as the hours slowly pass, my love,
I hear cadences from oboes and cello,
Distant, distinct, sanctified and mellow,
As a sweet, scented breeze
Graces our naked knees
From the linden trees above.

Your song is a compelling, melodious flower,
Which wavers gently through the alabaster parlor,
On autumn afternoons when the piano is caressed
By soft, slender hands, resplendently dressed.
With the liberties of summer, glowing and gold,
The myrtle-scented breezes outside renew the old,
As they swirl around the oak trees with a misty, leafy ring,
Absorbing the lutescent sunlight,
Amid bending, bright boughs, wavering.
Your fingers of white
Upon the ebony keys
Breed a manifold delight, a mosaic of rapture,
As your halcyon fragrance reaches out to capture
From beneath your pretty, naked knees
A poet and a sage.

What symphonies bleed in this timeless age
Down the wall of vines,
Of stucco, terra-cotta and violet wines!
Your rhapsodies
Are as zephyrs which languishing flee

Elysian Meadows

To the redolent seas
Of ecstasy.

And after your recital in the vast music hall,
We shall wander on the grass,
As the tender hours gently pass,
Like sunlight on the vine-clad wall.
We shall picnic on the verdant lawn,
And your hair, of a dreamy, summer dawn,
Parted in the middle, shall on your shoulders lay,
Long, straight and raven, darker than the night.
And beholding such a beauteous sight,
I shall be rendered mute as a work of clay.
And I shall love you there beneath that Kendal-green tree,
As you gaze upon the conservatory,
And its lily-white chasm
With liquid-filled eyes,
Struck with a fair, delicious spasm
Beneath the absinthe-tinted skies.

Elysian Meadows

The Duchess

What did I find in a snow-clad grove of pines,
More gilded than gold, beneath a bending, emerald bough,
Which brought an excess of joy, more than earth does allow,
More serene than a pond, more mellifluous than wines?—

Half-sleeping, upon a marble divan, swept by the wintry air,
I found a rosy-eyed duchess reclining in that scented land.

She possessed the gaze of a portrait graced by God's benevolent hand,
As breezes laced with mignonette touched her sacred, raven hair.

What did I find within the woolly softness of her greenish, watery, youthful stare?
A royal haven for a princely poet roving through a cold December.

She wore a ring from the House of David, and was clothed in the finest fur.
Then she gave me her hand to kiss. I knelt in the pearly snow, in that good, majestic air,
Above all splendor, above the glory of all arts.
And we walked betrothed, like two leaves, lifted high upon a wondrous gale.
Ave Maria, Ravisher of Hearts!
And Holy Catholic Heaven, Hail!

The Garden II

In the golden tuft of the morning flower,
In the delicacy of spring, in the fragrant hour,
When green boughs sing in the florid bower,
We shall wander by the yew trees,
By the rolling, blue stream,
And inhale the many symphonies
Which lead us to dream
Of a wedding in the sun,
Where we, as lovers, hand in hand,
Shall become evermore as one
As a mystic rose,
Within the glistening garden-close.
A sanctified and sacred band,
United beneath a canopy of lights
Shall take us to where rare candlelights
Are lit in the borders of the bright enclosure.
Beneath paradisal heights
Where our ardor is secure,
We shall fathom our eternal bond
Amid the lilacs of the azure square,
And I shall kiss your lips and roving hair,
Glimpsing realms beyond
That wistful garden there.
Then with a whisper, the Mycenae breeze
Called me back to the port, to the song of the seas,
Where I sat in a garden next to the harbor,
In a wistful arbor
Of ecstasies.

Elysian Meadows

Ghost Ship

Every hand on deck had faith in his sword,
Every hand on deck that climbed aboard
A ship that left Boston in a swirling snow.
In three days' time it attained the open sea.
And all hands on deck met their destiny
In the abyss of The Atlantic, in its dark billows below.

The schooner was tossed upon the waves
Like a mad, orphaned cork dancing on the blue terrain.
Its wheel turned blindly, assailed by wild rain,
Until the water was stilled over its graves.

Then silent as a whisper, a skeletal clutch
Took the helm and turned the ship to the east.
A malevolent guest, this mysterious beast
Reveled in the deaths which felt his touch:
The last thing they knew before the mad sea
Swallowed their bones so adamantly.

And in some days' time the ship arrived in Spain
Where eager sailors got on board
To take to Boston their gold and grain—
And every hand on deck had faith in his sword.

Elysian Meadows

The Grave of Arthur Rimbaud

Among the cryptic, emerald darnel that plays,
In the umbrage where wavering lindens scent
Tall grasses and reeds, slender and bent,
An alabaster tombstone slowly decays.

And there, asleep, beneath the sun above,
You, bohemian wayfarer, cradled in your crate,
Smile as the sun shines upon the ghosts that love,
Tormented by fire within the graveyard's gate.

As an eternal poet you take your purgatory well,
For you lived with anguish for a forty year spell,
And so you slumber as the flames consume your sins.
(The dour moon arises, and the doleful night begins.)
And in the dark, a fresh bouquet is laid upon the dewy grass.
By me, Rimbaud, your prodigy!—Your pains shall surely pass!

Elysian Meadows

The Graveyard

The tombstones were covered with a dense, gray fog.
A white mausoleum and a nebulous bog
Greeted my apprehensive gaze
With grim, dreadful, wayward, wanton ways,
As I proceeded down the cobblestone lane.
The cemetery was vast, and the cold, autumn rain
Pelted the grass; and the caskets below
Became soaked by the brine as a few flakes of snow
Fell upon my overcoat and my longish hair.
I thought I saw a wraith, a ghost,
Leap into the amber air
In the fit of a languorous, lewd despair.
(He was a dark and grisly host.)
"Why do you walk in the land of the dead?" —
He said in a way that chilled my skin.
"Do you wish to cross The Acheron in the living state that you're in?"
"Yes," I replied, "For every true bard is off his head.
And since I have had enough of the world outside,
I have changed my address. It is here I reside."
At that he left me, alone, amid the graves,
Where sobriety set in, amid the stark
Shadows of this hallowed pair,
Where the boon of darkness truly saves.

Elysian Meadows

The Grove I

Far from the cities, the towns,
The statues in the square,
I strolled to a grove of chestnut browns;
Butterflies glimmered in the summer air.

There were gourds which gleamed
Where I beheld the gods of old;
Hermes and Osiris appeared in garments of gold,
And in the rays of Phoebes I dreamed.

Ascending with the tremulous stars came Artemis;
I laid my head in the dew-clad grain.
I awoke to the moon, and strolled down a rustic lane.
I passed by the viny lattice of a wooden trellis.

Suddenly a storm arose, consuming the wild sky;
Fair, beloved Iris commingled with my muse,
And with a rhapsody of varied hues,
Painted bowers within my verse,
Until my inkwell went dry.

Elysian Meadows

One Hallowed Eve

The ashen clouds race,
Thrown forth by tepid winds in the skies,
To amber, southern fields,
Over the hills, where angels pace.

I am at one with your dusky, raven eyes.
The soft perfume your body yields
Blends with the redolent breeze
Which ferries through the linden trees,
In the silence of the hallowed eve.

All willowy boughs begin to grieve.
And winter soon shall take the summer's place.
In nights such as these
I find your face
To be at one with ecstasies.

Elysian Meadows

Love IV

I laze on the beach, careless,
Eyes full of the infinite.
Onto faraway places in time!
The white billows, breathless,
Cease to interpret
All nature, her benevolence,
Her malevolence,
Her crime.
I shall be in the world's greatest academic.
I shall turn my windy sophistries,
All scented with the dancing muse,
Into a gilded polemic,
Into rubies in June.
I shall infuse
A new global awareness
Of what is truly holy and good.
And of what is truly evil and bad.
I am Tom Thumb, a dreamer lad,
Who lives in the woods,
Relishing its bareness,
Blinded by the brooks that meander in the sun,
Struck with visions staring drunk at the moon.
With all of nature's secrets I am one.
There are no more mysteries to uncover.
I stroll beyond the ogive to where the lindens hover.
And I lose myself in every boon.

Elysian Meadows

Lady of the Bastion I

She slowly brushes back her long, sable tress,
Casually smoking in her grand, palatial room,
Gazing on her bower where the roses are in bloom,
Donning in the blossoming eve an alabaster dress.

The mountain to the south of her bastion
Speaks to her of many a romantic thing:
A troubadour might present to her a nuptial ring,
Before the dawn, in chivalric fashion.

And in the scarlet fragrance of the rapturous nights,
She walks among the statues in the marble square,
Where splendid fountains rise in the summery air,
Pining as she pines, supplicating the heavenly heights.
And I have seen her wandering there—
My future bride of love and lights,
Sighing a sigh of ardent bliss,
In the leafy shades of longing where I witness
The hope of a pure and sanctified kiss
From the lips of this woman, my goddess.

Elysian Meadows

In the Summer She Paces

In the summer she paces on the promenade,
Among the blooms of the enclave in the garden.
She gazes on the distant grasses of the glen,
Walking in the breezes of the cool, fragrant shade.

And when perfumes of the park flow through her hair,
She pines for the dark and a kiss beneath the fronds.
In the sanctuary of the vast, marble square,
She roves among the roses, and the blue, scented ponds.

Her heart is liberal, she is courteous and kind.
The garden's blooms entrance her eyes, and fill her mind
With dreamy thoughts of night, and boons of the season.

She strolls in the moonlight, consumed with only love.
She sings to the blue jays in the tall trees above.
And she lauds God alone, the crown of her reason.

The Palace II

Roving on the bright, spacious lawn of the palace,
I have come to behold the lady clad in white,
Who steps onto the balcony in the bold sunlight.
I stand below entranced, drinking gold from a chalice.

Amid the gray cast of ancient stone she appears,
As a breeze blows back the long tresses of her hair.
I am drunk with quatrains and the summery air,
With my lady and with wine, with regal belvederes.
Many billows from God are flung to the north.

The silhouettes of basswoods, of dark, turquoise-blues
Shed their shadows near the palace, on broad avenues.
Descending from the terrace, my lady comes forth,
And we wander for a rapturous hour,
As I finish my Chablis,
Through the garden, through the bower,
In an atmosphere of sanctity.

Elysian Meadows

The Queen

I roved among the fields and furrows.
I was tan in the sun of the golden day.
At the end of the my trail, at the edge of the meadows,
I found a blue pond, enclosed with hay.

Tall, yellow reeds wavered and swayed,
And fragranced the wafting, summer breeze,
Sailing like honey through the linden trees,
Blessing the courtyard there where I stayed.

Suddenly a queen ascended from the bowers,
In a garment of carmine and glistening white.
Her mane was raven, splendid, long and bright,
And her eyes were of a song which poured wine upon the flowers.

Her gaze was one of a statue's: deep, dark and grave.
Her lips were of Elysian woods, soft, red and glossy with scent.
I knelt before her, beneath the fronds, green and redolent.
She stood there in silence; although her tresses did lave
Blue, caressing gales, which came from the ocean.
We knew naught but ardor and its every emotion.
And the pond was struck with a gust from above.
She took my hand in hers, and accepted my love;
And as if in a dream,
We passed through a curtain, an ethereal light,
By a silver stream,
Beneath the full, starry moon,
White, round and pale,
Which eclipsed the trees, the courts and the lagoon,
Leaving us to the breezy sea,
As we departed from this weary old vale—
To a rapturous height of ecstasy.

Elysian Meadows

One Sacred Night

Where breezes grace leaves, in the solemn grove,
Through boughs and blooms, touched by the sun,
We wander through the dales, as lovers, as one,
Dreaming in trances, as vagabonds rove.

And in the somnolent depths of the sacred night,
When fountains in the courtyard sob and sigh,
To majestic blues in the glittering sky,
Bestowing to the statues a radiant and silver light,
Your gaze of amber, sable and soft
Graces my own, rising aloft
To paradisal heights as we kiss and embrace
As only regal angels know
In the sumptuous, white glow
Of the moon's adoring, crystal face.

Elysian Meadows

The Shade

Music permeates the late afternoon.
The shadows where you walk in are bathed in felicity,
In contrast with the dazzling daylight,
Above the myrtles rises the solitary moon,
With a languishing solemnity,
Preparing for the sacred night.
Your hair, raven and long, frames your fair face,
As all scents combine about your body and your dress.
The sighing umbrage is an amorous place,
Where you lean against the bough for a kiss and a caress.
Beneath a cloak of somnolent leaves,
Your beauty commands these autumn eyes.
And you leave me speechless as I behold
Your tresses of dusk, your gazes of gold.

The Sky is so Blue

The sky is so blue, so pure, and soft.
My dreamy mind ascends, gently, aloft.
The breeze stirs the boughs above my head,
As I recline in the dahlias of a flower bed,
In a vast, majestic courtyard, ringed with mountains,
Where tall, ivory statues glitter among the fountains.
And around their slender, slivery spray,
Beneath the lindens, bowed and bent,
A princess wanders in the golden day,
With raven eyes, and long, black hair,
Which lends its lovely, scarlet scent
To the wafting wind, in the summer air.

Elysian Meadows

Song of Your Love

The song of your love
Is of branches, of leaves,
Of flowery sprays,
Of Victorian eves.

Your sonata of the sea
Calls to me
With a sonorous voice
Of felicity.
And I have no choice
But to run to you,
My sable haired princess
Who hath possessed me so.
Our mutual reverence
Shall take wings and grow,

In the sacred silence
Of the garden-close.
And our kisses shall sanctify
The mystical rose.

The song of your love
Is of branches, of leaves,
Of flowery sprays,
And Victorian eves.

Elysian Meadows

The Square

T he jets of the fountain sob with ecstasy,
In the vast, marble courtyard, graced with statues of white.
A stream there flows for our delight,
As the sunshine exalts all solemnity.

And the emerald lindens which wavering, rise
To the lavender-tinted, weeping skies
Clothe the many florid boughs
As paradise allows
A glimpse for us to see
Into the boundless realm of infinity.

Starlit Night

Y our voice is dreamy, sad, like canticles of old,
Taciturn, like us, weavers of the rhyming word.
In the somnolence of the park, it can be heard,
Sifting through the branches, pensive and gold.

Yet your heart is young, and of an elevated air.
Sweet in your slumber, you dream without care,
In a lavender peace, my fair, exquisite one,
In a billowing tuft of leaves, redolent, of the setting sun.
Let us hold each other's hand in the Elysian gray.

Of the vague and nebulous starlit night,
And rove by the terra-cotta mansions in the moonlight.

Every rapturous thought, sea-borne, of the wind,
Rushing through bramble, reeds and the tamarind,
Shall said through our romantic minds, like twilit chardonnay.

Elysian Meadows

To Mary I

The willows sway, slowly,
Over the sea,
With a rapturous, solemn sanctity.
You vanquish me with one
Glance of your mellifluous cadence,
Which pours forth like honey in the sun,
From the silky radiance
Of your eyes and a raven tress,
Which graces your fair neck as a sable lace.

You saunter in an alabaster dress,
In the vestibule of a sacred place,
In the joyous marble square,
Where glorious fountains
Rise in the aromatic air,
Surrounded by a wreath of emerald mountains.

You have conquered me, my beauteous Queen.
And I am never to be the same.
Your bosom is a dew-clad meadow,
Safe and soft, and most serene;
And I go as one lost in a troubadour's dream,
Mystified by your reverent name,
Beside a descending, turquoise stream.

The redolent perfumes of your pearl-white hands
Are sweeter than all Elysian lands,
And your loving bands
Are more exalted to be served in eternity
Than it would ever be
To rule over kingdoms, regimes, the plains, the sea.

And so I go with hymns of thee
Rejoicing deep within my heart, ferrying to your home,
With boundless bliss and felicity,
Nevermore to roam
Like a wanton, mad sailor on the wild, boundless brine.

Elysian Meadows

Your kiss is an immaculate, thrilling, sacred wine,
And your look is of a statue's gaze:
Solemnly bewitching of a regal woman's wondrous ways,
Who walks as a goddess, beneath the lindens and the birch,
In the splendor of the cloister, in the court by the Cathedral,
In the fragrant umbrage of your magnificent church,
Where your citadel
Is one of a lover's tender reign.

And I forever go,
Wherever your Siren-like breezes flow,
Lost in the ocean of your dusky, Jewish, royal mane,
And the paradisal reflection of your pristine face
Which commands every pond and lake,
Possesses in my heart such a pious grace,
To be touched by your beauty, for your own majestic sake.

And the willows sway, slowly.
Over the sea,
With a rapturous, solemn sanctity.

Elysian Meadows

To One in Heaven

Must I live in the loneliness at such a price?
I have seen her there again
In paradise.
Amid glorious dreams,
She consumes my dreams
As I behold her walking beneath diamond beams,
In radiant gardens of silver and gold
Where all is new, where naught is old.
Her hair is long, straight and black,
There angels praise the beauty of her face,
Her fair, soft back,
And her eyes of grace.

And all my days are misty hours
Of longing sighs and mystic showers,
Rising to where fountains bend
As my cries ascend
To those heavenly bowers.

Elysian Meadows

To You, My Love

All night, when I am alone,
Your sweet voice I hear,
Angelic and dear,
Of a heavenly tone.
And when your soft perfume
Wafts in from the sea
Your fragrant gaze of ecstasy
Enters like a psalm into my room.

Through curtains of white,
I behold your face and form,
As billows rise in the starlit storm,
You appear in a ray of glowing light.
And when my hair you caress
As a moonbeam gleams
Through your dress and its ruffled, ivory seams.
To you, my love, I give all that I possess.

And then comes your ardent kiss,
As we wander in the courtyard's shade,
By the alabaster statues, near the oceanic glade—
Enraptured in an eternal bliss.

Elysian Meadows

Torment (The Guest)

I

Cigarette after cigarette,
With Sirens around me and a blond coquette,
What torments arise
After the bleeding of a dreary sunset!
The land and the skies,
Weary of my tepid life
Have left me in an isolated strife
Where there reigns in the dales of my tortured mind
Harpies of a raven, horrid kind.

II

In the endless corridors mad flames flicker.
Satan's legions in the black bile snicker.
And all my chambers are chilled and barren.
I am haunted by the shadows of my wife,
Who lives in paradise, beyond the stars.
O, my Karen, my lovely Karen,
Why must you touch with your fair, dead fingers
The glimmering bars
Of the fire which lingers
With an ominous glow
In my study, where the cold winds blow
From the frightful gape
Of my half-open window.
Must you move each ghostly, pale-white drape?
For the curtains moan as they flow to and fro,
With languorous wafts of nostalgic rapture.
For they carry on the evening breeze
From without, from the grove of walnut trees,
Your sweet perfume which only I know.
Like a thief it glides about my form to capture
My lonely soul within my parlor; it calls to me,
To resurrect our affinity,
Recalling to my battered psyche

Elysian Meadows

Kisses given in sunny glades.
Why does the moon in purple shades
Defy my reason on nights such as these?
Why must you recall our ecstasies?

III

And the grasses outside sway with the gales,
Beneath the boughs of sighing trees,
As you fill my head with ancient tales,
Of ethereal love, and tortured seas.

Elysian Meadows

Tremulous Seas

Melodious hymns of my ardor's fire
Silvery and blue, descend from above.
I sailed upon a carrack, to find my only love;
She lives in Normandy, in a bastion's spire.

Her face and the aspects of her eyes
Speak of hallowed symphonies.
There are tremulous seas—
Within her sighs.
And she passes slowly,
Beneath the boxwoods' scented leaves;
Her spirit is holy,
And her dear heart grieves,
To the ring of a cathedral bell,
As she searches for me, on the holly-green dell.
We meet beside a hallow pine,
Aside the freshets of a broad, bright stream,
Amid the wandering vine,
In the wondrous rapture of an endless dream.

IX

The Gilded Sun and Other Verse

The Gilded Sun and Other Verse

Introduction

 When I began to compose the verse contained within this volume, my primary goal was to translate the ineffable essences of both the practical and ethereal aspects of life into attainable visions through inspired terminology. As *The Gilded Sun* progressed, I realized that the stanzas which most achieved this attempt were inspired by a higher power and hence were not solely my own. The poems which make up this collection were written in the sequence in which they appear, and form a composite and chronological whole.

       ~John Lars Zwerenz

For Mary

The Gilded Sun and Other Verse

The Gilded Sun

Her long, dark locks wavered in the breeze.
As my soul ascended above the trees,
All became a diamond light
Brighter than any sun.

I beheld her hair through a brilliant fountain,
As her pitch-black tresses were overcome
By the shine of flaming, silver pearls,
Until I fell into an azure sea
From where I saw her walking,
Walking very slowly,
Beside a teeming, stone wall
Adorned with gilded vines.

She passed with the ineffable gracefulness
Of an angel immersed in gold,
In a dress of regal white,
As billows soft and laced with fragrance
Kissed her hair with tears.

A Lovers Song

Roving beneath the dew dappled trees,
Hand in hand, in a sacred rapture,
The statues and the fountains gently capture
The scent of your lips in the scarlet breeze.

Your name is of an angel's languorous song,
And your face is of the azure tinted skies,
Where beauty reigns in my adoring eyes—
Lauding your mane, mellifluous and long.

And in the starry, bejeweled, nascent night,
When the silver moon sobs on the terrace where we stand,
Your kisses yield an ecstasy, borne of glistening, sunlit sand,
Redolent with wine, as billows struck with light.

Heaven II

Heaven is of golden cabins, clad with redolent, diamond snow.
Gilded, angelic streams, through tall, slender grasses flow
To bright, majestic groves of myrtle trees which sway below
Turquoise skies, fulfilling dreams, where lavender-scented breezes go.

Theologians say that paradise knows no change nor night—
Only the cloudless firmaments of an infinite, immaculate day.
Yet the astonishing evening reigns in the starry regions of the north,
Bejeweling the sanctified brooks that joyfully tally forth.

Let us go, let us go, my princess, my lover, my only love,
To where the sacred woods are glowing with dappled, silver boughs;
Let us wander there enraptured, as long as love allows—
Lying in the regal reeds, exalted from above!

A Reverie

When the wavering cradle of the soft, amber field
Inebriates our kisses, as showers commence to descend
Upon our naked knees, where slender briars bend,
We inhale the mystic wind which the meadow's reeds yield.

And as the nascent moon rises in the curtain of the west,
Over the splendid, emerald crest
Of the pine clad mountain, strewn within our dream
Of a courtyard and a brook, a statue and a stream.

The Gilded Sun and Other Verse

A Sailor's Song III

To and fro,
Broken with grief,
My footsteps go,
Like an arbitrary leaf,
Where the borders of the river flow
In swirls of purple, cold, beneath
The solitary myrtles, the dying oaks, the weeping birch.
I sit alone in a vine-clad yard,
In a swirl of leaves, which makes a wreath
Around my boots, beside the church.
And all that I regard
As true
Which still has life,
(Like the thought of my wife
Inhaling all the blooms of a scarlet hue)
Merely haunts me in my reveries of you,
My sable-haired angel of rapture and rue.
And so Saturn ascends,
As the over-brush bends
Beyond my pea coat, tasting of brine.
I shall drown myself in the ocean's soft wine,
And steal from its Sirens songs of bliss,
Sailing to the East—to the shores of Boston,
To the grasses of Harvard—to a state of ephemeral happiness,
Where I, Dionysus, married you, the Apollonian!

The Gilded Sun and Other Verse

A Walk With You

In my countless walks I have never seen
A more gilded face than your own—so fair;
The noonday sun lauds your hair,
As my gaze unites with yours—serene,
In the gilded sheen of Juliet's square.

The Latin breeze which trails like a diamond fount
Brushes your parted mane, as your kisses thrill,
Gracing the Italian courtyard and its every distant, modest hill.
(To the north, your love does touch the crested snows of an alpine mount.)

And when the stars alight, sobbing on the balconies and streams,
Our love is understood, where the moonlight in Verona gleams,
In the solitary wood, in the vast, sighing, silent park.
We hold each other's hand in the silhouettes of the mist-clad dark,
And we walk as angels, beneath the glory of ivory Roman colonnades,
In harmonic raptures of our own, hidden in boons of immaculate shades.

A Winter's Night

Take my hand, where the white petals play,
In the caress of the soft, winter breeze,
Which winnows through the snow clad trees,
Beneath the sky of a gilded gray.
Kiss me, my love, in the rapturous field,
Behind our cabin where the fireplace does hold
The promise of embraces, strewn with gold,
For which we live, when we mutually yield
To one another's lips, to one another's heat.
We shall be higher than the angels, enthroned, complete.
And when the dawn shall rise God shall find me there,
My head upon your bosom, my tears upon your hair.

A Winter's Wood

I beheld you in a vision,
In the calm of a winter's wood:—
You passed beneath the enchanted boughs,
Dreaming as they gleaming stood,
Laden with their heavy snow,
And shaken by the roving wind;
The last of the sunset
Upon your face
Graced you with soft, amber hues,
As you went wandering,
Free from all care,
Beneath the white clouds and bohemian blues,
Happy as an angel—
Snug within your scarlet wool,
With blushing cheeks
And elegance,
Bearing a countenance
Ineffably fair—
In the billowing chills
Of majestic air.

After Our Deaths I

The potent Sangria of your dusky, French eyes
Rushes with passion to the snow clad pines,
Dispersing fragrant, cherry wines
Beneath the lavender tinted skies.

The clemency of your ivory hands
Releases many sacred things:
Diadems of wedding rings
Form a circle around our amorous bands.

And your hair of an angel's, conceived in black,
By God's majestic Triune brush
Glitters like a fount, Marie, when the starlight's hush
Illuminates your smooth, alabaster back.
We shall ferry beyond our cabin to the slopes,
No longer needing faith nor hopes—
For glorious billows pass above us as our coach arrives.
No more shall we think of superficial, lowly things.
Behold how all our sufferings
Were eternal blessings to our lives!

The Gilded Sun and Other Verse

Our Walk Amid the Reeds

The breeze is cool,
But it does not bite.
The world regarded us each a fool,
But there is no longer a reason to be contrite.
Let us stroll beneath the crimson blooms
Which laugh above the brooks of white.
And after our walk amid the reeds,
Let us retire to our palatial rooms,
Among our busts and vases;
Let us look out our grand bay window,
To where swirling siroccos softly blow,
Out upon the moonlit meads.
There, surrounded by fine tapestries,
And the most majestic, eternal art,
In between our lips' bated pauses,
We shall witness blue jays ascend in ecstasies,
As they flutter and dart
To the immaculate seas.
I have waited for this moment all of my life
To possess you as a woman, more than a wife.
For as angels in a crystal palace we dwell—
In the boon of God's most highest citadel.
Let all tongues be silent.

Am I Fine, Am I Beautiful?

Am I fine? Am I beautiful?
I possess many rubies
And I dine with kings.
I own many fair things,
And my face is young and fresh to the eyes.

Handsome musicians vie for my gaze,
They tell me so in secret ways,
Beneath the blue, enchanting skies.
So tell me then, if I am fine?

The perfume of my body is of delicious wine.
So tell me truly,
Am I pretty, am I fine?

My lips are round, and are redder than the rose.
Even the poet in his cloister, in his flowery close
Writes of me this hour.
Tell me, then, do I have power?
O poet of every starlit season,
O bard of greatness, use your reason,
And tell me, then, if I am fine.

"No," the poet solemnly said,
"For within your spirit you are naught but dead."
And so, with scorn, I walked away,
To find another bard to say:
"Thou art lovely, thou art fine,
More gloriously beautiful than the goddess-like sway
Of mighty Aphrodite, walking in the sunshine.
Thou art lovely, thou art fine!"

The Gilded Sun and Other Verse

My Reader

"He leads me in the paths of righteousness for His name's sake."

Psalm 23

This sonnet is for you, my reader, my lover of Anne and poetry,
Who peruses these pages like a wanton sailor does the wild and unbridled sea.
What wrongs can you claim? What abominations done
Were wrought by your hand under the all-knowing eyes
Of the grand and gold, omniscient sun?
Could it be you have forsaken the bright, celestial, holy skies?
Have you turned your back on virtue, offending everyone?
Perhaps. Or by grace your life has been lived in a pure and saintly wise?
For never were you at rest to sing the glorious strains
Of a brisk summer eve, in a Venetian gondola, cool, and kind.
For there are always demons which knife your psyche in the scorching rains!
So judge your past with reason; it is a certain promise of future gold.
And dispense with the confusion, the cobwebs' kiss of the dreary old.
And you shall know what it is to be bold!

Winter

Upon the riverside dale,
The moonlight, pale,
Blends with the infinite,
And a soft, majestic gale.
Poetry writ
In books of old
Soothe me
In the wintry cold.

The demands of winter's sanctity
Knell from the bells of Notre Dame.
As I sit by the ancient bank
Of the cold and windy Seine.

Upon the riverside dale,
The moonlight, pale,
Blends with the infinite,
And a soft, majestic gale.

The Gilded Sun and Other Verse

Death at Sea

The crest of the waves, furious, they rise
To the glittering stars, to the arch of the skies.
Some ships sail into the safety of the bay,
With small, feathery masts—
When seen from far away.
From the valley of Neptune
Comes the blasts
Of briny winds.
And from the north Thor
Batters the prows and the sands of the shore,
As Artemis ascends with a merciless moon.

These are the nights when captains clasp every wheel,
Calling to all hands, their rain-soaked sailors,
To avoid stern and port where the wild currents reel,
All are called to deck, all sea-loving whalers.
And Poseidon laughs with spite
As some heroes in their height
Are cast into the swallowing blue,
Forever to sleep beneath the waves,
Forever to sweetly slumber
Beyond the realm of watery graves.
And soon we shall be one with their number—
The likes of me and you!

The Gilded Sun and Other Verse

The Cult of Dionysus

Dionysus, blissfully,
Drunken, yet a sage,
Erected, like Hadrian,
A radiant temple for the global stage:
The ivory colonnades of the Parthenon,
That vast, Doric treasury;
The alabaster jewel of Hellas;
The embodiment of felicity;
Athena's fair cello, bought with the coins of Zeus.

For where did Pericles
Receive his Delian wage,
If not from the hands of Maenads
Whose gold and silver they found
From the flowing well-springs of the sacred ground,
From the fountains
Of wine,
From the fine,
White streams,
Which descend upon the Macedonian mountains,
Where bright, insane, fantastic dreams
Met with ecstatic wanderings.

And when grapes do sing
Their fragrant, minty strains
To Persephone who strolls
In the sunlit rains,
In the bowers of the spring
For rapturous hours,
With fair Dionysus
Who laughs among the melody of colorful flowers,
Which wavering, glow in the gold
Of sun showers—
The wine-possessed
Resurrect the old!

The Gilded Sun and Other Verse

And when young Dionysus
Was raised by Rhea,
After the Titans removed his head,
He grew to manhood
In the moonlit wood
Where the sky was painted by Zeus' hand
With scarlet, carmine,
And a bold, pubescent, burgundy-red.
His spirit, effulgent, majestic, grand,
Emancipated with wine,
Mated with the ghosts
Of Thanatos,
With his own Semele,
And he raised them from the dead.

And as Simonides writes
Expansive and flowery, then concise and terse,
Weaving his florid, chiseled verse,
Euripides declares the nights
Sacred for plays,
And wanton ways.
And Socrates, awake,
Likes to think of a moonbeam,
As the spinning, blue earth
Gives a miraculous birth
To another gilded stream,
Where the Maenads take
Another gold drink, from another mad dream.

The Gilded Sun and Other Verse

The Princess II

Gales of incense,
Gales of thyme,
Enrapture every sense,
With nature's use of pantomime.

The gardens and their old, iron fence
Are open for my little, wandering stroll.
I shall dream upon a path of stone,
As the passing hours of the summer toll.

In those scented breezes I walk in bliss,
Beside the massive, splendid sea.
Verily, I tell you, *her name is Marie.*
Through those spacious gardens I rove alone,
Searching for my medieval princess!
And with all the flowers that I behold,
Whether red or ivory, yellow or gold,
I shall awake in their petals a new felicity,
From their ancient, sleeping dew,
From each drop of their despondency,
Born of the balconies which sob in the night,
In the long silhouettes of the languid moon.
I shall bequeath upon them all a crimson light.
And I shall rejoice with them at noon,
Regal, bold and new.
The skies are joyful and cloudless,
Of a heavenly and perfect blue!
And as I recline
In the reeds, in their amber wine
Near the soundless,
Turquoise pool
An immaculate symphony stirs in its azure deeps,
In the soft, summer breeze,
Pleasant and cool,
As my princess sleeps
In a throng of grasses,
Beneath the scented linden trees.

The Gilded Sun and Other Verse

And as daylight passes,
She lies like Shakespeare's Ophelia, drifting in her mind
With tender reflections of a summery kind.

And as I approach her, ever so near,
I gather rosy blooms near the old veranda, the belvedere.
Awake to your prince, *my beloved Marie*,
Awake to the gleam of the sky above,
Awake to the vast and fragrant sea,
My only, my lover, my dear,
My love!

Meditation

I beheld you wearing a white and gold sweater,
In the realm of paradise, sitting at a table.
Your eyes were of brown, your tresses were of sable.
I was free from all pain, from every worldly fetter.

Behind you was a window, looking out to a purple sea,
Over verdant meadows, gleaming in the astonishing daylight.
With an adoring cadence, I kissed your hand as you gazed upon me.
Our sacred love was effulgent, sanctified and bright.

Then, along with Venus, the nascent, glowing night
Serenaded you on a balcony where melodically there wept
Mellifluous strains as vows were made, secrets there were kept.
And as the cherubim beheld that sight,

I kissed you among the tall, slender fountains,
In the courtyard of gold, amid the mountains.

Gales II

The wandering gales which gently pass
Sway the gleaming, emerald grass.
A remembrance of an evening past
Is married to a schooner's mast,
As it sails in the calm of the gleaming harbor.

I reminisce in a florid arbor.
How precious was your languorous kiss:
All autumn gales are made of this;
The things of heaven which we, on the sand,
Lulled by the weeping, somnolent willow,
Sipped like wine, each receiving one another's hand,
Where the fragrant, wafting waves did billow.

The wandering gales which gently pass
Sway the gleaming, emerald grass.
A remembrance of an evening past
Is married to a schooner's mast,
As it sails in the calm of the gleaming harbor.
I reminisce in a florid arbor.

The Palace III

Dreaming on the bright, spacious lawn of a palace,
I have come to behold the lady clad in white,
Who steps onto the balcony in the soft sunlight.
I stand below alone, drinking from a chalice.

Amid the gray cast of ancient stone she appears,
As a breeze blows back the long tresses of her hair.
I am drunk with quatrains and the summery air,
With the lady and with wine, with regal belvederes.

Many billows from God are flung to the north.
The silhouettes of basswoods, of dark, turquoise-blues
Shed their shades near the palace, on broad avenues.
Descending from the terrace, my lady comes forth
As we wander for a rapturous hour,
As I finish my Chablis,
Through the garden, through the bower,
In an atmosphere of sanctity.

The Death of the Pagan Gods

Let Apollo speak out with displeasure
On our mortal amour which is quiet in its leisure.
Let him rend the canvass of the sky's rapturous blue
With his bold, Olympian retinue.

Let them swallow the light
Which was made for only us.
Ah! We shall discuss
In the sweet, lively, solemn night
With glorious Dionysus
How to defeat this king
Of the summer sun.

For I own a princely, gilded ring
Engraved with grapes!—Ah, me!
Let us converse
In the deserts of the universe
With the Maenads,
By the boundless sea.
We shall consult
According to their orgiastic, forested cult
How to set fire to the moonlight's desire
To reign in the drunken, happy night.

We shall use the moon's goddess as our midnight friend.
As she paces highly upon the diamond height
With her wayward lantern, in her Orphic light.
We shall hide from Artemis
Zeus' impregnating kiss,
The mortal work of Semele,
And take her to our theatre by the sea,
Where Euripides sails in a moat with no end.
Showing her nothing but the pure divine,
We shall give to Artemis an alabaster flask
Of newly fermented, poisoned wine,
Poured in the dark,

The Gilded Sun and Other Verse

With a specious mask
Of godliness alone, wrought from the vine.

And once her eyes become all alight
It will be too late to know wrong from right,
And as the bright, gilded day repels the dark, starry night,
She will cast that sun god into the sea
Where Poseidon waits so enviously.

And the gods shall rage
One against the other, once their sun brother
Has truly died.
And they shall in this age
Engender the others' malevolent pride.
Death to Dionysus!
Death to the Roman gods as well!
Death to Egypt's tall tales of Osiris!
Death to them all!
All to hell!

For if you loosen one peg, so all does fall.
Death to Venus and Roma, perdition to Iris!

Artemis shall cast down her moon into the ocean,
And Poseidon shall raise a tempest
In his furious protest.
All the gods shall trade reason for emotion.
Athena's wisdom shall finally be revealed as fake.
The Parthenon shall splinter, tremble, and quake.
Aphrodite's lust for her son, Adonis
Shall offend the ire of Zeus.
Then Hades, with his greedy hands
Shall with gluttony
Swallow the entire Pantheon,
And all the other myths of pagan lands.
And with bold Apollo dead and gone

The Gilded Sun and Other Verse

We shall rejoice in the perdition his old, loathsome legacy,
Defeating the past, demonic desires
Which no longer reign on the Olympian mount
Of that impious throng!

We shall wander beyond their corpses
Among a row of roses and a silver fount,
In our court by sandy campfires,
Serenading God with a Christian song!

Dreaming

Walking through meadows I shall dream,
Wearing a sailor's coat, of soft, raven wool.
I shall bathe in summer breezes, scented and cool,
Sprayed by the happy froth of a stream.
I shall meditate on only love,
And make my way to a church by the sea,
To kneel by a shrine, dedicated to her majesty,
Beneath the radiant sky above.
And when evening comes, docile with the pace
Of the silent shoe of a vagabond,
My dream shall ferry me to the grand beyond,
Above the realm of time and space.

The Gilded Sun and Other Verse

Spring

It is a blue-butterfly day here in spring.

Robert Lee Frost

We shall sit on a swing
On the porch in the spring,
Half-sleeping,
Just resting,
As butterflies of blue
Go fluttering
Beside you.

Looking out upon a tuft of grass,
The summer breezes gently pass.
How I love your eyes, my lovely lass;
They take in the skies, like old, red wine.

Around the old,
Colonial post
Climbs the holly green vine.
(It is you I love the most.)

Let us laze in the yellow sunshine,
As siroccos blow,
Upon the brook and its dewy eglantine
We shall find rapture in every saffron billow,
As you place your tender hand in mine.

And we shall sit on a swing
On a porch in the spring,
Half-sleeping,
Just resting,
As butterflies of blue
Go fluttering
Beside you.

The Gilded Sun and Other Verse

A Voyage to Spain

My boots are of leather.
I am a buccaneer.
My spirit is devoid of fear,
I sail on furious, thankless brine,
In dangerous, windy, wild weather.
Though I am never drunk with rum nor wine.
I worship neither Poseidon nor Pan.
None but God do I adore.
I seek a pious woman and a sandy shore.
I am glad that I was made a male, a man,
Masculine to my very core.
I ferry on a schooner over the raging North Atlantic.
I manage the wheel, every tackle and mast.
I am destined for the verdant meadows of Spain.
My dreams are blissful, ethereal and fantastic.
I welcome the sound of the thunder blast,
The jagged lightning, and the down pouring rain.
I possess secret ales
Within a silver flask.
I have met the rocky port,
And collapsed are all my sails.
I have roving as my only task.
(My mind is of a wandering sort.)
My ship is ruined, so be it—good!
I shall pick my teeth with is splintered wood,
And walk to a tavern near the town of Seville.
My state of affairs shall be one with the skies
Of a young señorita, of brown and dusky eyes.
In Andalusia all is tranquil.
I sit in the back of the inn,
Within an old, wooden booth
Of piny, stained mahogany,
Removing the bark
From my pirate's tooth.
I pursue the good, and avoid all sin.

The Gilded Sun and Other Verse

And with the rain-swept, morning lark
I hum an ancient seaman's tune:
A vagabond's joyful rhapsody.
(It is the jig jog of the moon,
It is the song of the sailor's sea.)
I leave the din
Of the rustic bar, finishing my frothy beer.
I travel on foot, and I travel far,
Although I know my love is near.
I travel south in a horse-drawn car.
And I stroll to a boundless, amber field,
To where ancient potions
Wistfully yield
Immaculate furrows and grassy oceans!
I sleep in the hay
In a farmhouse not far
From the moonlit pier,
By the sea, near the bay.
And I awake to a voice, youthful and dear:
"I am your wife to be—do you hear?"
She was a peasant girl from the south;
Her name was none other than my fair Marie.
I kissed the slopes of her red, lovely mouth,
And I loved her in the umbrage,
In a corner of the stable.
(She was an angel, in the prime of her age.)
Her legs were ravishing, smooth, and fair,
And the hypnotizing tresses of her hair
Were scented, long, and sable.
She possessed the wisdom of Saint, a true sage.
Her eyebrows were black,
And the fair, white lily of her soft, Latin back
Struck me with its astonishing beauty.
Her fingertips and toes were of a glistening hue.
And her Spanish gaze of majesty
Was written in the dew.

The Gilded Sun and Other Verse

We sipped from her carafe a heavenly brew
Of burgundy, flowing, mellifluous and chilled.
Her embrace
Was angelic, of a redolent sea,
And her bosom thrilled
The very heart of me.
And her face
Was flushed with satiation.

In a haze of elation,
We wandered to the bounding
Of the massive, beauteous plain,
In our vast, florid surrounding,
Wet with redolent rain;

We walked to the mountains,
To the whistling tune of a lover's strain.
And I rested, rhyming quatrains
And the other verse, some prose here and there,
In the wondrous winds of the Spanish air.

We ascended a down which gleamed like sand
In the bold, summer sun, where towering and grand
Stood a vast, stony bastion,
Massive and Castilian.
And as the breezes died down,
My heart became lost in her raven eyes of brown.
And I knelt upon my knees in that good, green grass,
As time stood still. Not a second did pass.
And I presented to her gaze
A sanctified ring
Of diamonds and jade.
And the lovebirds still sing
Of that day
In their way
Of the eternal bond we so happily made,

The Gilded Sun and Other Verse

Freely,
And completely.
And the lovebirds there still sing, still sing,
In the holy light of spring.

The Gilded Sun and Other Verse

The Music Room

Astrophic cadence flows,
Of meandering verse and prose,
Touching my heart,
In the conservatory, in the chamber,
Where gales glide in from the large, open windows
Before they depart
With thoughts of her.
A piano is kissed by fair, white fingers.
From its keys arise a wistful song,
In the hazy music room,
Where the bloom of her perfume
Conquers me as it lingers,
In the sunny afternoon, wavering and long.
What is it in her mane's bouquet
That renders my spirit weak and trembling,
As the moon ascends
Above the hemlock which bends,
In the twilit gray,
Dispersing the billows,
Dissembling
In the day?
What is it in her face's unspeakable rose
That weeps in languish a haunting mode
Veering to the window with a solemn, mysterious ode,
Dying in the greens of the cloistered close?

It is Snowing in Town

I have come from the village, it is snowing, my dear.
Let us walk to the inn, let us have some beer.
And after we leave the din of the tavern,
We shall walk among the frozen brooks,
In voluptuous nooks,
Beneath the full, wintry lantern.
Oh, indeed, my love, it is snowing in the town.
Let me gaze astonished
Into your liquid eyes
Of ebony-brown.
And when I am finished,
Beneath the cold, dark skies
In the excitement of the wintry chill,
We shall wade through snowy piles deep,
And I shall kiss your crimson lips until
All the townsfolk are asleep.

My Poetry

I, a martyr, give to you, the world, my poetry,
Written to release you from the burden of time.
And if my stanzas instill in you a dream with rhyme
I have sacrificed rightfully my life for beauty.
For I paint many landscapes with an architect's flare;
Statuaries, courtyards, and castellated bastions,
Teeming high and clad with vine, gleaming in the fragrant air.
Onto faraway places and new-born passions!
Tell me, what is your need for Homer and Shakespeare?
It will not be long before I cease to serve you here;
And who among our day can out-duel me with the pen?
After my death, do you know, what then?—
Will there be burgeoning, gifted bards to follow?—
Or will their poor prose and rhyme still render you hallow?

Beauty is Her Name

By the lapping, deep lagoon,
Beneath the mist of the hazy moon,
On a silent, serene, breezy day,
In the early part of June,
I came upon a beautiful queen,
Lazing in the starlit hay.
On a soft, scented patch of turquoise-green,
She dipped her raven head
In dappled, grassy flowerbeds,
Amid the sunlight's setting violets, and its descending, swirling, carmine reds.
There, among fragrant inlets,
Purple and streaming,
She pondered many sanctified things;
For in her reveries were wanderings.
She beheld a castle, and a gold, cushioned carriage,
Dreaming of silver wedding rings,
Calling her to a sacred marriage.
She awoke to the night,
Gazing out to sea,
Next to the mansion and the marble
Of the square.
And when she did alight
In the sweet, summer air,
Her mane of sable
Gracefully
Blended with the scent of mint and rosemary,
In the vast garden-closes,
Among a throng of roses,
Next to the solemn statuary.

Recollection

The breeze above the rippling ponds
Wanders through the trees and their bright, fragrant fronds,
As the reeds, blown back, scent the morning dew.
I walk in the bower, thinking of you.
Your gaze, of hazel and almonds, are of astonishing hues,
They capture my recollections
With rapturous reflections,
As I pass on the grass beneath the myrtles and the yews.
Yet what if we married, what then, my dear?
Our hearts would grow wild
As a swinging chandelier,
With or without a child.
The gilded sea and its sky are blue,
Blue as in eternity.
(For I shall never forget you.)
Onto the mansion, where our memories revive
Your kisses, my dear one, and my friends here and now.
We shall sip heaven's wine upon every solemn balcony,
Beneath every leafy bough,
Glad to simply be alive,
Loving as long
With an angel's song,
As long as eternity does allow.

Our Chambers

The splendorous ocean, the broad, vast sea
Billowing beneath the arch of the sky,
Enraptures our souls, as we sleep and sigh
Engulfed in a radiant harmony.
The courtyard by the grotto, clad with vines,
Where the white statues made of marble rise
With slender fountains, in a solemn wise,
Serenades the mountains, laden with pines.
The pleasure of the peaks, in somnolent array
Refreshes our gazes, and our hearts which pray
For bliss come the vespers, the stars and their plumes.
Now that the rivers swoon with rosy blooms,
(Below the bright terrace, they flow in the light)
We shall kiss in our rooms, in the moon glow of night.

The Gilded Sun and Other Verse

An American Montage

Vegetarians are plentiful in Beverly Hills
The lens of their cameras like to keep themselves lean.
Flying down the highway kills,
As do hotel rooms with many pills.
(Just ask Monroe and Dean.)
From a book depository came
The oblivion of Vietnam;
A bullet through the temple
Wrought the day's present reign.
So Oswald can claim
The death of a Republic's calm,
Having ended the innocence
After making a decision,
Taking a bull's-eye aim.
With demonic precision,
Firing thrice on a plaza with awe.
And the orphaned world was set all aflame, with a wild, pungent fragrance
When The Beatles came,
After Johnson swore in his day of infamous fame,
On Air Force One, a blue and white plane.
Now men lurk the alleyways, and rich women pay.
The pyramid is off its head.
How hazy are these present days,
When our leaders laze,
Grazing by the laughing Potomac,
Drunken near a flowerbed.
And all the nations of the world,
Including the few,
Remaining red,
Present to you a circus-like fanfare.
Some Elysian, strange, Utopian world
Is setting off fireworks in the eastern skies.
(In a very clever, specious wise.)
The western hemisphere
Has relinquished its once authoritative air,

The Gilded Sun and Other Verse

And with many tears has unfurled
Its flag of old presbyters with somnolent sighs.
The wild winds whip up a fit
Ruining cities with their terrible tide
From furious gulfs at night.
O, lamenting American,
When will you admit
That neither side
Was right?
In the now and here
I listen to the tomb of Lincoln,
Pining with a plaintive cry.
I wander into a rustic, old tavern
In Baltimore, to drink a toast to Poe.
Yet I become nervous, for fluttering
Is heard in his raven's descending wings.
For broad, hungry, craven things
Are waiting for the moment to cast into confusion
Mantles of freedom, of speech, of the press,
Assembling in a dire distress.
A firm and ancient, bold resolution
To hold sacred honor, a glorious constitution:
It is being betrayed by Satan's revolution!
And I visited the cherry blooms,
Where Jefferson still looms,
Patrolling in his wanderings,
Among a throng of temples and tombs,
White—with violent stirrings!

Terror

Baudelaire terrified me to the very bone
When he wrote of hell's complete despair.
Beyond the horror of any fiery dream,
The prisoners of Hades, unable to scream,
Walk very slowly,
Silently on the grass
Of the eternal, fallen graveyard.
On fire, creeping, they pass,
Wearing burial shrouds, all tattered.
There resides nothing holy
In that netherworld of gray.
Please pray
For me solely,
Dear reader, now—**today!**

A Carolingian Ride

Bright, flushed-faced equestrian,
Welcome the sun in your saddled stride,
And the soft, romantic strain
Which flows from the river as you ride.
My princess and my youthful, young bride,
We shall as Carolingian invaders take the reedy sands,
Which gleam as gold next to the flaming tide;
We shall conquer every sea as well, all the European lands.
And when we retire,
We shall climb the carpeted,
Persian stairs,
In milky, Zoroastrian airs.
And in the chambers aglow with the balconies' fire,
Lit by the streaming, summery moon,
We shall fall into dreaming, in the dazzling boon
Of raptures gleaming, of passion, desire!

Let Us Cross the River

Let us cross the river and walk to the Louvre,
You as my lady, I as your bard.
In its terraced bower we shall be in love.
And after leaving its sunny, old, vine-clothed yard,
We shall admire the canvasses of Fragonard,
And pace the corridors, the artistic halls,
Of white and gray,
Among the drapes of artistic fuss,
Where Watteau
And Leonardo
Grace the endless walls,
For the likes of us,
Our naiveté.

The Lady of the Garden

In the soft, summer sun she paces on the promenade,
Among the blooms of the enclave, of the garden.
She gazes on the distant grasses of the glen,
Walking in the breezes of the cool, fragrant shade.

And when the perfumes of the park flow through her hair,
She pines for the dark and a kiss beneath the fronds.
In the sanctuary of the vast, marble square,
She roves among the roses, and the blue, scented ponds.

Her heart is liberal, she is courteous and kind.
The garden's blooms entrance her eyes, and fill her humble mind
With dreamy thoughts of night, and boons of the season.

She strolls in the moonlight, consumed with only love.
She sings to the blue jays in the tall trees above.
And she lauds God alone, the crown of her reason.

My Irish Love

I sailed to a port near the ancient rock of Hags Head,
Where I met by the rolling billows, you, my lovely lass.
We walked among the shells of the gold, breezy beach,
And we sat beneath the willows, upon a soft, grassy bed.

We roved through splendid bowers as the hours did pass.
Your lips were of the Gallic rose and of the blossoming peach.
I produced from my pocket some old, romantic rhyme,
And I read some lines from Yeats as the day began to die.

We beheld purple finches, leaving their nooks to fly
Over white, wandering brooks, in the brisk, Celtic clime.
We waded in the waves and sipped the crested brine.
Then we walked into town, and sat at a mahogany bar,
Of an old, wooden inn, where hidden from every orb and star,
Your wedding ring glowed, gleaming among the flowing wine.

The Lost Art of Poetry

What of a castle?
What of this?—
Expressing through words such verse that lauds
The pursuit and attainment
Of noble bliss,
Of timeless ages,
When courtships and chivalry
Composed the best of pages.
Truly there have been
And shall be better ages!
Yet of what do my contemporaries
Wish me to write?—
Of this day and age?
Of what
Indeed!—
Hedonism and perversity
That reverberates, unfurls;
Do they desire that I set these things to rhyme?—
The tragic constant news of monotonous crime;
Of madness and murder,
In the severed, sordid, urban night?—
Yes, I believe indeed they do.
Yet which of these worlds
Would most edify you?

A Nocturne Song

I slept upon white pillows
 In the lonely, old carriage,
 Aside the haunting willows
Which in their gloomy dew
Spoke of you,
So far away,
And the promise of day,
And a happy marriage.

The Gilded Sun and Other Verse

A Soul in Purgatory

Haunted in my study,
I turn from drink to drink.
In a dour attack of madness,
I am only compelled to write
Of sordid beauty.
I cannot reason with clarity
Nor can I think
Of anything but the mire of sadness,
Of the pools within my terrified sight
Where drooling from the walls
Are paintings in the candled halls.
I am Schumann, Mozart, Byron, and Baudelaire.
There are specters which seek my very soul
In the icy chill of the midnight air.
God help me if I fall into despair!—
I hear the bells of a chapel knoll,
In the blackness of the unforgiving night.
Shall we dance, you terrible wrath and I
Until the hazy, Orphic moon
Swallows me soon,
Long before I see the dawning golden light?
I shall be taken by the nymphs of the sea,
Where my washed, floating body will lie.
There shall be nothing left of me.
Until I am kidnapped by my omnipresent ghost,
I shall remove the candle from the wall,
And dance like a gypsy down the deathly hall,
Suffering as a saint,
Without complaint,
For the Virgin, my dear, the most,
And for you, one and all.

The Gilded Sun and Other Verse

A Walk in the Dawn

On a rustic trail lined with emerald gauze,
At one with the dawn,
I met a giddy, drunken faun
In an ethereal pause
Beneath pillars of gray.
The new, astonishing, carmine day
Wrapped its rays around the purple trees,
And their leafy, sunlit filigrees.
(Last night I was one with the hunter's moon,
In a vast, glowing bower,
Awaiting the noon,
In the somnolent boon
Of the Shepherd's holy hour.)
I continued down my path of bliss,
Seeking out a princess and her tender kiss,
As the waves rolled in from the pining sea.
I found her among the darnel and the reeds,
Where she gazed upon me,
Fulfilling all my needs.
And I proposed to her there,
Upon my knees,
In the soft, redolent, oceanic air,
In a rapturous glee—
Of ecstasies.

La Villa au Bord de la Mer

It was an enchanting stay.
Although it was the summer of 1993,
It seems I was there only yesterday.
With the tall, gray mountains as a backdrop,
And the Mediterranean lapping below
Every whitewashed, long, open window,
Every night and day the bottles would pop,
Flowing with bright champagne and chardonnay.
You wore a short dress of carmine-red,
And danced to every song until the moon went dead.
I kissed you that summer endlessly,
Upon the many terraces, upon every breezy balcony.
Ah!—Drinks were of plenty, plenty.
And when the ballroom lights went dim,
We followed the pipers, the mad Seraphim
Down to the shores of the blue Rivera.
We were surrounded there by many marigold blooms.
And when we were sated with the fresh Sangria,
We would return to the airy dance rooms.
I was your drunken Byron, your Poe,
And you were my girl.
How the wine did flow,
With a wish and a whirl!—
Remember riding
In your sister's black car?
What fantastic orb or beaming star
Did we not behold go gliding?
We rode through the hills
With the radio streaming.
Your breast were pointed daffodils.
Am I still there, or am I dreaming?
Down the mount, over the glen
Our wheels did roar.
Our days were the things of dreams.
Such folly now it seems?—
O, tell me, then,
What was life made for?

The Gilded Sun and Other Verse

Hyde Park

We walked among the spacious villas of Sydenham Hill,
Before I came upon the grand entrance of the park.
I met with the scent of many a lily and daffodil,
In the gold, gilded dawn which effaced the purple dark.

I strolled beneath the pillars and arches of gray,
And soon, as I paced on the long, regal Rotten Row,
I sang a sailor's song, and met a girl with a scarlet bow,
Clipping black, braided tresses which gleamed in the day.

We wandered in the wafting wind, fragrant with the peach,
To the tall, glassy walls of the grand Crystal Palace.
She asked for a sip of port from my chalice,
And we swung like monkeys from the Weeping Beech.

The Drinking Horse found us drunk and in love.
We found the Italian courtyards, and kissed in its rocky dens.
As the old moon arose, we left for Kensington Gardens,
By way of a florid close, beneath gold fronds above.

We were married in Knightsbridge, there in London Town,
And stayed at The Lanesborough, opposite the park.
The starry, English skies filled your liquid eyes of brown,
As French champagne arrived with strains of the morning lark.

Morning

Dawn's romantic overture
Scrapes the scarlet from my eyes,
Ever expanding,
Like a jeweled, mellifluous cloak,
Of ascending, regal diamonds
Thrown upon the dismal tenements
Of ashy lamentations,
Echoing in the dusky streets
Like sacred, sobbing cathedral bells
Met with indifference—
Unheard and forsaken.

The Gilded Sun and Other Verse

An Elopement

From the tower's height,
To the sun's delight,
A gypsy-blue,
The courtly hue
Of the queen's
Noble retinue,
Reflects on the greens,
On the cloistered sheens,
On the silhouettes of the avenue.
This majestic palace of china blue and white
Shall find me below your terrace tonight,
Awaiting your gaze, my young lady fair.
We shall elope, we shall run
Before the arrival of the summer sun
To the port of the sea, in the brisk, cool air.
And before her mother finds us there,
We shall cross the Channel and sail to France,
Where poets write and lovers dance.

Dante's Saloon

I wandered out beneath the full, white moon
Near Denver, Colorado,
As a desperate desperado,
To a mysterious inn,
To a cryptic saloon.
I sat in a booth among the lively din,
And refusing to drink from the ales of God's ire,
I avoided the wines of Purgatorial sin,
Along with its Stygian tide,
That place of ephemeral regret.
I merely requested water with ice,
And I repented and sought naught but Paradise,
Where I now reside—
Along with my desire,
For my belly met
With a rifle's fire.

Cafés

Tambourines in the city street
Blend With joy and sorrow's end,
Where musicians and Parisian poets meet
In sunlit cafés,
In loquacious ways,
They are charmed by the trees
Which ferment the perfumed breeze.
Conjuring up rare harmonies,
They take up a bassoon and fiddle within their minds,
They are mad as adders, drunk with wines,
Lost in all the sunny pageantries
Of Paris and its liveries,
Polishing their perfect lines.
What literary school
Of yours, dear professor,
Shall we place them in today?—
As a rule,
As their confessor,
I will certainly have to say,
They are Symbolists, Romanticists,
Decadents at play.

The Gilded Sun and Other Verse

My Politics

I walk in my sailor's coat,
Upon a cemetery mound.
Sober and sound,
Acutely aware of my imminent death.
The brevity of this life,
And the assurance of my final breath.
Such is my political foundation.
Whether of a liberal or a conservative persuasion,
We either love one another
Or else we shall perish,
From ocean to ocean, from sea to sea,
Along with the dimorphism of our dying society.
And so now it has been said.
From the falls of Niagara to the Mississippi's mouth,
New York and California Vote blue unlike the south.
(For Hamilton and Jefferson
Still duel for our nation's head.)
Nevertheless, we shall all see eye to eye
From San Francisco to the Texas sky,
When comes our final days.
Meanwhile in the Federal laze,
Republican powers are rapidly declining,
The Democrats are spending whilst dining;
Discotheques
And the ghetto's pall
Still dance a jig to the left,
While Wall Street jives
To the vanishing right.
Congress is in a haze.
And America is bereft
Of reason, of a visionary gaze.
Children weep in the streets today.
The western world is wild.
You!—Young, male seducers,
Without thought you conceive a child,

The Gilded Sun and Other Verse

The women are but your easy prey,
With whom you casually mesh.
And after they surrender to the weakness of their flesh,
To your bold enticements, to your beauty, to your seed,
To your words, to your looks, to your natural charms,
You trade yourself in for what the government renders
In place of the basic need
Of a loving father's tender arms.
And you!—Spineless statesmen,
Intolerant of all other ideas,
Save your own, small, tiny, microscopic specks,
Hypocrites, all!
You shall spend our every dollar
Until we are all in abject poverty.
Wait come soon some terrific summer,
Come some horrid autumn,
Come some miserable, terrifying fall,
The crash of '29 will seem like a sunny Saturday.
The dollar will cease to hold a penny's sway.
It will be a colossal, collective ruin,
This savage bruin,
This future rue,
This approaching monster from out of the blue.
(Just add, my dear economist,
The sum of two and two.)
For what happens when the tide of debt
Reaches those with gold,
The aristocrats, the young who are privileged,
The poor, the sick, the young and the old,
The poet who scribbles verse in the air,
The pilot of a jet?—
Now no one seems to care.
(Because it has not happened yet.)
But then, too late,
All factions will abate
Upon rocky, tragic shores.

The Gilded Sun and Other Verse

Even Presidents, Senators,
And Congressmen
Will become outright mendicants
Wandering on a homeless glen,
Begging for dimes in corridors;
Suburbs and cities
Will join their disaster, their downfall, their fate;
For they shall resemble broken caves
Crushed like sand,
Beneath a storm of tidal waves,
With their greed and contraband.
And the farmer
With his fiddle,
Brown, with a bow,
Mahogany and long,
Shall serenade our wavering grain
With the pain
Of a sorrowful swan song,
Beneath our once brave, noble skies
Of a rich, dark, dour blue.
Yet after all that I have been through,
Knowing that to give is to save,
If our final fate shall be as Greece and Rome,
At least I shall have a home
In the silence of my grave.

The Gilded Sun and Other Verse

Romance in Town

The bay looks up from the tawny, ancient sea,
Upon the steely, silver majesty
Of Manhattan's famed skyline, on its vertical mastery.
The red, green, and gold
Of the sky high casements
Of the Empire State Building are exquisite to see
At Christmastime.
Yet traditional sentiments
Are but a story that is told;
Although the birds in Central Park still sing,
Their song withers in the urban cold;
For the old New York is truly fading.
Still, Cathedral bells chime
From the gray of Saint Patrick's ornate towers.
Yellow taxis dart throughout the hours,
As horse drawn carriages
Clip clop up and down Fifth Avenue,
Celebrating wine,
Romance and marriages.
(In a black coach we recline,
Drunk with our passions,
Enraptured on cushions
Of white and blue.)
From tiny, metal carts
Hot dogs steam;
Many chestnuts and pretzels are bought.
As we are brought
To the stills of uptown
To where the poets dream,
Beneath the boughs and branches of brown,
To the fine, aristocratic museums of the arts;
We shall gaze at Rembrandt and Monet,
Until the gates are closed for the day.
And when the night is over,
We shall wander by the Hudson to the west,

The Gilded Sun and Other Verse

Where you shall sleep upon my grateful breast
Beneath the emerald fronds which quiver as they hover.
And underneath that wavering tree
All of the city's majesty
Shall be stilled as we kiss, for I love you best,
My only one, my lover.

The Gilded Sun and Other Verse

South of Florence

The bay looks up from the tawny, ancient sea,
Upon the steely, silver majesty
Of Manhattan's famed skyline, on its vertical mastery.
The red, green, and gold
Of the sky high casements
Of the Empire State Building are exquisite to see
At Christmastime.
Yet traditional sentiments
Are but a story that is told;
Although the birds in Central Park still sing,
Their song withers in the urban cold;
For the old New York is truly fading.
Still, Cathedral bells chime
From the gray of Saint Patrick's ornate towers.
Yellow taxis dart throughout the hours,
As horse drawn carriages
Clip clop up and down Fifth Avenue,
Celebrating wine,
Romance and marriages.
(In a black coach we recline,
Drunk with our passions,
Enraptured on cushions
Of white and blue.)
From tiny, metal carts
Hot dogs steam;
Many chestnuts and pretzels are bought.
As we are brought
To the stills of uptown
To where the poets dream,
Beneath the boughs and branches of brown,
To the fine, aristocratic museums of the arts;
We shall gaze at Rembrandt and Monet,
Until the gates are closed for the day.
And when the night is over,
We shall wander by the Hudson to the west,

The Gilded Sun and Other Verse

Where you shall sleep upon my grateful breast
Beneath the emerald fronds which quiver as they hover.
And underneath that wavering tree
All of the city's majesty
Shall be stilled as we kiss, for I love you best,
My only one, my lover.

The Gilded Sun and Other Verse

A Morning Song

The furrows are alive with crystals and jades.
I wander as a troubadour through cloisters by the sea;
Near oceanic orchards, I dine on oysters blissfully.
Come the night I sleep in reeds, in grasses, on the glades.

I have within my pocket a volume of romantic rhyme,
Snug within my sailor's coat, I write of love and travel.
Roving on the beach, I kick the sandy gravel,
Free from every weight of places and of time.

There is a lady that lives in a castle high.
I behold her now, along with a sigh.
She is clad in a long, alabaster dress.
Her lips are of wine, of bliss; enchanting;
She sings of fair love in the warmth of spring,
As I pine for her kiss and her soft caress.

The Meadows

The cool wine cellar, furnished with your sighs,
Shall leave us drunk and dreaming
In the summerhouse at night,
Beneath the arch of lavender skies,
After our kisses are sated in the gleaming,
Gold-tined meadows, we will be dreaming
Of the gilded, bright
Rosy scented daisies,
Fireflies, briars and mystic grasses.
We shall go, hand in hand,
As the dawning passes,
Among the radiant and grand
Warm, scented gales.
We shall rove like poets on the dales,
And refraining from all thought,
We shall glide among the emerald-hued vales,
On the boundless fields by the rising ocean,
Immersed in naught
But love and emotion.

A Troubadour's Song

When the moon was full, round and fair,
I sauntered through the breezes of blue
Whistling a cheerful troubadour's air,
To lovely, charming thoughts of you.

Now the lamppost, doleful,
Somnolent, and woeful,
Receives the misty rain,
Which kisses every bough with tears,
As it has done now for countless years,
Under the long, gray curtain
Of billowing, heavy skies.

And tears are certain
For the gaze of my eyes,
Sadly and full of pain,
Wanders madly like a breeze,
Wayward and winding,
Beneath the wet
Silhouette
Of gloomy linden trees.

And yet,
With nothing apparently binding,
I call to mind my reveries
To render some portion of the day
To the realm of joy,
As I would do as a boy,
Dreaming of light in spite of my sorrow,
Hoping for a bright, golden tomorrow,
Lost in an amber bed of hay.

I Once Lived in Luxury

I once lived in luxury,
A king, I reveled, below the ornate porticoes.
Drinking from the royal ponds,
A plaything of the fronds,
Of the teeming trees,
I lazed among wells and fantastic seas.
All seasons were my ecstasies.
My loves were all sated,
All!
And every kiss was more than fine.
My every emotion was elated,
Every vineyard yielded flowing wine.
Then came one winter,
Which possessed a chilling breeze.
It froze my throne,
And my kingdom fell.
The death bells did knell,
And I found myself alone.
Now I rove as a pauper goes,
Amid the harrowing wind
That freezes as it blows,
Below those teeming porticoes.

Landscapes

The commencement of voyages,
Begin with florid, marvelous landscapes,
And beautiful maidens in gleaming towers:
These are the things
Which sanctify my hours.
I know of many mystic, misty rings.
A tree immersed in flowers
Is clothed in a cloud, where Indigos and alabasters
Seen in a marble square bequeaths
A sweet, melodic, angelic air
Into my ears, with silver wreaths.

October Nights

My dwellings are haunted,
Every room, and every floor.
The sole candle flickering upon a girandole,
Whispers in a deathly tone down the long, endless corridor.
The gloom of this mansion possesses me whole.
Derelicts rise from their grisly graves,
Amidst moonlit caves.
Strangely and morose,
One particular, ghastly, pale, cruel ghost
Welcomes himself to my ancient house.
And considering himself the bastion's host
He takes me beneath the cryptic clouds,
Conversing with the other wraiths,
In flowing burial shrouds.

And frequently,
When the fingers of the dawn
Rise in the east,
Near the ominous sea
By the dreadful lawn,
After these October nights,
Bereft of normality or delights,
I am often a meal
For a zombie's feast.
And these poems are nothing less than real.

Madness

The chandelier sways
Ominously.
The moonlight plays
Mysteriously
Upon the boughs of the cryptic, weeping birch;
On the panes of my chamber,
Its baleful branches pat and lurch
With frightening hues of dark, blackened amber.
The hallway is ghastly
And uninviting.
I could swear I saw a specter hiding
Outside on the furrow,
On the grave-like meadow;
The light on my candlestick is dying.
In the abysmal wind I hear howling and crying.
I believe that ghosts from their crypts are rising.
My wooden desk is far from bright.
My verse is poisoned in the hellish night.
And all my soul is sighing.
Hallucinations are abounding.
The bell of death is suddenly sounding.
I fall faint with terror on the hard, marble ground.
All is madness,
As I hear the sound
Of mortal waves of dire sadness.
I shall nevermore know neither sunshine nor gladness!
In the dour evening, heavy with fog
I am carried in my mind to the swamp, to the bog,
Where every tree is clothed in misery.
The night is darker than grimy coal.
There is no place to run;
Damnation has killed every remnant of the sun.
And the cryptic crypt awaits my soul!

My Lady

I scurry carefree on the emerald dawn,
To purchase Chablis in the rustic town.
The winds are from the north today.
I am in love with a beautiful lady.
Her face is angelic, her eyes are dark.

Her hair is of diamonds, her mane is black;
Her tresses recline like fleece upon her back.
At peace with all nature, she sings with the lark.

She resides in a bastion by the tranquil sea.
Her gaze is of silver, at one with the moon.
She sings to the stars a blissful tune,
With a radiant voice of harmony.

London, 1969

Smoking a cigarette on Abbey Road,
In the West of London Town,
My gorgeous brunette goes walking by,
She is the apple of my mystical eye,
Passing by a wall of brick and brown.
Gracing my heart with joys of gold.

Angels in the sky
Are dressed as my lady,
Clad in white,
Above the shady,
Sweet, dappled shadows
Where I wait to hold her in the moonlight.

Then suddenly, she clasps my hand,
In the light of a state of peaceful bliss.
And the golden wonder which is born of her kiss
Makes a bright, true heaven out of eves like this.

The Gilded Sun and Other Verse

Juliet

Black haired beauty
Of Verona's carmine blooms,
You lean upon the marble stone
Of your vine-strewn balcony,
Inhaling the soothing, summer perfumes
As you dream among your palatial rooms,
Content to be alone.
On your gilded terrace
Near the boundless, Roman sea,
Your lovely, white face
Blushes as it blooms,
As the stars revolve above you with an ageless majesty.
And far below the willows of blue,
Romeo intensely pines for you,
As his heart does woefully implore,
And you gaze far beyond him, to the ivory moon,
To the firmament of blue,
As though he was nothing more
Than a mere statue.

The Gilded Sun and Other Verse

On Poets

Some write copious volumes
Of prosaic verse and prose.
Yet they know not the poet's life.
They are blind to the rose,
And they flee from ecstasy,
And dire strife
When the carmine reds of sunsets mystically close.
They refuse to shed their blood
For golden pages
That transcend every place and time.
Their rhyme when used rings falsely.
They fail to revere sanctified things.
Their writings are merely a hobby—
Their lines become tired, boring and old.
Their dim flirtations are of flighty birds.
And such ephemeral infatuations
Never grow the wings of angelic words—
Unlike the songs of eternal gold.

The Lane

We wandered along down the sleepy lane,
Which descended to a rushing, blue rivulet;
The breezes were scented with mignonette,
And with the bright, lapping stream's morning refrain.

You walked beside me, gracefully in the autumn sun;
You inhaled the majestic wines of the good, sweet air,
Of roses, of grasses, of carmines and saffron.
We went to a picnic in a garden there.

Aside the brook, beneath leafy, old trees,
Tall reeds wavered around your smooth, white knees,
As the ivory moon arose, full, round, and fair.

Then you tuned to me, ablaze, dreamy yet aware,
Of our mutual need to serve and to please,
Our love in a haze of ecstasies.

The Gilded Sun and Other Verse

Your Mane, Your Eyes

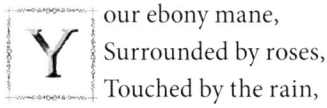

Your ebony mane,
Surrounded by roses,
Touched by the rain,
In garden closes,
Wafting through red leaves
Bequeaths a sweet refrain,
To the cool and magical, brisk, autumn eves.

Your dark, brown eyes,
Surrounded by the ocean,
Touched by lavender, autumnal skies,
Are filled with emotion,
As you gaze at blossoming, mystic shrines,
And charming strains of bating sighs,
More sanctified than sacred wines.

Silhouettes

In the hush of the evening, the opaque rivulets
That sigh to the moonlight in scented flower beds
Produce a thick mist of grays and violets,
Amid silhouettes of leafy, dark reds.
The courses which they flow through are of briars
And grasses, slender and long,
Ending in the starlit bay,
With passionate fires,
Not far from the statues' enchanting song,
Which grace the regal courts above,
Of deep, starry blues, of infinite love.

My Lady is Lovely

My lady is lovely, my lady is fair;
She walks in the noonday, glistening light
To the square, to the veranda, dreaming of the night,
In soft, saline breezes which sail through her hair,
Perfuming her tresses, gleaming in the sun.
She wanders amid the statuary,
Gathering blooms with delicacy,
Where slender, lavender brooklets run.
They are sweet and of the evening, gently do they glow,
Like rain upon the streams, which glitter as they flow.
She meditates on love alone, pining with a sigh.
And when the alabaster moon ascends, she strolls amid the ponds,
Beneath the fragrant boughs, beneath the minty-scented fronds.

Summer

When summer's emerald liveries
Are astounding in bloom,
And the forest's florid filigrees
Gleam beneath our balcony,
Below and beyond our palatial room,
We shall ride in a luxurious carriage,
Down the lane, into the country.
We shall rejoice within our band of marriage,
As we ferry passed the breezes which swirl
Around leafy throngs of the lindens' silhouette,
With a circular, scented whirl;
We shall inhale the gold of a red sunset.
And when we reach the expansive, azure sea,
Beneath the turquoise arch of the splendid skies,
We shall love one another rapturously,
And I shall drown in the pendulous ocean
Of your dusky, delicious, Elysian eyes.
We shall abandon our mind
And savor only emotion,
Immersed in our passion
Of a tender kind.
Then, returning to our bastion,
The moon, of a liquid, pristine light,
Shall fall upon our balcony,
Beneath the lindens' emerald sway,
With a wistful cadence, a wavering melody,
As it does in the night,
As it does in the day.

A Walk After Painting

Our passion, tempered by the daylight,
In the art room, where skins, wet with paint,
Scent the breeze from the window,
Pungent yet faint,
Awaits the raptures of the lovely night.
I shall undo your long, sweet, braided bows,
As we drink champagne where the sunlight glows.
Colored like Van Gogh,
In the zenith of the summertime.
After we are done, we shall rove amid the purple vine,
Your soft and tender hand, gleaming, holding mine.
And as the slender, sobbing fountains ascend
Above the scented, green fronds that waver and bend,
We shall be caught in their pearly, silvery spray,
When the somnolent evening shall gently arrive,
Along with the bees and their buzzing hive,
As the sun retreats, and the fireflies stray.

An American Girl

Vermilion waves,
Rolling, ascend, descend and sigh,
Beneath amber, jades and blossoms
Brushed against the twilit sky.
Each billow paves
A river in the sands,
Where little children wade,
Splashing at the brine,
With their tiny, little hands.
Like a princess you recline,
Beside me on the beach,
Grasping every star of silver and silk,
Within your tender, feminine reach.
The sunlight streams like mother's milk,
Iridescent, luminous, gilded and gold,
As you close your gaze,
Slowly as you laze,
In the tender hold
Of the late summer haze.

The Gilded Sun and Other Verse

The Shade III

Music permeates the late afternoon.
The shade where you walk is heavy,
In contrast with the setting daylight.
Above the myrtles rises the solitary moon,
With a languishing solemnity,
Preparing for the sacred night.
Your hair, black and very long, frames your fair face,
As all scents combine about your body and your dress,
The sighing umbrage is an amorous place,
Where you lean against a log for a kiss and a caress.
Beneath a cloak of drowsy leaves,
Your beauty commands these autumn eves.
You leave me speechless as I behold
Your tresses of dusk, your gazes of gold.

Candles

The candles in our silent room,
Flicker like gold,
And light the past.
They celebrate the new, the present, the old,
And our soft affections which shall always last.
Your cheeks in bloom
Are of a lovely cast,
As I kiss you as the sun descends,
Outside our mansion, where the fleeced bough bends,
Sending us into raptures, timeless, and true,
As the moon ascends majestically, into the blue.

Epilogue IV

And now, dear reader,
I have written my rhyme,
In a cloistered yard,
Beneath a redolent, leafy, summery cedar;
I have fulfilled in my time
The duties of a lifelong bard.
Enough of fair poetry,
Enough of chiseled verse,
Enough of the word, our mystic ruby,
Enough of traveling high and low
Throughout the varied realms of the universe;
Enough of sun, the rains, the snow.
Now I am free to freely go
Into a reticence called wisdom.

I shall laze by the sea,
In the solemn glory
Of another celestial kingdom.
And so I end my soliloquy.
Fini, fini, au revoir, fini.

X

Mystic Wines

A Word From the Author

Mystic Wines is the tenth and next to last book poetry featured within this Anthology, comprised of roughly forty poems. This volume was begun and completed during the summer of 2018 with the hope that it would be written according to the inspirations of The Holy Spirit, to the Good Will of God, in keeping with His providential wisdom. When *Mystic Wines* was completed in every literary aspect, in July of 2018, I hoped with a longing that did not disappoint me that the afore mentioned aspirations had been achieved, at least to a significantly laudable extent, and I was confident that the other, more incidental aspirations of this new collection were also realized and brought to a successful conclusion. My vocation of being called to write poetry by the will of God occurred in a high school library in the midst of my seventeenth year. I was then struck with the revelation as by a lightening bolt that in order to become a *true poet* entailed a life pursued and lived within a solemn and reverent spirit of self sacrifice, in service to God above all, and to my neighbors. In this art form there is and never should be any room for furthering one's own name, to seek fame or renown, or to pursue money for money's sake, nor to display one's apparent talents as if they belonged to or stemmed from oneself, when in fact they are exclusively unmerited gifts given by God from His benevolent hands.

I wish to sincerely and humbly thank my wonderful publisher, Katherine Bizzoco, for all of the exceptional kindness and professional support she has shown to me during the creative process of this anthology and to the litany of my many precious friends, teachers, and family members who have supported me throughout the years in my service to the public as a poet. I am forever indebted to these many wonderful people, and indeed to many more. The poems which comprise this volume are true to the same highly esteemed principles which make up the rest of this exceptional volume. Finally, all the verse you will find within *Mystic Wines* appear in the order in which they were written, and adhere to form a composite whole.

~John Lars Zwerenz

To Mary

Totus tuus ego sum, et omnia mea tua sunt.

Introduction

I first met John Zwerenz in September of 1986 when he entered my humanities class that golden year when he was a senior in high school. A colleague had recommended him saying, "I am sending you an amazing student." I placed that student in the back seat of the last row because his name began with a Z, but I saw right away he was listening intently. Here was that rara avis in a classroom, a genuine learner.

It is an axiom that poetic flames burn brightest in a poet's youth. The "real world" has its way of stealing imagination's thunder and imposing its peculiar drabness over the poetic faculties. Not so with John. Life became a school with many classrooms and his humanities class broadened into Humanity's Classroom. Now, at the age of fifty, the one time student poet who sat in the last seat is enjoying a final bloom of autumn.

Long ago I remember him stopping by my desk to compliment me on my Sappho lecture. Soon after he began to share his fondness for French Symbolists like Verlaine and Baudelaire. He was also steeped in advanced theology.

But poetry was his mistress. It dominated his thoughts and actions. One day he missed class because he had overslept on a bed of grass in the cemetery adjacent to the school, having fallen asleep musing on death. For John, death was the nexus between poetry and philosophy.

As for philosophy, John was reading Nietzsche at the time, along with Pluto, Kant, Sartre, Aquinas, Augustine and many others. Yet it was poetry which dominated him, fired his emotions, and consumed his energy.

He always carried some book of poetry in the halls. Poetry for him was like kindling wood. Beside poetry, math and science for him were banal.

Of himself at that time, John writes, "*I was 17 years of age that spring, and from that day onward I immersed myself in just about every poet of renown I could find. Aside from the French Symbolists of Rimbaud's era, such as Verlaine, Nerval and Baudelaire, I also fell in love with the great romantic bards of Victorian England and America such as Byron, Shelley, and especially our own Edgar Allan Poe. By the time I entered undergraduate school at Queens College in New York, I was thoroughly proficient in composing great, metered, rhyming poetry. I truly began to bloom.*"

In the second to last segment of this anthology, John the wanderer looks for a place to rest.

The choice for him was the same as it was for The French novelist and art critic Charles Marie Huysmans, whose friend had observed, "There can only be one of two endings for such a writer, the gallows or the cross." John has chosen the latter.

~Paul Franzetti,
Professor Emeritus, Saint John's University, New York, 2019

The Regal Dawn

On sumptuous evenings in late July,
I would scamper down diamond-studded dunes,
Beneath an azure confusion of ethereal moons,
And I slept in the sand where linnets would fly.

I drank from a silver cup a cosmic brew.
I drowned myself in pelagic brines where cathedral bells would ring.
In my raptures of ecstasies, I heard a chorus of seraphim sing,
Wrapped in curtains of green, and petals of dew.

And when I awoke to the splendid phantasms of the regal dawn,
I witnessed our Deity resplendent and bright,
In command of all love, from morning until night
As I sat in astonishment, on a gilded, gold, eternal lawn.

Mystic Wines

Ode to Bram Stoker

Our sallow hearts, they crave true peace,
And so our carriage sallies forth
To the regions of the mystic north,
To the rocky shores of Whitby's sand
Where Stoker wrote his masterpiece,
Hidden in that haunted land.
Do you all not know
That every monster in embryo
Is borne from an ill played piano?
Its airs do spread like vampire wings
Over poorly protected, humble things.
And when the wild harbor glows at night
With an odious, translucent, ominous light
The colored panes of Saint Mary's show
Reds morose, upon the doomed archipelago
Warning us all of what exists down below.
And Stoker, drunk, over his morbid manuscript
Attempts to raise Lucifer's clan.
Saved or sullied, kept or ripped,
He hands the pages to the swallowing, tan
Dusk that has taken his psyche to the east,
To the Northern Sea, that boundless beast
Filled with hungry Sirens, all craving blood;
Their teeth, ivory as the Roman colonnades,
Their hearts, older than the freezing Celtic glades
Fill Stoker's ink well with the all consuming blood
Of a despair far darker than of Dante's mind.
For literary fancy has become unkind—
And worse than real—
Which no desperate dawn can appease nor reveal
The slightest possibility of hope
As the author doth wail
He flees to the grasp of a tightly wound rope—
Dare you place your dear self in his horrible tale?

The Garden III

Your long, exquisite hair,
Resting upon your naked back,
Parted, straight, ineffable, and fair,
Engraves upon my scarlet heart
Its ruby tinted tresses of black.

With a feminine decision,
All the tears I have shed forever depart
With one lover's acquisition.
For your unspoken sermon,
Solemn and true
Permeates the winter around me
Creating all anew.

Yes, now is the sacred hour,
Devoid of every haunting rue.
For all does bloom like a glimmering bower.
And your sable gaze and your soft, scented mane
Which, in time, I shall eternally ascertain
Exudes the tones of a sacred cello,
Hyacinths and the crimson rose,
In melodies which are sweet and mellow,
In the still of our sunlit garden close.

Mystic Wines

Dusk II

Wavering myrtles and mountainous boons
Rise to your palatial rooms
On a cliff, free from cares, in dusky hours,
Upon your marble squares, and radiant bowers.

Curtains of purple which grace your chambers
Sway and part as autumnal perfumes
Waft in to touch your dwelling's members:
Your baby grands, your vases and blooms.

And every staircase you descend
In your dress of white, clad with lace,
Beams with the sun, as your pristine face
Reflects the pillars and the boughs which bend.

Now is the time when the grand beyond
Flows in through the hush of stained glass panes,
As tender as a symphony, rising from the wild plains
When every scarlet hue and longing correspond.

My dear beloved child, my sister of the redolent breeze,
The night, umbrageous and blessed with melodic accords
Has claimed your bastion, as its loyal and loving lords
Summon your carriage,
As you pray upon your naked knees,
To take us to a sanctified marriage,
Among the bliss of holy trees.

The Song of John Keats

In the late, expansive breezes of the fall,
When humble poets seek to learn
Wisdom from the secrets of a Grecian urn
Streams of zephyrs through tall trees call.

What is that poignant melody
Which beckons the bard with its luminous art
Moving my all too sensitive heart
To the sunlit terrace, looking out to sea?

What are those lofty symphonies
Which tremble through my iridescent rooms
Emitting an air which, scented, blooms
Like the rose from my inkwell's rhapsodies?

The Grove II

The sandy grove dressed with cherry trees
Wears carmines and other hue's, delicate and yellow.
It stands among a stream, azure, soft and mellow
Which glimmers in the sun, caressed by the breeze.

I arrived from the isles of the bright Floridian Keys
On an ancient vessel in three weeks time,
Landing on the coast of Normandy in France,
Weaving mystic, gilded, visionary rhyme,
In a sailor's pining, romantic trance,
In search of regal pleasantries.

I happened upon a rustic, old inn
Where I heard the sweet strains of a violin.
And, behold, I met a maiden, doubly fair,
And I inhaled the blossoms of her raven hair.

She brought me a glass of Belgian beer
And sat down beside me
In a redolent, mahagony booth,
And my eyes, they shed a tear,
Of gratitude and eternal truth
As the haunting moon kissed the sea.

Then we walked onto an emerald dale,
Where the purple sun set beyond the red farms.
With tender kisses and open arms,
We loved one another as the day did pale.

And as the moon rose in the firmament, ever higher
Into the star clad canvass of the astounding night,
We found ourselves immersed in a sacred light,
And we met the evening's midnight with a lover's pyre.

The Ghost Ship

My vessel left Boston, seaward in the rain,
As I ferried to the east, to the vast, Italian main.
Half way across the ocean,
In a tempest, my emotion
Turned from tranquility to disdain
As I witnessed a commotion—
A vision reserved for the rabidly insane.

For above thick, nebulous billows,
Which clapped over the emerald sleep,
Like a shroud of gloomy, dreadful pillows,
Dark clouds did amass, foreboding and deep.

In the distance, barely seen on the watery court,
Sailed a cryptic schooner, wooden and old;
It swayed to either side in the maritime cold,
Wild and wavering from starboard to port.

And without rhyme or reason,
Devoid of any tangible treason,
This ship of ghastly vacancy
Revealed to the eye not a soul on board.
And without a trace of clemency,
It leveled the waves like a terrible sword.
And then, to my abject horror I beheld
An animated corpse with skeletal hands
Clasping the wheel, on deck, alone,
Save for spiritual contrabands,
Which possessed that devilish specter's groan.

The horrid wraith did reel with the wind—
And an ominous rush, a poisoned zephyr,
Did cling to my neck, with the dusky scent
Of an ill and tainted tamarind,
A grand and dreadful, dark disease.
And then, with a hatred I had never known before,
His dead and steely eyes had bent

Mystic Wines

Over the infinite, oceanic floor
Before he exclaimed to me,
Through the black and dour, briny breeze,
Unhallowed, untamed on the ferocious sea:
"I am death,
And your hopeful desire
To reach the shore safely
Shall now expire
As I take your down—
To eternal fire!"

Diadems

I fashioned the wings of my spirit
With the ethereal tears of black, spotted butterflies,
Intoxicated with the noonday sun.

I greeted the most egregious heresies
Committed by austere tyrants,
And, using spiritual alchemy,
By mercy, transformed those savage apostates
Into pious servants, one by one.

I wandered beneath the brine kissed stars;
Endless trails of grass
In mystic woodlands
Opened like ecstatic dahlias;
Each one promised eternal happiness
By appearing as moonlit, mysterious sands,
Clad with wondrous forms of reedy hopes.

I took all dawns as miracles;
On summer nights, on fire,
I resurrected chivalry
From the pages of my poems,
Writ in streams with leaves for a pen,
Every line dedicated to the servants of The Virgin,
And to her seven dolors, those noble plights.

I warned the black, Saxon knights
In their mad, metallic arrogance
To beware of Dante's circular hells:
Nine in number, never knowing an end.

Forsaking sleep, I conversed with angels.
All romances became waterfalls.
And my bride descended like a paradisal queen
From the heights of Jerusalem, adorned with diadems,
Of regal purples, jades and gems.

The Lane II

We walked as angels in the rosy breeze,
Among holly green hedgerows (just us two).
The lane was gold and the sky was blue,
And we heard through the boughs rare symphonies,
As the grasses framed your naked knees.

Descending from the leafy branches, each note borne from above,
Graced our enraptured hearts, flowing like a joyful stream,
As we lost ourselves in a wondrous dream,
Immersed in the meaning of eternal love.

The Shrine of Saint Anne

After the rain had fallen on the town,
Beyond the maze of city streets,
Where sounds become suburban retreats
I found a shrine upon a down.

Silhouettes of oaks, and an iron fence
Found me amid blooms which marked the entrance.
With dappled rays, the sun did set
Over my trail, as I crossed a rivulet.

Slender fountains and marble floors of white
Bathing in the umbrage of the wavering trees
Emitted a concerto in the redolent breeze.

And in one corner of the shrine's pure light
I beheld the spirit of good Saint Anne,
And discovered what it means to be holy man.

The Window Bay

The window, half open, looks out upon the boundless sea,
While a black baby grand plays in a minor key
A melancholic air,
Enamored with rhyme.

It speaks of a former life,
A solemn ardor, banished by time,
Calling to mind the eyes of my wife.

And every time I hear it played,
My heart becomes younger, and less afraid
In the broad, omniscient, yellow sun,
Streaming from the cosmic sea,
Over the grotto, where love birds sound their summery voice,
And once again, our hearts are one,
Forever to rejoice—
Triumphantly.

Mystic Wines

Stilled by a Sigh

Her veil is long, modest and white,
And more than just merely lovely and fair.
Her speech is terse, yet debonair.
Her braided tresses are long and black,

And rest like gems upon her back,
In the reticent boon of the tranquil night.
Her gaze, it gleams like jewels in the shade,
On the arboreal, scented misty shore.
Her kisses are of cinnamon, and her voice is one of gold,
I pine as I implore,
To hear her Christian, melodic ode,
Beneath the Roman promenade.
Atop the mounts, the stars on high
Along with the moon bestow their light
To soft siroccos as they sanctify the night,
As her song is sung with a Celtic sigh.

Her Silken Kiss

I wandered through the countryside at night,
In search of a virtuous, pious bride,
A true and faithful holy mate.
On a rustic lane, with diadems on either side,
I beheld a sable, scented mane, gleaming in the moonlight.
Her tresses were enchanting, redolent, long and straight,
Her eyes were deep, profound and dark;
She appeared as an angel, in that solemn park,
And her voice was grave, of a statuary's tones—
Pure and profound, of exalted rubies, gems and other precious stones.
She took my hand in a garden close,
Where the scent of lilies, emitted from her lips,
Sent my psyche into rapture, as my silken heart took sips
From her soft, silken buss borne of sunshine and the rose.

Mystic Wines

The Half Opened Window

How many days in the year
Must I live without you?
My bride, my love, my only, my dear.
The gold, summer sun shines above and about you,
And in the scented, solemn breeze I hear
Over the somnolent ponds of blue
Effete, acrostic rhythms which flow
From your iridescent, luminous bower.
They glide in through the opened window—
Hymns of a resolute, relentless flow
Which permeate this hallowed hour.

They haunt me so, those melancholic airs
Sacrosanct, allotropic, like a mysterious sun
Filled with the lethargy of a dim despair,
As they enter my chamber, with imprecision,
Calling my soul, morose yet immortal,
To poignant thoughts of days gone by.

And the minutes pace, and the hours weep
Like sands in a glass, as I resolutely keep
Your angelic face within my mind
Born from the gardens that wistfully sleep
In an atmosphere untouched, unkind.

After Many Sullen Years

After many sullen years
Of numb confusion and abject pain
I have become inconstant as a weather vane.
And my bitter tears
Trailing from blind eyes
Which sees evil and good
With an identical gaze
Gives rise to hollow, remorseless cries
In the forsaken wood, my wayward ways
Ascend to empty, clueless skies.
And my faith does pale
With each passing morn,
As I go hither and there, wanton and worn—
O, the sad and tragic tale!

Isolation II

The iridescent sky
At the peak of its beauty
Reigns like a cosmic oligarchy
Knowing every when, where, and why.

And the reedy trail, bathed in sunlight
Which I travel upon, as a vagabond,
Beckons me to contemplate the great beyond
Where infinite peace is married to delight.

There are pianos playing in the trees by the piers
On either side of the breeze blown lane.
There are mystic wines within the rain,
Which sanctify my pages, wet—as with tears.

One Fine Day

One fine, glorious, golden day,
Donning a sailor's coat, happily,
Treading through majestic garden closes,
I wandered freely as one can be,
Amid mellow daisies, and scarlet roses.

I passed by a wooden trellis of white,
Strewn with ivory, and struck by the sunlight,
On my way to the regal village square,
To a royal wedding by the sea,
Where a young, handsome man and his maiden fair
Enraptured in the noble, amorous air,
Shall pledge eternal vows of true fidelity.

And they walked as a true king and queen
For one glorious day.
And from balconies above,
Made from stone and clad with florets of green,
Palms of victory did joyfully sway
To celebrate their love,
In the quaint little town, by the blue, rustic bay.

Mystic Wines

Robert Louis Stevenson Samoa, 1894

I shall go to the wine cellar
And retrieve some cold Chablis
In this dreadful chill of winter,
Encompassed within a dour ennui.

Outside on the frozen dales,
Aristocratic ladies daily change their faces
In eerie, haunted, dusky places
As the overwhelming daylight pales.

Yes, the tangerine sun—
It weeps and waits,
Delightful to no one;
Oh, these doleful, maddening tales!

If I could only find a gate,
I would gladly assassinate
My ghastly imaginations,
Filled with innumerable specters of self hate;
And bitter, cold recriminations.

Perhaps it is too late?
My dear, I am in the basement;
Do come down here, and witness what I can not prevent.
Every slice of the decaying casement
Has left my breath without a vent—
And all has turned to a fatal malice.
And my face—Is it changed?
Is this fate heaven has arranged?
O God, is there no solace
For the damned and the deranged!?

Mystic Wines

Byron's Ghost

In the furrows Byron, I roved alone,
Through a throng of oaks and shady willows.
Beneath a firmament of viral billows,
I approached his mansion of dark gray stone.

I inhaled his many deaths as I did dare to dream,
Passing through an ominous silhouette I went,
Beneath an ancient ogive, where its boughs were long and bent.
Its rusty iron gate hovered over a cloudy stream.

The foyer was lifeless, and the panes were dark.
In the hall no life existed save spiritual contraband,
A solitary candle was lit by a hand
Unseen to the eyes. Outside, in the park
I imagined I glimpsed a phantom of hate.
The boughs, by harsh gales seemed to relate
Perdition as they crashed together.
The sky grew dim, and I wondered whether
I should leave the realm of that haunted estate.

And then, I beheld a horrible sight:
For Lord Byron's ghost descended down the stairway;
His countenance was white and I could hear him say:
"You will not survive the coming night."

Then, from the graveyard, from each pale, sickly reed,
I heard empty voices bereft of all hope
Rise from coffins, from the dreary slope
Which surrounded the house, as my brain did bleed.
And Byron smiled as a maddened bard.
The moonlight bled through the ashen glass
And I fled to the foyer, into the black yard,
Mad beneath the rusty pass,
Hearing Byron laugh as the horrid night
Consumed the entirety of the accursed land.
And my own fate, doomed, passed from my soul
Forever un-whole,
Into the horrid grip of his frozen hand.

Mystic Wines

Saint John's Wood

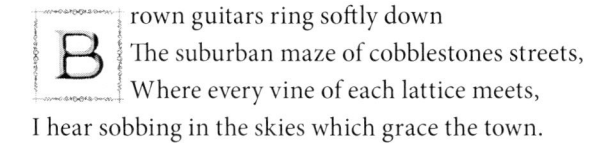

Brown guitars ring softly down
   The suburban maze of cobblestones streets,
   Where every vine of each lattice meets,
I hear sobbing in the skies which grace the town.

In long, cryptic shadows, in the redolent shade,
Hidden in the shade of the boughs' disguise of dying trees,
Beneath their fading, bended heads wavering in the breeze,
Far off, solemn vows are reluctantly made.

Singing in a minor key,
Two lovers walk in the languorous rains
Where obscure beauties gleam on the plains
Reflecting their dreams tenuously.

Uncertain of their nuptial designs,
To and fro, they wander as warm gales
Glide through their hair as daylight pales
Over old, silent houses, serenading their minds.

And then the moon, in its profound luminosity,
Reveals each to the other's admiring eyes
Their nebulous doubt—which lives and dies.

The approaching dawn hearkens beyond what they can see:
Holding a future concealed behind a veil,
Whispering in the wind, as yet, an untold tale.

Mystic Wines

Saint Paul's Cathedral

In the shadows of Saint Paul's Cathedral,
Beneath the gray stones of its ancient wall,
I embraced your hair and its braided bows.
Its raven tresses out shined the stars,
And thrilled my soul from head to toe.
And all my years of unyielding woe
Were changed to airs borne of white guitars.
And then I hear you speak my name,
With a softness no poet could ever pen.
As we walked into your warm, cozy den.
With a gentle hush the moonlight came,
And it rests upon your sable mane.

Now a soft concerto of violins
Fall into your gaze like an angel's wings,
Into the deep dark browns of your immaculate eyes,
Which speak to me of mandolins.
And all the pure and humble things
(Which grace your chamber, along with my love)
Are lit from above,
As a holy Saint complies
With the very hues of heaven
Which live within your eyes.

Sailing

I set off for London from the coast of Normandy,
I an old, wooden schooner,
Laden with gold.
The billows were cold and chilled the sea.
And the brisk, rising evening fell much sooner—
Much sooner than I had been told.
The stars were drunk with cosmic wine,
And the firmament was boundless and bright.
I was immersed in a canopy of mystic light,
In zephyrs of china bluish brine—
Which endowed the deck with the scents of night.

Ode to Saint John

Living with Mary, in a rural place,
Saint John was but a diadem
In the golden crown of her royal grace.
And there each utterance was a sacred gem.

With unspeakable beauty she tended to the home.
And John, her faithful son, never thought to roam.
And on winter nights, beneath the stars,
She would kneel and pray, beside the glowing, wooden bars.

And when they were forced to suffer a bitter goodbye,
(For he was exiled in Patmos, an isolated isle.)
She still retained her lively faith and gorgeous smile,
With a longing and a grievous, pious sigh.

And upon Saint John's return
Her heart did yearn
To see her Son in Paradise:
And the glory of God, Holy Thrice!—
How God's tender heart did purely burn!

The one evening, solemn and mild,
The the time for grieving had come to an end
For both John's mother and him, her beloved child,
For he witnessed her rise
Above the dell where the reeds did bend.

With the moon at her feet,
Surrounded by twelve brilliant stars,
In the ineffable realm of celestial skies,
Her glorious Assumption was complete.
And so does end the sacred tale.
Ave Maria, gratia plena,
And holy Catholic heaven hail!

The Farmhouse

I arrived in a Portuguese port at dawn,
And wandered to a rustic inn.
I sat in a booth amid the lively din;
A chandelier above me lit my view of Fatima's lawn
And the meadow beyond, of dew and grain.
I ordered an ale from a pretty waitress,
With dark, black ringlets in her hair.
We walked to a farmhouse in the summer rain,
And I loved her until noon—resting on her dress.
The fragrance of her dew clad breast laced the aromatic air
With scents of thyme and mignonette.
We found peace in the hay—
A lovely coquette,
She haunts my psyche to this day.
Then we roved through a garden, a florid square.
Where terra-cotta statues stood beside the vines
Sprawling heavenward to fantastic columns, gleaming in the light.
And we fell into one another's visual wines,
Devoted to our hearts of fire, and kisses of the night.

Mystic Wines

The Storm II

I awoke to a storm in an ancient time.
The rain fell upon the branches and the vines,
And filled the streams of eglantines,
As in my notes I penned metered rhyme.

The moon up high did weep with a tear,
Upon the land, in a silhouette of the silent wood.
Willows and roses wavered where I stood,
As the fragrant breeze tasted of beer.

And in the hour when the sun went down,
Over the plains of a distant, tawny, chestnut brown,
I beheld a lass, more beautiful than life.

She smiled as an angel, and took me by my hand,
Sighing like a siren, upon the grassy land,
And I knew from her kiss—she would be my wife.

Chillingham Castle

Hungry from my excursion, and thirsty from the sun,
I came upon an immense estate,
Nestled far from this very world of strife.
Indeed, it seemed severed from life,
And it looked as though I was the only one
To find this place, but alas to late—
For I saw not a soul to aid my condition.

The entrance was imposing to sight and to sound,
For the loneliness of such a cold, dark place
Made my dizzy head spin round and round.
I beheld no forms, no voices, no face,
Which resembled a human over the entire ground.

I made my way to the keep of the mansion.
Where I made a discovery, dim and dour.
For a grave with an inscription there,
In the horror of that bastion,
In the terror of the stifling air,
Indeed, spelled my name, as I passed through a veil—
With a pitiful and desperate, helpless wail—
In the dire blackness of my final hour.

Blossoms in Her Hair

How lovely her grace seems to me,
When she wanders through the courtyard
In a state of precious grace.
There angels praise the symphony of her face,
As she walks near the undulating sea,
Where the briny wind speaks of her masculine bard.

How delicate are her braided bows,
Where a stream from paradise gently flows,
Crowning her a queen, as she kneels in the square;
For from sanctity she will never part,
With ardor in her sacred heart,
And cherry blossoms in her hair.

Mystic Wines

Roses on the Waves

On my way to meet you,
I gathered and brought a new bouquet,
Of the earth's finest florets,
From a gilded dale of gleaming hay.
And knowing you lived upon an isle,
I had to swim from my boat to the rocky moor,
And while I swam to you,
I lost every rose in the sounding sea,
In the shower of a violent downpour.
And so each bloom was graced with a potion,
Like a dappled poem of a mystic shore.

Now that I have recovered from the brine of willows,
Where the waves were strewn with those scented petals,
Beneath the firmament of azure blue.
Swirling in circles, in the summery sun,
Please accept these redolent souvenirs from the oceanic blue,
And the fragrances they bestow upon you,
As they unite our perfumed hearts as one,
Your face as an angel's, our love as true.

My Love

My love can not be found in the verse of Poe.
Nor in Shakespeare's litanies of the wise man's woe,
Verily, I tell you that you will not find her there,
Resting upon a balcony, in a state of swooning, mad despair.

For nor Romeo can lure her from my arms.
(She yields her secret charms
To me and to my heart alone.)
The sunlight beams on her bastion made of stone,
Where she walks to her royal carriage,
Dreaming of a sacred marriage,
And a knight (none but I) she can truly call her own.

A Sanctified Flame

I must have lived a long time ago,
When your long, black hair met the contrast of the snow.
And your smile of an angel's filled my heart with a sacred flame.
Into my life, as a blessing, you came,
As a musical sunlit sirocco.
And my psyche and heart have never been the same
Ever since I beheld your holy sight.
For the cadence of your flowing name
Renders dead my rues of plight.

On Soft, Spring Nights

On soft spring nights,
When the sun is in the west,
Dying over the saffron crest
Of the purple, jagged mount,
On the passing clouds I count
The blissful boons of the April lights
When my every kiss can love you best.
And when my eyes do run their sacred trail
From your raven tresses to your silver feet,
There begins the holy, chivalric tale
Which makes whole our ardor, triumphant, complete.

Mystic Wines

In Shadows on Foot

In shadows on foot, I strolled alone,
In search of true love and an inn for rest.
I drank mystic liquors which I found in the breeze,
In a wondrous grove of walnut trees,
And I declared you as my solemn queen
Whom I would serve, whom I loved best.
For on the banks of a wide, lush ravine,
Where a rivulet splashed over stone,
I saw you picking rare, bright flowers,
Hyacinths and purple roses, yellow daffodils,
With joyful tears, in the scented shades of misty, dusky hours,
In aromatic dells, on brilliant, mystic hills,
When God reveals His healing powers.

Peace III

I ventured out, one cold winter's night
To an isolated furrow, to a holly green pond.
I looked up high to the grand beyond,
And saw rumbling from the sky a tremendous light.

No passersby did see me, no human eye did know
That I came to seek my Maker,
In the sun and on those trails of snow.

Still I heard no sound from Him.
Then I pleaded for a sign.
And I heard from God a distant voice:
"I am yours, and you are mine!"

Tears

Another bitter dawn,
I am alone, forsaken, cold and forlorn.
One priest did say
I will never see her
In a lovely way
When in heaven we shall forever live.

Beyond all years,
Beyond all strife,
The one, sole comfort I have had in this life
Is having shed so many tears.

The Courtyard II

I will tell you truly with my heart
Just how lovely you are, my dear.
The rain clouds fade,
And slowly depart
Under the gold of the sun's chandelier.

The descending gilded stars, over every ancient rampart,
In the courtyard where you wade,
On the marble silhouettes, over every colonnade,
Praises with grace your angelic face.

Near fountains which sob, rising slender in the shade,
You touch every precious beam, in the firmament of grace.
Your regal countenance, looking out to sea,
Overwhelms my psyche,
Which transfers to my soul
Things which words can not express.

For you make my spirit whole,
As you dream among the statuary, holy in that sacred place,
Donning a bright and splendid dress,
Clad with frills and lace.

The Driest Place

Yes, there are many tears to cry.
In our collective orphanage,
In our common well
That has run dry, verily as the driest place.
Wherefore art is our love and our duty to our
Thrice good, holy, omnipotent Sage?
And of destiny, who can tell,
Whence one's death in the final hour?

Tell me, then,
Will you attain that gold, bright garden,
That holy and heavenly, infinite bower?
Or will you find it horrid an odd
To have your soul
Swallowed whole
Sharing the fate of Marquis De-Sade?

And when you die,
Will you leave in grace?

Yes, there are many tears to cry.
And yes, this world is the driest place.

Mystic Wines

The Good Road's End

I wandered beyond many thankless hills to a barren wood,
Beneath frozen firmaments; and as often as I could
I would warm myself in the boons of a hearth's gold flames,
Encompassed by many leafless trees, yet each devoid of names.

A silhouetted reticence reigned in the night.
Every sanguine bough was shaken by the merciless cold.
Gales bended branches like thieves at twilight,
And I heard in their echoes a sapience of old.

My worn, brittle boots breached the untouched pall
Of the vast, virginal meadow, as sheets of snow began to fall.

Every flake spoke of reason, coupled with grace.
Their silent epiphanies clothed the umbrage of the mead,
As they covered the hidden browns of every chestnut reed:—
One often finds God in a lonely place.

The Ascension

I

Hades
I began the long journey with one weary advance,
As a homeless villager, quite alone in the world.
As subterranean pits unfurled,
I opened my psyche to the endless, dreadful dance.

There were demons on fire with a lust for unkindness
As they turned from truth and indulged in blindness,
Turning the damned over coals in fire,
In Satan's black chapel where he rules in pain.

His entire existence is one lived in vain.
For he chose to murder, his only desire
Ever since his inception, envying man:
Fashioned in God's likeness, born for God's plan,
Destined for a celestial body, to be another god.

The devil could not suffer this, and so the rebellion began.
"I will prevail!" he swore, in his witless, infant mind.
And though it might seem obscure and odd,
Nothing but fire did the demon find.

Afraid of all below and above,
He prowls and travels as an arsonist on leave.
(So he thinks.)
And the only moments he can bare is when he drinks
Vodkas, rums, and biles from the slums,
He knows naught of how to love,
He knows naught of how to grieve.
(To hatred alone he utterly succumbs.)

Mystic Wines

II

The Countryside
And as I raised a toast in the knell
Of a rustic and old, quaint French inn,
I decided I had enough of hell.
So I danced with a waitress, in that blessed place,
To the happy chime of a distant church bell;
So we took a covered carriage
To the festivals and to the quaint, old squares,
And our romance did begin,
Destined by God for a sacred marriage.
(She wore an ivory dress, made of the finest lace.)
I left her more than mirthful, playing rosy, classical airs,
On an old and russet mandolin.

III

The Dawn
As the dawn crept over the greenery,
I awoke to my notebook for the very last time.
And I took in the hills, the canvass and its scenery,
Seeking, like a beggar, a nickel or a dime.

My God, Thrice Holy

Holy Trinity
Help my poor soul,
And never abandon me
To myself;
For no one but Thee
Can render my spirit whole.
In the consecrated furnace,
Before the witness of the angelic host—
Here upon the earth.

Spare me from purification
After death,
And O, by Thy Kingly might
Welcome my being into the radiant sight
Of your thrice victorious face,
In this life and in eternity—
Of charity, peace, and ineffable grace.

In Nomine Patris et Filii et Spiritus Sancti
Amen
The End

XI

Cathedrals in the Rain

Cathedrals in the Rain

Preface

    This anthology now concludes with a fresh volume of verse which I composed during the spring and summer of 2019. The rhyme contained within *Cathedrals in the Rain* is unique in my lifelong catalogue of poetry books in that it exclusively pertains to the ethereal aspects of this life and of the next, espousing on the existential essence of those things in existence which are and remain *unseen*. In order to bring out of the darkness these things which mankind is privy to on one level of consciousness or another, I first had to venture out of my psyche's normal state to discover, through mystical visions, the forms and characteristics of these entities which, until now have been largely ignored, both in literature and in life. Having completed this final segment of The Complete Anthology, I can state with a deep and solemn gratitude to The Virgin and to God that the experiment was successful, and those things of wonder, beauty and terror remain unseen no more.

~John Lars Zwerenz
New York, 2020

To Mary, Most Holy

Cathedrals in the Rain

If You Give Your Heart Away

If you give your heart away
Then consecrate with certainty.
Make your union for eternity,
For more than just a passing day.

For if her hair is of the skies,
And her tresses are of the blissful sun,
And her kisses unite you as truly one,
Then bury your head into her sighs.

And if her eyes are of the sea,
And resemble endlessly God's faithful love,
Then go, ascend to her abode above,
Where rapture reigns with ecstasy.

Ecstasy (A Sonnet)

On the woolly fleece of a wide, wintry down
When powdered, descending, white, crystal snow
Graced every hemlock and pine as I did go
Roving blissfully and cheerful on a frosted lane to town.

Boughs brushed flakes together as the sun set in bliss
Blooming like a bower, russet, vast and gold.
Its nascent, starry dusk renewed in the wondrous cold
Memories of your love, and of our first true kiss.

You wore a soft sweater, and your face did blush
With the warmth of a lover's angel, soft, sweet and fair.
Mutually given gazes, in the brisk, majestic air

Would fire our united blood among the forest's hush.
And when the moon did ascend, over the silent, azure sea,
Your eyes would over brim with sighs, with a timeless ecstasy!

Cathedrals in the Rain

The Courtyard III

Far beyond the gloom of shadows and graves,
The sun sheds red through the boughs of the lindens.
Teeming, ivory billows, and the rosy waves
Weave in from the nearby, tremulous sea.
The marble, alabaster enclaves
Which cradle the likes of you and me
Exalt the fountains of the square and its gardens,
Crowning their immaculate majesty.

For just as love does never force,
Though it glows as the nascent evening arrives
When statues gleam, and leaves take their course
Beneath the azure tinted skies.
While the moonlight beams, they gracefully endorse
Our eternal love, which rising, dives
Into those heavens which immerse our eyes
With concertos of rapture, and an angel's sighs.

The Baby Grand

The black baby grand,
Caressed by slender fingers,
By a young, red-haired's fair, small hand,
(With her russet curlicues in a bow)
Emits a cadence that languishing, lingers
From the royal nook of her regal parlor,
Where she gazes through the stained-glass window
Upon the lagoon and the turquoise harbor;
(A wave ascends, then reels,
Circling down to the watercress.)
Her patrician dress
(One might confess)
While modest, reveals
Her soft, lavish knees,
Where lily-scented harmonies
Rise from that medieval chamber,
Out into the garden below,
Through the half-open, bluish panes,
Where the dahlias, slumbering, waver,
Now to and fro, now high, now low,
Kissed by those amber, ghostly strains.

Cathedrals in the Rain

The Duchess (A Sonnet)

In the softness of the warm and sunny, sunlit spring,
Up high, upon the dappled cradle of a terrace,
Above the vast wood, where the gleaming streams race,
I can hear the tender voice of my duchess sweetly sing.
Her mane is long and black, and her face is fair, divine,

And the many beauteous aspects of her soul's felicity
Graces her every song of the breeze with sanctity,
Which enchants every willow in the redolent air of wine.

And as the cool, nascent evening rises with the moon,
My heart falls into a rapturous boon
Struck by her eyes of a brownish, bright hue.

She descends from the balcony, as the sighing, elysian dew
Rejoices in the shadows where all ecstasies await
As my lover's' lips draw near, through her garden's open gate.

Behold

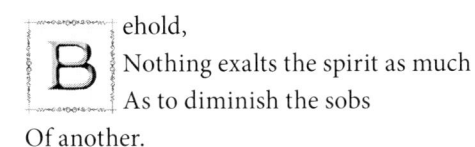

Behold,
Nothing exalts the spirit as much
As to diminish the sobs
Of another.

Verily,
Nothing bequeaths as many gems
Upon your eternal crown of glory
As consoling your brother
In a fit of distress.

For I have seen all of humanity
Weeping in pits of isolation,
Too proud to confess
The horrors of our torrid night:

Behold, my saintly troubadours,
We are called to be ambassadors
Of peace, good will—and infinite light!

Cathedrals in the Rain

Love V

Loves that have been separated in time
Like one majestic voyager, rended in two
Are reunited above the boundless blue
As the spring does revive the eternal vine.

Our lips shall meet once more in the light,
And pain will not even touch our memory.
The mansions shall be tiered in rings of seven.
We shall be transformed in palaces gleaming bright.
For this life of agony possesses only brevity.
Loves doused out by the night are rekindled in heaven!

Cathedrals in the Rain

Who Doth Seek Me When I am Near?

Lord, I was ill; my life was gray.
And you came to me.
And I heard you say:
"Who do you not seek me when I am near?
Do not let the vastness of the sea
Encumber you with needless fear.
O, my precious son, who do you not seek me
In the anguish of your darkest nights
When I command the good sweet lights?"

And then His mother, clad in blue,
Said unto me: As surely as heaven is thine
I have always known you.
Truly I am yours, and truly you are mine.
For regard, my son, the dawn comes after the night.
And when you were in darkness I graced you with light.
In my mothering arms,
Free from all alarms,
Grace upon grace I showered upon your soul."

And I thanked the merciful Lord
For creating such a wondrous mother
Who never fails to make me whole
Always in accord
With His will alone,
Always, always, as no other.

And the sun it ascended,
And His love was proven true,
As the nascent dawn gilded the blue
In the sky above my anguish ended.

Cathedrals in the Rain

My Love, She Sleeps

My only one, my dove,
My love,
She sleeps.

The bells, they chime
Their endless rhyme.
As I go
Through the snow,
My heart—it weeps.

On a lantern lit lane,
Which glows despite my dire pain,
I surrender to The Lord,
To His infinite glory,
To His providential symphony,
To the pulse of its soft refrain—
As our hearts do beat
Of one accord.

And all of the sufferings which I meet,
Which fall from the sun kissed, astonishing trees,
Render me mute, as a work of clay.
And although your touch is faraway
I can still hear the cadence in the beauty of your name:
Its eternal gems shine forever the same
In the mystic enclaves of the falling rain,
In the redolent air
Of the wild breeze,
Which sobs its quatrain,
Now here, now there,
Reciting only ecstasies.

Cathedrals in the Rain

One Summer's Dawn

The sanctuary where you dream as a maid,
Among the terra-cotta statues which gleam in the shade,
Surrounded by slender fountains
Which sob in somnolent jets
To the fathomless immensity of the China blue sky,
To the crest of the teeming, emerald mountains,
Knows of the love between you and I.

And the azure rivulets,
Which glitter as they flow
Beneath the countless willows' fleecy glow
Bathe your pretty, fair white feet
Where your joy is profound,
Holy and complete.
And love is all around.
(For I verily know)
We are one forever, forevermore.
As I kiss you with reverence all the while,
The cosmic, bold dawn rises with a smile,
Shedding its gold on the old, amber shore.

Your Face II

The opulent roses,
The tall, slender vines
Wed the wooden trellis with summery wines,
As daylight closes,
With eglantines.

So near,
The grace
Of the mellifluous blues
Of the bright belvedere,
And the terra-cotta statues
Which clad the marble square
Have nothing to compare
With the wandering gaze of your tender face,
Now smiling, debonair,
Glancing at the rumbling sea,
Now here,
Now there—
Into the very heart of me.

A Sonnet of the Shade

A hazy melody permeates the late afternoon.
The shade in which you wander is bathed in felicity;
It lies in sallow contrasts with the setting of the light.
Above the silhouettes of sycamore trees ascends the sacred moon,
With a languorous solemnity,
Preparing for the starry night.

Your hair, raven and long, frame your fair, white face,
As all scents combine about your body and your dress.
The sighing, sobbing shadow is a sanctified and amorous place,
Where you lean against a bough for my kiss and my caress.

Beneath a wreath of somnolent leaves,
Your beauty commands these cool, autumn eves.
And, speechless, you leave me, as I with awe behold
Your tresses of dusk, your gazes of gold.

Lady of the Bastion II

Her rosy tinted windows shine
On the bastion's tallest tower.
They reflect pure light upon the bower,
And scent her streams with mystic wine.

I have come from many miles away,
From northern lands to see her face,
Her smile of gold and her lips of grace.
I wrote of her in the diamond day.

And now that I found her in the gilded sun,
Happy as an angel, lost in reverie,
Her gaze runs through the very heart of me,
Down to the blooms where the vines are one.

Pensive is her mind, and blissful is the time
When we, as bride and groom to be
Are lost within an azure sea
Of holy love and sacred rhyme.
And when the moon does live and die
Over the boughs of emerald trees
With the solemn reverence I have for her
The fountains over the courtyard stir,
Sobbing to the starlit sky
With operatic symphonies.

A Litany to Mary

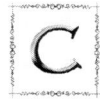

I

Conceived by the very heart of Our Lord,
In Judea's sun,
In the womb of Saint Anne,
The immaculate miracle of Our Holy One
Overshadowed her in humility
To usher in the Son of man.

In a state of ineffable mystery,
Our Lady born, of David's lineage,
Married perfection to humanity
For every age,
For all to see.

And if you can pierce through
His Majesty's mind
You will gladly find the sage in you
To understand the reason why
Eve mistook fruit for a god.

Rejoice in that propitious fault
And acknowledge the strange and apparently odd.

Celebrate in the Redeemer's saving hand
Which transformed all death
And every cobwebbed vault
Into opened gates of eternity,
Into a boon for every imprisoned land,
For the wretched likes of you and me.

II

And when Gabriel came
With love devoid of the slightest stain,
With a trembling flame,
Mary did not hesitate
To see her life

Cathedrals in the Rain

As one of a glorious fate.
And despite all strife
She would live in pain
For the mendicants and the reprobate.

III

And at the station of the bloody base
Of her only son's cross of wood
Where He suffered to erase
Our impossible debt (Which the thief did steal)
Our Lady did feel
Every terrible trace
Of His radical sacrifice.
(More than any man
Possibly could.)

And her agonies did breach
All understanding in the minds of men
Which is now within reach,
Today, *unlike then*.

For no more is her sacrifice veiled and unseen.
Hail, Holy Queen!
Amen, Amen.

Cathedrals in the Rain

Advice From a Father to His Son

Remember my beloved son
If you will not become a priest
Then please (for your own sake at least)
Heed this verse from a wiser one.

For if you choose to marry (if you truly must)
Keep in mind that most women are driven to mate,
And they try without care for their husbands' fate.
For they are deceiving—and live for lust.

For though her face may an angel resemble
Her heart can be a home for insatiable need.
She may seek to own all the trappings of greed,
And from such crimes your soul may tremble.

And when the specious gloss of her eyes fade away
You will likely regret
That dismal hour in which you met
Your lady of the devil—in the bright noonday.

Cathedrals in the Rain

The Autumn Leaves are Falling

The autumn leaves are falling
From each and every moonlit bough.
O, how little time does life allow
For us to reach our calling.

The diamond stars are silently keeping
Their ancient course over reedy dales.
As the sunlight, grieving, slowly pales.
The swollen streams which flow are weeping.

Yet sorrow is a precious gem.
It fortifies our fragile being,
Transforming blindness into seeing—
For all sad souls—for all of them.

For surely secret pains do cure
Our weak humanity by making pure
Our spoiled hearts which rebel and complain—
While God is drying all the rain.

Cathedrals in the Rain

My Dead Wife (1814)

A ll ships left Boston's forbidding harbor.
I brought gold brandy in a flask.
To go to sea was a troubadour's task.
My mind was filled with blooms of an arbor.

The dreadful sun on the sails did glare
Upon my schooner, made of wood.
As the daylight died over the hills
I felt naked in my coat and my head was bare.
I would have chosen to stay if I could,
But the ocean promised to cure my ills.

The caravan leapt into the waves
Like knives into a throng of billowing bread.
The captain pointed to the stars, then said:
"We sail to capture Negro slaves."

Oh, how the Atlantic seemed endless to the eye!
Our creaking masts did tremble in the breeze.
Like a grove of sullen walnut trees,
They shook as they kissed the starless sky.

Neptune, Venus, and the Kraken's den
Awaiting to consume every soul on board
Yawned into one nebulous chord
Of a dismal hymn voiced by a Siren.

At the center of the freezing brine
Which we reached in the span of three days time
I began to hear a queer stanza of rhyme
Which rose from the waves like forbidden wine.

Like Euripides' plays or Cicero's lines,
Like the dreams of Poe and Byron's sin
A terrible cold of horrors dove in
To my inner being, replete with signs:
Maritime warnings, of a vengeful ghost,

Cathedrals in the Rain

A fearful, briny, ghastly bride
Of anguish, agony and every dire emotion.
My sudden urge, my desperate impulse
Was to dive overboard from my ship into the tide.
Yet that was what SHE wanted most!

And my soul was thrown into the boundless ocean,
To a nameless fate
The Greeks call Hades.
And in that dark and baleful place
To my stark amazement I beheld her face,
Living only for eternal hate.
And then I recalled one black summer's eve
When I killed her with delight,
In a graveyard's isolation, where true death was wrought,
Bereft of all light,
And devoid of a witness (or so I thought).

And in a prison beneath the oceanic floor
Each torrid moment is impossible to keep,
As I burn and weep
Forevermore!

Cathedrals in the Rain

The Vagabond

Wandering through the countryside,
All things to my eyes became sanctified.
My old sailor's coat became sacred too!
I dipped my hand into a stream of china blue,
And walked into a wood where the chosen reside.

I drank mystic ales from that good grove.
In the sun, as a vagabond, I did rove
To the outskirts of a gleaming plain,
In the redolent rapture of the falling rain,
Where the summer breeze removed all pain.

And at the foot of a castle, where moss clad stone
Gleamed among blooms kissed from above,
I ceased to feel the coldness of being alone
For there below a terrace of sunlit vines
I had found the essence of eternal love.

For a lady demure with an angel's face
Of purity, light and timeless grace
Possessed a gaze of golden wines,
And the world became a sacred place.
Now every blossom sings from the branches and the vines.

Cathedrals in the Rain

Ode to Paul Verlaine

Verlaine, Verlaine, where did you go?
My thoughts, today, blown by the wind,
Saw you in a Kendal Green tamarind,
Which swayed in a drunken sirocco.
I can see you now, in a majestic court,
Where dream struck lovers wade by the sea,
In an immaculate state of felicity,
All bards, like you, of a mystical sort.
And your verse—ah! It was truly of your heart!
Never color nor hue, but nuance (in blue)
Gleamed upon the reeds you walked upon in rue.
How you wept in the dales when your love did depart!
Now the libraries' dust covers the king
Who made a heaven out of suffering,
And noble marble out of formless clay.
Oh! How I shall rejoice,
When, with a singular voice,
We shall be as one in the eternal day!

The Glory That is You

Come to me my braided angel of the light.
Your tresses are darker than the raven night,
And your kisses are of the sunlit sands:
Sallow and soft, more precious than all elysian lands
On which you rove through the diamond hued reeds.
All of my heart and its spiritual needs
Outshine the countless stars which run
Down slender, gleaming streams upon your glittering back.
We have always breathed in the breezes as one,
As I have always worshiped your stunning mane
And its every ringlet of rapturous black.
Your adornments of purity keep me sane,
For the golds of your gaze which never lack
That gilded magic which renders me
Mute as a statue in a courtyard of blue,
Next to the broad and endless sea,
For the depths of our love, for the glory that is you.

Cathedrals in the Rain

The Piano

Her maple airs glide to the autumn sheets:
The curtains which introduce the perfumed bower
Which sob up the vine clad wall into the still of a solemn hour,
Makes her dear heart tremble as her psyche entreats
The faded balm of her old lover's kiss.
(And more than merely this.)
This melancholic melody taps like tears upon the panes,
(And outside upon the misty lanes.)
She can feel his palm on the keys which disassemble
The billows of her memory to a certain time, to different skies,
When the leaves in the fall of his chivalric gaze,
Fell into the pools of her own brown eyes
Like tranquil, solemn, wistful waves.

Ophelia

In the still of her bedroom
Candles on her mantles glow.
They quiver and gleam
As a demon does dream
In the fog near the sheets
Which cover her window.

And on the terrace where she meets
The solitary moon
The nascent night
Arrives too soon
With gloomy clouds
Which traverse the firmament.
Like burial shrouds—
All death is permanent.

A hopeless sinner moans and dies
And is banned as he crosses the despairing skies
In silence over the wintry dales
Where the last of the sunlight
Perishes and pales.

And in Ophelia's lifeless, stony, gray eyes
There dwells no sadness
No sobs, no cries,
As she retreats into her chamber of sin.

A wanton madness
Wanders through the rattling din
Of her vacant soul,
Unchaste, un-whole,
As a baleful breeze
Sails through her hallway as a dark disease.

For evil reigns whenever it allows
The laughs in her head
For her husband lies dead—

Cathedrals in the Rain

Damned in a lake of scarlet red,
Where he lies stabbed twice in a bath of fleas
Outside, below the boughs
Of leafless trees.

My English Love

My soul is always shaken
By my English lover's almond eyes.
And my heart is always taken
To her regal land, beyond the skies.

And whenever her smooth, cherry hued lips
Condescend to savor mine,
My entire being takes languorous sips
From her warm and sanctified, russet wine.

She was born to a duke in Cornwall,
In a bastion of stone, ivy clad and white;
She saunters in the liveries of the fall,
Among her courtyard's fountains,
Amid the statuary, ringed with mountains,
In the sacred boon of the solemn night.

Cathedrals in the Rain

Dresden

An ancient jewel of Europe's proud past,
Blasted and bombed into a heap
Of scattered rubble, miles deep,
Has been restored, in part, at last.

The churches, the heights of each baroque palace,
The Zwinger, its glory, and the old opera's lights,
The city's regal castle, now stretch to the sky.
No longer the seat of Nazi malice,
After being obliterated from the German eye,
The remainder of the city's old charming nights
Have returned to Saxony despite Hitler's plan
(To raze to the ground all the lovely sights
Given from the hands of God to man.)

And the moon rises over Dresden's stony towers,
Its dappled trees and its nearby hills.
All of its squares despairing, once on fire,
Are now redolent with the fragrant dews of choice daffodils.
The city's new grandeurs, its gardens and its timeless bowers
Now waft fresh perfumes to heaven, as they touch every spire.

Who were we to judge the poor babies sleeping,
Born into a state of atrocious crimes?
Instead of learning nursery rhymes
Their lives were one of death and weeping.

The Rain it Fell

The rain it fell on roofs and walls,
Soothing lonely hearts with a wistful rhyme.
I once wrote a book of mignonette and thyme
Amid a sea of waterfalls.

And in the dusky sky of red
Heavy with tears, there with majesty descended
From regal heights, from high above,
A melancholic, angelic tune
Which sang of your love
In the glory of the moon.

Cathedrals in the Rain

A Wedding to Be

An exalted castle gleams as one
With radiant courtyards, redolent with blooms.
They shine beneath tall, stony towers
Where a melody's choice and rare perfumes
Sail over a statuary's solemn bowers
To your soft and grand palatial rooms.

And on your bed below its canopy
You dream of a handsome, Saxon knight.
As a hunter's moon bestows delight
Upon your pining, lovely face
Ascending with a nascent grace,
It kisses the mounts,
And a wedding to be.

And all of the slender, rapturous founts
Rise like billows, glimmering on high
As they sob to the sky
With ecstasy.

Sable Eyes

The rain it falls gently on the town.
I loose myself in your tranquil gaze,
In lovely, soft and rapturous ways,
In the raven pools of your eyes of brown.

And in those boundless, sable seas
I have become well acquainted with ecstasies
Which emanate like diamonds from your glances.
The universe rejoices and providence dances.
And all of my living comes to this:
A fire lit cabin and a nuptial kiss.

Cathedrals in the Rain

The Ghost

Alone in my castle, a plaything of the breeze,
Indolent and tepid, my leisure filled hours
Lead my soul astray from the good, narrow path.
In the black tiers above me demons mock and laugh,
As more of them assemble below in the leafless bowers:
Those ghastly dark gardens bereft of scarlet trees.

I wonder if the November night
In this timeless lassitude of pain
Reserves for my all too sullen heart
A melancholic trail to the light
To allow me to depart
From the tumult of the ceaseless rain.

Lo! What is that specter I behold wide eyed
Carrying a noose with a candle in her other hand?
She is none but a ghost full of Satan's contraband
To place that rope around my neck—*coming forth to have it tied!*

She Walks Beyond

She walks beyond the vine-clad stone,
In the English shade, to a garden of sun.
Her spirit and her flesh are exalted as one;
She walks in peace, to the glade, alone.

There are ebonies which call her
To epiphanies of yellow light.
And when the scented breeze
Through the willow trees stir
She reveals herself as royalty
Upon her humble, bended knees,

In the diamond glow of heaven's sight.
And then,
Next to a bench of marble in the garden,
Where statues stand, among the watercress,
A fountain rises to the cloudless sky
Rejoicing in her beauty,
With a silver sigh
As her dark eyes gaze upon her ivory dress.

And all the earth is a symphony
As every star gleams with majesty,
Fair and solemn, sacred and of glory;
She walks upon the promenade,
Pondering rapture, and ecstasy
In the melodious bower of the sanctified glade.
Her thoughts are of felicity,
As the lavender sunset touches every rose,
With a summery grace,
Bestowing gold upon her face,
Where she walks in the little garden-close.

Cathedrals in the Rain

To Mary II

Walking in the meadows I shall dream,
Wearing a coat of soft, raven wool.
I shall bathe in the breeze, scented and cool,
Sprayed by the happy froth of a stream.

I shall mediate on only love,
And make my way to a chapel by the sea,
To kneel by a shrine, dedicated to her majesty,
Beneath the azure sky above.

And when the dying day does slowly depart,
With the silent shoe of a vagabond,
My mind shall ascend to the blissful beyond,
Where angels praise the Virgin's heart.

Cathedrals in the Rain

The Murderer

Once there was a handsome, young, pretty maid
Who knelt in front of her father's tomb.
Her fate was one of eternal doom.
For behind her stood her husband there within the shade.
A malevolent sort,
He lifted up high his long, silver blade
And plunged it without mercy through her coat—
A thin, old jacket which he bought.
And it ripped through her back.
She couched up blood, and died from the impact.
And the murderer reveled in the death he wrought.
He fled to a jetty,
To the refuge of a dismal port.
And left for Yorkshire in a little boat,
Arriving at midnight to a castle by the sea.
This house on a hill
Where the wind was always still
Welcomed this fiend who knew only to kill.
And at midnight in the tallest tower,
He looked below into the dour
Bower of dead reeds beside a glen.
And then, to his horror, he beheld a ghost,
His victim who arose from the tawny brown
Of her pitiful grave, stained with a sanguine red,
This once lovely maid he hated the most.
She looked at him with steely eyes
Both alive yet dead.
And then came a dark and baleful surprise.
For she ascended up the stony old wall,
Without any mercy, no mercy at all.
Her face was torrid and livid with hate.
And lo and behold he met his fate,
As she returned with the same silver blade,
Gleaming in her hand with its handle of black
In the moonlit night bereft of shade,
And she plunged that knife into his back.

Cathedrals in the Rain

Andalusia

Andalusia,
I have come to see you,
From far away,
Seeking a lady of regalia,
Beneath your radiant skies
Of azure blue.

I have heard her pining, royal sighs
From a moonlit ship docked westward
In the soft, Spanish cradle
Of a deep, tranquil bay.

Her hair is of a raven sable.
It is redolent, wavy, graced and long.
Her name is of a sacred song.
At night I hear her angelic voice sing.
Her soul is of Juliet's terraced wing,
More enchanting than that lover's fable.

She is the daughter of a generous lord,
A survivor of The Carolingian line
Who rules with a kind and kingly hand
His vassals who labor, reaping dreams from wine
In the scarlet dappled land,
In the sun among the vine.

Cathedrals in the Rain

After Our Deaths II

The breeze is cool,
But it does not bite.
The world regarded us each a fool,
But there is no longer a reason to be contrite.
Let us stroll beneath the crimson blooms
Which laugh above the brooks of white.
And after our walk amid the reeds,
Let us retire to our palatial rooms,
Among our busts and vases;
Let us look out our grand bay window,
To where swirling siroccos softly blow,
Out upon the moonlit meads.
There, surrounded by fine tapestries,
And the most majestic, eternal art,
In between our lips' bated pauses,
We shall witness blue jays ascend in ecstasies,
As they flutter and dart
To the immaculate seas.
I have waited for this moment all of my life
To possess you as a woman, more than a wife.
For as angels in a crystal palace we dwell—
In the boon of heaven's citadel.

An Angel's Song

We ventured out in the gray of night,
From the summerhouse, drinking wine in the breeze,
On amber furrows beneath linden trees,
Where the gales caressed your naked knees,
Smooth as a stream, and kissed by the moonlight.

The fountains which sobbed in the marble square
Bequeathed to the brisk, aromatic air
A somnolence of grace, repose and song,
As I worshiped your black and braided hair,
Which sighed to the stars, mellifluous and long.

Cathedrals in the Rain

The Duchess

There are long, circular stairs
In a mansion by the sea,
Where a duchess of regal chivalry
Walks down its Persian carpets
In an atmosphere of royal airs.

She leaves the grand foyer to wander in the squares,
Where the lively scent of mignonette
Surrounds the many ancient fountains
And the terra-cotta statuary,
Which hypnotizes as it gleams
By the many pristine, china blue streams,
Among a ring of emerald mountains.

And in one sleepy corner of the park,
She steps into her carriage
And sails into the shadows of the dark,
Born from a crimson silhouette.
Dreaming of a sacred marriage,
Her aristocratic state is of an innocent coquette.
She wears a long, white, pearly dress,
With lovely, embroidered frills.
Her breasts posses the scent of blooming daffodils,
As she glides by the lakes and the glittering watercress.

The bowers of the summer sun
She passes slowly one by one,
Gazing at the tops of majestic trees.
The forest is made of symphonies,
As song birds sing and sigh in the breeze.

Maples, lindens, the oaks and the birch
Frame the wooden pane of an old, Catholic church
Where she pauses to kneel by a Marian shrine.

Her heart is of an angel's, and her mind is of Cabbala wine.
She weeps as she prays, for her lover is far away at sea:
None other than the likes of me.

Ladies

After I listen to the Holy Spirit's whispered name,
I open my book, and compose anew:
And my soul is immersed in a hardy brew.
I am engulfed in every aspect of grace, form and the narrow lane.
For order and measure, meter, words and rhyme
Are what I hear when cathedral bells chime.
But my verse is torn by a sudden, hungry breeze,
And ferries to the endless, billowing ocean,
Near the female rupture of the willow trees.
It is taken by this maiden whose maw is insatiable—orgasmically red.
She becomes naught but thunder and emotion,
Whose passion is violent, inviting the dead.
Then still a more potent, furious hue
Possesses her heart—and all becomes a fire, baneful, hot and blue;
The Eve in her lust becomes all aflame.
Her clutches transform into a wanton gale:—
Which discards the sun, and makes the moonlight pale.
She rejects true love as the hobby of a fool.
And the specious cadence of her spoken bliss
Betrays her urge for an unlawful kiss,
Clasping with the licentious grip of her tool.

The Day Still Does Rise

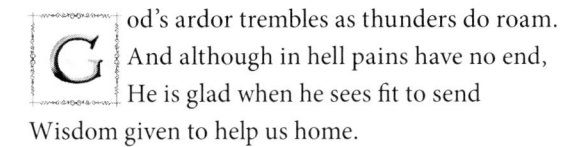

God's ardor trembles as thunders do roam.
And although in hell pains have no end,
He is glad when he sees fit to send
Wisdom given to help us home.

For I was cast out among the devil's mead,
Savagely bruised in a toxic rain
Where his cold and furious, mortal disdain
Procured for him a smile as a Saint did bleed.

Yet the sunny dawn of day still did rise
Over hills and castles wonderfully lit again,
Housing pretty young maidens and cheerful old men
Tending to an ever new empirical surprise.

Cathedrals in the Rain

Ode to Elizabeth Barret Browning

In my wanderings to the south of Spain,
I met Robert's faithful wife, in the warmth of the Portuguese sun,
I picked every hyacinth, one by one,
In honor of their eternal love,
To bequeath to sweet Elizabeth, to soothe her dire pain.
The canvass of the sky was cloudless above.
And we walked as true poets, as a wild storm arose,
Hand in fair hand, where rainbows did grace
The sonnet drenched light of her beauteous face,
In a garden where the vines are married to the rose.
And when comes our next existence
Who can say,
When we go at the end of our stubborn insistence
That we live not in vain, neglecting to pray?
So let us walk in peace,
Robert, you and I,
Beneath the bold and regal sky,
And allow our fears to finally cease;
Let us all transcend this vale of oblivion, of fire and of ice,
Unafraid to earn heaven's glory, its highest paradise—
Through the grace of your holy rhyme,
Elizabeth, my friend,
Let us all ascend to our ineffable end
In splendid, gilded, golden days,
In true poetic, wondrous ways,
Beyond the weight of time.

Cathedrals in the Rain

Two Ghosts

Once there was a castle, perched high upon a mountain
Which towered over a courtyard's fountain.
And when the moon arose, shadows fell upon the lanes.
No light did ever glow
From the square nor any window—
Except for two candles' dimly lit flames.

Held by hands cold and dead
Two ghosts tried to summon up the past
And the night alone heard the words they said.

The pale, old master cried: "Ah, here we are together at last!
Does your heart still beat for me? Do you love me still?"—
His maiden replied: *"Why do you ask?"*

"Let us drink to our ardor from this flask,
And once more let our passions thrill!"
He said.

But deader than the dead,
She slowly walked away,
Down the silent, hollow hall
Caring not at all
For her lover nor the lark,
Vanishing in the dark,
Never to see the light of day.

Night by the Bay

My darling, my princess, won't you stay?
The tall sails of white spike the placid bay
By the wooden jetties, beneath the gleaming stars,
Where soft, nylon, ivory guitars
Play classical odes heard from the beach.
The moonlit rays and their cosmic reach
Grace your dress as you lay reclined and dreaming.
All the hovering, silver orbs are gleaming
In the heights of the firmament, bereft of all pain.
I shall kiss your lips, and caress your mane.
And your eyes shall ascend above the seas
Where raptures blend with ecstasies.

Dusk

Languorously, the stars ascend
Over your nude, exquisite back;
The heavens of gold turn to black
As the last rays of dusk, where grasses bend
Die in the west, over the farms,
Seducing your mind, free from alarms.
Knowing nothing but the evening's ardent pleasures,
The russet, telling blush of your tender breasts
Release their redolent, pink nippled treasures
As they gently heave with silken sighs,
To pursue true love as your dark gaze rests
In the ocean of my opened eyes.

My Sailor's Daughter

Come to me, my only one,
My sailor's daughter, born at sea.
O, come my lover, come to me,
Countess of the moon and queen of the sun.
Let us wander among the maples which gleam as they sway
Beneath the clouds of cotton which dream to release
Their misty sheets of rain where angels of peace
Above, rejoice in heaven, in the endless day.

Blossoms in Her Hair

How lovely her majesty seems to me,
When she wanders through her regal garden
In a state of pristine, gentle grace.
There angels praise the symphony of her face,
As she kneels in prayer near the undulating sea,
Where ivy and vines meet the trellis on the glen.

How delicate are her braided bows,
Where a stream from paradise gently flows,
Crowning her a queen, as she roves in the square;
For from sanctity she will never part,
With ardor in her sacred heart,
And cherry blossoms in her hair.

Cathedrals in the Rain

The Eve

When the brandy scented breeze
Sways your long tresses
As you smile in your chamber,
Arranging your dresses
A throng of gilded myrtle trees
Sheds gold, green and amber.
Yet in the eve when candles gleam
In the hallways of your castle's gloom
A dead man comes into your room
And makes your life a horrid dream.

The Castle

The wind swept with violence against the dreary panes,
In my castle perched high among the mountains,
Overlooking the square devoid of all fountains,
Surrounded by woods bereft of paths or lanes.

From my cryptic chamber of incessant gloom
I gazed down the candlelit corridor;
(My blood it turned from hot to cold.)
For leaving my dour, barely lit room,
I heard creaking in a threshold,
Lacking any door.

For once, quite very long ago,
As I vividly remember so,
My lover met death kneeling in despondency
Where she placed a bouquet by her father's grave.
I reached into my coat, and raised a silver blade,
And stabbed her in the back where no one did see,

Cathedrals in the Rain

And her evil soul became Satan's slave.
(Such was the end of the malevolent life she made.)

Now four year hence I wander our estate,
And on February nights when the halls echo death
And the ominous sycamores clash in the breeze
I hear her heart beating with a mortal hate
And there, near the curtains I loose my bated breath
As I behold her ghost, down below beneath the trees
Clutching the knife I used that day.
My nerves they fail, and I try to run away,
Out through the window on the castle's other end.
But before I could leap
She appeared in a dreadful wise,
With hatred in her heart, and demons in her eyes.

And she plunged that knife
Within me deep;
And so ended my life
As I forevermore keep
The company of Satan
As I groan and weep.

Cathedrals in the Rain

Your Song

The song of your love
Which descends from above,
Is of branches, of leaves,
Gracing cathedrals, where boughs are bent.
It is of flowery, redolent
Victorian eves;
It is of a wistful, splendid, pristine scent.
Your sonata of the crested sea
Calls me like a siren's, enchanting, full of melody;
My soul becomes yours by your sonorous voice.
I am enraptured, captured, without a choice,
By your sable eyes, my princess,
Which hath possessed me so.
In a state of angelic, wondrous grace,
Hither and there, like a breeze I go,
Beneath your battlements, in the wintry snow,
I behold your face,
And your flowing, white dress.
Among the streams and watercress,
As the sallow sun dies,
Among the slender fountains' languorous sighs,
In your courtyard by your bastion,
Where the statues' gazes resemble your own,
With their loving looks, from living stone.

Cathedrals in the Rain

Your Name

The grass that wavers in the gales
Tossed by the whirls of those seaside glades
Carries mignonette and thyme
As the sunlight dives and dies and pales.
And all the earth and her glory fades
Like timeless woes and ancient rhyme.
Yet a thing unseen forever sails
Over founts and mounts in a mystic clime.
The cross of God heals all with His wine.
As does your name: pristine, divine!

Your Majesty

When the sky is enamored, flushed with a pristine gold
And the slim, springing fountains in the courtyard sob to the trees,
When Bach's symphonies serenade me in the soft, summer breeze
I breathe within the harbor's wind in the clasp of the gilded cold.
As a Carolingian wanderer I was faithful to thee
In the liberty of the boundless summer's sun
I brought each dappled petal, one by one
Into the fair, white hands of your regal Majesty.
And when the sprawling silver moon spread across the bay
We would hide amid the flora, in one another's arms.
And I felt your kiss as fire, free from all alarms,
As the spirits of the angels blessed us in the eternal day.

Lucifer

All of the ocean was at the mercy of the wind.
I sailed at top mast, and tasting infinity,
The sun glared upon me like an Orphic tamarind,
And on all the glossy mirrors in the kingdoms of the sea.

The whispering ghost of a demon's soul
Played host in the gleam of the midnight hour.
Like a baleful dream, a black, briny power,
He spoke not a word to the mind he stole.

Yes! My mind was taken by this phantom's wrath!
In the maritime cold, on a starless path
My schooner rocked from starboard to port.
I felt his icy clutch. A terrible sort
Of terror itself cruised through my veins
As the bile of his watery, endless plains
Rushed upwards with its billowing, wavy disdains.

Drearily, I muttered.
My speech, it failed and fluttered
As I begged to hear his horrid name.
"Lucifer!" he said,
With the empty echo of a witch's spell.
And knowing I was dead—
I was thrown into the well
Of an infinite, red
Eternal flame!

A Courtyard's Sonnet

On tepid evenings, when fountains descend like rain,
Tall, ivory statues glitter in the moon glow,
Amid ancient colonnades, where rivulets flow
To ponds of mystic wines, devoid of any pain.
And when I kiss your lips of the sun
In the shade of russet myrtle trees,
Our hearts unite, and marry as one
In the azure cradle of the scented breeze.
Then your gaze becomes solemn, grave and still,
As all of our sorrow forever departs.
And your eyes begin to speak with ecstasies,
With angelic tears shed from rapturous seas
Imbuing within our bating hearts
The holy hues of rhapsodies.

Cathedrals in the Rain

The Bells of Amiens

Cold rain descends like mystic rhyme
On the rustic, old town, forming a stream.
Over cobblestone streets where lamplights gleam,
Tall willows hover as church bells chime.

I wander as a sailor through slender, amber reeds,
Clad in a pea coat, raven and worn.
The dusk had died, and the night is born.
My stanzas, they pine. My spirit, it bleeds.

In a barn I stay, where the breeze exhales
The scent of mignonettes which mingle with the moon,
Fermenting potent liquors, of a summery boon.
The hour has come for witches' tales.

Now that my lover has gone away
The stars which dance in the arched, nocturnal hues
Carry my psyche to Parisian avenues
Where we first embraced in the gilded day.

Nostalgia

When the purple drapes of the nascent night
Cover the veils of the mountainous greenery,
I wander amid the fountains and the statuary,
Lost in reflective pools of light.

And when the moon ascends to the sobbing sky,
Alone in the starry firmament of black,
I recall the ringlets upon your smooth, white back,
When the spring evenings blessed us, you and I.

How profound was our felicity,
How deep was our joy,
When we danced in the meadow as girl and boy,
With an ardor that shone like diamonds on the sea.

Now the drab days slowly pass,
As I walk upon the wan, old grass,
Beneath the cradle of the weeping trees;
In the darnel, wavering, high, then low,
Through the wilting, tremulous reeds I go,
Haunted by your name, which scents the wild breeze.

Death

Dying as a nervous wreck
Is not the way to go.
I will not quiver at the quake of death.
I will ascend as a diver from a joyful deck.
I will leap into the azure freshet
Where the gleeful waters flow.
And my final, victorious breath
Shall be bravely met
With a merited bravado
Borne from decades of grief.
Yes, a glorious death is my crowning relief!
So why should I be afraid?—
The soul goes where it goes.
The stream rises where it flows.
And the spirit ascends as the body is laid!

Cathedrals in the Rain

The Villa by the Sea

Ah!—The villa by the boundless shore,
It was a lovely, enchanting stay.
And although it was the spring of 1984,
It seems I was there only yesterday.

With the tall, gray mountains as a backdrop,
And the bold Mediterranean lapping below
Every white-sashed, long, opened bay window,
Blessed us every night when the bottles would pop,
Flowing with sanguine, cool, bright Chardonnay.

You wore a dress of carmine red,
And danced to every song until the moon went red.
Oh, how I kissed you endlessly,
Upon the many terraces, and every breezy balcony.

Ah!—Drinks were of plenty, plenty.
And when the ballroom lights went dim,
We followed the piper, the seraphim,
Down to the shores of the blue Riviera.

We were surrounded there by marigold blooms.
And when we were sated with the fresh sangria,
We would return to the floors of the airy dance rooms.
I was your drunken Byron, your Poe,
And you were my girl.
How your dress did flow,
With a whoosh and a whirl!—

Remember riding
In your sister's black car?
What fantastic orb or star
Did we not behold go gliding?

We rode through the hills
With the radio streaming.
Your breasts were sunny daffodils.
(Am I still there, or am I dreaming?)

Cathedrals in the Rain

Down the mount, over the glen,
Our wheels did roar.
Our days were the things of dreams.
Such folly now it seems?—
O, tell me then,
What was life made for?

Cathedrals in the Rain

A Poem Written in Heaven

Heaven is of golden cabins, clad with redolent, diamond snow.
Gilded, angelic streams, through tall, slender grasses flow
To bright, majestic groves of myrtle trees which sway below
Turquoise skies, fulfilling dreams, where lavender scented breezes go.
Theologians say that paradise knows no change nor night—
Only the cloudless firmament of an infinite, immaculate day.
Yet the astonishing evening reigns in the starry regions of the north,
Bejeweling the sanctified brooks that joyfully tally forth.
Let us go, let us go, my princess, my lover, my only love,
To where the sacred woods are glowing with dappled, silver boughs;
Let us wander there enraptured, as long as love allows—
Lying in the regal reeds—exalted from above!

All Save for Heaven

This passing world is a dark, dark place,
And impressions of darkness are hard to efface
To enlightened minds that perceive only gloom,
Even in the specious light of day.
Fallen humanity wallows in the loom
Of miasmatic ponds where fireflies stray.
Cryptic boughs are bereft of bloom
Marking dusky graveyards where caskets lay.
And that end, inevitable, approaches soon,
Beneath the solitary watch of the cold, stony moon.
All save for heaven ends in decay.
And impressions of darkness are hard to efface.
Yes, this world is a dark, dark place.

Cathedrals in the Rain

Sunlight

When the sun streams through the psyche of your spirit's heights,
And the moon is hidden from the earth's blue face,
Take the precious time to solemnly trace
Heaven's pure and wholesome lights.

And when you hold my hand beneath the trees
Of lindens, oaks and yews in the late afternoon,
Remember that love is the only boon
That can save us from the night's cold breeze.

And when Bach's concertos ring in your mind
Like the sound of angels gliding through the square,
I shall take you by the pines and kiss you there,
And reveal to you truly all that is kind.

Cathedrals in the Rain

The City

In urban songs
Where the vagabond longs,
When the blissful day is done,
And the prom queens are dressed in lace,
I've seen the good from goodness run
From God's celestial face.

The One Whom You Admire

I've seen the good from goodness run
In the grand dance hall, with your heart afire,
As your wandering gaze meets with the moon, astute,
The evening of the prairie arrives with a cheerful lute.
(I know the very one of whom you quietly admire.)

You humble him and the starry skies.
(The meads appear like crimson ice.)
For him your eyes outshine the sun,
For in truth thou art his holy one,
His bride from God,
His paradise.

Cathedrals in the Rain

Come

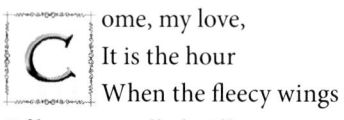

Come, my love,
It is the hour
When the fleecy wings
Of breeze cradled willows
Turn their heads away
In Reverence.

Come, my love,
Endure with grace
The sacred moment
Prior to our kiss.
Let us be the channels
As God's Divine face
Smiles as He in sanctity—
Creates!

Cathedrals in the Rain

A Belgian Tale

Exalted higher than all noble Flemish fables from above,
In the corner of a park, where gardens, amazing
Grow. A ducal lady, majestically clothed and gazing
Looks out upon the brine to glimpse the ship of her true love.

Fair is her countenance and pure is her heart.
She admires the best of Holy Roman art.
Her mind is of the Renaissance, gilded and gold.
Standing on a wall, next to the ocean,
Tilting near terraces beside the boundless sea,
She awaits for her Saxon lover in the cold.
She is intact with her reason, and every emotion
Increases the charms of her modesty.

Near an enchanting veranda where she waits
She hears a clock strike two.
The moonlight in the firmament quickly abates
And the rippling, small lagoons glimmer in blue.

Hidden in the hedges is a nuptial ring.
She has placed it there to greet her poet king.
The windmills swirl like London's Big Ben.
Her thoughts turn to slumber, yet, just then—
Beyond the chambers of her palace a ship appears.
Conjuring up visions of jades and emerald billows,
Meteoric comets and spheres of wild willows,
She leaps into the air, as her handsome lover nears.

As a buccaneer, a demigod, a son of mighty Pan,
A youth in his prime, his eyes shine like the dawn,
Fearlessly he walks upon the marvels of the lawn,
More than just a sailor, he exceeds the rank of man.

In the cradled silhouettes of Poseidon's proud elation,
The two endure for a moment in the cool and shady sand
An anguish of anticipation
As their hearts of one do throb with a hot and grasping hand.

Cathedrals in the Rain

Yet before their lips do meet, safely and secure,
The dawn approaches from Istanbul,
Certain and for sure,
Along with the ageless insanities,
The sinister thieves,
Who in Satanic disguise
Paint false reliefs
As the last of their innocence is blemished—
It perishes and dies:
Along with their sacred vows,
Along with their beliefs.

Her Cadence

After I listen to the Holy Spirit's whispered flame,
I open my book, and compose anew:
And my soul is immersed in a hardy brew.
I am engulfed in every aspect of her face, her mane.
And order and measure, meter, words and rhyme
Are what I hear when cathedral bells chime.
My verse is borne in the soft, scented breeze,
And ferries to the endless, blue, splendid ocean,
Near the rapture of the willow trees.
It wavers like my maiden whose ardor is fair and true.
And all becomes naught but thunder and emotion,
Whose passion is tender. Then still a more potent, violet hue
Possesses her heart, and she becomes all aflame.
Her kiss is of a melodic gale:—
Which enlightens the sun, and makes the moon pale.
And the harmonic cadence of her halcyon kiss,
Speaks of heaven and a rare, elysian bliss,
In the rapturous wave of her beauteous name.

The Rose Clad Bower

The melodies which emanate
From a mystic mandolin
Evokes the many strains of an ancient violin;
And harmonies multiply, as the meaning of our fate,
Are laid open to our psyches in the pristine wood:
They croon in the Lethe of your scarlet kiss,
Where libertines are dressed—
In modest crimsons, as they should.
Your fragrant bosom, praised and caressed
Glitters firmly with ardor and with bliss;
For I have seen on tepid evenings such as this
Paradise confirmed, in the rose bedecked bower:
For as each lush petal's glittering mistress,
You long with love to capture every lovely flower.

The Black Night

The sun by the ocean
Always filled me with dread.—
For my every emotion,
Perceives only that
Which is dark—
Gloomy, oppressive—
And dead.

From the time my mother rocked me
In a crib of wool and wood,
Until I came of age—
I saw the sun as few men could.

Indeed that sun, over the sea,
Hovered with a blackened eye
So very very strangely.
And neither the angels that sailed up high
Nor my bride who kissed me
Here below
Could speak of this hellish blot I know.

And the world went spinning
In the tempest of my mind
As the clouds amassed
In a way so unkind
As to leave no remnant of that glow—
For the light, bedeviled, shines no more—
As I stare, astonished, on the sunless shore!

Cathedrals in the Rain

The Ghost Ship

Every hand on deck had faith in his sword,
Every hand on deck that climbed aboard
A ship that left Boston in a swirling snow.
In three days time it attained the open sea.
And all hands on deck met their destiny
In the abyss of The Atlantic, in its dark billows below.

The schooner was tossed upon the waves
Like a mad, orphaned cork dancing on the blue terrain.
Its wheel turned blindly, assailed by wild rain,
Until the water was stilled over its graves.

Then silent as a whisper, a skeletal clutch
Took the helm and turned the ship to the east.
A malevolent guest, this mysterious beast
Reveled in the deaths which felt his touch:
The last thing they knew before the mad sea
Swallowed their bones so adamantly.

And in some days time the ship arrived in Spain
Where eager sailors got on board
To take to Boston their gold and grain—
And every hand on deck had faith in his sword.

Cathedrals in the Rain

The Grave

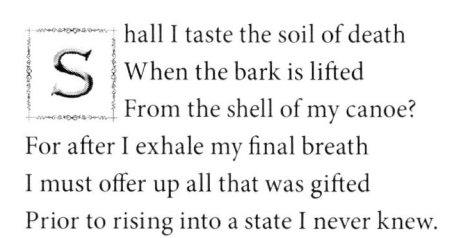

Shall I taste the soil of death
When the bark is lifted
From the shell of my canoe?
For after I exhale my final breath
I must offer up all that was gifted
Prior to rising into a state I never knew.

Shall I swallow with my mouth
That unhallowed earth
Falling quickly south
Departing from the finite route
Which began at birth
Before my soul shall be cast out
Into that realm of terrible doubt?

Or if, by Christ, may He choose to spare me
From that awful union with the mire
Be it with ice or be it with fire,
Not to be condemned to my requiem's attire,
To the baleful, endless, briny sea.

For if it be so
I shall escape from that fate
Before it be too late
Never to go
Into my rest
It will only be so at her bequest.

Yes, It will surely be due
To The Virgin Mary's merciful desire
To raise me into the blissful blue,
While cheating a hell so black and dire.

Cathedrals in the Rain

The Regal Palace

Roving on the bright, spacious lawn of the palace,
I have come to behold the lady in white,
Who steps onto the balcony in the sunlight.
I stand below entranced, drinking from a chalice.

Amid the gray cast of ancient stone she appears,
As a breeze blows back her redolent hair.
I am one with quatrains and the summery air,
With my lady and with wine, with regal belvederes.

Many billows from God are flung to the north.
The silhouettes of basswoods, of dark, turquoise blues
Shed their shadowy leaves near the palace, on massive avenues.

Descending from the terrace, my lady comes forth,
And we wander for a rapturous hour,
As I finish my Chablis,
Through the garden, through the bower,
In an atmosphere of sanctity.

Cathedrals in the Rain

The One I Love

It is not Juliet whom I adore,
Nor Beatrice, nor the florid, glistening lore
Of fair Aphrodite, nor Athena's fair face.—
No.
The one I love is dressed in lace,
And wanders silently beside the gilded shore.
And lo!—
She commands all the lilies in the glen,
Where she walks among the statuary,
In the cloister of the square,
On a path in the russet garden,
Where
Her felicity
Breeze blown, now here, now there,
Rides like a leaf in the redolent air.

Cathedrals in the Rain

Grace

I am drunk with waves, and majestic brine.
I have returned from Spain with gold and gems.
I have found my princess donning diadems,
In the courtyard where the stones meet vine.

She wanders as a Saint in the hallowed space of the vast and marble square,
Where slender fountains paint with grace the cool, enchanting, autumn air.
Her home is up high, on the terrace of a tower,
Where she sings of fair love to the trees above the bower.

And like Juliet, from Shakespeare's pen, she pines for her lover's masculine kiss,
When the nascent moon shines like a ring within her dusky, raven eyes.
For her swooning hope is to be betrothed in a tender throng of effluent sighs.
Her longing, chaste and sanctified heart, acquainted with only a pious bliss,
Reaches out into my own, warmer than eternity
As our rapturous gazes intertwine,
Like gold within an endless sea,
Like red, redemptive, sacred wine.

Cathedrals in the Rain

Our Love

Our love was an ivory boon,
Which reigned with the angels in the night.
We would kiss beneath the moon,
Among the statues in the light.
But your death arrived too soon,
And so soared our felicity out of sight,
Which was once so gold, which was once so bright.

Now all that I can ponder,
All that I can see,
Is your fair face over yonder,
In a court of majesty,
Surrounded by slender, radiant fountains,
Where in a haze, you dream,
In the square beyond the mountains,
Lazing by a falling stream.

The Christian

If you could pierce through shades of dismal gray
Ringing tall towers clad with parapets of stone
Which languish in the specious day
You would see I defeated Zeus alone.

And if you could perceive beneath the curtained glow
Which beams among glades which frame the sea
In the boon of night, in a vein completely
In the merit of verse I conquered Poe.

And if you traveled to regal places of birth
Where their greatest boasts are their earthly kings
Compare their gems with my Christian rings
And you will find them devoid of every worth.

FINI

About the Author

John Lars Zwerenz (1969 -) is an American journalist, musician, song writer, and poet renowned for his classic romantic, impressionistic, and mystical works. Described as the "Monet of the Muses," his poetry inspires the reader to feel the powers of spiritual and physical love. He left graduate studies to travel and write, and has been doing so ever since. Author of eleven books of verse, Zwerenz is a true classic American poet. This anthology includes his newest unreleased collection titled "Cathedrals in the Rain." John lives, loves, and creates in Glendale (Queens) New York. Visit John on Facebook @JohnLarsZwerenz.

About the Illustrator

Steven Anthony D'Ascoli (1968 -) was born in Queens, New York. Although he majored in economics at Columbia University, he also studied oil painting and architecture. He went on to work as an adjunct professor of information technology at the City University of New York. His artistic interests include portrait sketching, the romantic art movement of the 1800s, and art of the medieval, baroque and Renaissance periods.

Index of Poems

A

A Bonny Lass 172
A Carolingian Ride 452
A Christmas Poem 116
A Coquette 176
A Correspondence 147
Adam and Eve 383
Advent 185
Advice from a Father to His Son 709
Advice to Young Poets 305
After Many Sullen Years 667
After Our Deaths I 577
After Our Deaths II 729
After Our Walk Amid the Reeds 332
After the Rain 270
A Garden in Paradise 513
A Grecian Tale 139
A Gypsy's Life 143
A Journey 384
A Kiss 48
A Lady Fair I 43
A Lady Fair II 412
A Lady in the Park 203
A Lady Most Lovely 381
Alchemy 134
A Litany of Roses 232
A Litany to Mary 707
Alone with Renee 290
A Lovers Song 571
A Lover's Sonnet 153
A Maiden Fair 158
Ambrosia 50
A Melody 522
Am I Fine, Am I Beautiful? 579
A Morning Song 474
Amour 388
An American Girl 492
An American Montage 449

An Angel's Song 730
An Autumn Eve 593
An Autumn Sunset I 106
An Autumn Sunset II 493
Andalusia 728
An Ecstasy 21
An Elegy 56
An Elopement 464
An English Sonnet 283
A Night in December 189
A Night in Hades 166
A Night in Paris 264
An Invitation 222
An Irish Garden 308
A Nocturne Song 457
An Ode to Keats 136
A Pantomime 175
Apathy 215
A Picnic 287
A Reverent Night 109
A Reverie 572
A Rhapsody 323
A Roman Garden 239
A Sailor's Song I 70
A Sailor's Song II 414
A Sailor's Song III 573
A Sanctified Flame 681
As I Await Her*f* 221
As in a Dream 20
As I Wander 128
A Sonnet of the Shade 705
A Soul in Purgatory 458
As the Sun Descends 30
A Stream of Stars 120
A Summer's Day 144
A Supplication 33
As You Lay 22
A Troubadour's Song 475
At the University 73

A Tuft of Daisies 375
August 274
Autumn 435
Autumn's Cellos 196
A Veil of Sorrow 152
A Voyage to Cyprus 417
A Voyage to Scotland 236
A Voyage to Spain 440
A Walk After Painting 491
A Walk Beneath the Stars 211
A Walk in Spain 233
A Walk in the Dawn I 379
A Walk in the Dawn II 459
A Walk in the Garden 171
A Walk in the Square 524
A Walk in the Town 355
A Walk Through Paradise 240
A Walk Through the Graveyard 190
A Walk with My Lady 69
A Walk With My Love 525
A Walk With You 574
A Wandering I 188
A Wandering II 367
A Wedding of the Sacred 65
A Wedding to Be 722
A Winter's Night 575
A Winter's Wood 576
A Wistful Strain 209
Azure Heights 294

Index of Poems

B

Baby Grand 523
Ballads 218
Beauty 398
Beauty is Her Name 446
Beethoven's Ghost 270
Before the Ball 288
Before We Met 57
Behold I 697
Behold II 698
Belgium 292
Beneath the Archway 397
Beneath the Boughs 45
Beneath the Green Palms 25
Benediction 122
Benedictions 214
Beside the Stream… 36
Billowing Reeds 538
Blossoms in Her Hair 678
Blossoms Once Bright 113
Boughs 413
Bouquets 107
Bourbon 259
Browns 15
Burgundy 64
Buried 302
By a Wall of Stone 265
By Hazel Eyes 111
Byron's Ghost 670
By the Bay 86
By the Lake 333
By the Manor House She Walks 24
By the Seine 38
By the Winter Moon 127

C

Cafes 466
Calm 301
Candles 494
Canticles 402
Carol 186
Central Park (2012) 296
Chablis 260
Chelsea 231
Chillingham Castle 677
Claudie 291
Come, Let Us Wander 146
Coming Home 104
Consumed with Sighs 112
Conversion 269
Corridors 145
Currents 162

D

Dante's Saloon 465
Dawn 246
Days Now Gone 94
Death at Sea 582
Diadems 661
Diamond Stars 257
Dreaming 438
Dresden 720
Dusk I 312
Dusk II 656

E

Ecstasy 499
Emerald Billows 173
Emotions 413
Ennui 42
Epilogue I 407
Epilogue II 495
Eternal Streams 110
Ethereal Mist 126
Exile 281

F

Faded Candles 91
Flaxen Gold 35
Forest Park 238
Forlorn 97
Fountains 403
From the Balcony 29
Fruits of the Ascension 268

G

Gales I 197
Gales II 588
Gently Near She Comes 32
Ghost Ship 544
God 400
Golden Shores 389
Grace 201
Gray 194

H

Halos 272
Hamlet's Guest 266
Harding Court 161
Heaven I 98
Heaven I 571
Heaven's Dew 206
Her Kiss 349
Her Melody 521
Her Piano 67
Her Silhouette 89
Her Silken Kiss 665
Homer 277
Hope 199
Hyde Park 462
Hymns 217

Index of Poems

I

I Came Upon a Castle 433
If You Give Your Heart Away 694
I Hold You on a Bed of Gold 331
I Lay Down with Christ 354
I Met You in a Dream 336
I Met You in Paris 357
In an Hour of Silence 193
In Clement Ties 120
Inebriation 477
In Love's Eternal Realm 363
In Shadows on Foot 682
In the Bower 16
In the Candlelight 181
In the Evening I 224
In the Evening II 326
In the Field We Lay 124
In the Hush of the Morning 346
In the Lamplight 53
In the Summer She Paces 551
I Once Lived in Luxury 478
I Saw God in Your Tress 131
I Shall Call for You, My Love 424
I Shall Place You in a Garden 76
Isolation I 93
Isolation II 667
It is Snowing in Town 444
It Is the Season 420
I Trod Upon the Glade… 12
I Ventured Out Beneath the Moon 514
I Walked with Byron 528

J

Je Vous ai Recontré à Paris 356
Jones Beach 230
Juliet 485

K

Kingdoms 261
King Henry VIII 179
Kissing in the Woods 299

L

Ladies and Men 503
Lady of the Bastion I 550
Lady of the Bastion II 706
Landscapes 479
Late November 118
La Villa au Bord de la Mer 460
Le Chateau 350
Lethe 216
Let Me Sleep 37
Let Us Cross the River 453
Let Us Dream 71
Let Us Drink Our Fill 394
Let Us Rove 325
Little Girl on a Bike 100
London, 1969 483
Love I 286
Love II 425
Love III 502
Love IV 549
Love V 700
Lovers 219

M

Madness 481
Majestic Heights 34
Mary 339
Mary, The Mother of God 364
Meditation 587
Monet is Still Here 25
Moonlight I 229
Moonlight II 320
Morning 463
Music 184
My Best Beloved 125
My Black-Haired Queen 108
My Chamber 263
My Contrite Heart 28
My Dead Wife (1814) 711
My English Love 719
My Eternal Beloved 511
My Fair Love 347
My God, Thrice Holy 689
My Host 303
My Irish Love 455
My Lady I 310
My Lady II 401
My Lady III 482
My Lady is Lovely 489
My Love 680
My Love, She Sleeps 702
My Mansion by the Sea 338
My Poetry 445
My Politics 467
My Proposal 223
My Queen 115
My Reader 580
Mystic Wines 236
My Turquoise Soul 212
My Youth 101

N

New Hampshire 87
Night 289
Night in Paradise 376
Noel 151
November 55

O

October 128
October Nights 480
Ode to Baudelaire 300
Ode to Bobby Darin 275
Ode to Bram Stoker 654
Ode to Coleridge 246
Ode to Edgar Allan Poe 515
Ode to Henry David Thoreau 307
Ode to Lord Byron 297
Ode to Paul Verlaine 714
Ode to Robert Louis Stevenson 251
Ode to Robert Schumann 96
Ode to Saint John 674
Of a Dark-Eyed Lady 519
Of a Regal Grace 58

Index of Poems

Of She Whom I Love 520
Of Two in Paradise 319
O Mary 155
On a Winter's Eve 92
On Betrothal 307
One Fine Day 668
One Hallowed Eve 548
On Entering Heaven 327
One of the Mellow Dawn 154
One Sacred Night 554
One Summer Morn 250
One Summer's Dawn 703
One Winter Night 191
Only in You 90
On My Way to Boston 516
On Poetry 137
On Poets 486
On Soft, Spring Nights 681
Ophelia 717
Our Bastion by the Sea 390
Our Chambers 448
Our English Tudor 123
Our Souls Become One 123
Our Walk Amid the Reeds 578
Over the Windy Sea 165

P

Paradise I 220
Paradise II 342
Paris 39
Peace I 164
Peace II 401
Peace III 682
Poetry 130
Poets 93

R

Radiant Angel 46
Rain 476
Rapture 227
Raptures 121
Raptures of White 309
Rapturous Gazes 112
Recollection I 177
Recollection II 447
Reflections 293
Rejoice 160
Remnants 83
Rhyme 135
Robert Louis Stevenson Samoa, 1894 669
Romance I 80
Romance II 512
Romance in Town 470
Roses on the Waves 679

S

Sable Eyes 723
Sacred Glances 47
Sadness 202
Sailing 673
Saint John's Wood 671
Saint Paul's Cathedral 672
Saint Steven and Saint Paul 731
Sanctified and Bright 51
Sappho 247
Scarlet Breezes I 26
Soft Breezes II 506
Schoolgirl 157
Seen and Unseen 74
Serenity 382
Shakespeare 235
She Passes and I Sigh 204
She Walks Beyond 725
She Walks in a Russet Ray 210
Silhouette 41
Silhouettes 488
Snow 329
Soliloquy 168
Song of Your Love 556
Sonnets of Travel 278
Southern California, 1966 431

South of Florence 472
Spring 439
Starlit Night 557
Steven 228
Stilled by a Sigh 664
Suburbia 85
Summer 490
Sunlight 23
Switzerland 299

T

Tears 683
Terror 451
The Abbey at Dusk 192
The Acropolis 518
The April Rain 208
The Arbor 387
The Ardor of the Wise 200
The Art Gallery 285
The Ascension 687
The Auburn Dawn 262
The Autumn Lane 537
The Autumn Leaves are Falling 710
The Autumn Rain 54
The Balcony 378
The Ball 289
The Baroness 149
The Bastion by the Sea 252
The Billowing Reeds 418
The Black Concerto 539
The Blessed Dead Are We 253
The Bower 507
The Bride 40
The Carmine Hill 378
The Carriage 306
The Castle I 124
The Castle II 340
The Chameleon 303
The Chaste Wood 348
The Chateau 352
The Cliffs by the Sea 169
The Cloister I 62
The Cloister II 540
The Cloister of Kings 267
The Cloisters 341

Index of Poems

The Coach 61
The Colonial House 256
The Colossal Wood 362
The Composer 187
The Conservatory 429
The Countess 148
The Courtyard I 321
The Courtyard II 684
The Courtyard III 696
The Crypt 302
The Cult of Dionysus 583
The Dale 213
The Dance 304
The Death of the Pagan Gods 590
The Driest Place 685
The Duchess I 14
The Duchess II 542
The Farmhouse 675
The First Snow 178
The First Sonnet 536
The Flower by the Ocean 360
The Fountain 311
The Fruit of Igusau 404
The Garden I 322
The Garden II 543
The Garden III 655
The Ghost 724
The Ghost Ship 659
The Gilded Ball 334
The Gilded Sun 570
The Glade 95
The Glory That is You 715
The Good Road's End 686
The Grand Beyond 163
The Grave of Arthur Rimbaud 545
The Grave of Charles Baudelaire 504
The Graveyard I 505
The Graveyard II 546
The Grove I 547
The Grove II 658
The Half Opened Window 666
The Hallowed Beach 376
The Hallowed Eve 432
The Happy Fault 282

The Harvest Ball 237
The Holy Trinity 369
The Hurricane 301
The Infinite 427
The Journey of Aeneas 255
The Lady of the Garden 454
The Lake 415
The Lakeside 114
The Lane I 487
The Lane II 662
The Lavender Mist 183
The Little Flower 371
The Little Garden 195
The Lost Art of Poetry 456
The Louvre 119
The Mansion 271
The Mansion by the Sea 298
The Meadows 475
The Morning Dew 105
The Muse 526
The Music Room 443
The Outer Darkness 517
The Painter 263
The Palace I 60
The Palace II 552
The Palace III 589
The Palace Ball 182
The Patio 68
The Piano 716
The Poetic Dimension 23
The Pond 114
The Porch 118
The Priest 358
The Princess I 17
The Princess II 585
The Queen 553
The Rain 330
The Rain it Fell 721
The Regal Dawn 653
The Rosary 405
The Rose Garden 501
The Sacred Shrine 129
The Scarlet Breeze 127
The Sea Below the Forest of Pines 324
The Second World War 276

The Shade I 89
The Shade II 555
The Shrine of Saint Anne 662
The Sky is so Blue 555
The Snow-Covered Hill 249
The Song of John Keats 657
The Song of Your Love 399
The Spring 167
The Square 557
The Starlight Night 170
The Storm I 272
The Storm II 676
The Study 377
The Swashbuckler 180
The Thirteenth Sonnet 256
The Thirty-Fourth Sonnet 273
The Vagabond 713
The Veranda 81
The Visitor 295
The Voyage of Icarus 248
The Wanderer 66
The Way to Heaven 345
The Window Bay 663
The Zephyrs of the Paradisal Sea 363
Tinges 24
To a Dark-Eyed Lady 80
To Marry 72
To Mary I 558
To Mary II 726
To Mary and My Beloved One 63
To My Future Bride 510
To One in Heaven 560
To One So Fair 13
To Rebecca 421
Torment (The Guest) 562
To You, My Love 561
Tremulous Seas 564
Twilight 49
Twilight by the Shore 205
Two-Thirty 414
Two Women by the Shore 174
Two Years Ago 226

Index of Poems

U

Une Promendade dans la Ville 355
Unrequited Love 198
Upon the Bench 27

V

Vermont 284
Verse I 99
Verse II 254
Vespertine Fire 31
Vignettes 103
Violets 150
Violins 75
Virgil 234

W

We Shall Rove 437
We Shall Wander 436
When Music Ceases 159
When You Were Young 428
Where Roses Weep 49
Where the Sun Laments 52
Where the Zephyrs Flow 207
Whiskey 258
Who Doth Seek Me When I am Near? 701
Wind Chimes 117
Wine 18
Wines I 300
Wines II 419
Winter 581
Wisdom 156
Within Your Soul 54
Wreaths 44

Y

Your Eyes 380
Your Face I 88
Your Face II 704
Your Face in the Garden 368
Your Gaze 19
Your Hair 14
Your Hymns 82
Your Mane, Your Eyes 488
Your Name 396
Your Rose 84
Your Russet Wine 59
Your Sobbing Soul 97
Your Touch 81
Your Tresses Reposed 26
Your Wake 397

Made in United States
North Haven, CT
07 March 2022